Photographers of Old Hawaii

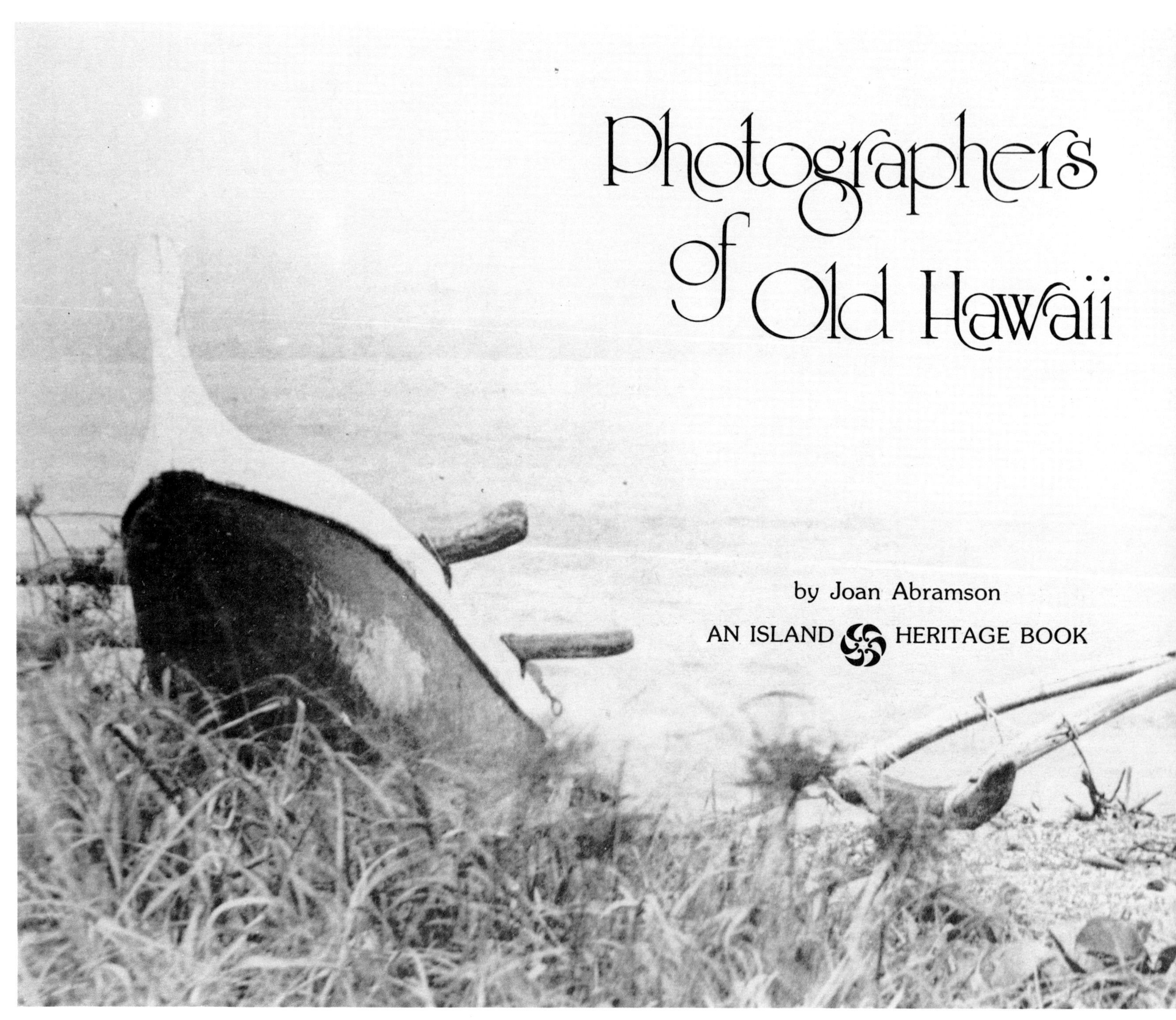

Photographers of Old Hawaii

by Joan Abramson

AN ISLAND HERITAGE BOOK

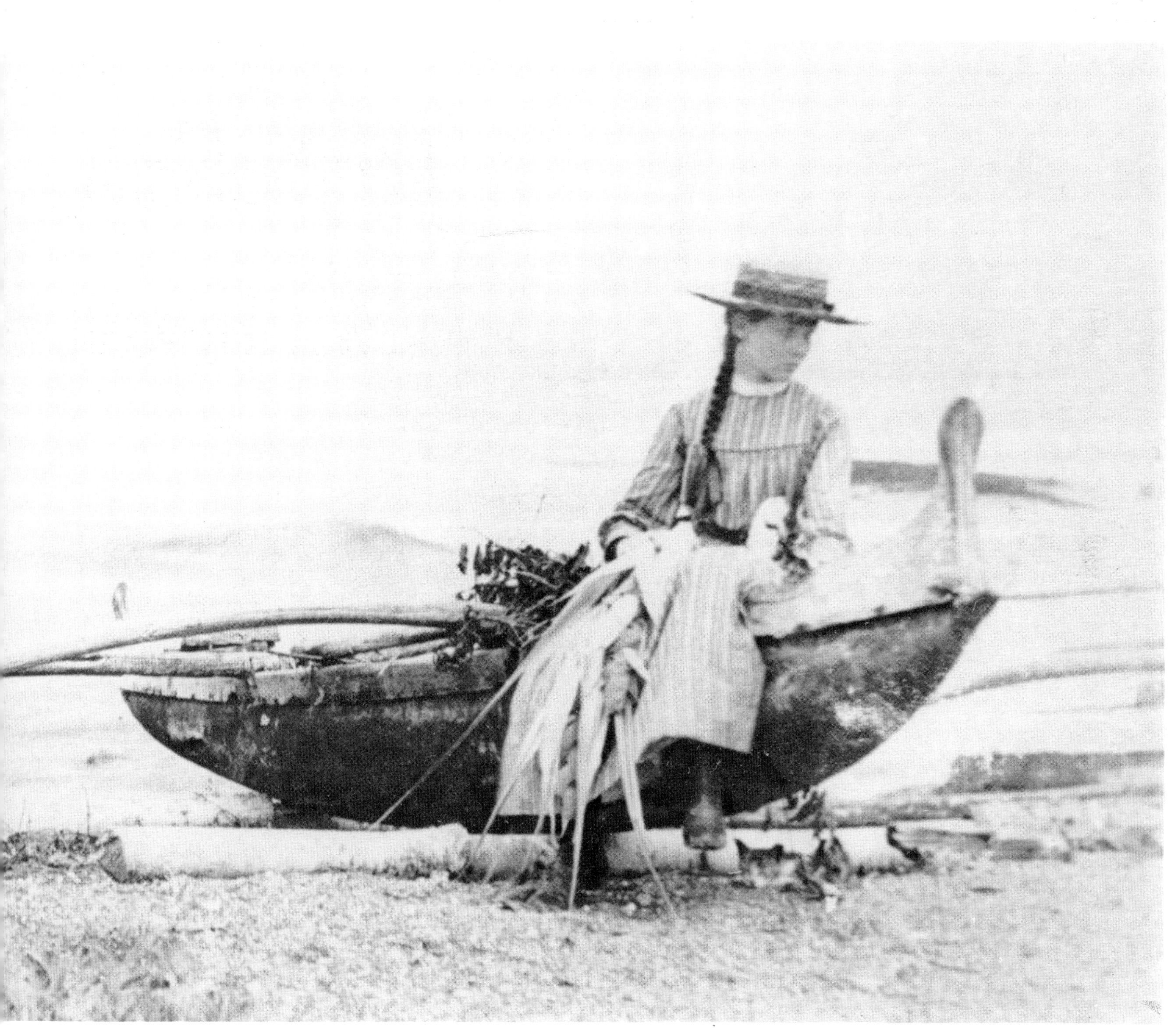

THIRD TRADE EDITION, 1981

Please address orders, editorial
correspondence and catalog requests to:
Island Heritage Limited
104 Ward Plaza/210 Ward Avenue
Honolulu, Hawaii 96814
Phone: (808) 526-1126

Printed and bound in Hong Kong
Library of Congress Catalog Number 76-1504
ISBN Trade 0-89610-082-0

for Norman . . .

Contents

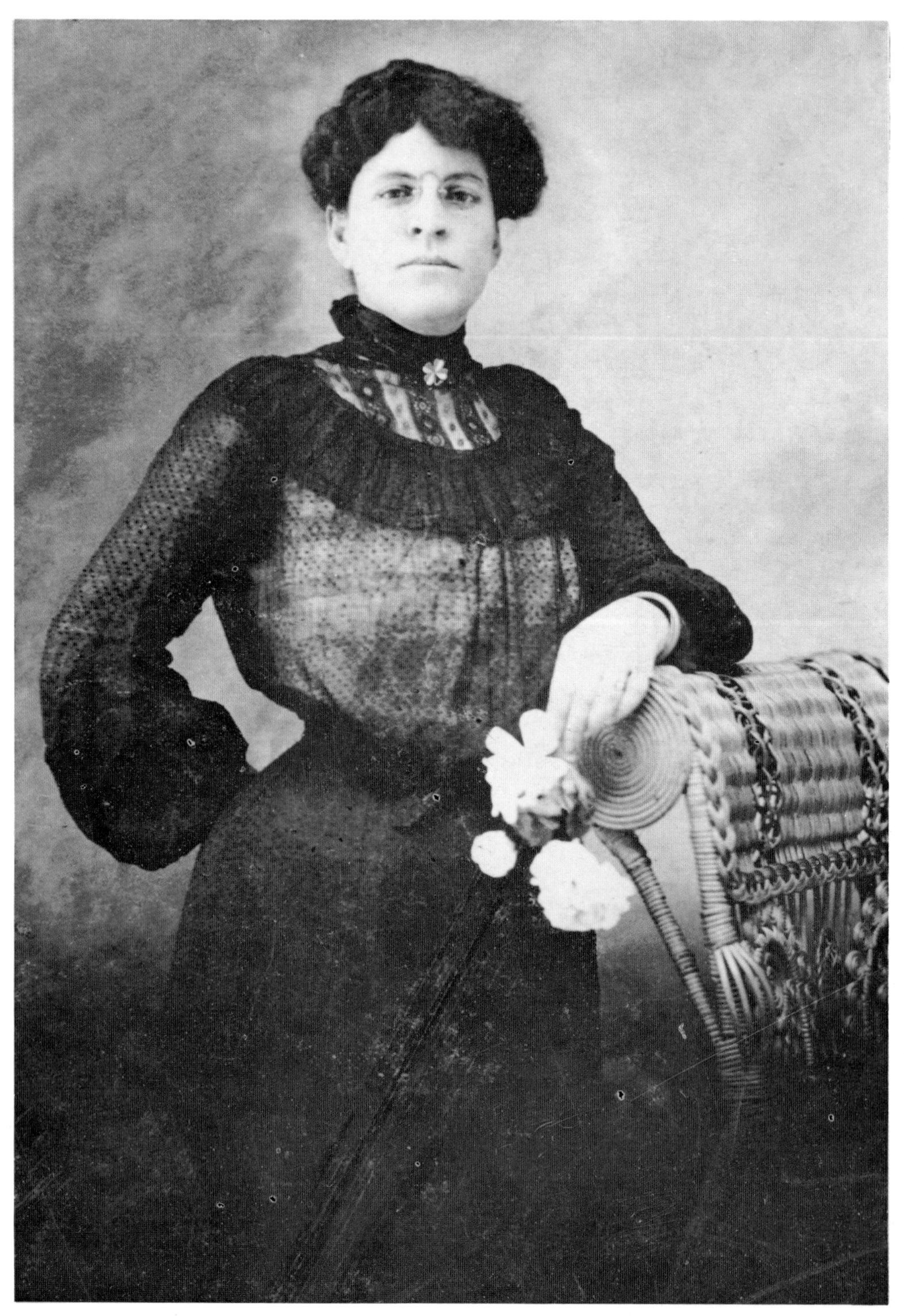

Honolulu woman, about 1900. A. Higaki. From Hawaii State Archives.

Introduction

On May 17, 1845, *The Polynesian* carried what was apparently Hawaii's first newspaper advertisement for photographic services. The modest notice was sandwiched in between an announcement about an auction of "THE good Sch. CHINCHILLA, 70 tons burthen, copper and copper fastened" and an advertisement for ISRAEL H. WRIGHT, PAINTER, GILDER, AND GLAZIER, Will execute with neatness and despatch, HOUSE, SIGN, SHIP, COACH & ORNAMENTAL PAINTING." In the photographic advertisement, one Mr. Theophilus Metcalf "begs leave to inform the public generally, that he is now prepared to take LIKENESSES by the Daguerreotype, at his Rooms, over the Polynesian Office, every fair day, between the hours 9 and 1." The Metcalf announcement continues: "The dress of the sitters should correspond as far as practicable with the complexion. His terms are $10 a picture, and $2 for a miniature case. Honolulu, May 17th, 1845."

The announcement of a daguerreotype facility in Honolulu, so soon after the process had become practical enough and cheap enough to interest the public, seems surprising. The daguerreotype process was made public only in 1839 and was by no means practical for portraiture until at least 1841. Even then, exposure times were uncomfortably long: sitters were required to stare into the camera while their heads were kept still by a metal neck brace and the resultant likenesses were all too often severe and unflattering. Despite its shortcomings, the daguerreotype appears to have traveled with great rapidity and the number of daguerreotype operators seems to have grown with even greater speed.

But what is as surprising as a daguerreotype gallery in Honolulu in 1845 is the fact that the gallery and its owner apparently attracted very little notice. None of the local newspapers paid great attention to Metcalf's enterprise and, three months after it began, his announcement in *The Polynesian* was discontinued. Mr. Metcalfe either disappeared from Honolulu or, according to one report gathered by early 20th Century photographer, Ray Jerome Baker, became a surveyor. If any of Metcalf's work remains in public collections in Hawaii it has not yet been identified as his.

Metcalf's early attempt to interest the public in the daguerreotype was followed 18 months later by a somewhat more successful attempt by one Senor LeBleu. LeBleu is apparently one and the same with an F. LeBleux, French national and priest by profession, who, according to Baker, was listed as a passenger aboard the Chilean brigantine *Beatrice*, which arrived in Honolulu on December 22, 1846. But whether LeBleux or LeBleu, by February, 1847, the Senor was doing a booming business taking the likenesses of Honolulu notables.

The February 3, 1847 issue of *The Sandwich Island News* took note of LeBleu's success in a long article with interesting political overtones. The article noted that Honolulu citizens had been flocking to LeBleu's rooms and that "Instead of the ordinary greetings of the day, people enquire whether you have 'been taken yet?' or when you are going 'to be taken?' — questions which, to the uninitiated, have a somewhat omnious (sic) sound; and we confess that on hearing the other day, before we were up to the new order of things, that His Excellency the Minister of Foreign Relations had 'been taken,' an inexpressible shock thrilled through our entire corporosity, and it was with difficulty that we could sufficiently command our nervous sensibility to make the anxious enquiry whether it was with a cholic, a constable or a lucid interval. Our distress was presently allayed, however, by the consoling information that he had only been taken by Senor LeBleu, and that His Excellency's sole suffering had been the difficulty he found in getting upon so much of his person as could be crowded into the narrow compass of a photographic portrait, all the ornaments and insignia which his exalted office, the order in council, and his own strict sense of propriety, necessarily oblige him to wear." "His Excellency" was none other than Robert Crichton Wyllie, who served in a number of government offices during the monarchy and who was, in fact, pictured in a later daguerreotype, complete with gold star, gold braid and buttons, elaborate sash and tri-cornered chapeau.

The Sandwich Island News article also congratulated LeBleu on "the avidity with which our fellow-residents, naturalized and 'unnaturalized,' crowd to his rooms to exchange the current coin of the realm with his well executed little specimens of photographic immortality. We understand that he already has engagements for weeks in advance, and there appears a general panic among those at the caudal terminus of his list, on account of a most discouraging report which has gone abroad, that the artist's plates are not likely to satisfy all the demands made upon them."

Despite his apparent popularity and the fear that he might run out of the highly polished metal plates required for making daguerreotypes, LeBleu, like Metcalf before him, quickly disappeared from the Honolulu scene. It is possible that both were itinerant daguerreotypists who had intended to remain in Honolulu just long enough to satisfy the needs of those with ready cash before moving on to the next location. Certainly the itinerant "artist" was as common as the studio operator in the early decades of photography. Having one's likeness photographed, like having one's portrait painted, was not an everyday occurrence — indeed, it was something only for the well-to-do and, at that, something that occurred but once or twice in a lifetime. It took some time before imagination concerning the possible uses of photography developed and some time before the technology of the new art progressed to the point where photography could be put to broad use.

As is the case with Metcalf's work, nothing that can as yet be identified remains of LeBleu's work in Hawaii's public photographic collections. However, there is a possibility that small locket and ring daguerreotypes with LeBleu's name engraved upon them have remained in family collections within the state. Certainly such daguerreotypes would be of historical value.

After Senor LeBleu, Hawaii does not appear to have attracted any photographers, itinerant or otherwise, for several years. But in 1853, the local papers announced the arrival of Goodfellow and Stangenwald, who would be establishing themselves for a short stay before going on to Australia. It should be pointed out that Stangenwald and Goodfellow, even on their arrival, were behind the times. While they were setting up as daguerreotypists in Honolulu, the wet collodion process, discovered in 1851, was rapidly gaining ascendancy elsewhere. It took several years for the wet collodion process to catch up with Stangenwald and with other photographers who soon established themselves in the islands. But from the arrival of Stangenwald on, the tempo of photographic business in the islands picked up. Some photographers, like Stangenwald, came as itinerants and decided to stay. Others, like Goodfellow, quickly faded from sight. Almost all, it seems, were inveterate traders who exchanged business locations with one another with great frequency. They show up, for example, with confusing regularity "upstairs, over the Advertiser, next door to the Post Office."

With the spread of the wet collodion photographic process the early photographers were more able than Metcalf and LeBleu to leave a record behind them. The great drawback of the daguerreotype was that it was a direct positive and could not be produced in multiple copies. While some cameras were developed that could take several daguerreotype exposures at one time, the process was clearly limited by the fact that it produced no negatives: each daguerreotype was unique and most did not remain in the possession of the photographer. The wet collodion process, on the other hand, used a treated glass plate which was exposed and developed into a negative image. The negative could then be used to produce multiple positive prints on paper. The wet collodion plate could also be used to produce an image similar to the daguerreotype: the glass negative plate was treated and backed with black material to produce an apparent positive called an Ambrotype. The process was popular for a time for portraiture. But the Ambrotype had the same drawback as the daguerreotype, for the collodion plate, used in this manner, became in itself a single image. The use of the wet collodion plate as a negative was far more important for it was the first practical photographic process that allowed multiple prints from a single negative exposure.

The process was a step that not only popularized photography but also made possible a sizable change in the nature of the photographic record that could be left behind. While the photographic record in Hawaii can be said to date from the 1850s and Stangenwald, who left a small collection of daguerreotypes of people and scenes, the volume of photographic materials left for the historian increased greatly with the popularization of the wet plate print.

With the advent of duplicate prints from a single negative, the selection of images for a book such as this becomes most difficult yet most rewarding. Insularity has added to the richness of Hawaii's photographic record and there are tens of thousands of photographs by hundreds of professional and amateur photographers in island collections from which to choose. Far more must be left out than can be included.

Nonetheless, what has been included is a representative sample of the photographic work done in Hawaii during the last half of the 19th century and the early 20th century. At least it is a representative sample of that part of the photographic work from the era that has surfaced to date. It includes the work of some professional photographers and some amateurs. Professionals are represented exclusively for the earliest years, both because there were more of them and because most traces of the work of the early day amateurs have vanished.

Amateurs, who increased in number as photographic equipment became more readily available and as techniques became less cumbersome, are increasingly represented in the later chapters of the book. The period covered is roughly 1853, when Hugo Stangenwald first began to work in the islands, to 1924, when Tai Sing Loo, R.J. Baker and On Char were still at work.

Among the photographers represented are some who did little more than imitate the prevailing portrait fashion of the Eastern United States or Europe, and others who were able to free themselves to capture something uniquely Hawaiian in the faces of their customers. There are photographers who concentrated only on portrait work and others who carried their heavy equipment around the islands to gather albums of scenic views. There are some who left us extraordinary images of ordinary daily life in the islands and others who ventured into early photo journalism and thereby left us a record of unique events.

Yet, despite the variety of materials included, and despite the rich photographic record available from which to choose, Hawaii's photographic history remains barely tapped. In mainland states, easy overland travel and unclear boundaries have blurred regional materials. Except for photographs with clearly identifiable geographic and architectural landmarks, a great deal of material available on the mainland cannot be tied with precision to a specific geographical region. Hawaii's long years of comparative isolation have, in this sense, been a blessing, for the result has been that large collections of material have remained intact.

But ironically, despite the fact that Hawaii is blessed with one of the richest state photographic records, it remains one of the least developed records. And there are still serious problems connected with the development of Hawaii's photographic heritage in both museum collections and private collections of photographic materials. Those collections that have been donated to museums within the state remain as yet largely unexplored. While it is certainly commendable that so many collections have been preserved through donation to museums, it is clear that there has not yet been a viable method developed for making these valuable historical materials available to the public in any great volume. Unless some method for researcher access is developed, these materials are likely to fade from sight, self-ignite (in the case of nitrate negatives) or be overcome with mildew and fungus before they can be properly exploited for historical, cultural and artistic purposes.

The private collections present quite different problems. There are dozens of photographers who worked in Hawaii during the late 19th and early 20th centuries who have left barely a trace behind them. A. Higaki and Y. Yamamoto, two photographers represented in this introduction, are examples. Both men were listed as professional photographers in Honolulu directories at around the turn of the century. Both, from the handful of portraits that have drifted into the public collections, appear to have been skilled at their work. Yet the bulk of their photographic work is nowhere to be found.

In even more instances, not a clue remains beyond a name in a newspaper or directory. In a distressing number of cases the reason is the same: a commercial photographer or a hobbiest left his prints and negatives to heirs who failed to recognize their historic values and discarded them. In other cases, large collections of old glass plates and nitrate negatives are kept — and kept quietly — in the hope that some day, when they are old enough, they will be of great financial value. All too often, in such cases, Hawaii's climate has the last word. Before the hoped for financial gain can be realized, mildew and water damage often have their way and there is nothing left to exploit.

Such are the current problems in working with Hawaii's vast photographic history. It is to be hoped that they will be overcome in the near future and that the people of Hawaii will gain access to these materials before they forever fade from view. But despite such problems, the major difficulty in creating a book such as this stems from Hawaii's embarrassment of photographic riches. Of the hundreds of photographers who worked in Hawaii during the early days of the art, we have touched on only a sampling of the work of little more than a dozen. It would have been impossible to do more within the covers of one book. Certainly, then, this book cannot long remain the definitive work on photographers of old Hawaii — there were too many photographers; and there is too much photographic work yet unpublished that merits attention either for its historical or artistic value, and often for both. For this volume, choices had to be made. Photographers had to be left out. And other photographers, known only by a name in a business directory or not yet known at all because they were amateurs, could not even be considered. There was no way to cope with this problem except to mentally label this book "Volume One."

With our heritage largely untapped, we may yet see additional volumes of *Photographers of Old Hawaii.*

Joan Abramson, Honolulu, 1976

Family group in 1913 *(left to right):* Mary Madeline Seabury, Mabel Botelho, Philomena Seabury Botelho and baby Cecilia Botelho. Y. Yamamoto, Hawaii State Archives.

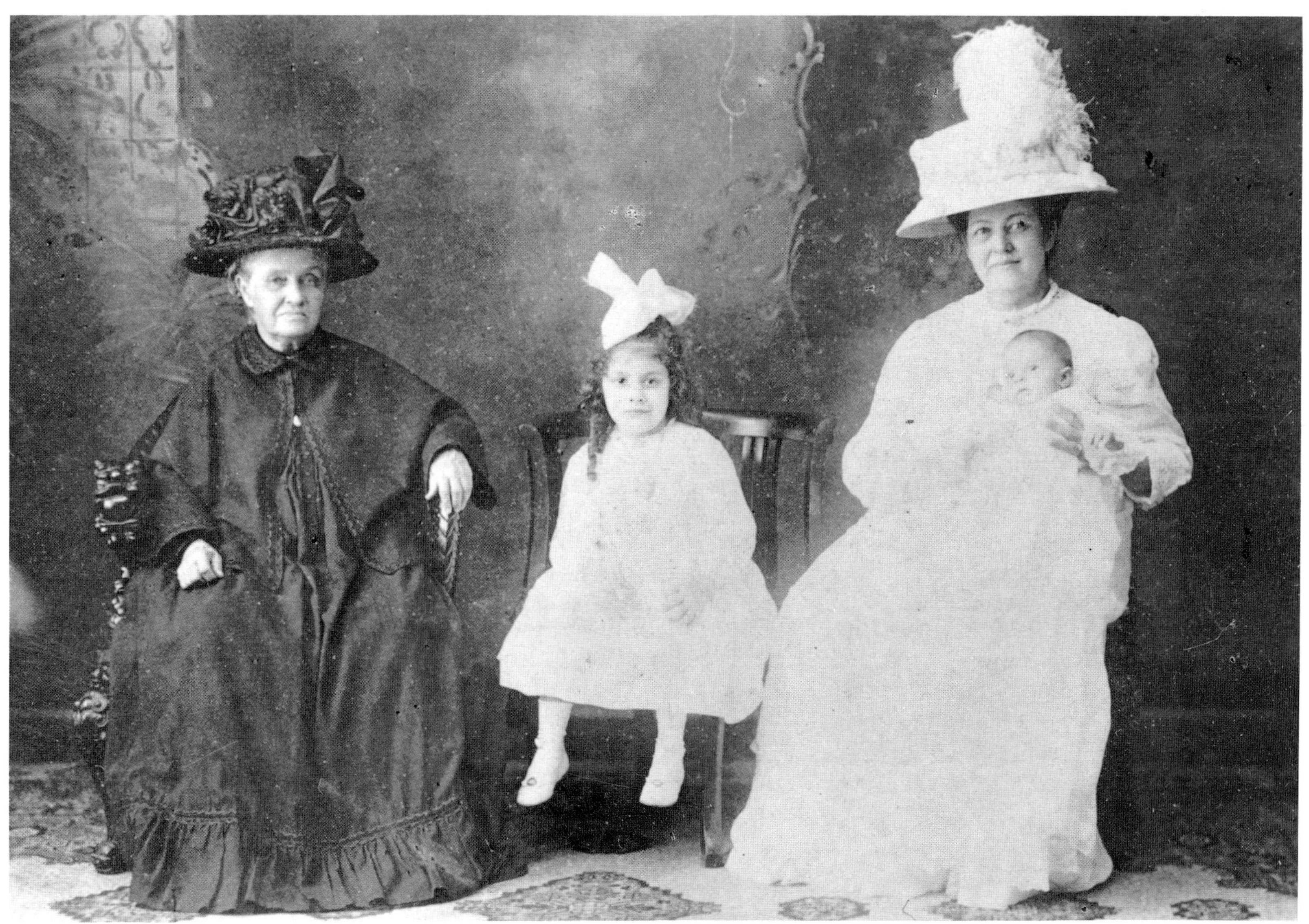

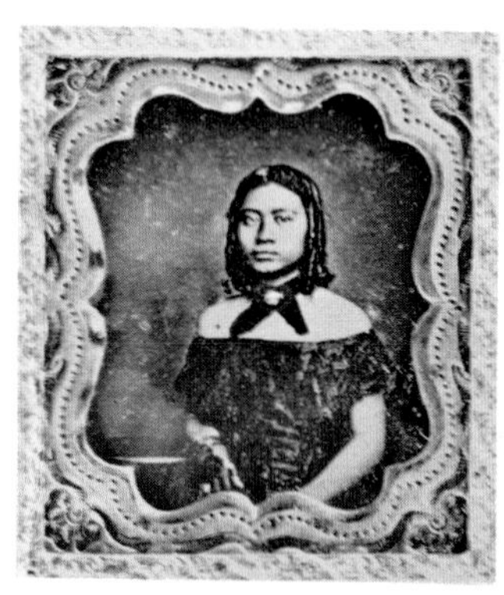

Daguerreotype miniature of Victoria Kamamalu, 1885. H. Stangenwald. Hawaiian Mission Children's Society.

Praise to the man who first employed
The orb of day, a ray of light
On silver plate quite neat and fine
To trace the human face divine.

Who boldly entered nature's field,
And brought at will her powers to yield,
That ours might be an image clear
Of those we love and hold so dear.

From distant lands and climes we've come
To this our far-off Island home
And many hearts do long in vain,
To see their absent friends again.

And there they mourn and weep and sigh,
When looking at the western sky,
When thoughts of past and happier days
Recall their friend's and brother's face,

When childhood scenes, the scenes most dear
In all their force and charm appear
And memory plays the magic art
A tune of old upon their heart.

How would they like an image true,
Reflected by the sunbeam's hue
To show your features plain and clear,
Their hours of solitude to cheer.

To send to them that precious boon
And have your picture taken soon
And quick their weeping eyes they'll wipe,
To smile on your "Daguerreotype."

Hugo Stangenwald

In 1854, most of the advertisements that appeared in Honolulu newspapers merely announced goods and services and politely requested a share of local patronage. The hard sell in poetic form on the facing page appeared in *The Polynesian* in October, 1854 and was, to say the least, unusual. The advertiser, and presumed poet, was Hugo Stangenwald, the earliest photographer in Hawaii to leave an identifiable record of his work. His advertising campaign was unusual even for Stangenwald, who had previously announced his services in the traditional and more subdued manner. And, from the available evidence, an emotional pitch for the sale of portraits was hardly necessary: Stangenwald appears to have had no serious competition in the photographic business in Honolulu until 1857.

Hugo Stangenwald began his photographic career in Hawaii as one half of a team of itinerant photographers. His arrival in the islands was announced in the March 26, 1853 edition of *The Polynesian*: "We are happy to announce the arrival in Honolulu of Messers Stangenwald and Goodfellow, Daguerreotypists, who have opened their rooms in the building adjoining the brick shoe store of J.H. Wood where they are now prepared to take miniatures in the first style of the art. We have examined numerous specimens of their work, both landscapes and miniatures and can recommend them as well taken and highly finished. See their advertisement in another column for particulars." A week later, another brief announcement appeared in the same newspaper: "Having gotten their apparatus in good working order, accustomed to the light &c Messers Stangenwald and Goodfellow are prepared to take pictures in a superior manner. We have seen additional specimens of their work taken and can recommend them as fine productions of art. Give them a call as their stay in town will not be protracted."

The April, 1853 issue of *The Friend* also took note of the arrival of the partners and pointed out that the two were merely passing through the islands on their way to Australia. Goodfellow, it is true, may have been passing through. Before a few months went by his name no longer appeared in the advertisements run in Honolulu newspapers. Where he came from and where he went remain a mystery. But Stangenwald spent the better part of a half century in the islands and there is at least a partial record of both his origins and his career.

Hugo Stangenwald was born in Germany in 1829. In 1848 he was a medical student in Vienna. And Vienna, during that year, was the center of revolutionary activity that shook the Austro-Hungarian Empire. Exactly what Stangenwald's role was in this activity has never been clear. But student agitation precipitated much of the revolutionary chaos that year and Stangenwald apparently was in the thick of things — so much so, in fact, that he was forced to flee Austria. Stangenwald spent some time in the California gold fields in 1850, but beyond the announcement in *The Polynesian* that samples of his work were "well taken and highly finished" we do not know anything about his career as a photographer before coming to the islands. At the time of his death, at least one obituary notice claimed he had first come to the islands in 1850, then returned to Vienna to complete his medical studies before settling in Hawaii permanently in 1853. If this is indeed correct it seems odd that the papers of 1853 failed to take note of his medical abilities and claimed instead that he was setting up shop as a daguerreotypist for only a short while before moving on to Australia. R.J. Baker, in his unpublished notes on early photographers, assumed that Stangenwald practiced medicine and operated a photographic studio on the side until the medical practice became too time consuming and the photographic business too competitive. Such dual careers were not unusual for early photographers. Indeed, one of the most notable double careers was that of a blacksmith-photographer reported to be operating in France in 1861. But there is no solid evidence that Stangenwald practiced medicine until 1861, well after he sold his photographic establishment.

Stangenwald set up his Daguerrean Gallery at the corner of Merchant and Fort Streets in 1853. During his first two years in business in Honolulu, he advertised daguerreotypes only and stressed his ability at taking miniatures. This would indicate that Stangenwald did not then possess knowledge of the wet collodion photographic process nor even any of the faster lenses that were in use in Europe and the Eastern United States. One of the early problems with the daguerreotype and with other early methods of photography was that a combination of inadequate lenses and inadequate chemical techniques made exposure times extremely long. Sitters for the earliest experimental portraits were forced to remain still for extended periods in full sunlight. One early way of coping with this problem was to reduce the size of the image. This concentrated the limited light available through the early lenses onto a smaller surface and thus reduced the amount of time necessary to obtain an image. Static subjects such as buildings could, of course, be taken on larger plates since the exposure time required to produce an image was not limited by human endurance. From the collection of Stangenwald daguerreotypes at the Mission Children's Society Museum in Honolulu, it is apparent that Stangenwald was able to take daguerreotypes with fairly short exposure times, for his images are quite sharp. However, none of the portraits that have been preserved are larger than 2 by 3 inches in size and a few are closer in size to postage stamps. The size of these images is a fair indication of the limitations of Stangenwald's equipment.

Interestingly enough, Stangenwald was making use of a technique that enabled him to overcome one of the major shortcomings of the daguerreotype, the problem of lateral reversal. Since the daguerreotype is a direct positive print, an image produced through the use of a lens was reversed from left to right. When Daguerre released his process in 1839, he offered no solution to this problem. Within a few years, two solutions were devised. In one, a system of mirrors was used in place of a lens to focus the light on the daguerreotype plate. This system both intensified the available light (thus reducing the amount of time required to produce an image) and did away with lens-produced lateral reversal. Its major drawback, however, was that it did not produce as sharp an image as could be obtained through the use of a lens. A second system, which merely used a reversing prism in front of the lens, was developed in 1841. The prism, when used with an improved lens developed at the same time, avoided lateral reversal and still permitted sufficient light to make exposure times bearable for portrait work. Stangenwald was evidently aware of at least one of these techniques when he began his career in Hawaii, for the April, 1853 announcement in *The Friend* points out that the Stangenwald and Goodfellow establishment could provide such items as "correct views of gentlemen's residences, vessels, machinery and parts of the city &c taken without reversing." It is surprising that the two techniques for the reversal of daguerreotypes were not known to R.J. Baker, who for the most part did a painstaking job of recording information about the work of his predecessors. In his unpublished notes on the early photographers, Baker speculated that Stangenwald may have re-photographed his daguerreotypes in order to overcome lateral reversal.

Stangenwald's Daguerrean Gallery continued in business at the corner of Merchant and Fort Streets until the middle of 1855, when he relocated at the corner of Fort and King Streets. At that time he was apparently equipped for the use of larger plates for he advertised that his new "increased facilities" would enable him to "operate in any kind of weather, and also attend the taking of families, groups &c." Unfortunately, none of these group sittings have drifted into Hawaii's museums. By this time, too, Stangenwald was advertising the use of other methods of photography along with the daguerreotype. And, in a nod toward the fading popularity of the daguerreotype, his ad also notes that he has a complete daguerreotype apparatus for sale and will give instructions to a buyer "desirous of visiting other parts."

In the spring of 1857, Stangenwald announced the sale of his business and his departure from the Hawaiian Islands. He remained away from the islands for three years and it is probable that he completed his medical education during this period. Whether or not he practiced medicine along with photography before leaving the islands in 1858, it is clear that after his return in 1861 he did not practice photography along with medicine. Early in 1861, a small notice began to appear in *The Friend*: H. Stangenwald, M.D., Dispensary Physician, member of the Medico Chirurgical College and Pathelogical Society of New York. Office over Dr. Judd's Drug Store, on Fort Street, Residence in Nuuanu Valley, opposite E.O. Hall Esq."

Dr. Stangenwald lived until 1899 and practiced medicine almost to the time of his death. From all indications he was a successful practitioner with a reputation for kindness and gentleness in handling his patients. His hobby over the years was chemical and electrical experimentation and his house was well equipped with experimental gadgetry.

But his reputation as a photographer faded over the years and by the time of his death it was all but forgotten. The obituary notice carried in *The Commercial Advertiser* on June 2, 1899, recalled his participation in revolutionary activities: indeed, it reported that in 1848 the then 19 year old student "served as a surgeon in the great revolutionary movement" — a somewhat unlikely claim. But the obituary made no mention of Stangenwald's earlier career as a photographer. *The Hawaiian Gazette* of June 2, 1899, reported on his research in electricity and chemistry and on his early revolutionary activities, but made no mention of his photographic work. Only *The Friend*, in the July, 1899 issue, recalled that "for several years he was Honolulu's chief photographer."

Ironically, little can now be said of Stangenwald's long career as an island physician. But the few Stangenwald daguerreotypes that remain mark him as the earliest photographer in Hawaii to leave an identifiable record of his work. For this reason alone Stangenwald deserves mention. But his work demands careful attention as well: his portraits and landscapes are beautifully preserved and technically excellent examples of the daguerreotype form.

Below: View of Charity School, Honolulu, looking toward Waianae Mountains, about 1853. Photo by H. Stangenwald. Hawaii State Archives.

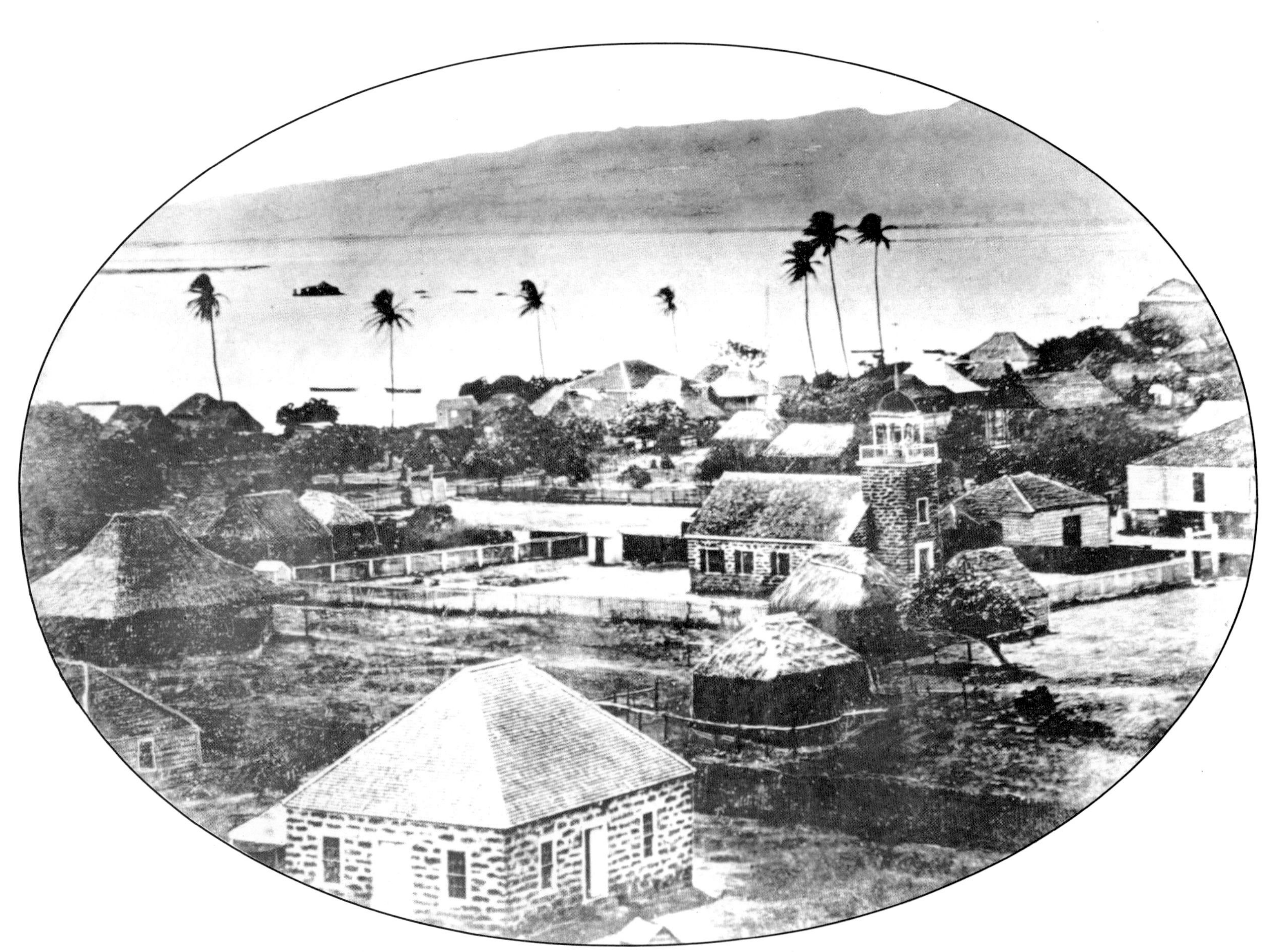

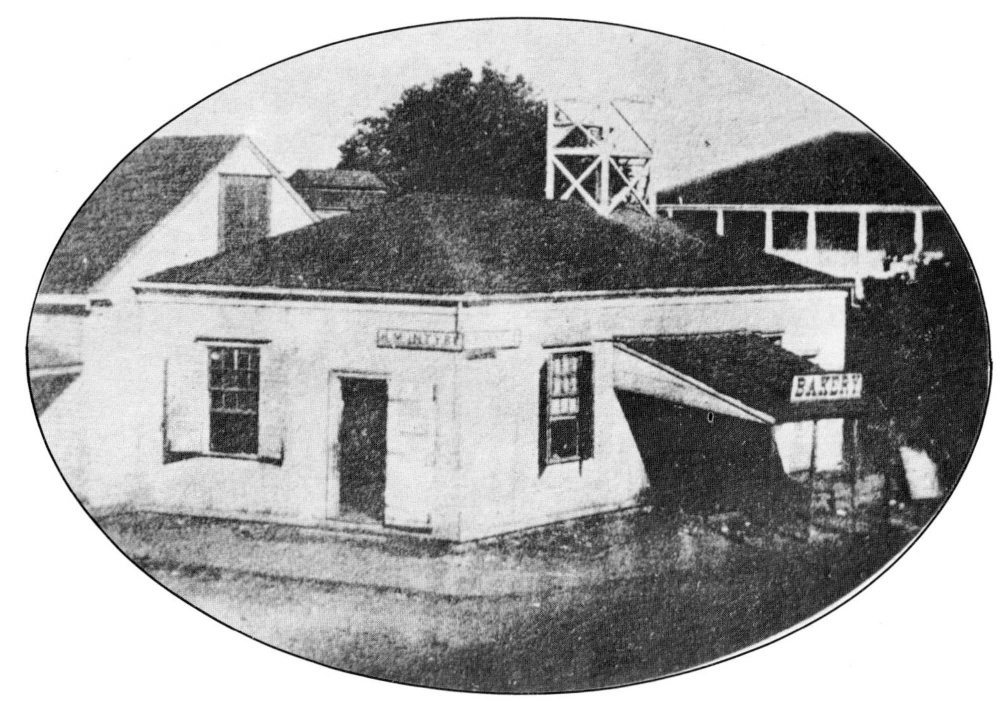

Above: The first McIntyre Building, Fort Street, Honolulu, 1856. H. Stangenwald. Hawaii State Archives.

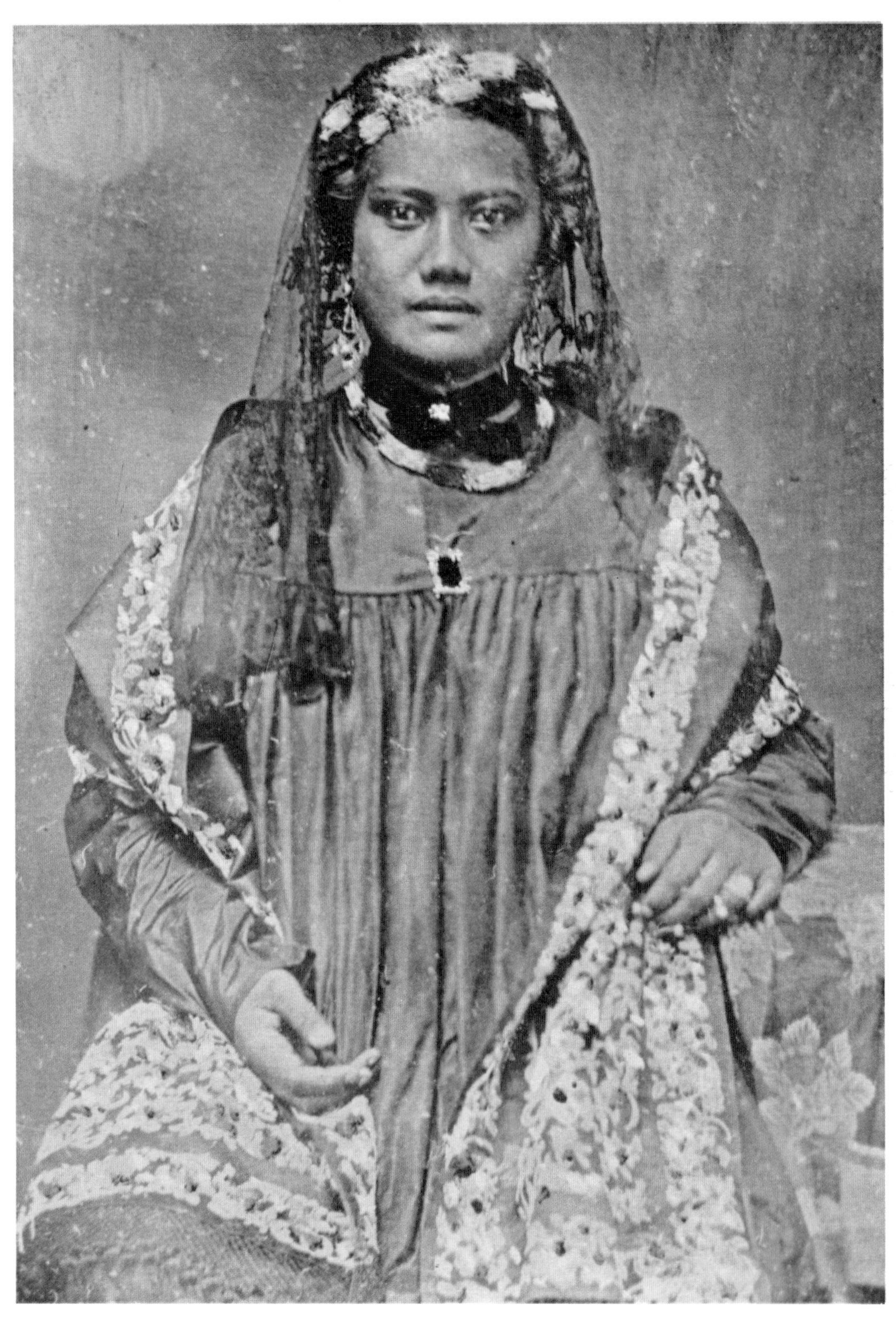

Hawaiian woman. The original daguerreotype is elaborately hand colored. Photo by H. Stangenwald. Hawaiian Mission Children's Society.

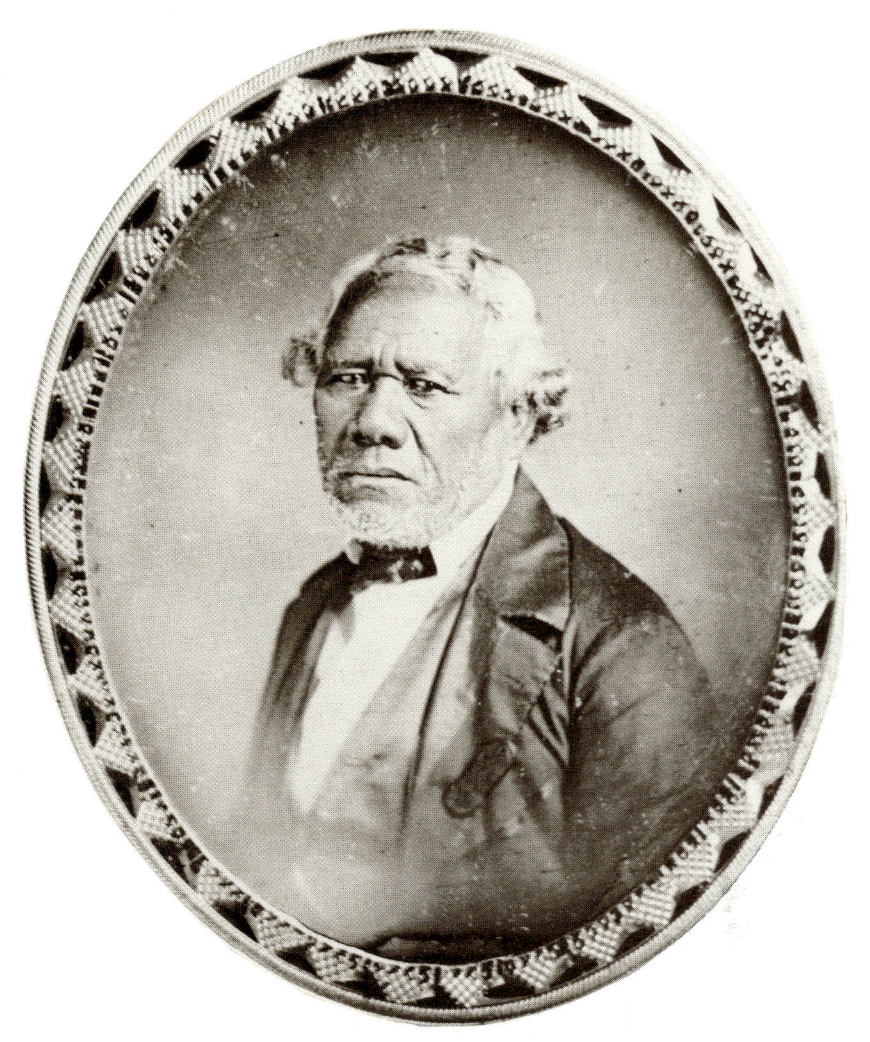

Above: Portrait, about 1855. H. Stangenwald. Hawaiian Mission Children's Society.

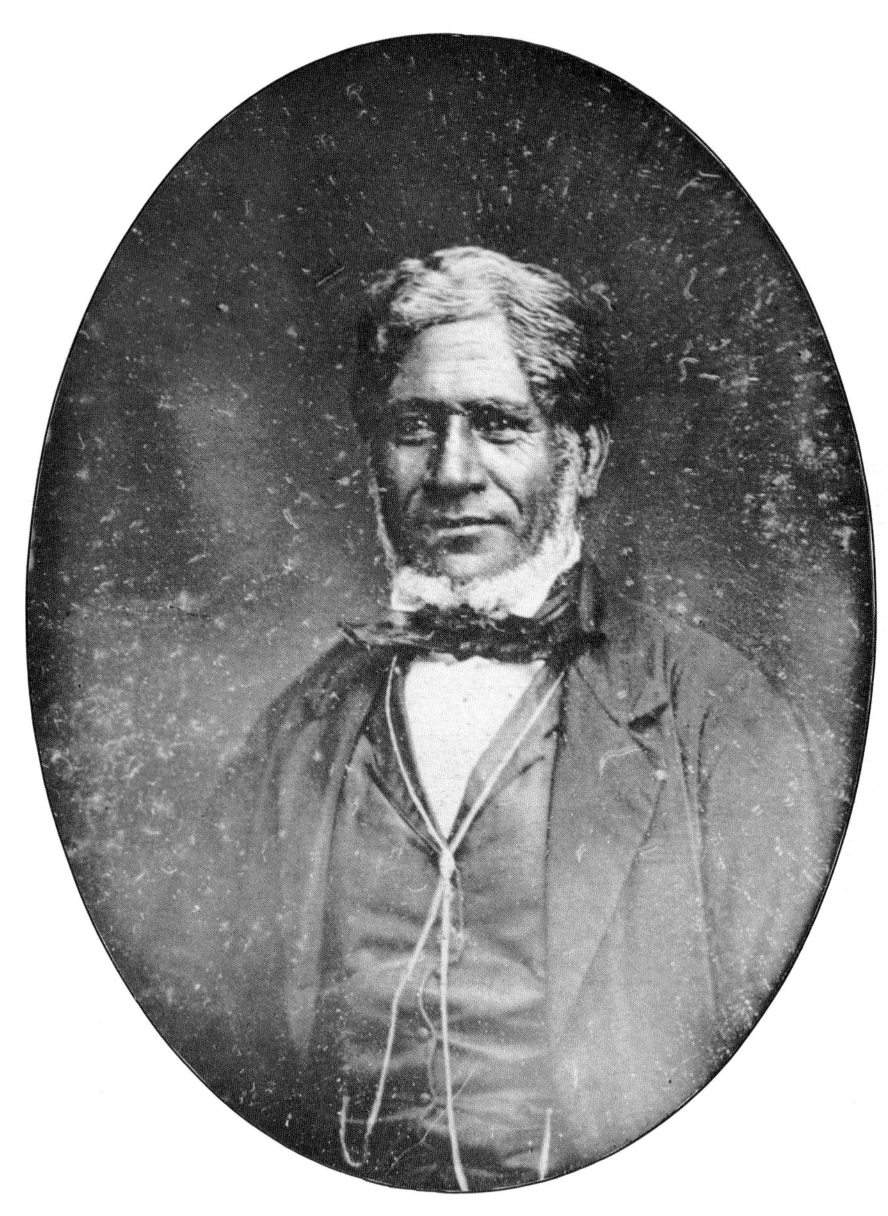

Hawaiian gentleman about 1855. H. Stangenwald.
Hawaiian Mission Children's Society.

A view of Honolulu looking toward Nuuanu Pali, 1853. H. Stangenwald. Hawaii State Archives.

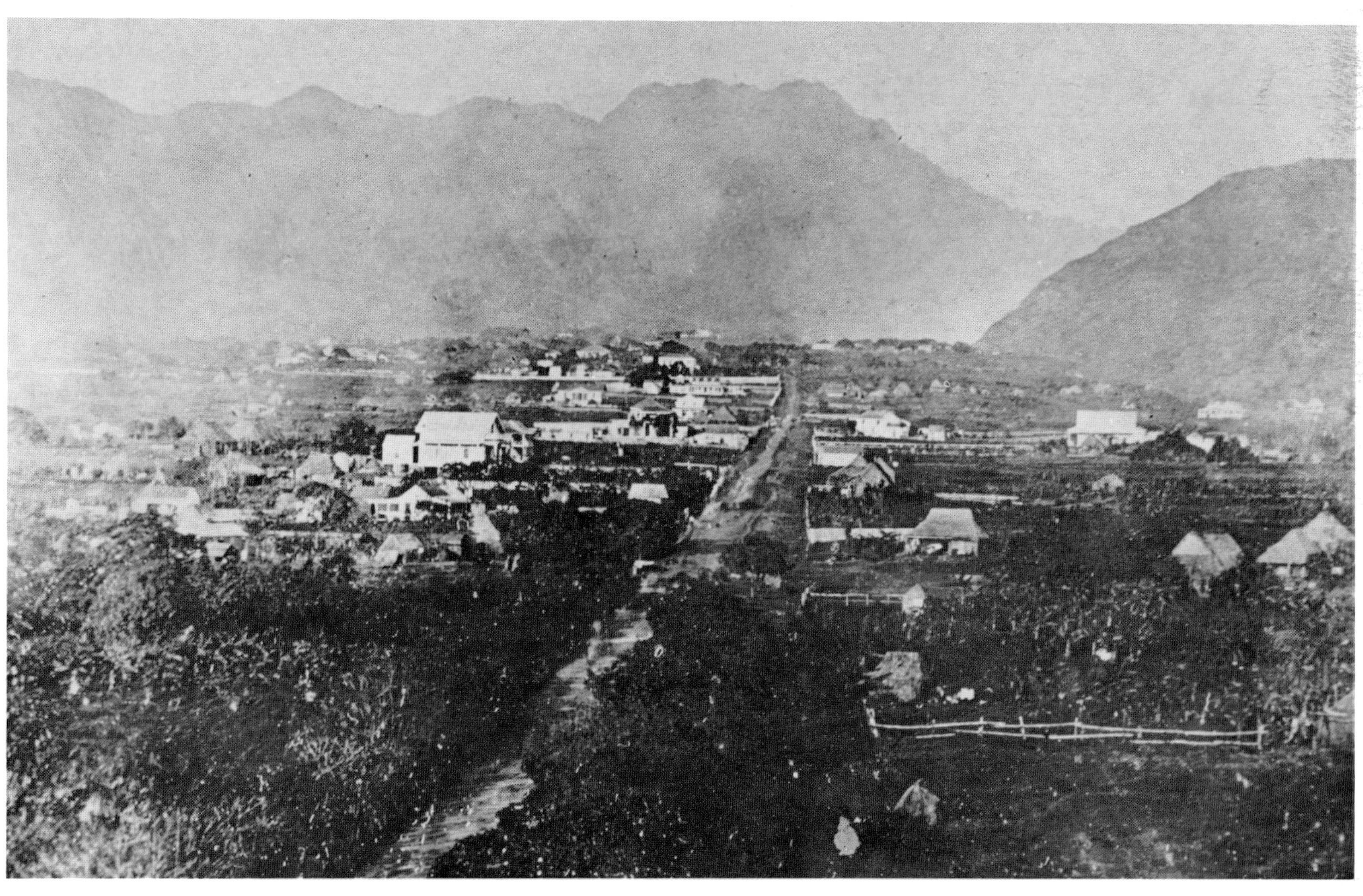

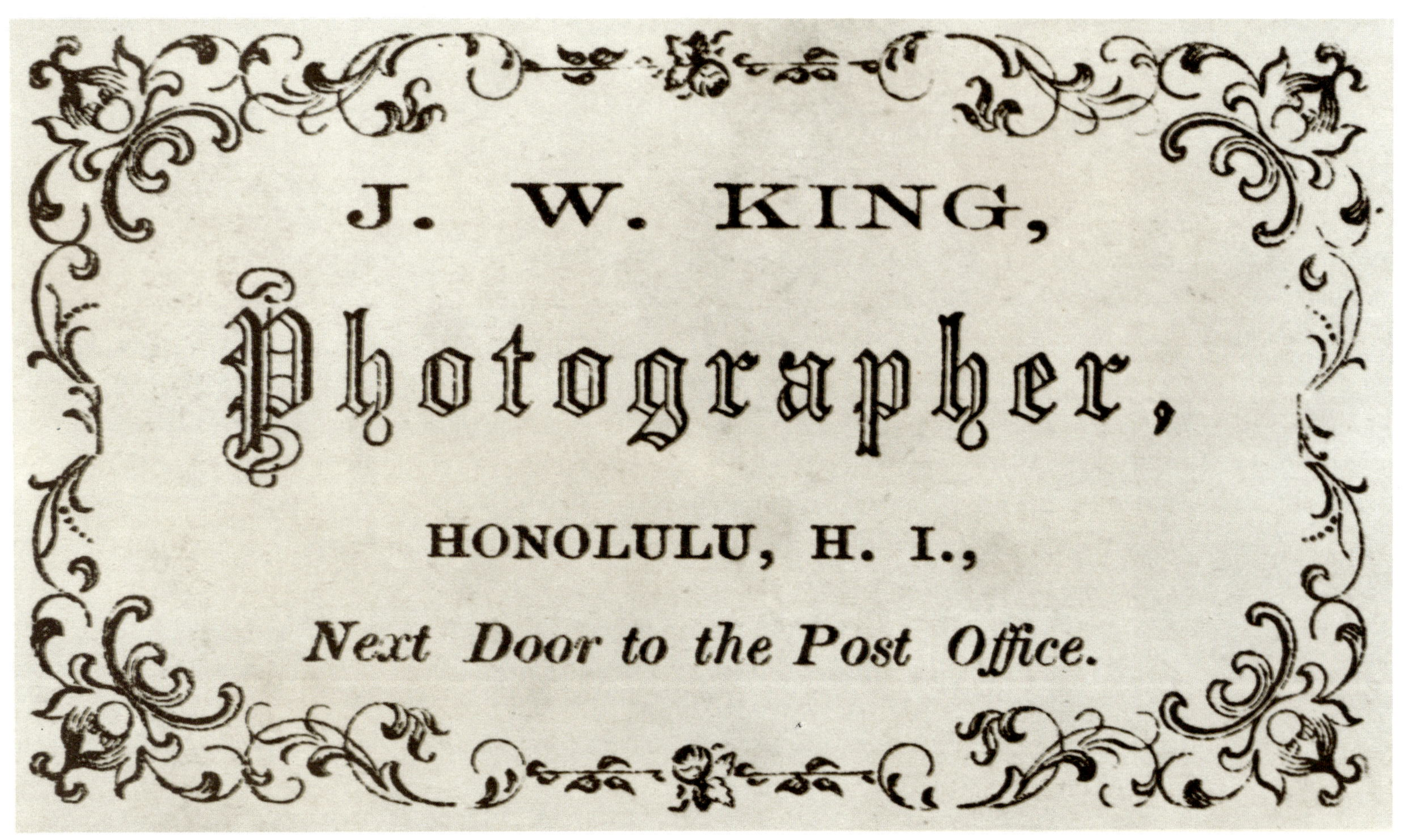

Imprint from back of Joseph King photograph.
Hawaii State Archives.

Joseph W. King

"WHAT NEXT! NEW YORK in Honolulu in the photographic line! Only one Dollar for as good a likeness as has ever been taken in Honolulu before at $2.50 and $3.00. HARD TIMES! and the effect of a large stock of chemicals and cases on hand which must be got rid of to make room for new importations. KING has come to the conclusion that his old (New York) style of taking pictures cheap and a good many of them ought to do as well here as in any other place and therefore invites his friends and the public generally to take the chance while they can of getting good Ambrotypes for less than half the old prices. Call and look at specimen pictures at the rooms. Photographic views of scenery, private residences taken cheap and with dispatch, in the rough or retouched. No one can say now they cannot afford to have their pictures and those of their friends taken at the extremely low prices when they get them as good in every respect as those taken heretofore at two and three times the present price. Only one dollar for a good picture cased, and put up in as good style as ever before in Honolulu. At KING'S Photographic rooms over the Advertiser office, next door to the Post Office, Honolulu, November 28, 1861."

Joseph W. King's advertisement, which appeared in *The Friend* in December, 1861, and January, 1862, was one of the few early advertisements to appeal to a mass market. Although King did key his business to the mass market, the ad, even for King, was somewhat unusual. For the most part, King's infrequent advertising was far more conventional in form, pointing out the excellence of his updated establishment, for example, as in the following advertisement from the August, 1862 edition of *The Friend:*

"PHOTOGRAPHIC GALLERY — King Street, Next door to H. Diamond and Son. The Undersigned having received his new photographic apparatus has entirely refitted and renovated the rooms occupied by H. Stangenwald (More recently by E.D. Durant) and hopes by strict attention to the tastes and fancies of his customers to receive a share of the public patronage. The Carte de Visite in either plain or fancy styles put up neatly and with dispatch. Joseph W. King, King Street, next door to H. Diamond and Sons."

In fact King's photography — or what little is left of it in the public record — is as conventional as most of his advertising. It features for the most part nattily dressed gentlemen and well corseted ladies in unsmiling poses. King's techniques were evidently quite up to date. He offered Honolulu customers the most popular forms and the cheapest forms of photographic images, most of them based on the wet collodion process. In one ad, he assures the public that he can provide the "best quality and latest fashion" in PHOTOGRAPHS — AMBROTYPES — MELAINOTYPES — LEATHER — LOCKET — AND RING PICTURES."

The Ambrotype, which largely replaced the daguerreotype by the mid 1850s, especially among photographers who catered to the mass market, was simply a collodion process glass negative plate that had been treated in a bleaching solution and mounted against a dark material. The result, usually packaged in a case similar to the daguerreotype case, had the appearance of a positive print. The Melainotype was a direct positive print made on tinned iron — the cheap, popular and tinny looking tintype. Tintypes were probably used by King to make the locket and ring pictures he advertised. The use of the tintypes in this form was extremely popular at the time. King's leather pictures, on the other hand, were probably not in great demand. While collodion prints on leather were possible, they were not the most successful use of that process.

King's entire career as a photographer is somewhat shadowy. No advertisements could be found for his studio before September, 1861, when he appears to have taken over offices formerly occupied by one W.F. Howland. Yet, King's 1861 ads implied that he had been in business in Honolulu for some time, for he "assures his friends and patrons that he will either satisfy them in their pictures or no pay." Some of the portraits taken by King that have drifted into the major collections also reinforce the thought that he set up business in the islands before 1861. On the backs of several of these, King's imprint is bracketed by two dates: 1858 appears on the left side of the imprint and 1869 on the right. It is possible, of course, that the earlier date refers to the beginning of King's career as a photographer — taking pictures in "his old (New York) style . . . cheap and a good many." But by 1869, King had been in business in the islands for sufficient time to gain a professional reputation. It seems likely that the two dates refer to the length of time he had been in business in Honolulu.

But the date of King's entrance on the Honolulu scene is hardly the most interesting aspect of his career as an island photographer. More interesting, by far, is the spectacular manner of his exit.

On August 6, 1870, *The Commercial Advertiser* carried the following story: "COMMON NUISANCE — On Wednesday Mr. J.W. King, photographer, was summoned before the police magistrate of this city on a charge of maintaining a public nuisance as described in Sec. 7, Chapter 36 of the penal code. It appears that Marshall Parke and Sheriff Dayton have been aware, for some time (months) past, that indecent and obscene pictures were being issued by some photographer of the city, and have used their best endeavor's to ferrit out the party. Some of the pictures coming into their hands, they arrested several of the female subjects represented, and after close interrogation, ascertained that Mr. King was the guilty party. They quietly accumulated evidence, and on Monday the Marshall made descent upon Mr. King's Gallery with a search warrant, and unearthed the negatives of a most disgusting assortment. To the credit of this community it should be stated that the demand for this style of picture is mostly foreign. We trust that an example which will warn others from a like course will be made of this party. The punishment under the statute is $500, fine or imprisonment for six months. We agree with the Attorney General that the punishment is inadequate to the offense. Mr. King by his Counsel, R.H. Stanley, Esq. pleaded guilty to the charge and asked 1 week delay in judgment, in order to make arrangements. Sentence will be passed on Wednesday next."

On August 13, the follow up story appeared:
"*Mr. J.W. King's Case* — On Wednesday Mr. J.W. King was brought before His Honor John Montgomery for sentence on the charge of common nuisance. His Honor referred to the plea of guilty, by advice of counsel, and said that it only remained for him to fix such a penalty as in his judgment was fit and proper under the circumstances; that after a perusal of the depositions of the females who, in the course of a disgusting traffic in obscenity, had been induced to expose their persons, and permitted themselves to be photographed in positions revolting to common decency, there can be no doubt but that the traffic has been carried on for a long time, and down to the period of the issuing of the

search warrant showing clearly that there was no remorse for the great wrong that had been inflicted; that after a close scrutiny of the evidence of this great iniquity the less excuse was found for any mitigation of the severest penalty of the law, (which is imprisonment) so far as the prisoner was personally concerned, and which would be imposed if he stood alone. But the consequences of this disgraceful conduct would fall with crushing force upon a person indissolubly bound to the prisoner, who is manifestly innocent of any possible complicity in the offense; a circumstance which he could not in common humanity overlook and whose peculiar position must enlist the sympathy of any man possessing a spark of humanity, and having in mind the command of high authority — that justice should be tempered with mercy — he had decided to empose a fine of $100. Score one for the Police Magistrate."

In May, 1943, R.J. Baker attempted to trace the career of the chastized King. He interviewed several members of King families in Honolulu and all were unanimous in denying any relationship to the miscreant. From the time of his sentencing in August, 1870, King seems to have disappeared from the Hawaiian scene. The "disgusting assortment" collected by the Marshal and Sheriff for evidence has apparently not been preserved, nor have the records of King's hearing before the police magistrate. For the curious, this gap in the court records and court evidence is indeed unfortunate for it leaves an unanswered question about what constituted pornography in the Hawaii of 1870. And strangely enough, despite his mass market appeal, even ordinary work by King is a rarity in Hawaii's photographic collections. One wonders if embarrassed upright citizens discarded work by King following his arrest. Perhaps the local citizens preferred not to have King's imprint on photographs collected for their family albums and perhaps some early censorship is responsible for reducing the number of King photographs that eventually worked their way into the public collections.

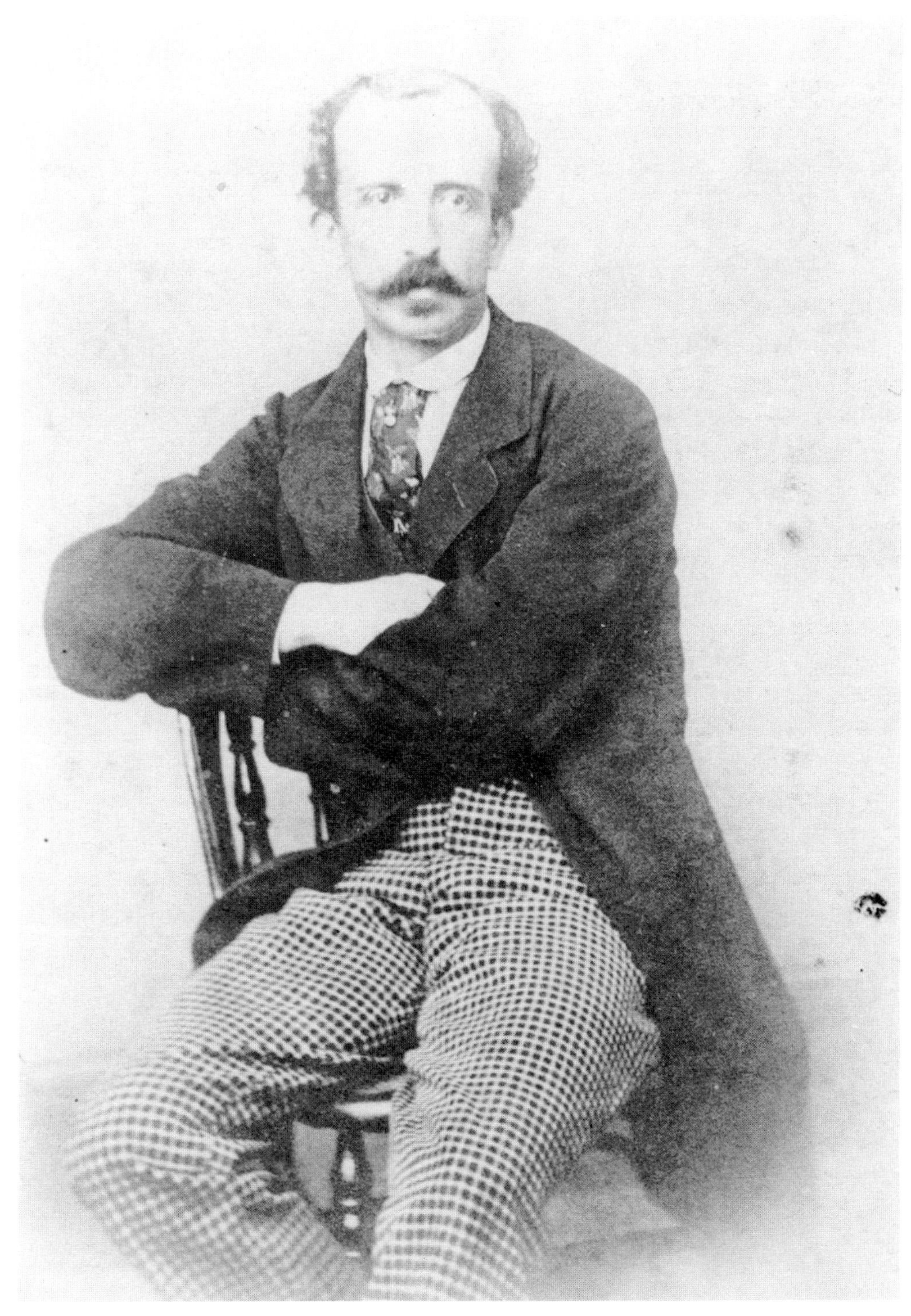

A Honolulu gentleman in the 1860s. J.W. King. Hawaii State Archives.

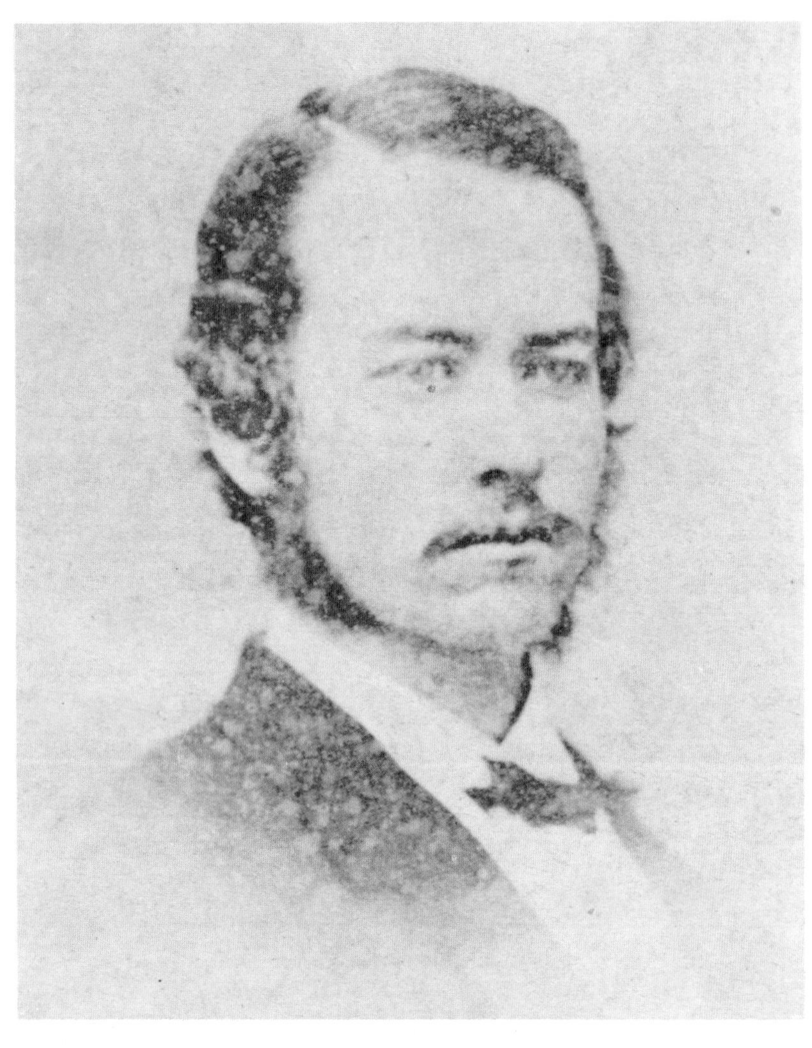

Portrait. 1860s. J.W. King. Hawaii State Archives.

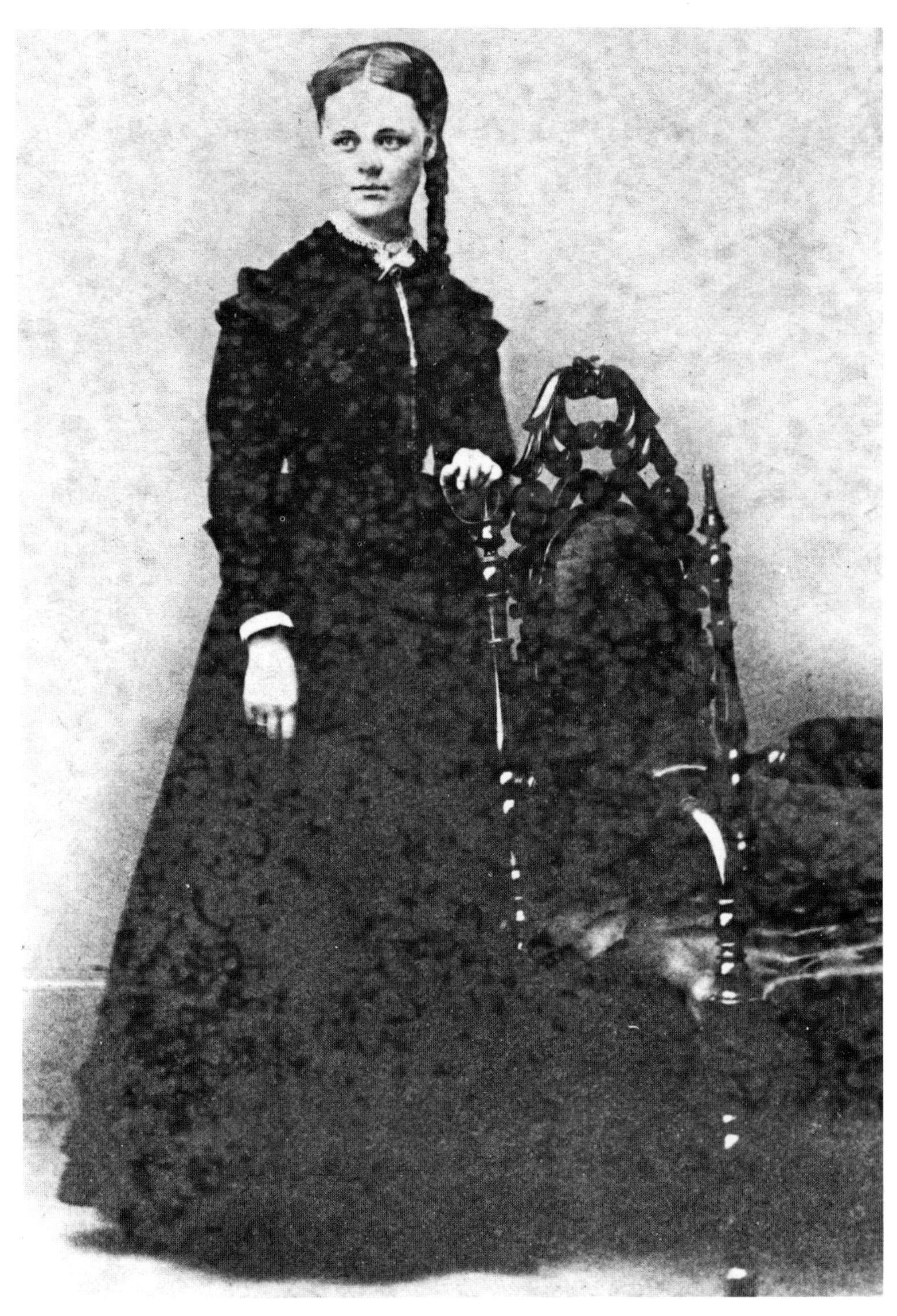

Miss Flora Jones, 1860s. J.W. King. Hawaii State Archives.

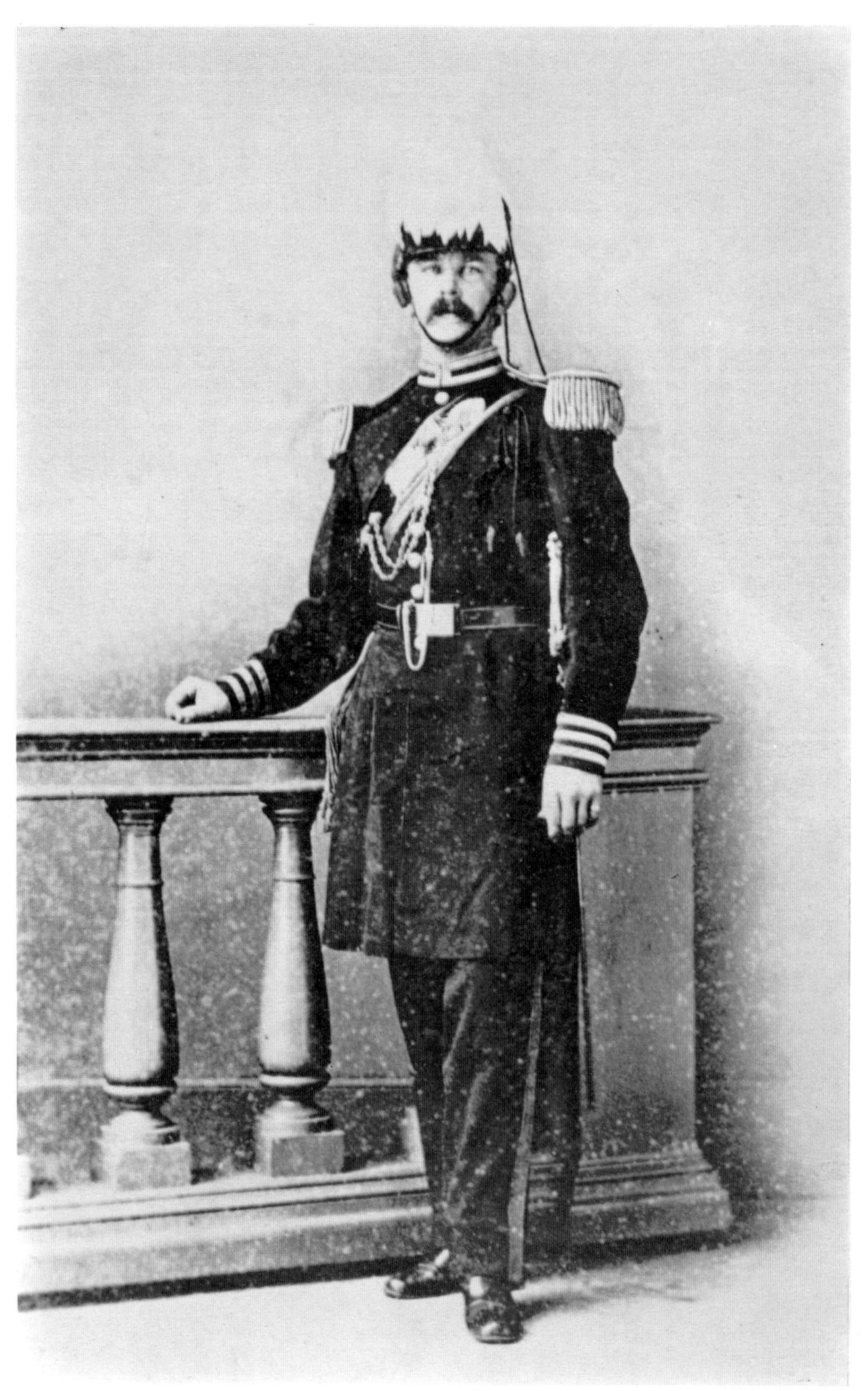

Left: Man in elaborate uniform, 1860s. J.W. King. Hawaii State Archives.

Right: Three young women, 1860s. J.W. King. Hawaii State Archives.

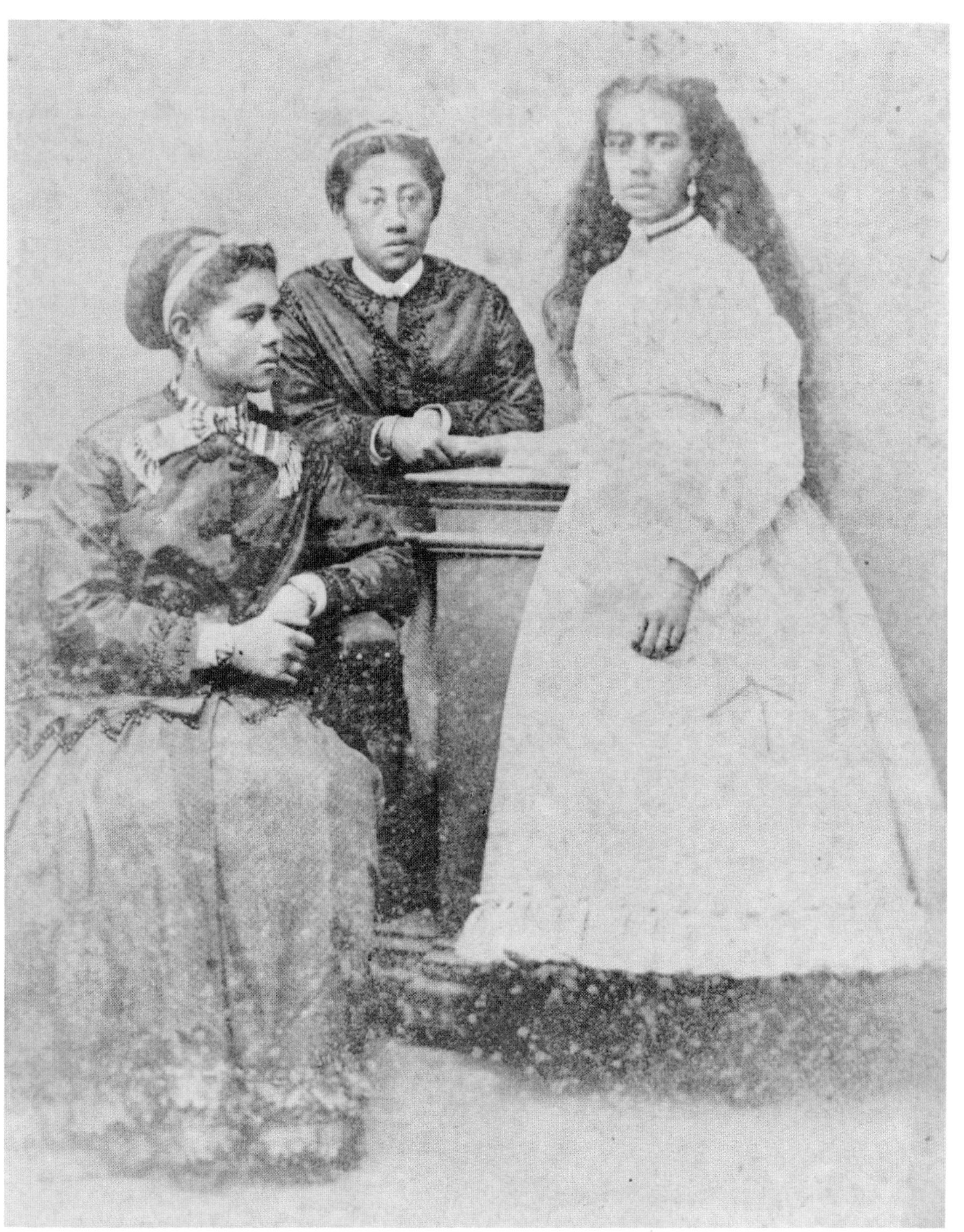

Fort Street, Honolulu, in early 1860s. Hale Paikii (house of pictures) on left is probably one of the business locations used by Henry Chase. H. Chase. Hawaii State Archives.

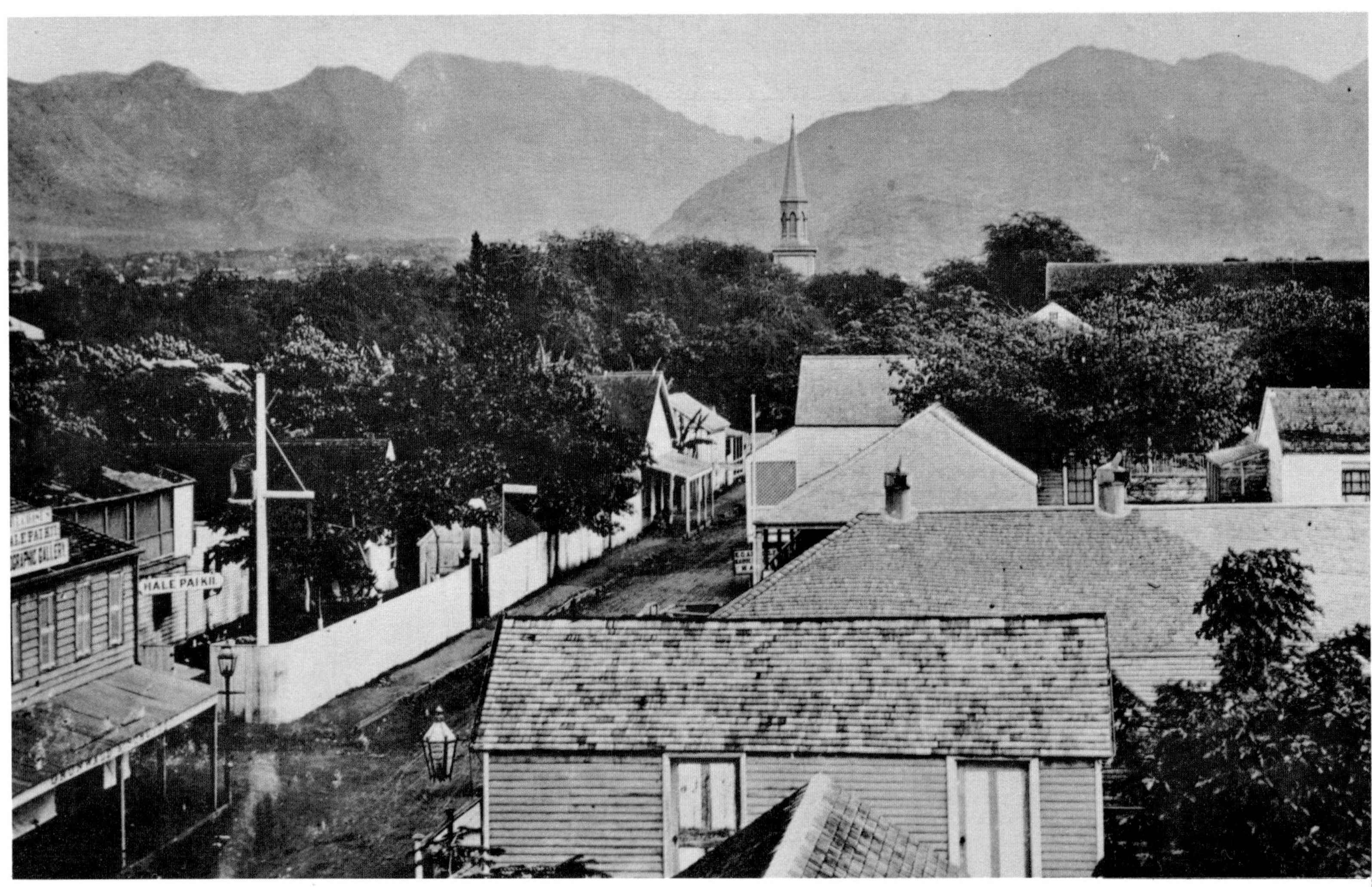

Henry L. Chase

In July, 1862, a small notice appeared in the pages of *The Friend:* "Photographic Rooms. We direct attention to the advertisement of Mr. H.L. Chase, in another column. Mr. Chase has purchased the establishment of Mr. King (Howland's old stand) and having on hand a complete stock of materials is prepared to hand down to posterity in correct, enduring and elegant style all who may favor him with a call. That he is skilled in the business he has undertaken a glance at the pictures in his room will prove."

Henry L. Chase began his photographic business in Honolulu as did almost all the early photographers: a small news column notice seemed inevitably to have accompanied the first paid advertisement. And Chase's first business address in Honolulu seems also to have served as the first location for a good many of the city's photographers, Hugo Stangenwald among them. Indeed, any effort to trace the moving about of Hawaii's early photographers can become confusing, for a number of them bought and sold locations and equipment from one another. Chase, at any rate, advertised his photographic establishment "Next door to the Post Office, Upstairs over the Commercial Advertiser Printing Office" and continued to advertise at that location for at least four years.

Over the years, Chase accumulated a collection of scenic photographs which he advertised for sale. In fact, Chase was a persistent and heavy advertiser. It is fortunate that he was, because, except for the clues provided by his ads, little is known of Chase. In 1864, in *The Friend,* his ad proclaimed: "Pictures taken in every style such as ambrotypes, photographs, Melaineotypes for lockets and landscapes, views of dwellings &c. at reasonable prices. Also on hand a good assortment of fancy cases, frames &c."

In 1866, Chase moved his establishment to a new location on Fort Street. He apparently made several more moves during the next few years, all within the same Fort Street area.

In 1866, *The Friend* carried an advertisement in which Chase featured "Photographs of the Kings Kamehameha and the Chiefs, also scenes of the Islands for sale, 25 cents each." In 1869, in the same newspaper, he proclaimed that "Improvement is the order of the day. Having constructed a new sky-light and made various other improvements I hope now to be able to suit the most fastidious with - A PHOTOGRAPH - of any size from a crystal to a mammoth taken in the best style of the art and on most reasonable terms."

By 1870, though still maintaining his photographic business, Chase had expanded into other fields: *The Pacific Commercial Advertiser* of January 1, 1870, carries the following notice: "H.L. Chase - Drugs and medicines, the best assortment in the city can be found at H.L. Chase's in Fort Street. Also Shaker Herbs of various kinds, such as are used in domestic practice."

And *The Hawaiian Gazette* of November 22, 1871, announces: "Re-OPENED The photographic Gallery, west side of Fort Street, corner of Hotel St. . . Satisfaction in every instance, A general assortment of views and portraits for sale."

These are but a few of the many advertisements that Chase ran in the Hawaii press. They indicate that Chase made the broadest possible appeal for his photographic work, offering everything from cheap tintypes and paper copies of photographs of Hawaiian royalty and views to portrait work for the "most fastidious." Like most photographers working by that time, Chase retained negatives when he was able, as a source of income from future sale of prints—probably in all instances when he was not selling ambrotypes or direct positives. And it is clear from at least one of his advertisements that this practice needed explaining to a public accustomed to walking away with an exclusive image. Chase concludes an ad that ran in *The Friend* for some time during 1865 with a footnote: "P.S. No one can purchase another's picture without written permission." The advantage of a process that permitted multiple prints was obvious to most customers. But the practice of retaining negatives probably generated concern. Chase's postscript was meant to reassure potential customers that their photographs would not be put on sale along with the "volcano Kilauea, the Kings Kamehameha, and a variety of scenes illustrating Island scenes."

The custom developed by the early commercial photographers of keeping large files of negatives has been most valuable to later day historians. And Chase's record of early Honolulu, the outer islands and the island people, would have been a treasure. But on March 18, 1877, a fire, apparently started by an oil lamp in his darkroom, destroyed all of Chase's equipment and supplies and, even more unfortunate, his entire collection of scenic and portrait negatives. R.J. Baker, in *Honolulu in 1870*, reported that the entire Chase Gallery was destroyed and that, except for prints in private collections and pre-fire stocks of scenes that had been sold to local drug and curio stores, nothing survived of Chase's 15 year collection of negatives and prints. The 15 year period, moreover, was one in which Chase was the most popular island photographer and the most prolific in taking and printing island scenes.

The loss, from a historical point of view, was enormous. There is no way to calculate how many early scenes taken by Chase have been totally lost. Indeed, those that remain to us are probably only a small percentage of his work that arrived haphazardly at various museums through donations of private print collections. And, even more unfortunate, Chase seems to have been better at taking photographs than at printing them: most of his original prints have faded badly, many almost to the point where they are useless from any point of view.

Though he re-established himself for a while at a Nuuanu Street location, Chase never completely regained his former footing in business. By 1880 he announced in *The Hawaiian Gazette* his willingness to take assignments on the neighbor islands: "Photography. H.L. Chase. The undersigned having now all the apparatus and conveniences for traveling, is prepared to visit any part of the islands and do either portraits or views to order at short notice. Only first class work will be done. Terms, cash or draft on Honolulu when the negatives are made." The announcement could not disguise the fact that for Chase, who had been an established Honolulu photographer for years, the willingness to do short notice, itinerant work was a step backward.

In 1888 Chase left Honolulu and took up life and the photographic business at Wailuku, Maui. In his unpublished notes on early photographers, R.J. Baker reported talking with a "Miss Green of the Library staff" about Henry Chase. Miss Green, he reported, had seen Chase in about 1895 in Wailuku. He looked very old, she said, and "in a very disreputable condition." Baker asked if she attributed his appearance to illness, poverty or drink and Miss Green replied that it was probably due to all three. He looked, said she, "down and out."

Henry L. Chase died on Maui on June 1, 1901. According to Baker's notes, he left only one relative, in Hilo, who could never be found and he died practically penniless: his estate consisted only of some photographic material and equipment, and two gold watches. His funeral was arranged at a cost of $40.

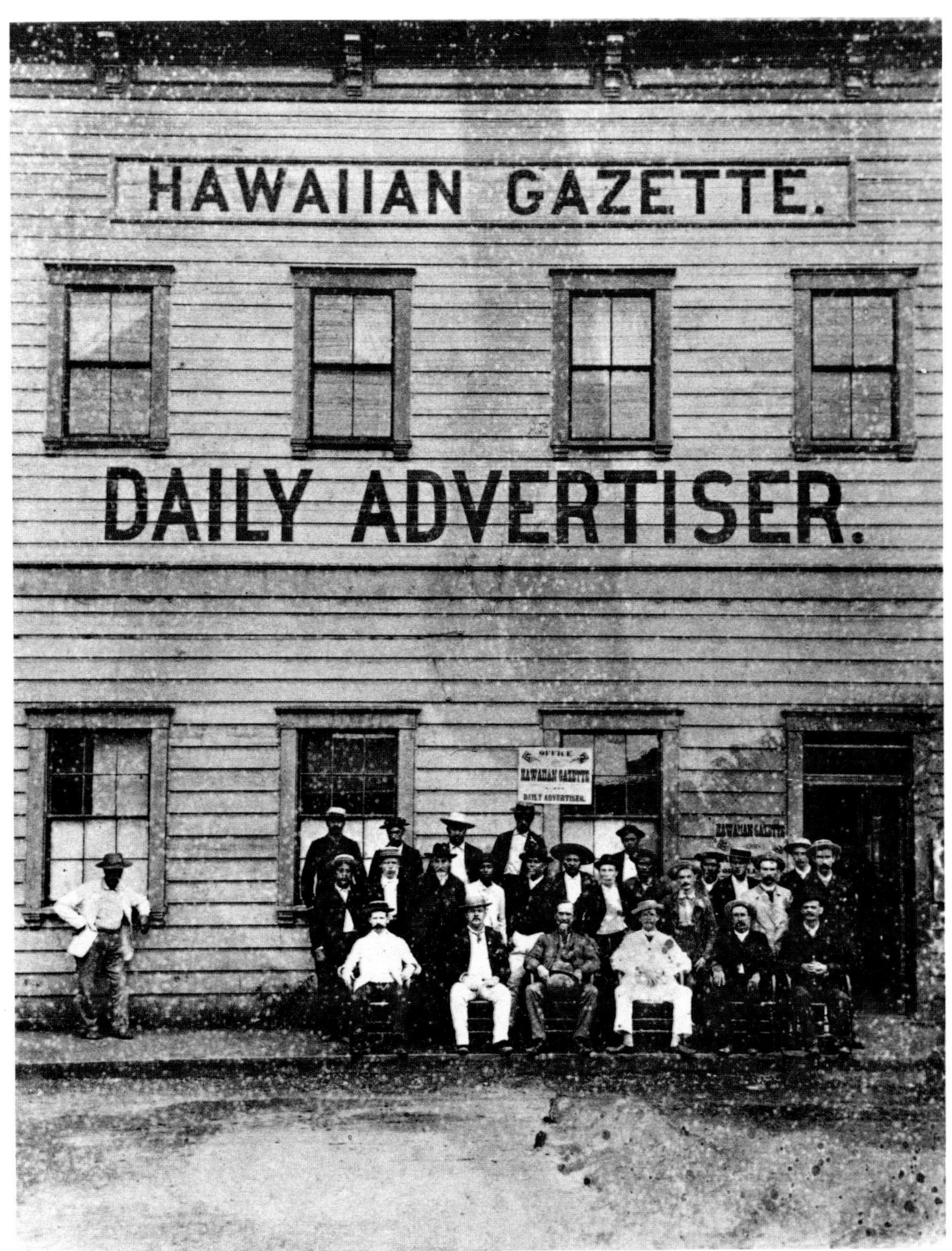

The Hawaiian Gazette and Daily Advertiser Building. An upstairs office in this building was used by several of the early photographers. 1890s. J. J. Williams. Hawaii State Archives.

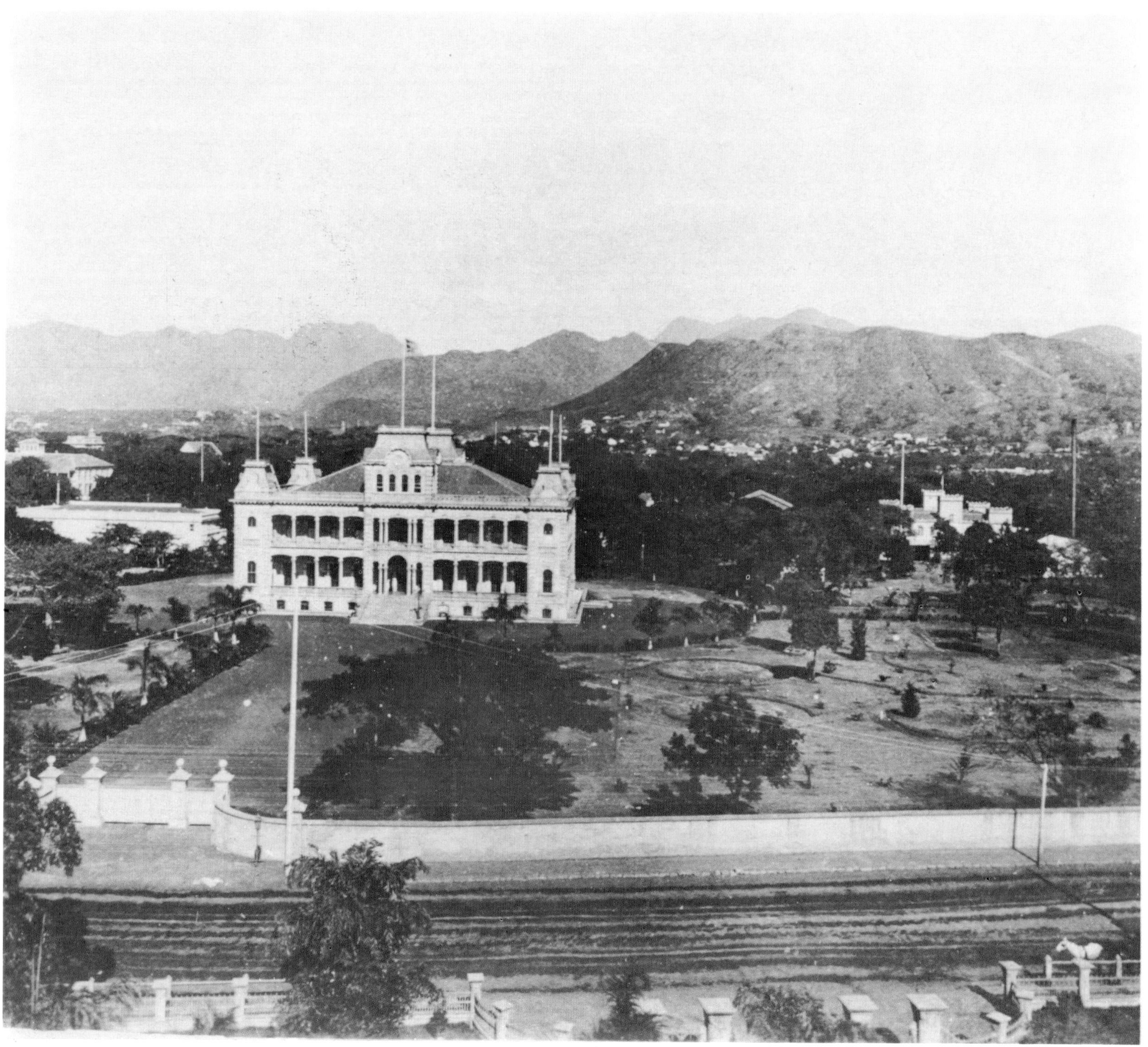

Left: Iolani Palace with Iolani Barracks in the background. Taken from the Judiciary Building, 1880s. H.L. Chase, Hawaii State Archives.

Below: Interior of Iolani Palace throne room, 1880s. H.L. Chase. Hawaii State Archives.

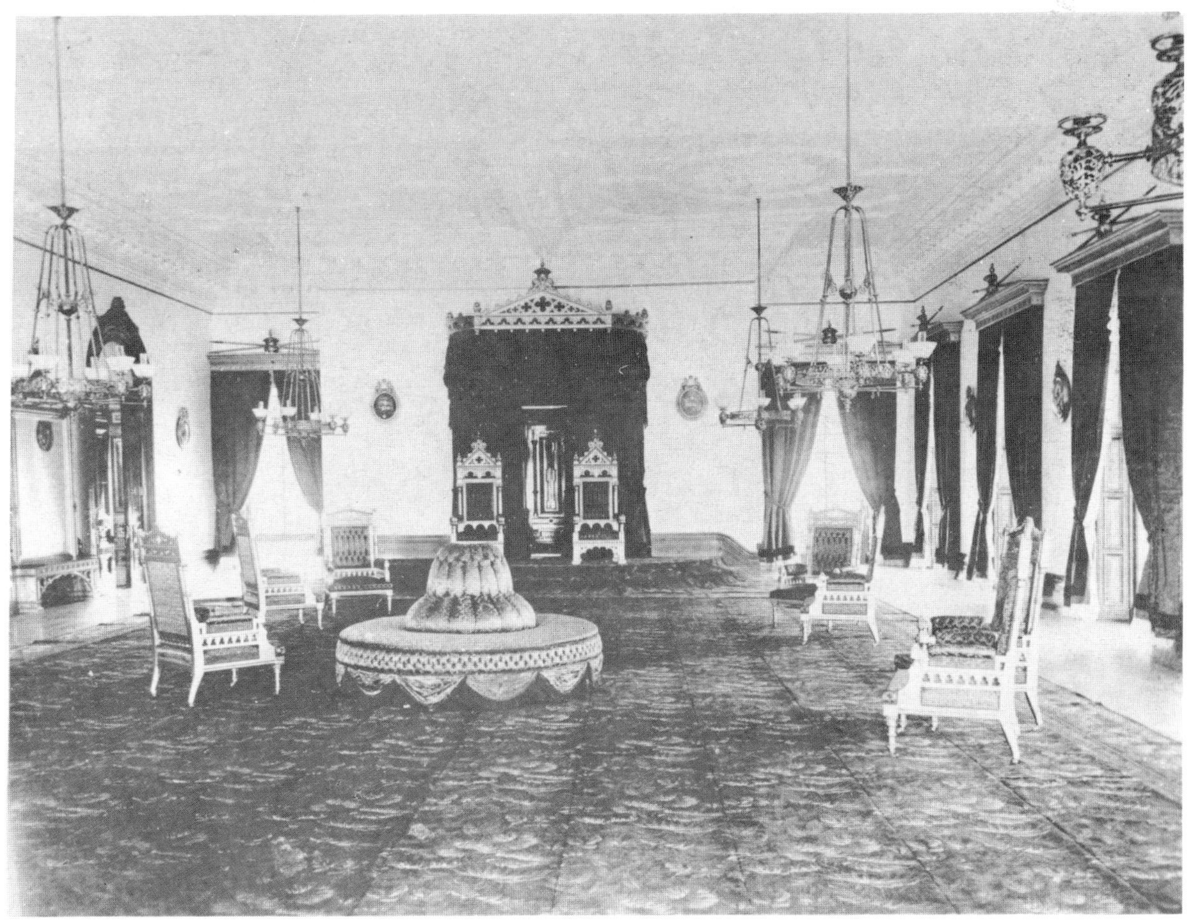

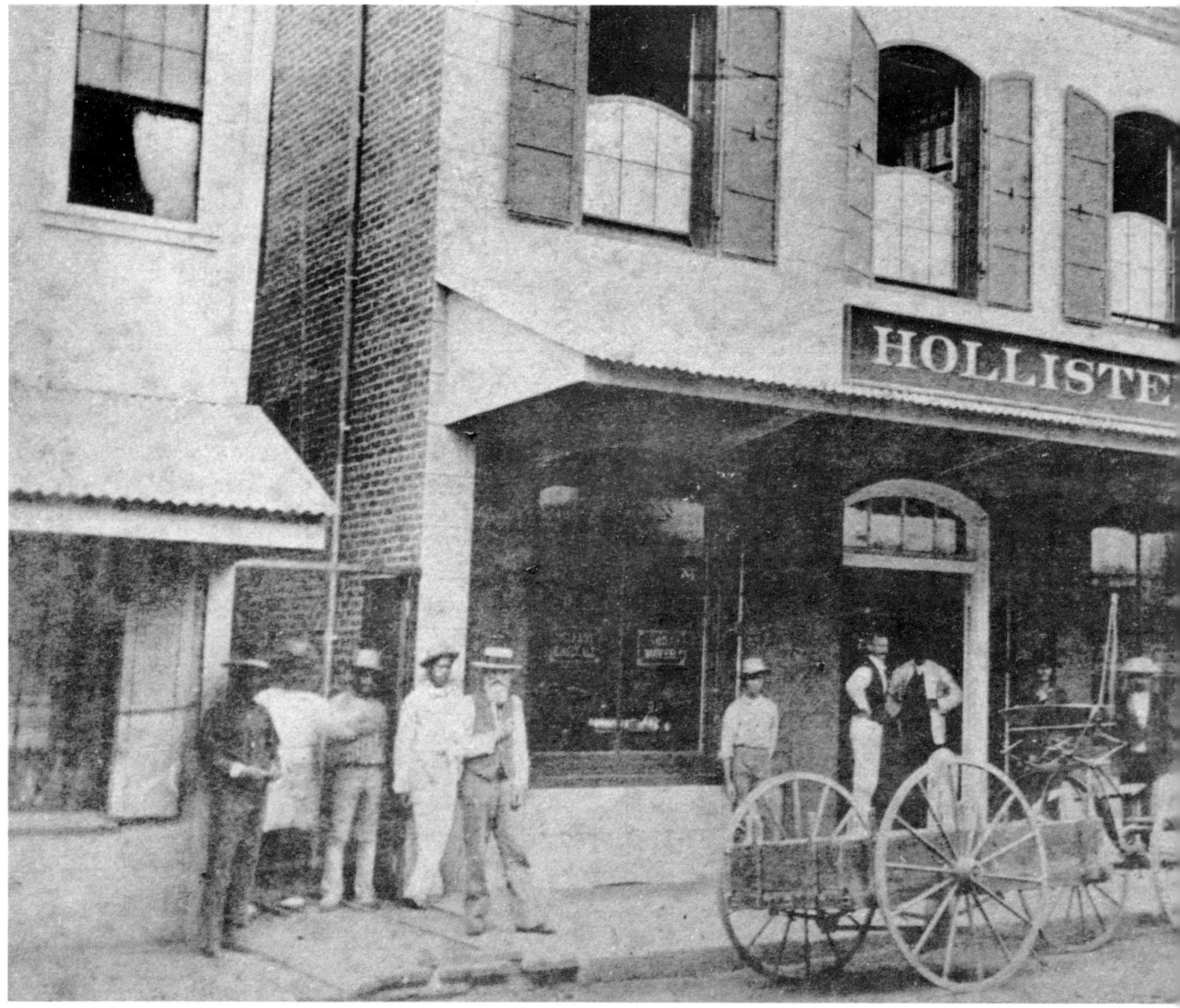
HOLLISTE

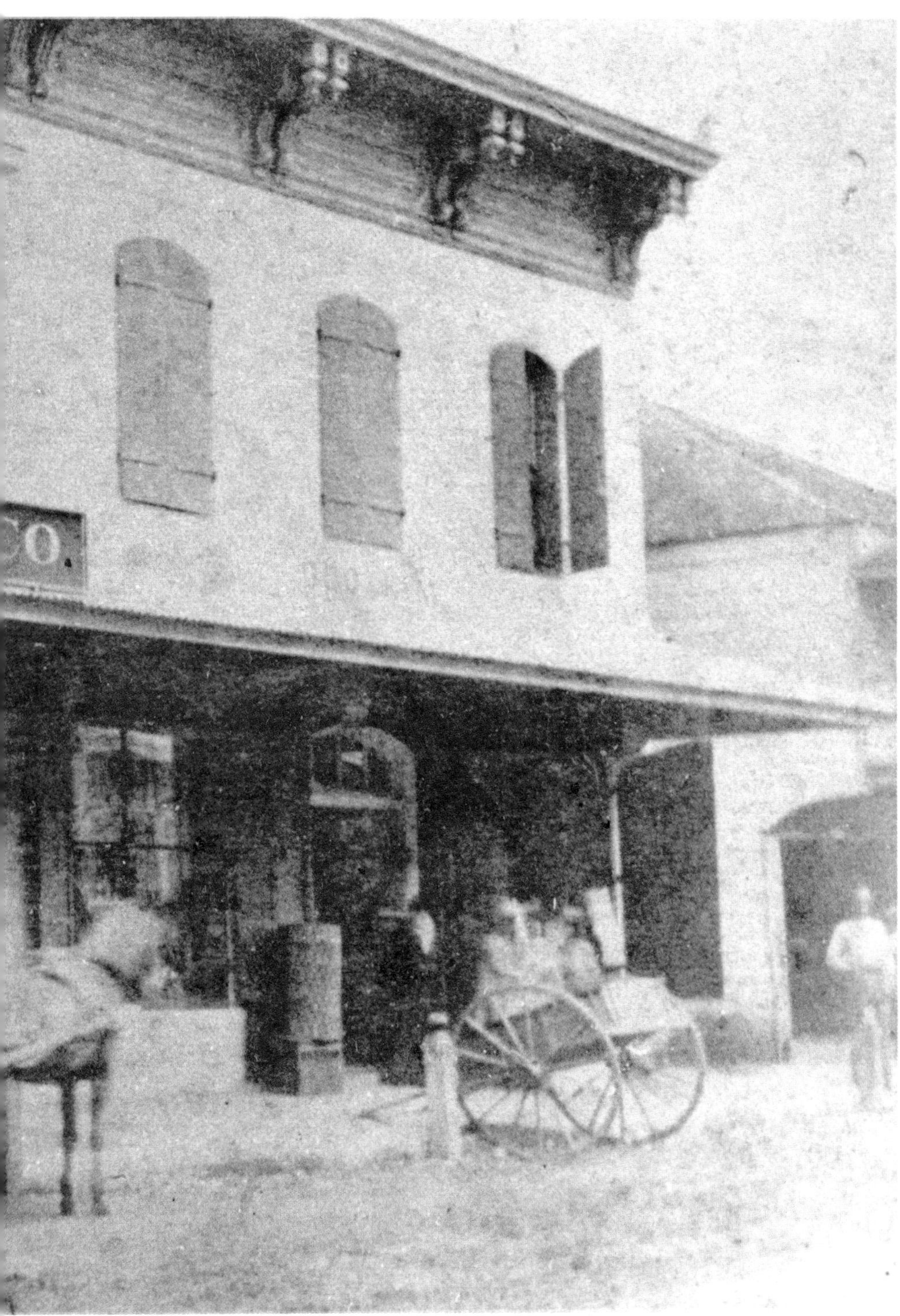

Nuuanu Avenue, 1883. H.L. Chase. Hawaii State Archives.

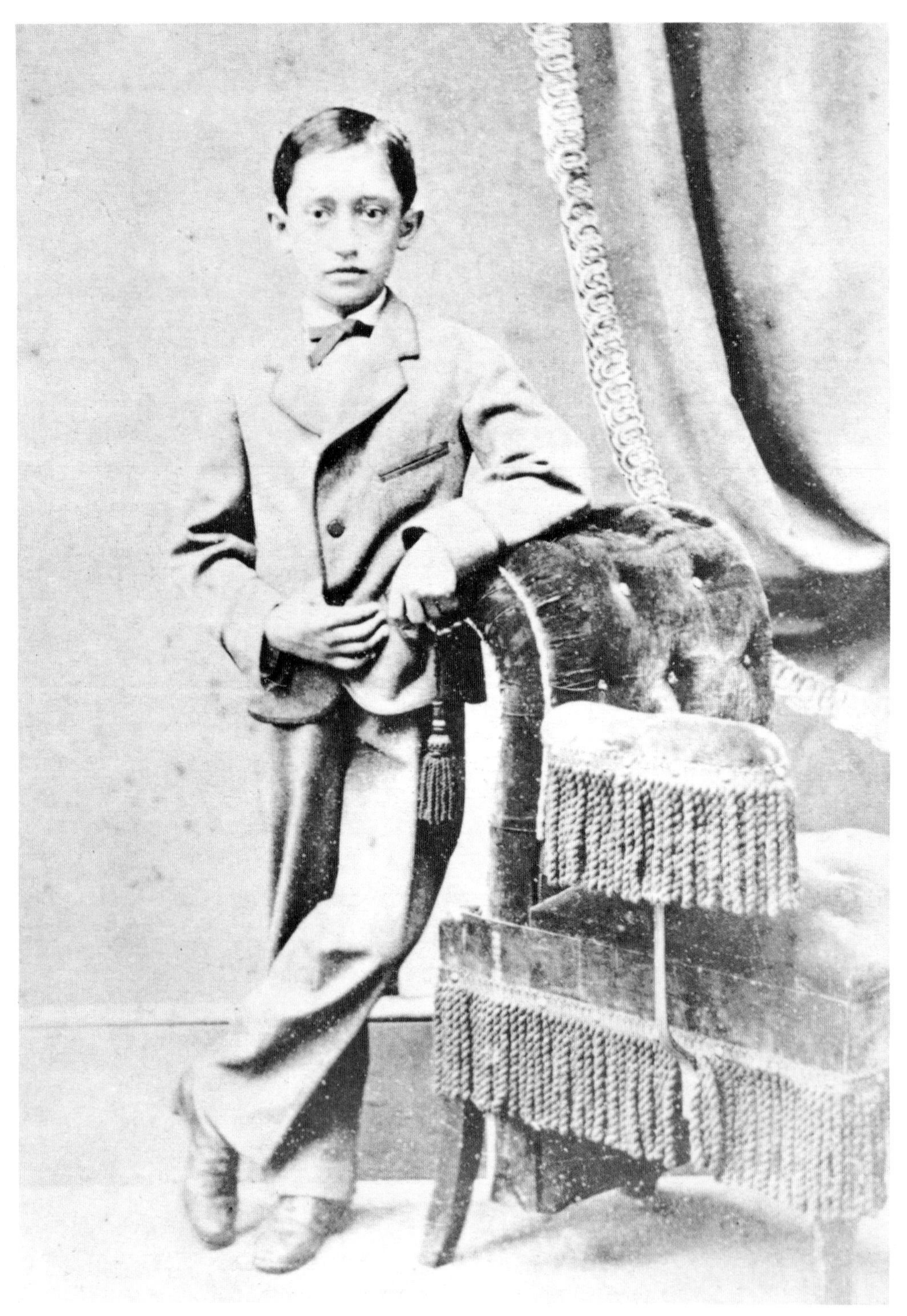

Young Master Wideman, 1875. Photograph by M. Dickson. Hawaii State Archives.

Menzies Dickson

Menzies Dickson should be recognized among the old photographers for two reasons. First, in 1867, he founded what has become the oldest photographic studio in the Hawaiian Islands. The studio was sold in 1880 to J.J. Williams and has remained in the Williams family through the present time. Second, he can be recognized as the photographer in Hawaii whose consummate skill was in a highly Victorian style of portraiture.

Menzies Dickson came to Hawaii in 1867, apparently from Cincinnati, Ohio, where he had lived for some years. He set himself up on Fort Street, as did a number of the early photographers. While he did not advertise as heavily as some of the other early photographers, at least one advertisement ran unchanged in *The Friend* from early 1874 through January, 1878:

"M. DICKSON, Photographer, 61 Fort Street, Honolulu. ALWAYS HAS ON HAND A CHOICE ASSORTMENT OF PHOTOGRAPHIC STOCK, A large Collection of Beautiful Views of Hawaiian Scenery, &c,&c. CURIOSITY HUNTERS will find at this establishment a SPLENDID COLLECTION OF Volcanic Specimens, corals, shells, war implements, ferns, mats, kapas and a Great Variety of other Hawaiian and Micronesian curiosities. PICTURE FRAMES A SPECIALTY!"

The excursion into curios was apparently the result of efforts by Dickson's brother, for in the June, 1871 issue of *The Friend* a small notice appears that calls public attention to the collecting genius of the Dickson kin:

"Hawaiian Curios — Strangers and visitors are often making inquiries for Hawaiian curiosities, specimens of lava, coral, etc. We are glad to see that the brother of Mr. Dickson the photographer is doing his best to meet the demand. Already he is able to make a good exhibition, and ere long we are disposed to think he will be able to gratify curiosity hunters to their fullest desire. His collection may be seen at his brother's photographic stand in Fort Street."

Like a good many other island photographers, Dickson left the photographic business but remained in Hawaii. According to R.J. Baker, he sold his business to J. J. Williams in 1880 and became manager of the Kawailoa Cattle Ranch at Waialua, Oahu. Dickson died in Honolulu in May, 1891.

Little else is known of Menzies Dickson but in an interesting way his photographs speak for at least a part of his life in Hawaii. Of all the early photographers, no one more consistently depended on velvet draped tables, fringed chairs or braided uniforms. And no one so thoroughly used that ubiquitous painted canvas backdrop of Diamond Head awash with crested waves and swaying painted palms.

The style that Dickson adopted, a style that has been labeled by a number of photographic critics as Victorian Trash, was certainly not original. Yet it captures an important dimension of the age: even in far off Hawaii the studied, uniformed young gallant, the serious and demure young lady, the angel girl-child with perfect blond curls and the Lord Fauntleroy little boy with perfect manners were apparently in great demand — in photographs at any rate. From the great popularity of Dickson's work, it would appear that at least a part of Hawaii's population was pleased to depict itself and its children as good, stern, proper, sober, serious and sincere. Indeed, if not for the much used canvas Diamond Head, a prop that seems to appear in one of every ten of Dickson's portraits, it would be difficult to tell that Menzies Dickson was in business in the middle of the Pacific Ocean. His prissy children and proper adults could just as easily, perhaps more easily, be identified as coming from the most complacent level of middle class British society during the height of Queen Victoria's reign.

Yet, despite the fact that this style of photography has been deprecated by so many critics, it holds a definite fascination for the modern viewer, telling us much about the times in which Menzies Dickson lived and worked.

The Dickson imprint, as it appears on the back of Dickson photographs. Hawaii State Archives.

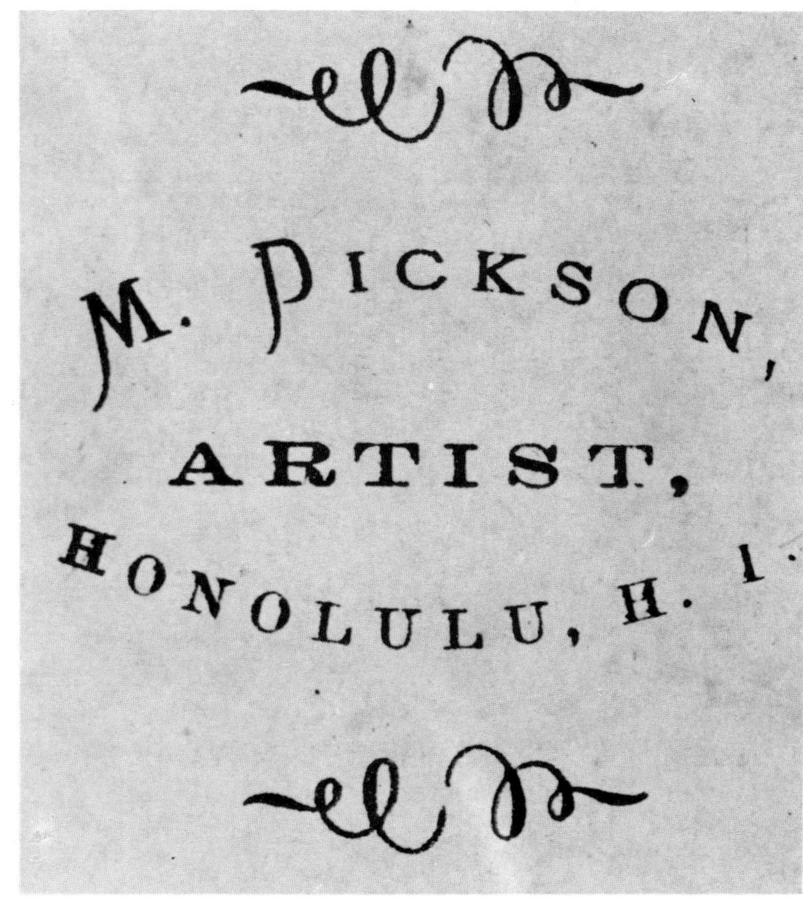

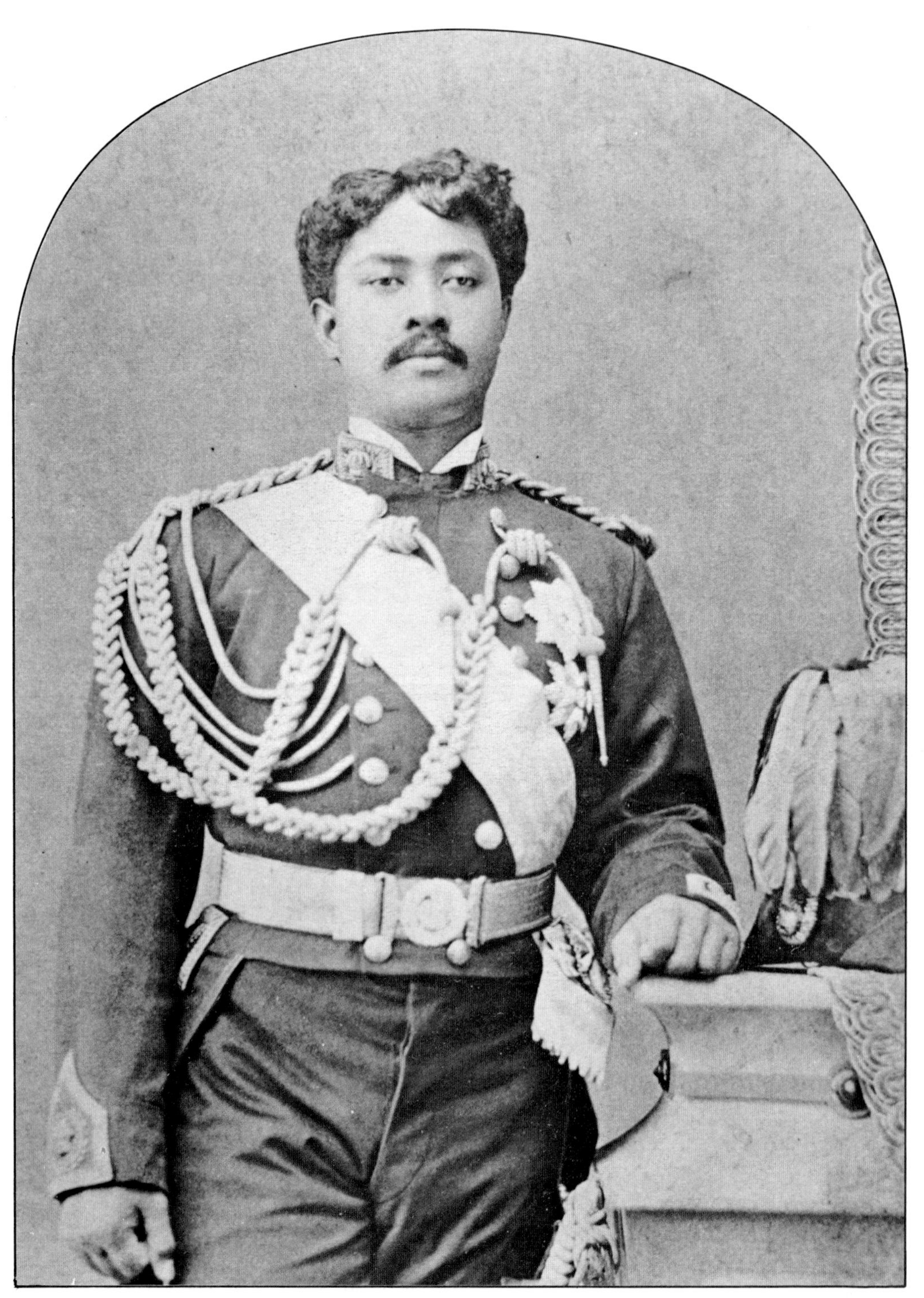

Prince William Pitt Leleiohoku, 1870s. Photo by M. Dickson. Hawaii State Archives.

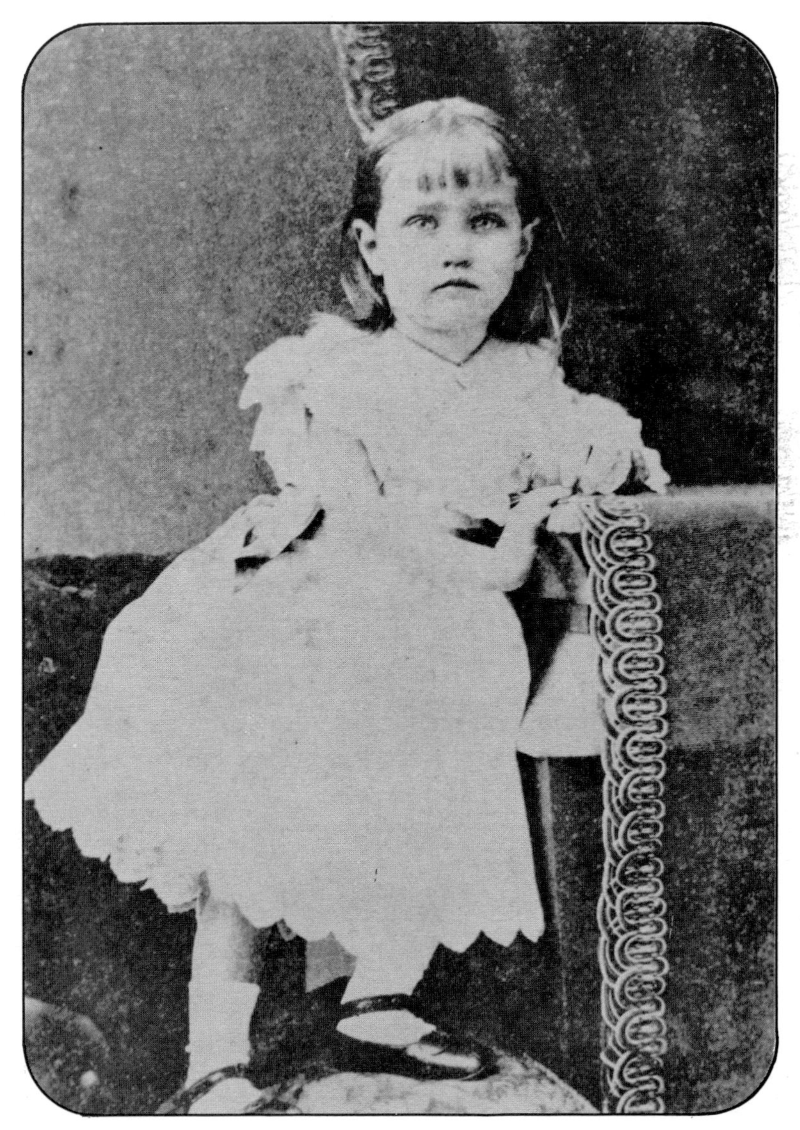

Studio photograph of young girl in about 1870.
M. Dickson. Hawaii State Archives.

The painted Diamond Head backdrop was a favorite with clients in the 1870s. M. Dickson. Hawaii State Archives.

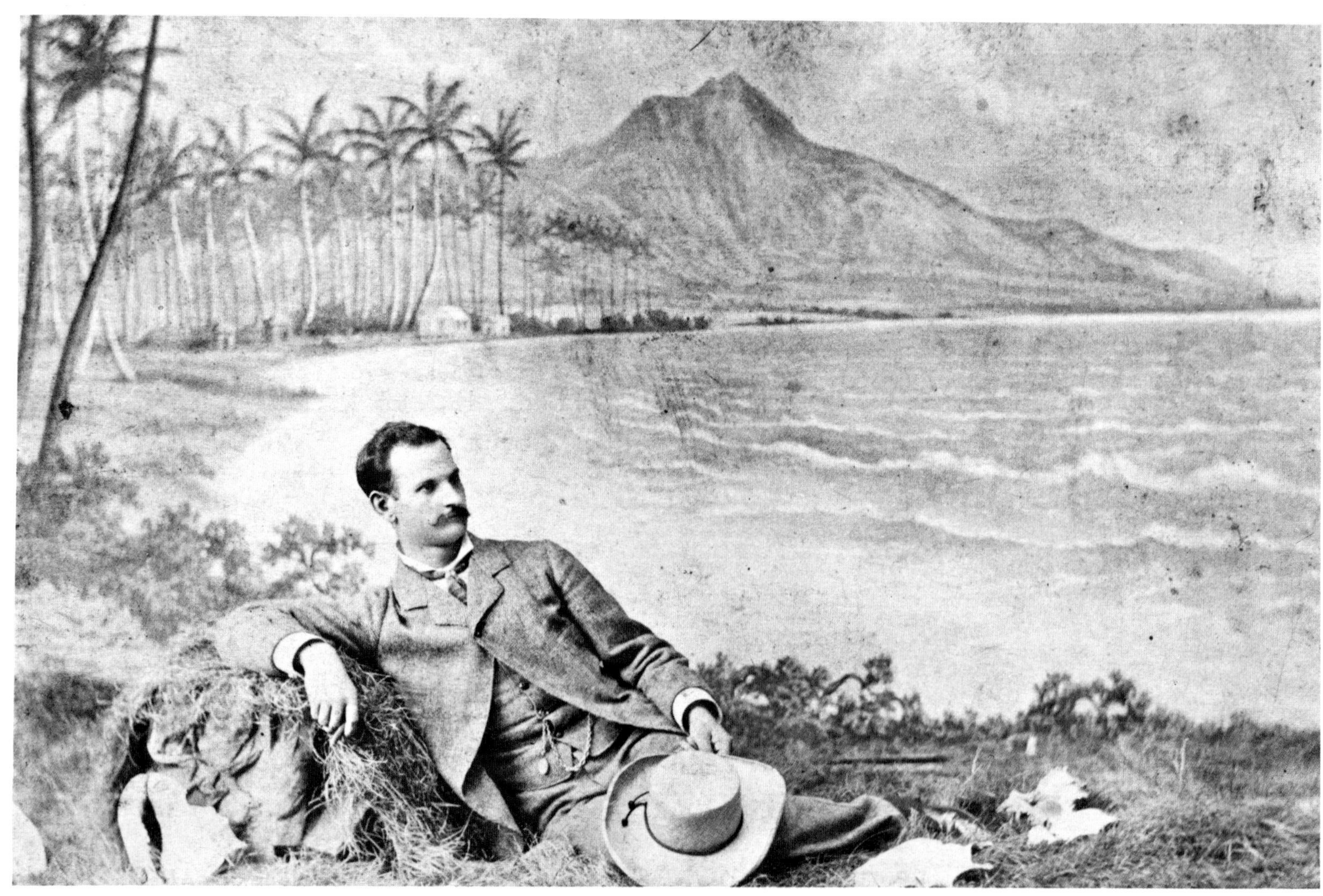

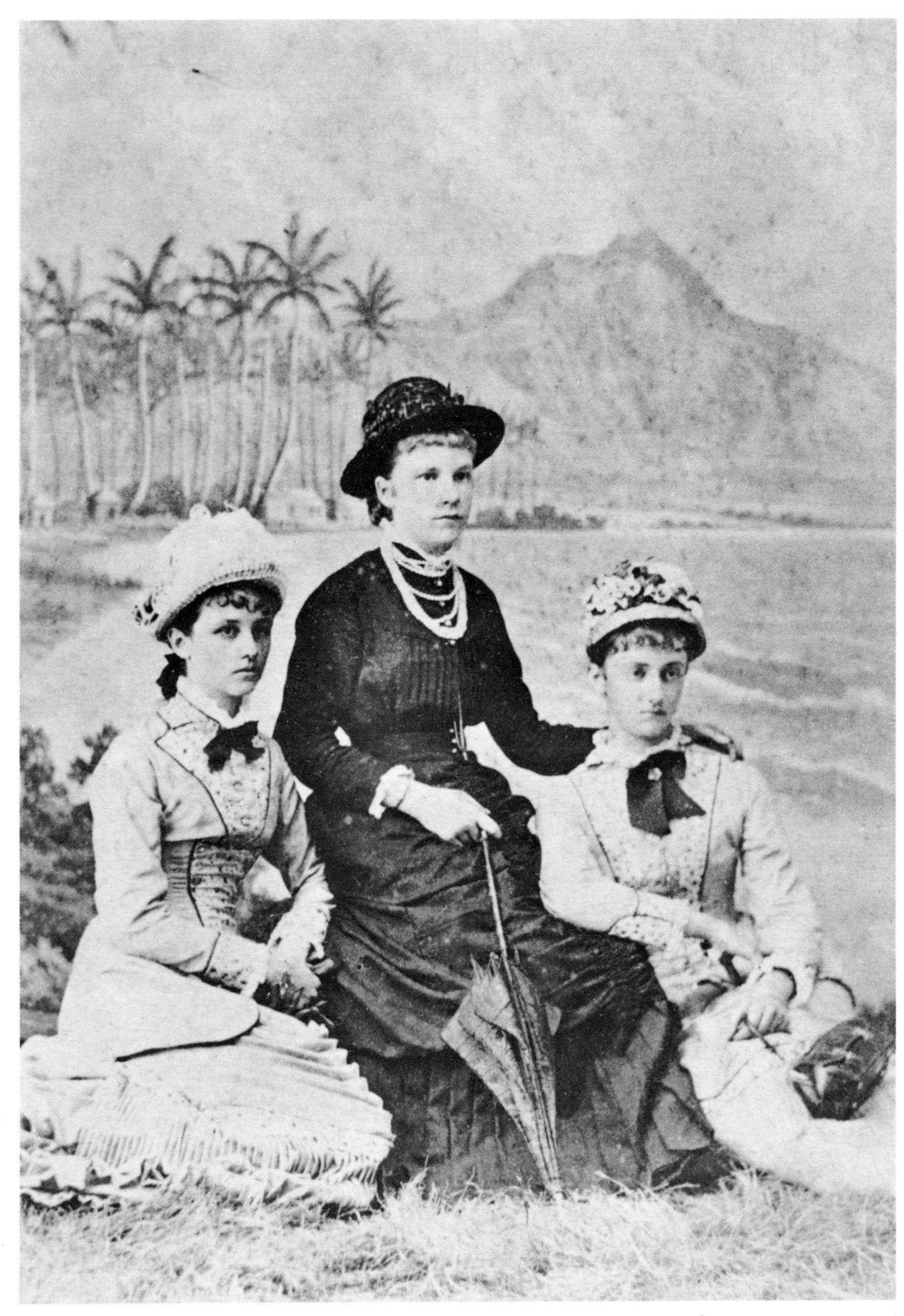

A canvas backdrop of Diamond Head sets off three young women about 1875. Photo by M. Dickson. Hawaii State Archives.

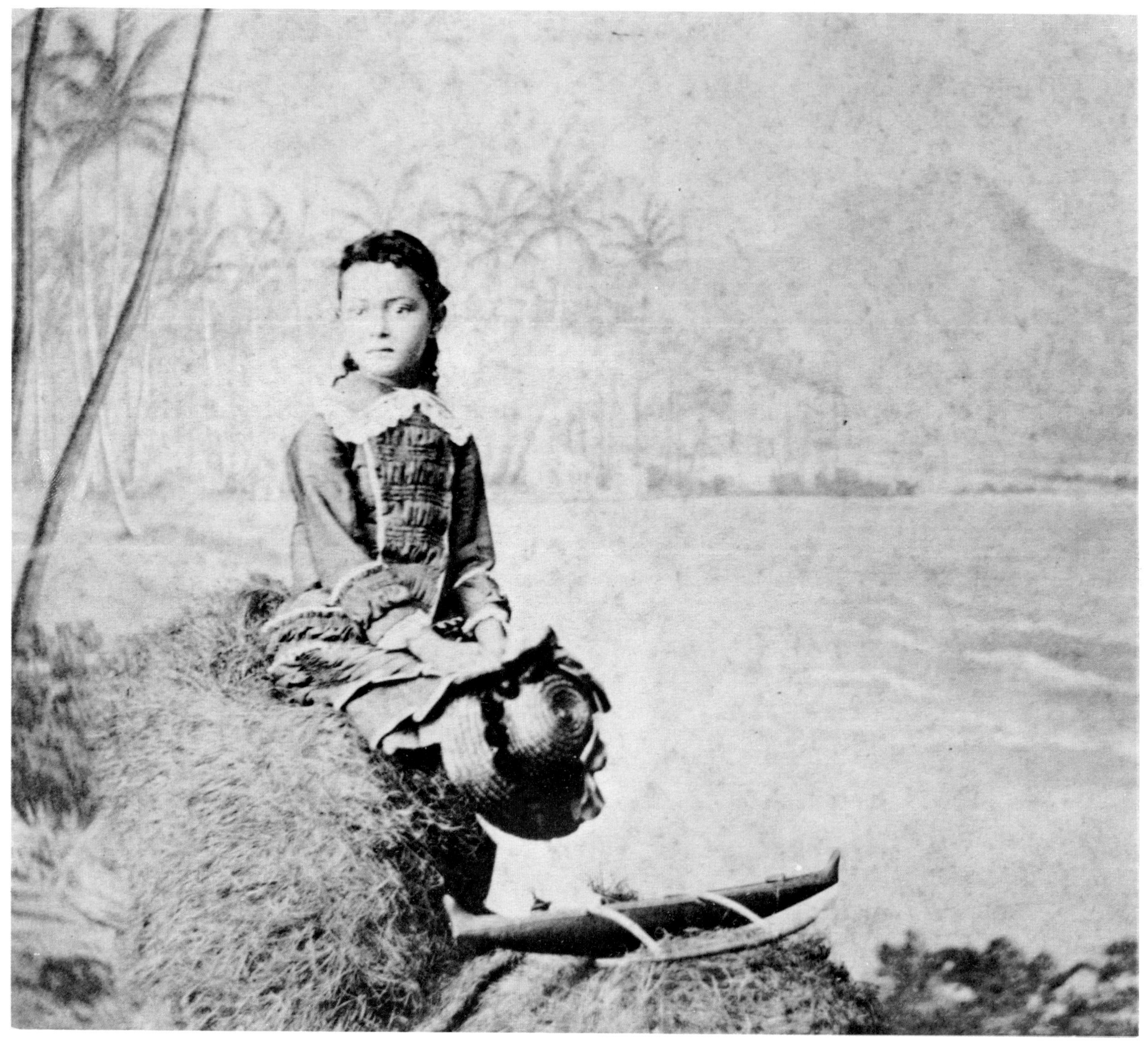

Left: Princess Kaiulani photographed before a canvas Diamond Head. This photo was probably taken shortly before Dickson sold his studio in 1880. M. Dickson. Hawaii State Archives.

Right: Boy leaning on a table. M. Dickson, 1870s. Hawaii State Archives.

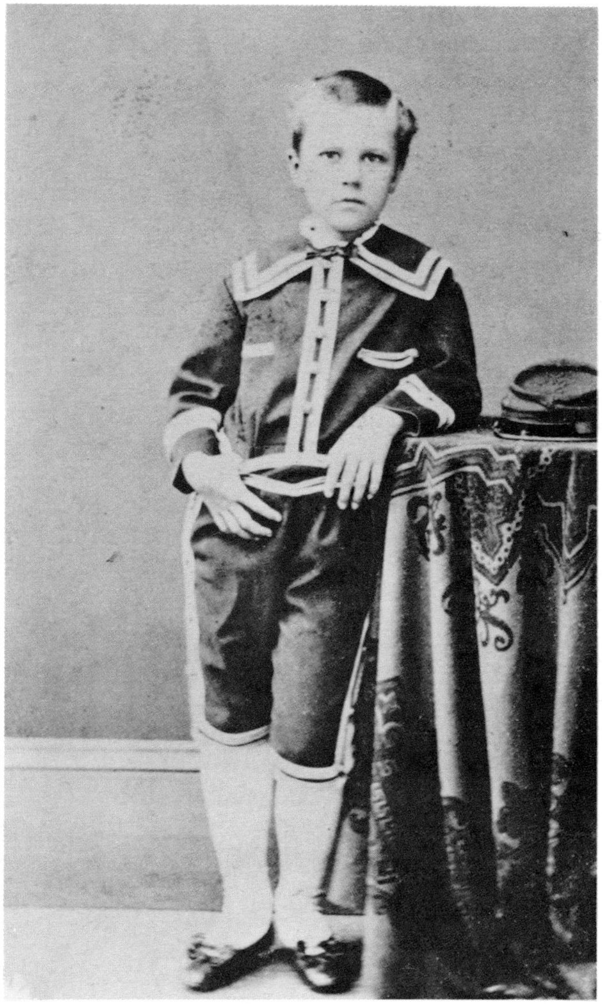

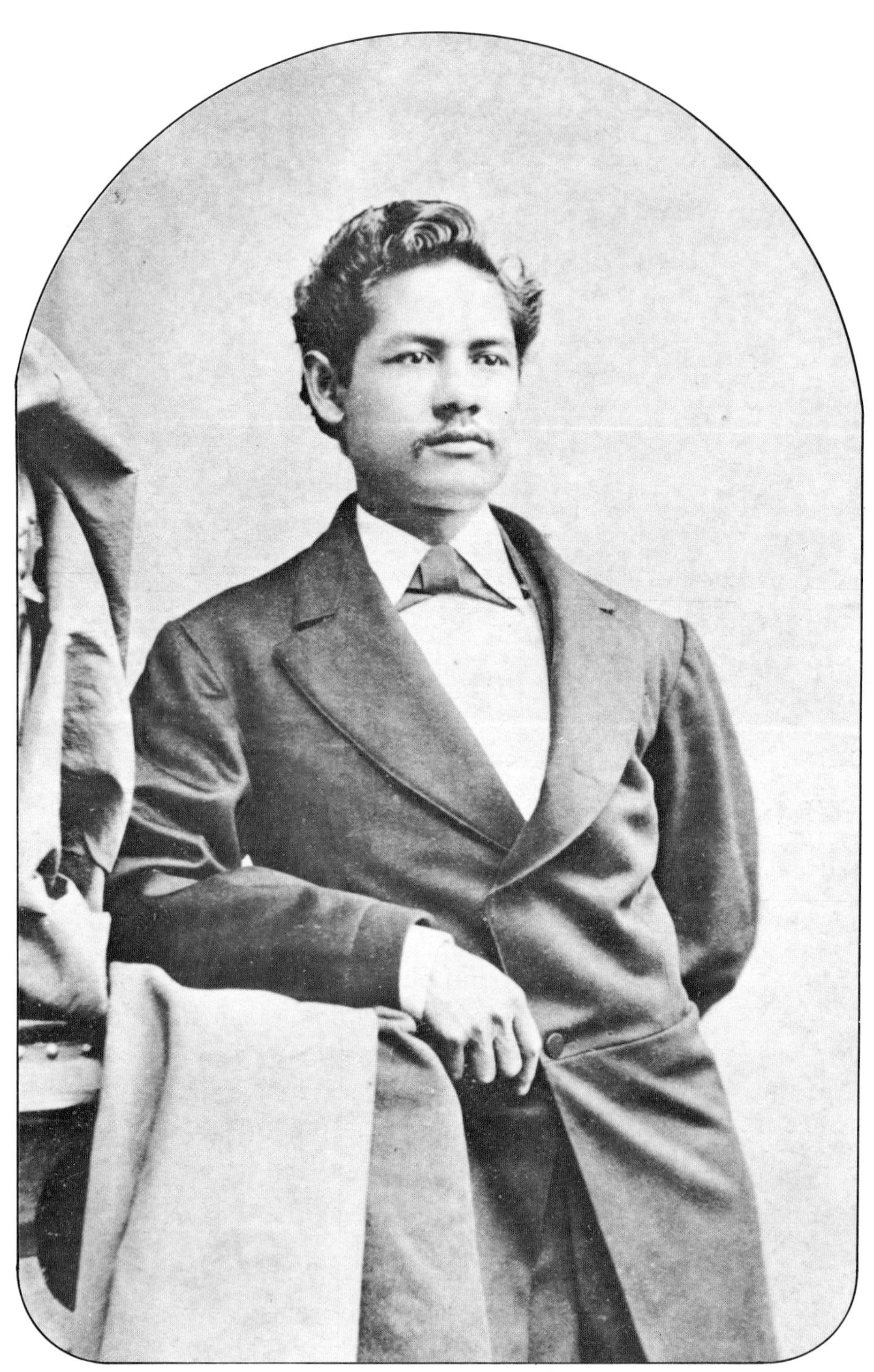

Self portrait, around 1880. Note the position of Montano's left arm. He probably held a device behind his back to trip the shutter. A. A. Montano. Hawaii State Archives.

Andreas A. Montano

Andreas A. Montano was unique among the early Honolulu photographers: he set up business at 87 Fort Street on his arrival in the islands in 1876 and he remained at that location until his retirement from the photographic profession in 1888. His departure from photography was permanent and he was listed in the Honolulu Directory, a few years after his retirement as manager of Kaipu Dairy.

It is unfortunate that little is known of Montano's life. R.J. Baker, in his interviews with old time residents concerning the early photographers, gathered that Montano was a "South American" by birth. And, according to an obituary notice in the December 2, 1913 edition of *The Pacific Commercial Advertiser*, Montano came to the islands from the Republic of Columbia, after he was "involved in a South American revolution, and was forced to flee from the country for his life . . ."

Baker refers to Montano as both an artist and photographer. *The Commercial Advertiser* article refers to him as an artist who "maintained an art store and studio at Fort and King Streets, and was the first one to introduce the art of retouching pictures in the Islands." It is only this reference to retouching pictures that gives the reader of this obituary an indication that Montano's art, or at least one of his arts, may have been photography. Yet, among the many Montano photographs that remain within the state's collections one can easily find many strikingly beautiful portraits.

Montano was married to Mary Jane Fayerweather Davison, a part Hawaiian widow with extensive and influential contacts in the Hawaiian community. It is probable that Mrs. Montano was responsible for her husband's initial popularity with the Hawaiian community: Montano was the only early photographer who seemed to have a predominantly Hawaiian clientele. But certainly it was the artistry of his work that kept his reputation alive and, for a long time, made his studio the most fashionable in Honolulu. Montano numbered many members of the Hawaiian royal family among his customers. Queen Emma returned to his studio many times for sittings and Kalakaua not only paid him frequent visits but also sent a steady stream of members of the royal household to have their photographs taken.

For those of us who are accustomed to the large size that is a feature of most photographic portraiture today, it is easy to thumb through a collection of old photos and entirely overlook those taken by Montano. All of the Montano portraits in public collections are small: some are about four by five inches in size — what was then called a Cabinet. But most are not much larger than a standard playing card. These tiny portraits were probably taken with a carte-de-visite camera that produced four or six exposures on a single plate. The photographer would then print all of the exposures, cut them apart, and mount them on cardboard backings about 2 1/2 by 4 inches in size. The carte-de-visite was introduced in Europe in the 1850s and rapidly became a popular form of photography. In fact, for a time, people collected carte-de-visite photos much in the same manner that children today collect baseball cards.

The finished carte-de-visite is, today, easily laid aside in any quick shuffle through hundreds of old prints. But careful attention to these tiny portraits and full length views by Montano reveals that they are exquisite. Montano had an eye for something beyond the physical presence of his sitters. The average portrait of his day told a great deal about the physical features of the sitter, sometimes more than the sitter wished to reveal. But it told little else. Somehow Montano's portraits, particularly of Hawaiian women, tell us more. It is difficult to describe what it is that Montano does that gives his tiny portraits an extra edge. His sitters somehow seem more at ease, more at peace with themselves, and they seem to reveal to us something of their inner nature.

Indeed, so exceptional are these tiny portraits that it proved difficult to make a selection for this book — one is tempted to include them all.

Andreas A. Montano died in December, 1913, at the age of 67, at his Manoa Valley home. He had not taken any photographs professionally for over 30 years and he had spent the last eight years of his life in bed, the victim of what appears to have been a paralyzing stroke. He left behind one of the finest legacies imaginable: a collection of portraits of Hawaiian women of rare beauty and soul.

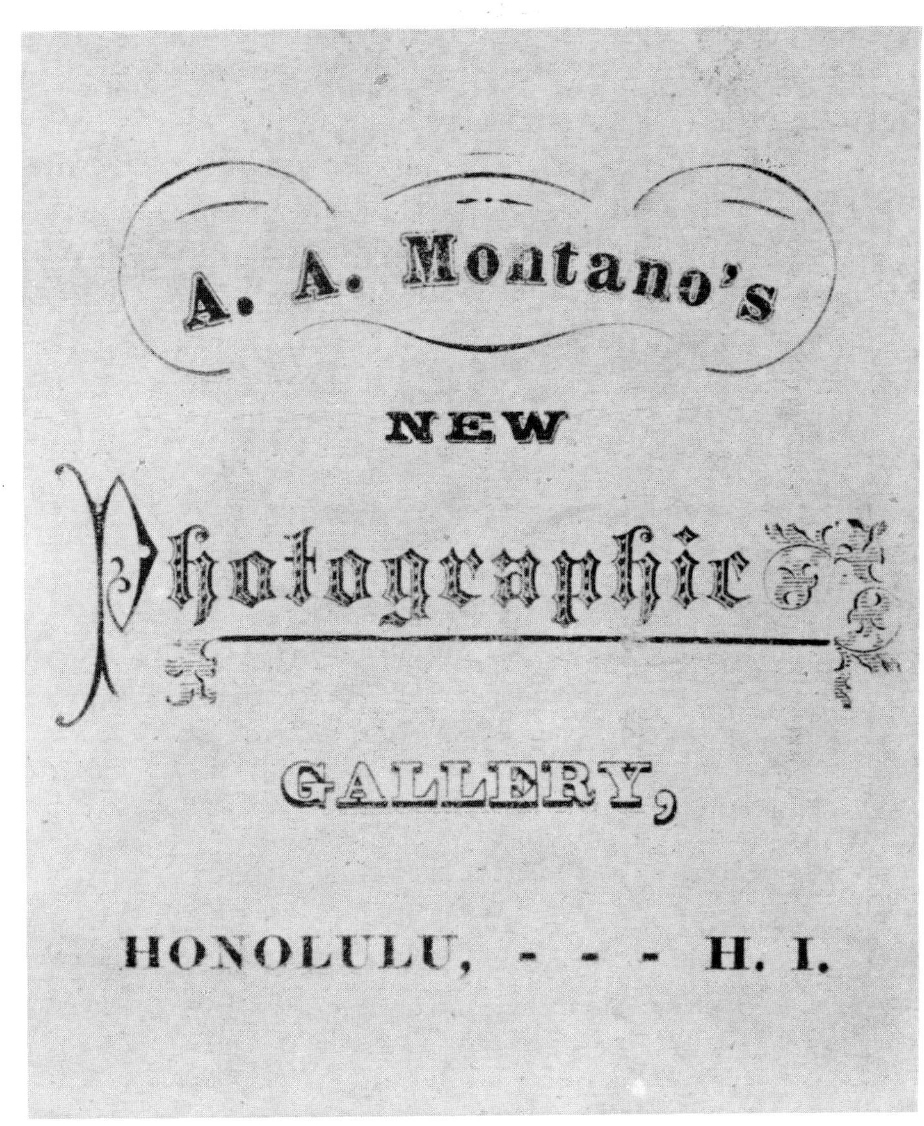

Enlargement of imprint used on back of Montano carte-de-visite and cabinet photographs. Hawaii State Archives.

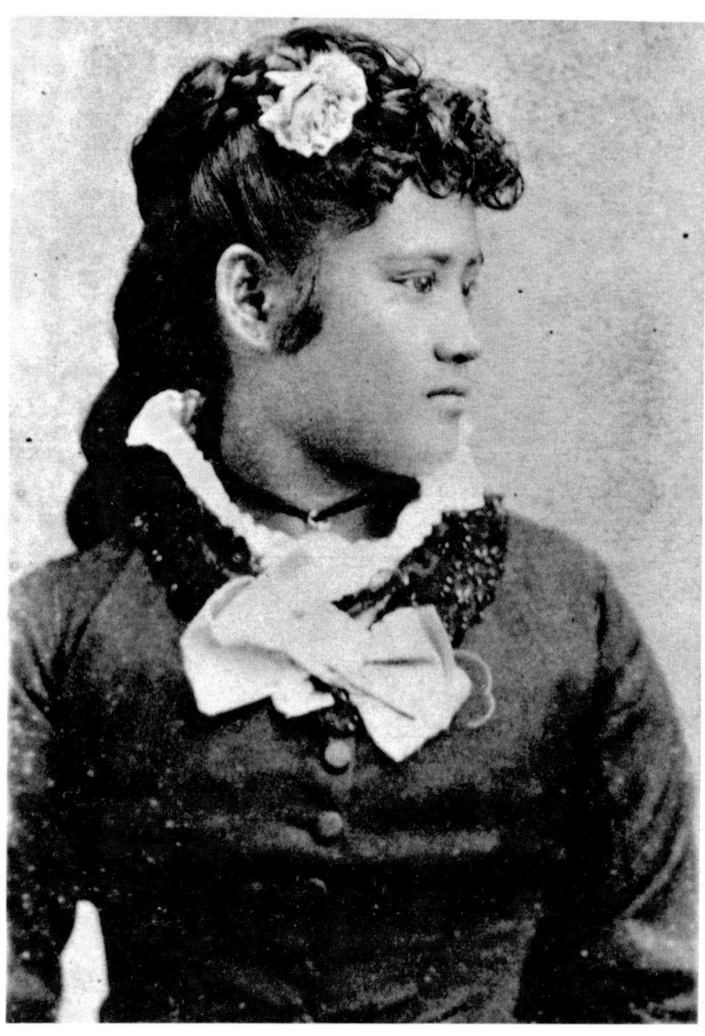

This photograph and most of the following photographs are reproduced from carte-de-visite miniatures. Portrait, 1880s. A.A. Montano. Hawaii State Archives.

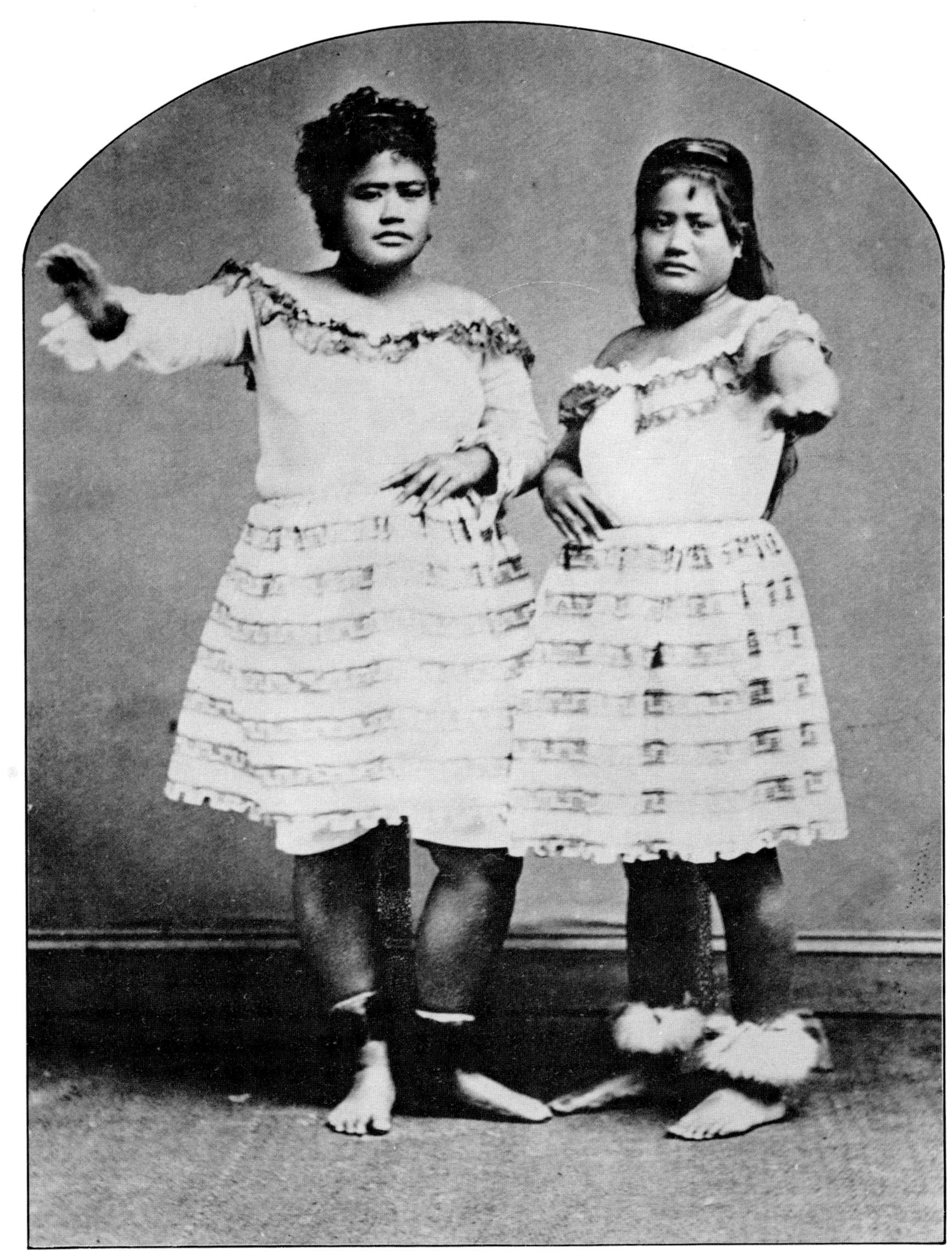

Two hula dancers, late 1870s. Photo by A. A. Montano. Hawaii State Archives.

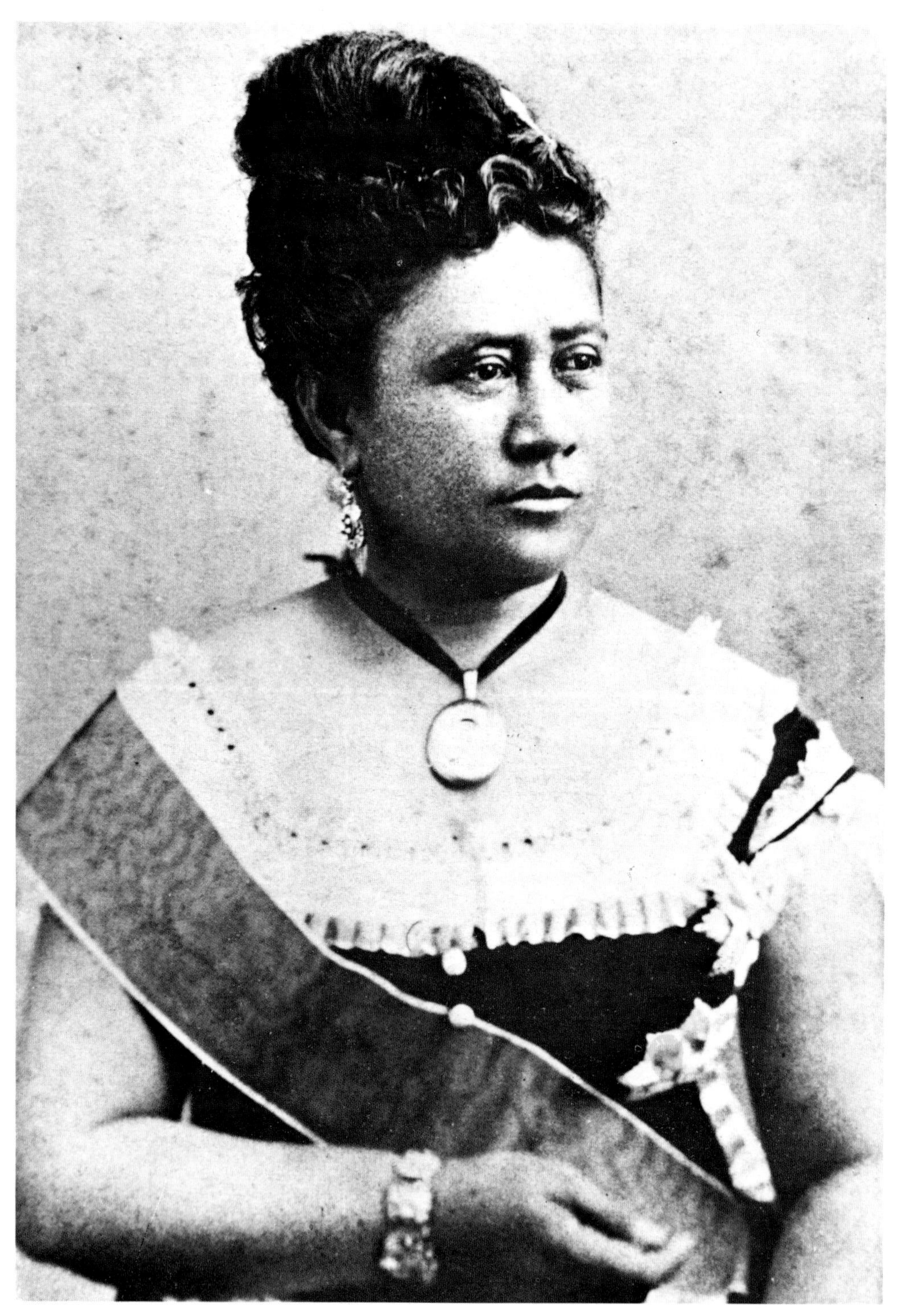

Queen Kapiolani, 1880s. A. A. Montano. Hawaii State Archives.

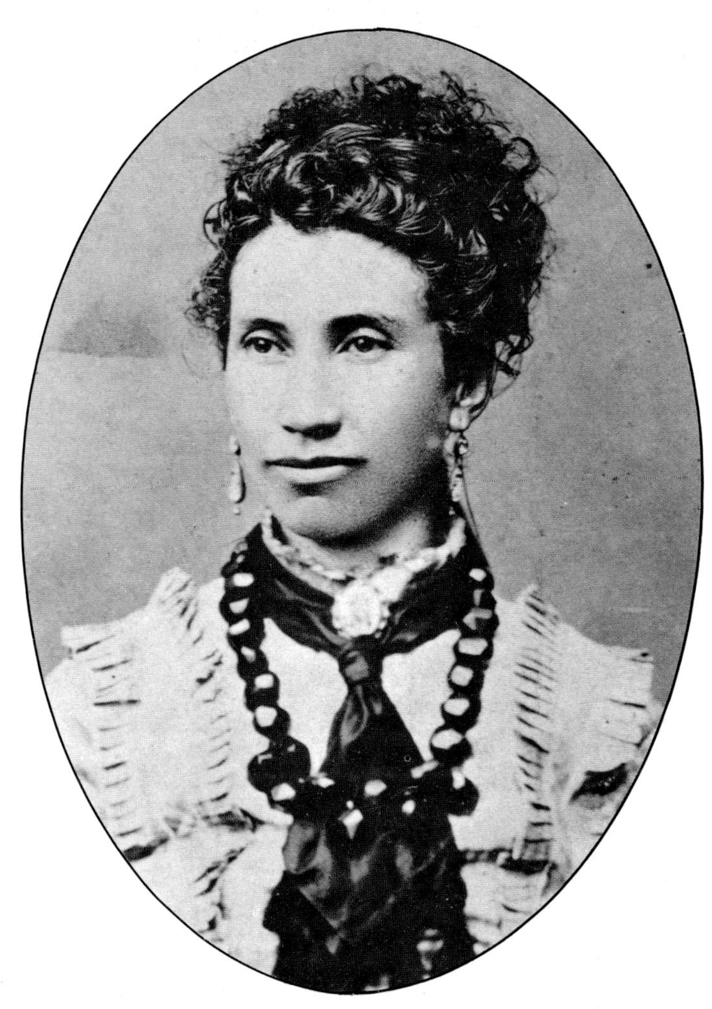

Mary Jane Fayerweather Davison Montano, 1880s. A.A. Montano. Hawaii State Archives.

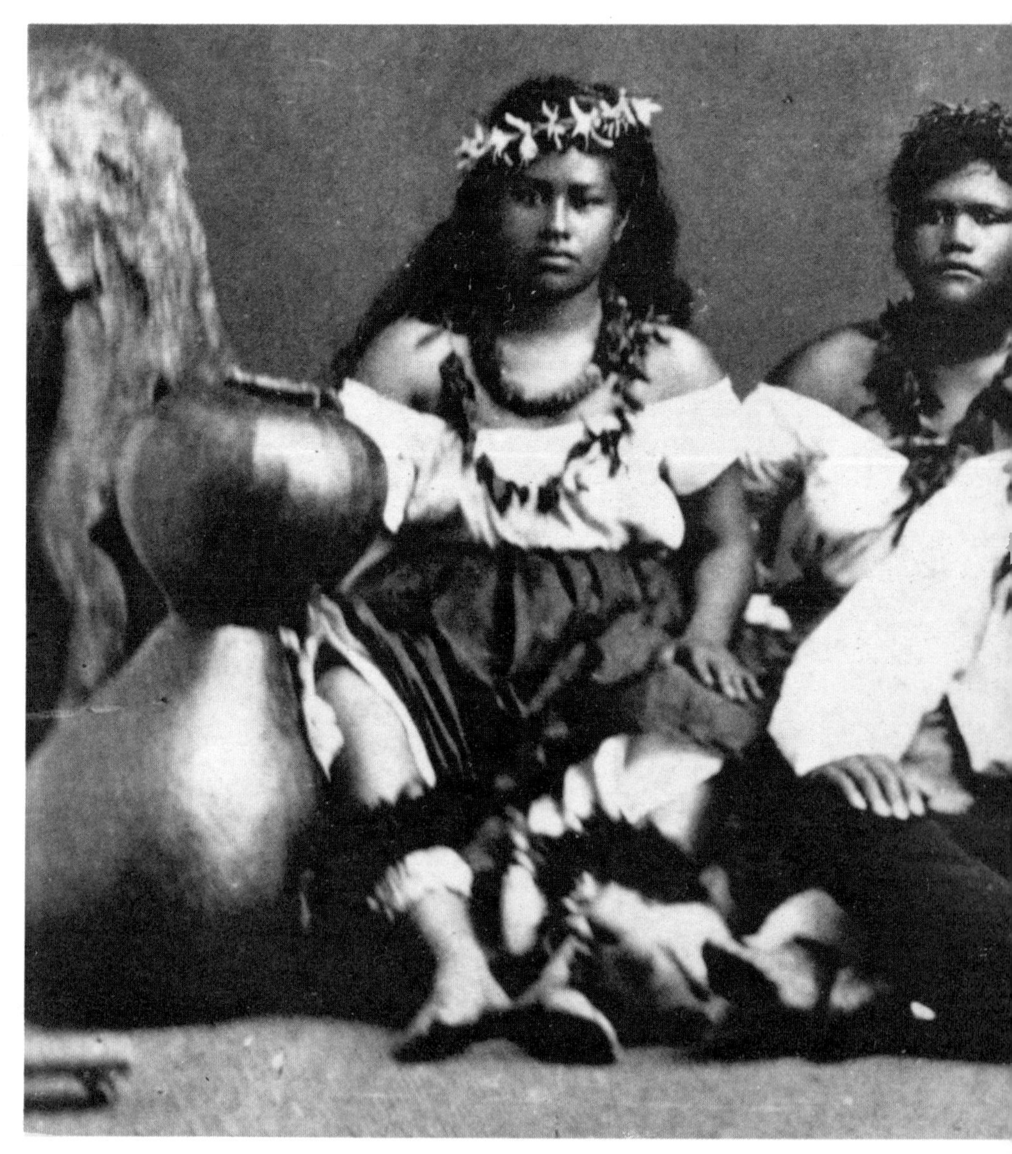

Hula troup with Ioane Ukeke, instructor, 1870s.
A. A. Montano. Hawaii State Archives.

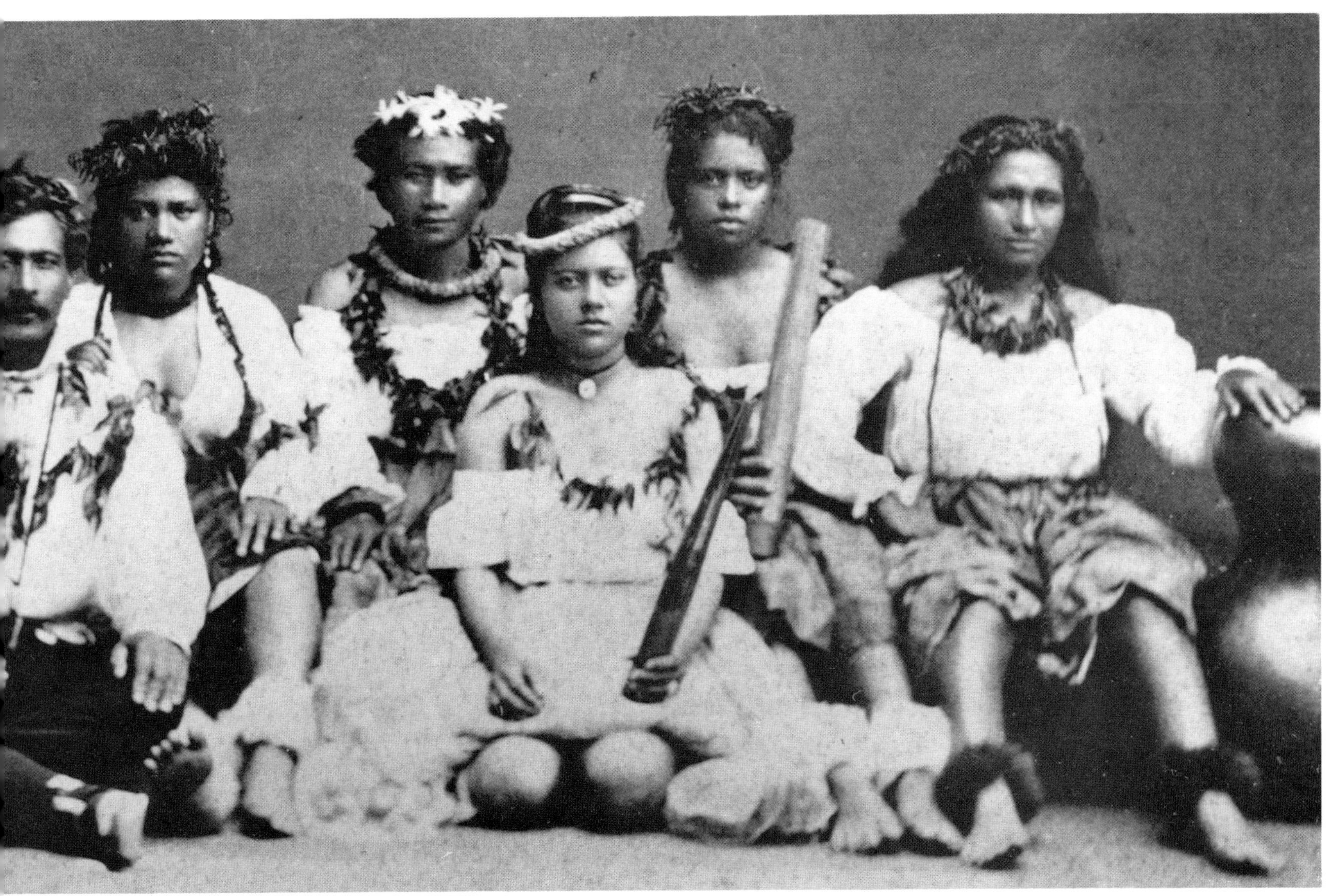

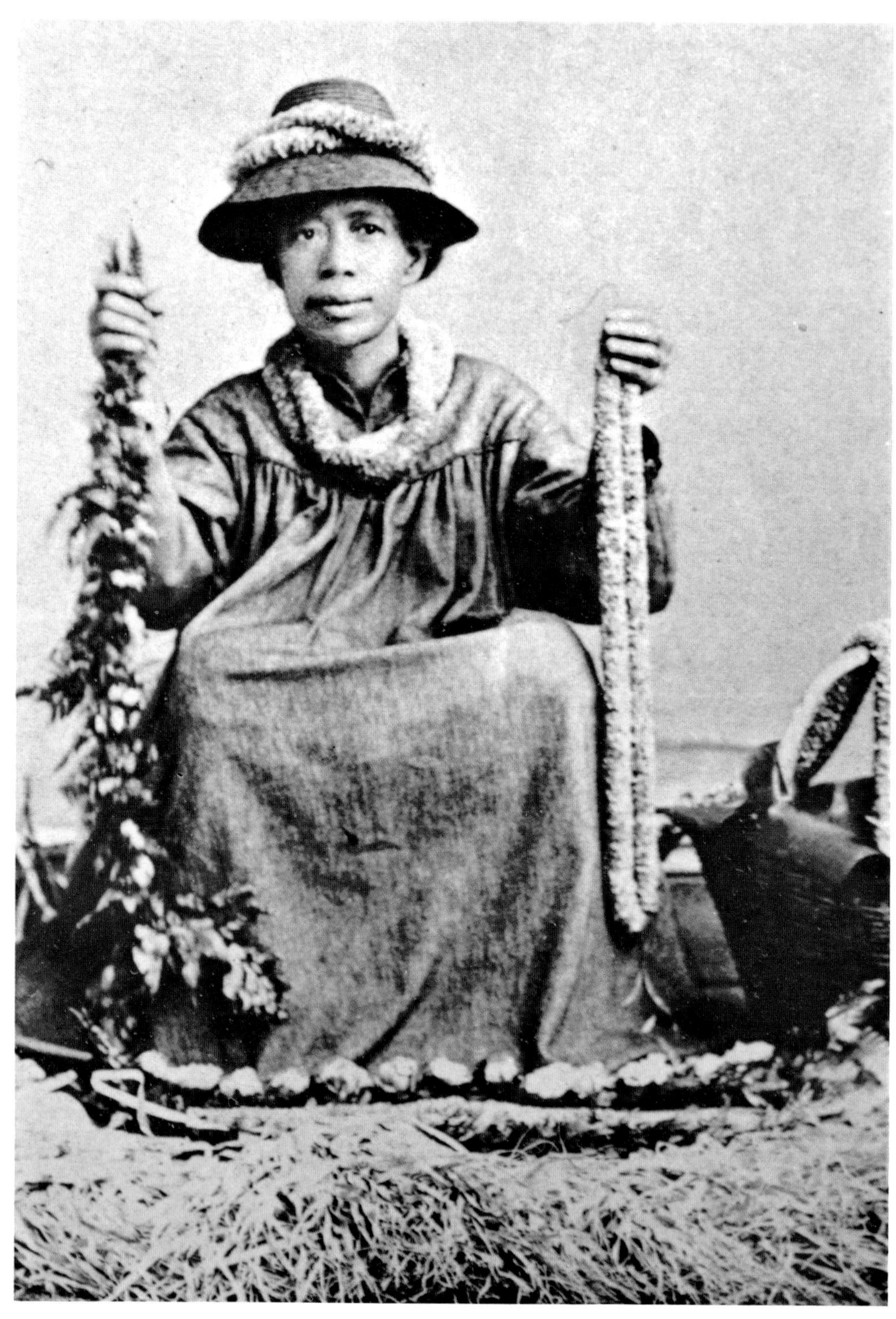

Lei vendor, about 1880. A. A. Montano. Hawaii State Archives.

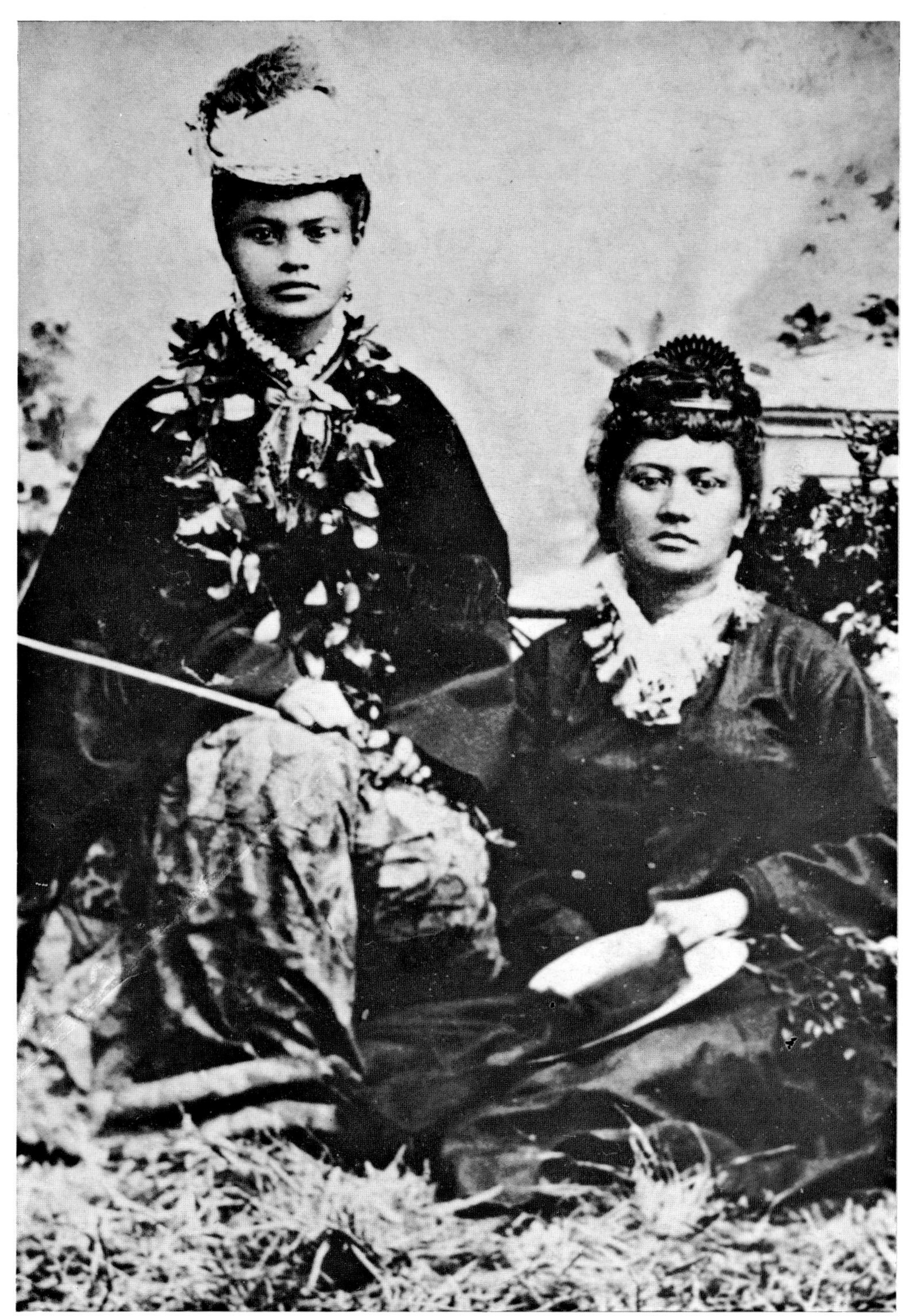

Two women dressed in pa'u riding costumes, about 1880. Photographed by A. A. Montano. Hawaii State Archives.

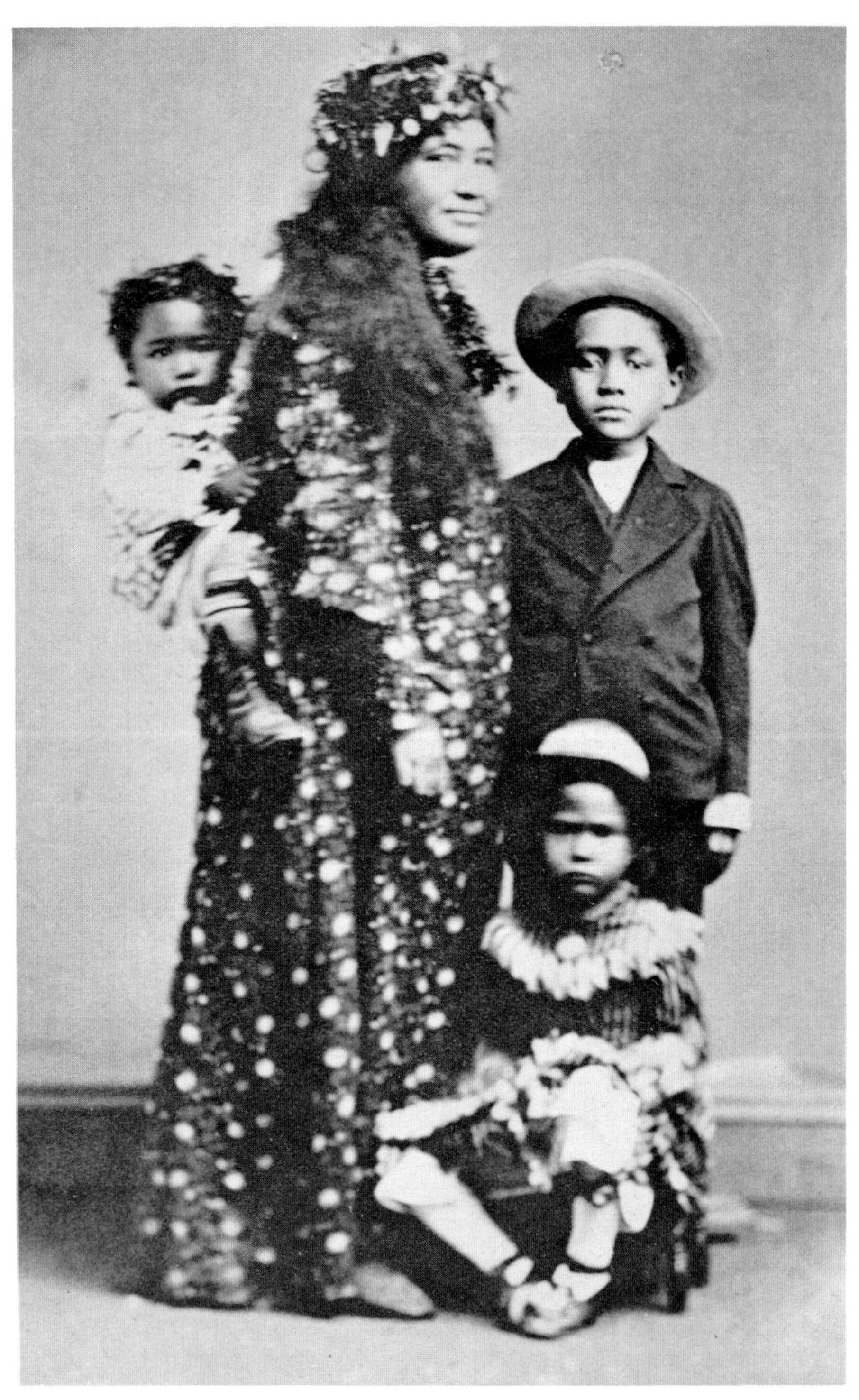

Mother and three children, about 1880. Taken by A. A. Montano. Hawaii State Archives.

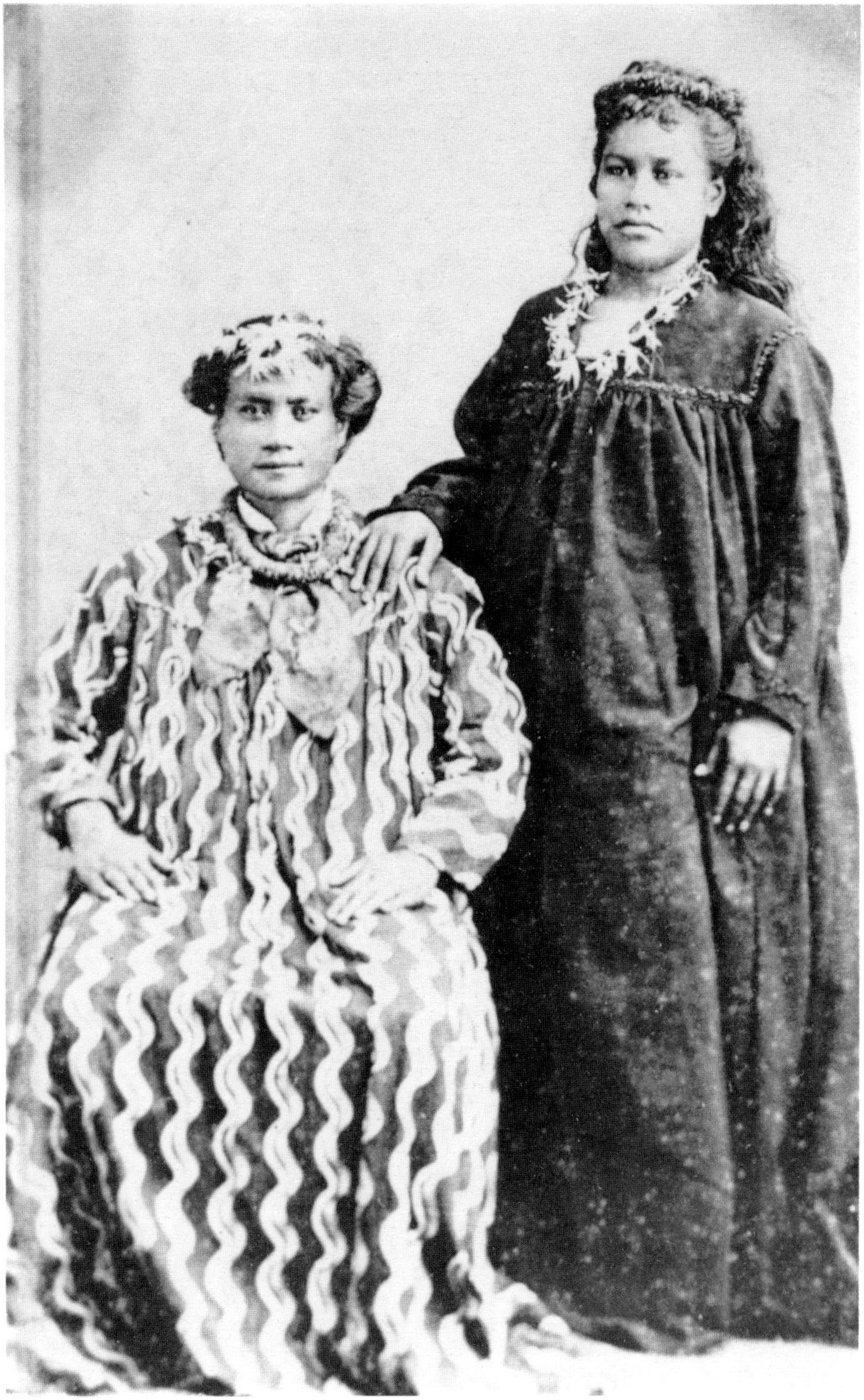

Women in early day muumuus, about 1880. A. A. Montano. Hawaii State Archives.

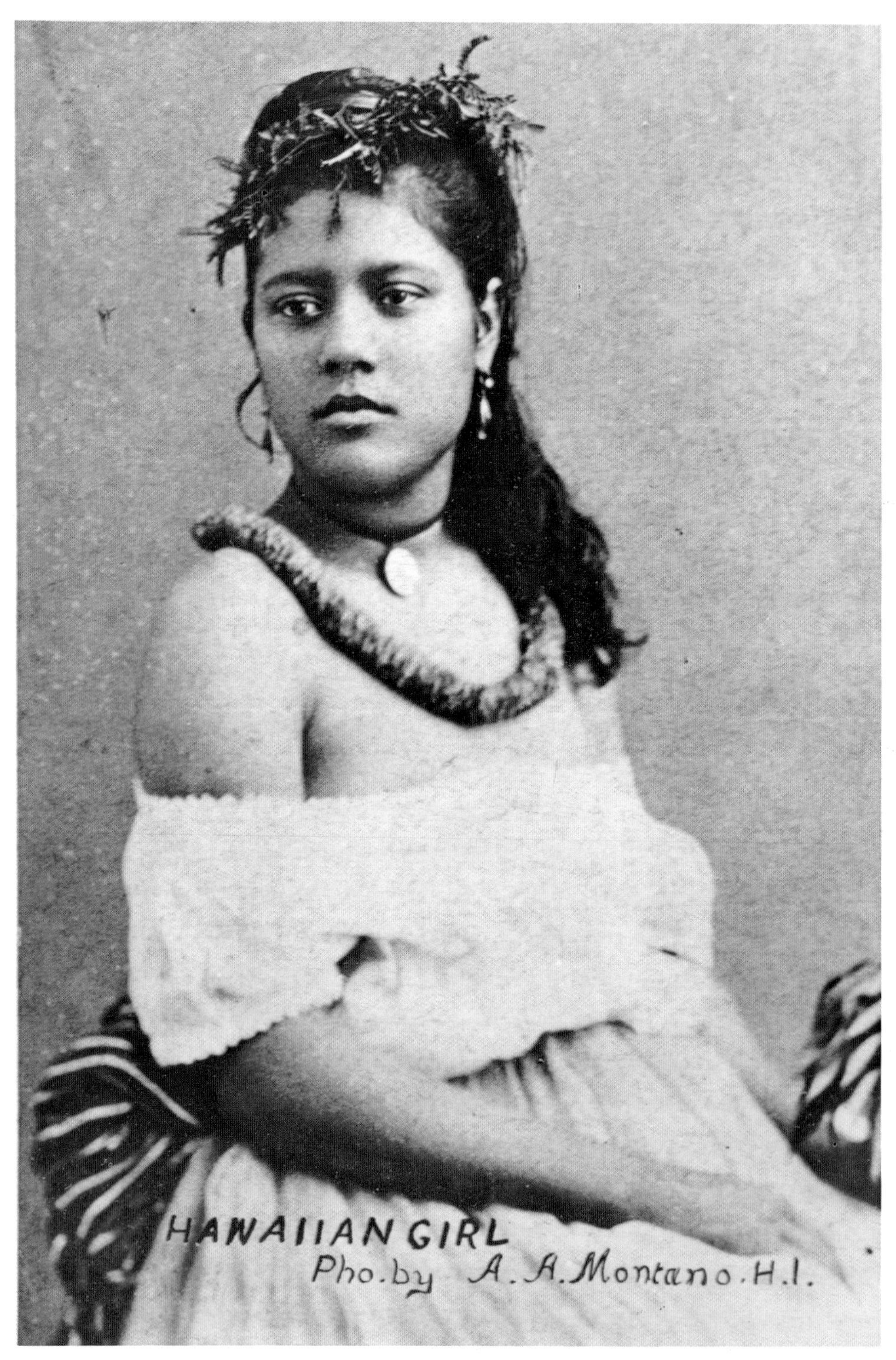

Hawaiian girl, about 1880. Photograph by A. A. Montano. Hawaii State Archives.

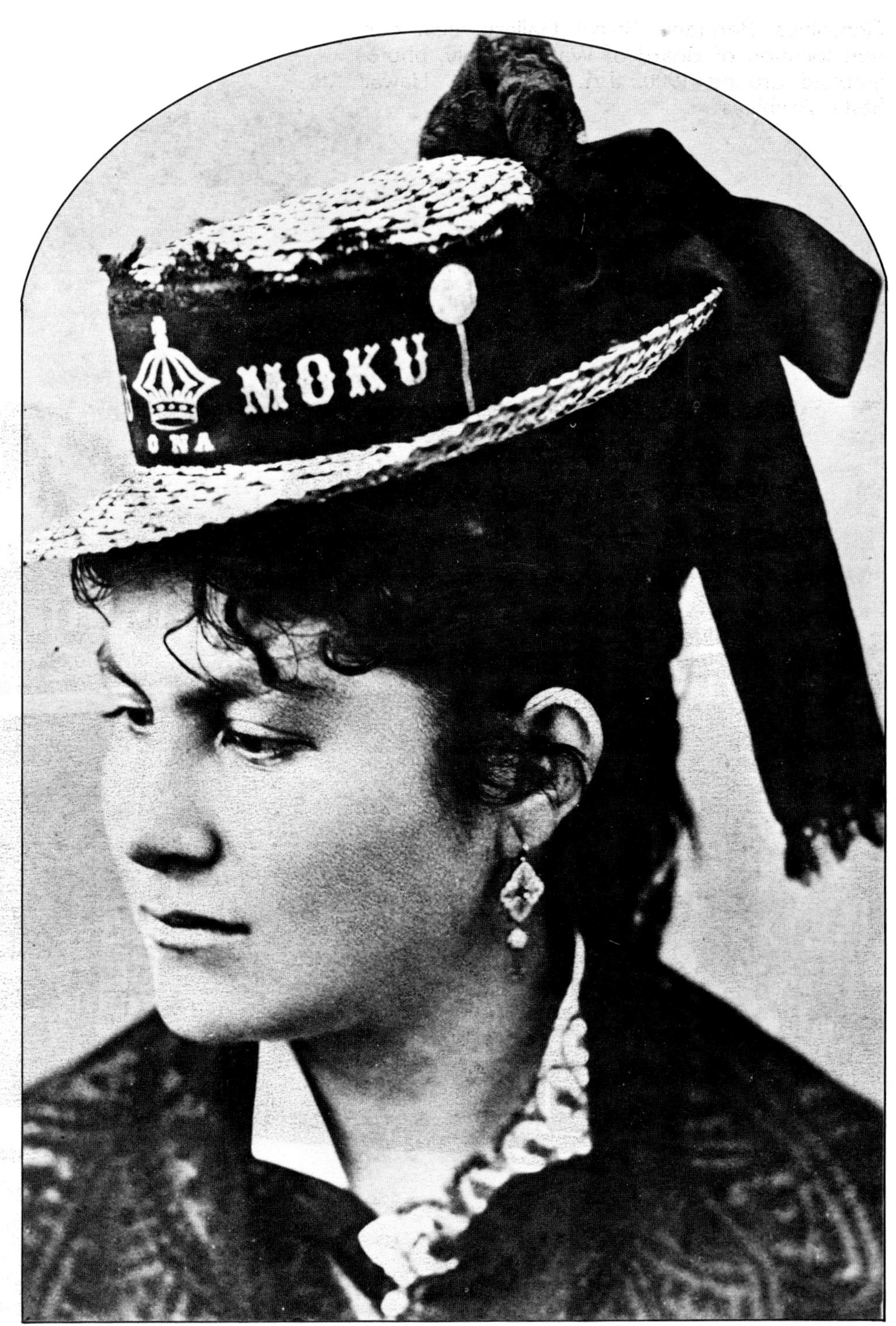

Jesse Kaai, about 1880. Photograph by A.A. Montano. Hawaii State Archives.

Gonsalves' Beretania Street Gallery, near current location of Board of Water Supply, photographed around 1900. J.A. Gonsalves. Hawaii State Archives.

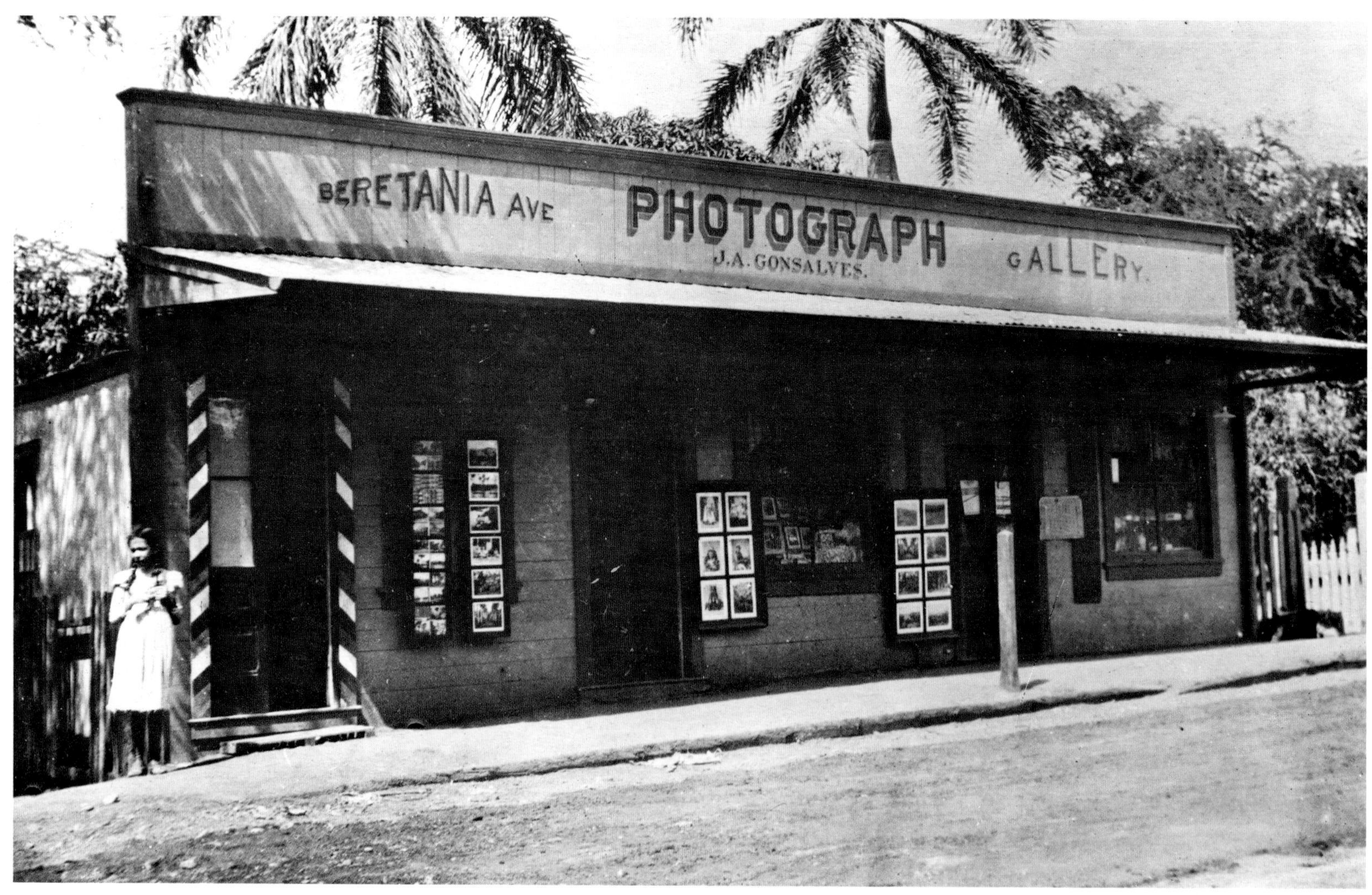

Joaquin A. Gonsalves

Joaquin A. Gonsalves was born in Funchal on the island of Madeira on August 15, 1855. He arrived in Hawaii in 1879, with the second group of Portuguese immigrants brought to the islands. It had been the hope of plantation owners that the Portuguese who, unlike most Asian laborers, were brought to Hawaii in family groups, would remain on the sugar plantations. But, as with previous groups, a great many had aspirations beyond the arduous labor of the sugar fields. J.A. Gonsalves was certainly one of these.

An obituary notice in *The Advertiser* of April 19, 1931, indicates that little is known about Gonsalves' first five years in Hawaii. It states only that he was one of 25 charter members of the Lusitana Society, a mutual benefit group formed in 1882 by Portuguese immigrants to Hawaii.

From 1884 until his death on April 18, 1931, the record is fuller. Sometime in 1884, it appears that Gonsalves went to work in the Fort Street photographic studio of J.J. Williams. Williams had bought out the studio from Menzies Dickson in 1880 and was apparently doing well enough in 1884 to require some assistance. Several years later, Gonsalves seems to have moved his activities to the studio of A.A. Montano — whether as an employee or as an associate is not clear. It is probable, however, that when Montano retired from the photographic business in 1888, Gonsalves took over the Montano studio. And it would appear that along with the business, Gonsalves gained the patronage of King Kalakaua that Montano had previously enjoyed.

The association enabled Gonsalves to do a considerable amount of traveling around the Hawaiian Islands, accompanying the king and taking photographs of his entourage. In fact, by the early 1900s, when Gonsalves had moved his business to 654 Beretania Street, he was able to advertise a complete line of island views for sale to the public. The association with Kalakaua, however, did not prevent Gonsalves from taking part in anti-monarchical political activities. Or, perhaps more accurately, Gonsalves' anti-monarchical activities apparently did not discourage King Kalakaua from using his photographic activities. For Gonsalves was a member of the Honolulu Rifles, the group that took up arms on behalf of the foreign community in 1887 in order to force the king to grant a constitution favorable to the foreign interests in the islands.

Gonsalves' activities on behalf of the foreign community continued into the 1890s. He took part in the dethronement of Liliuokalani in 1893 and served as a sergeant in the Old Guard, which maintained the provisional government of the Republic of Hawaii in pre-annexation days. And Gonsalves took part in the ceremony in which the flag of the Hawaiian Republic was lowered for the last time from Iolani Palace when formal cession to the United States took place in 1898. With the formation of the Hawaii National Guard, Gonsalves became a captain in Company "C", the all Portuguese contingent of the guards.

Despite his political activity, Gonsalves managed to find time to continue in the profession of photography until only a few years before his death. However, it is clear that during his later years as a photographer he did not enjoy the popularity that had come to him along with his purchase of Montano's business. According to R.J. Baker, the reason for Gonsalves' fading popularity was his failure to keep up with the latest developments in the photographic field. It is possible that Gonsalves simply felt more comfortable and confident with the old ways and saw no reason to change his equipment or style. It is equally possible that this failure was due to deep involvement in the politics of the time.

From the record of his work it is clear that Gonsalves never possessed the photographic talent of Montano. But given sufficient time, all photographs become interesting for they give us a sense of an age we have not ourselves experienced. It would have been an added and valuable plus had Gonsalves been equipped with an eye for composition such as the one owned by his predecessor. But Gonsalves' work is sufficiently important for its historical interest: he did get out of the portrait studio with great frequency and he has left some fascinating views of the islands during the several decades surrounding the turn of the century.

The flag of the Hawaiian Republic being lowered from Iolani Palace for the last time, August 12, 1898. J. A. Gonsalves took part in the ceremony and may be among the guardsmen pictured. Photographer unknown. Hawaii State Archives.

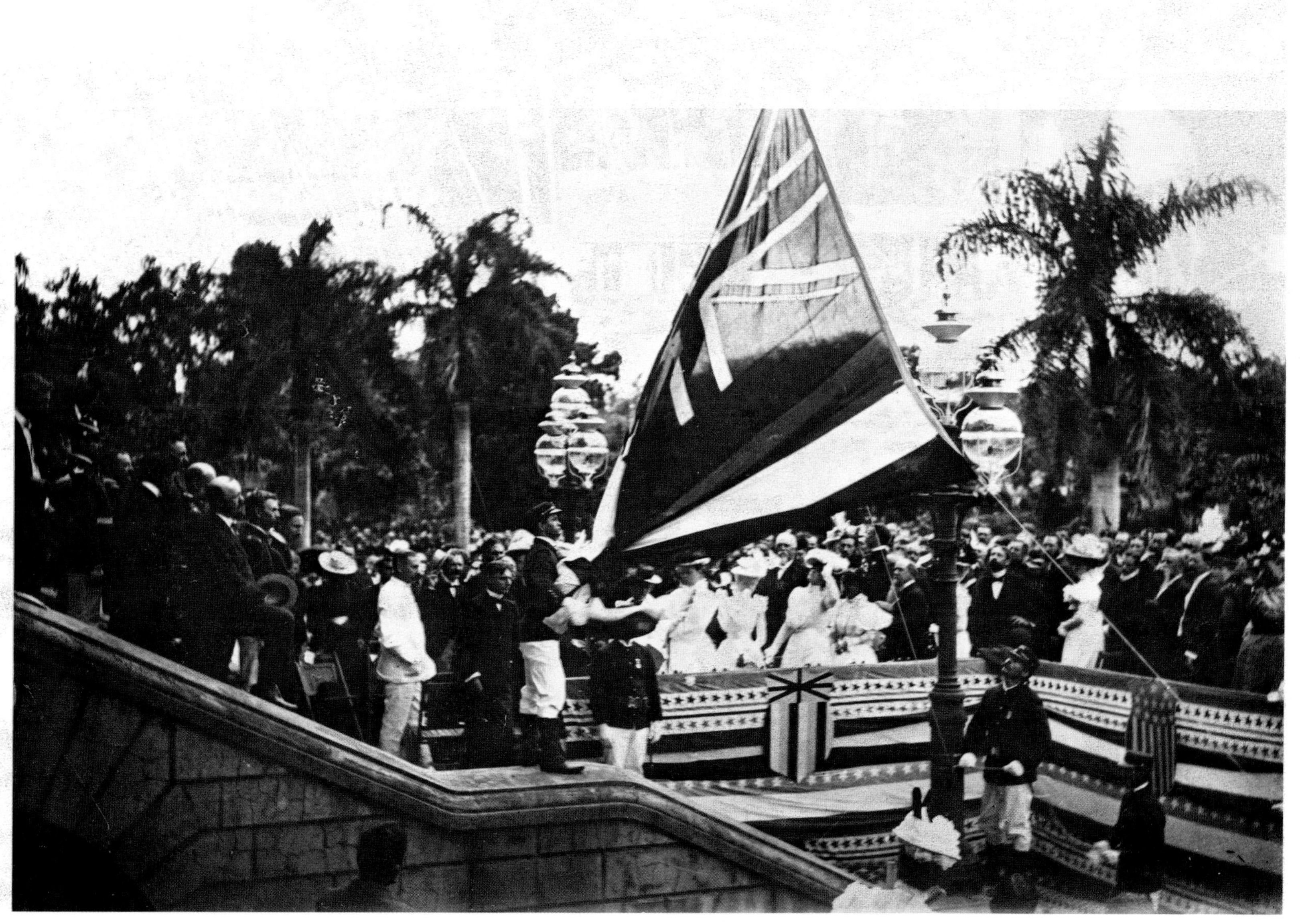

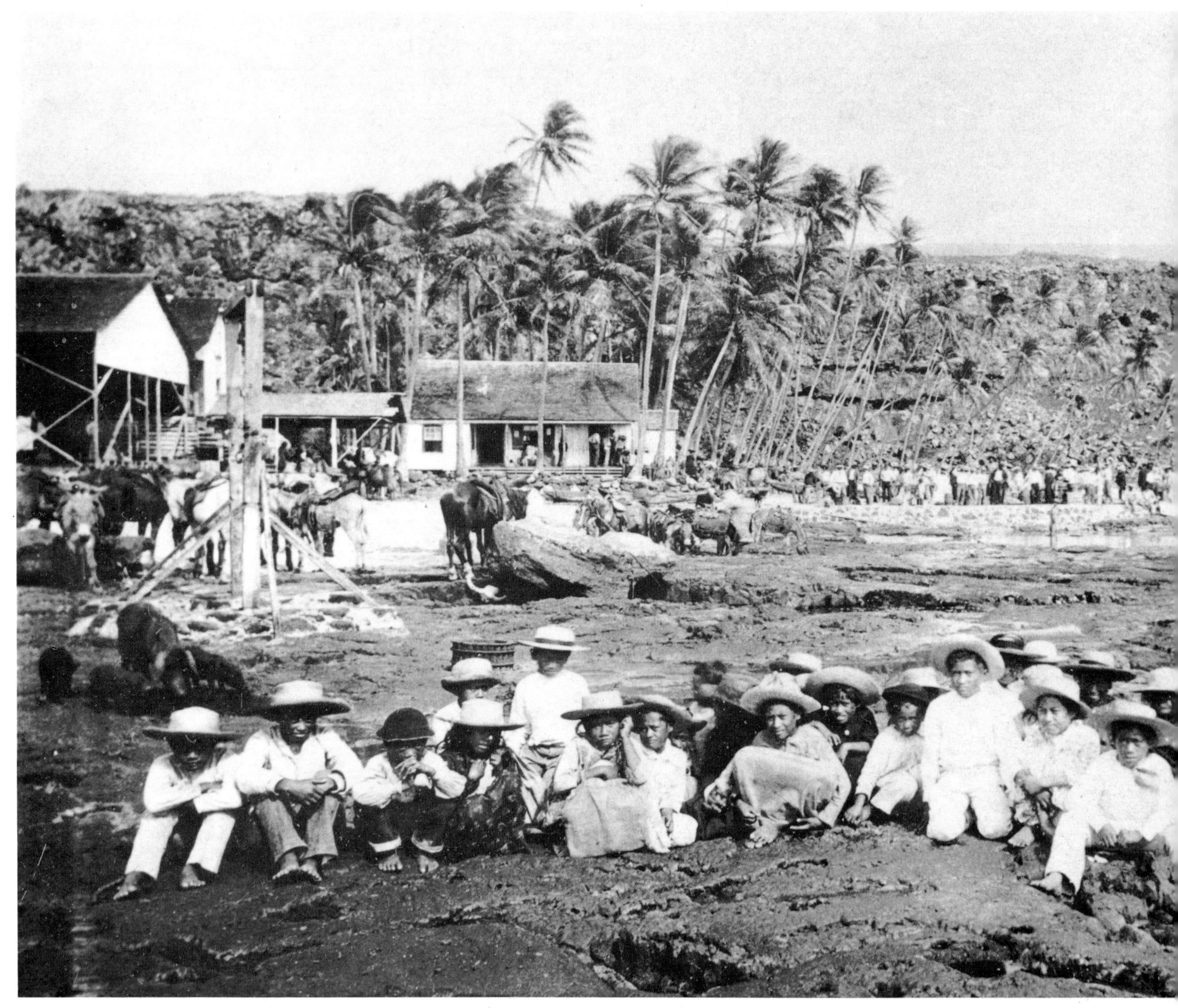

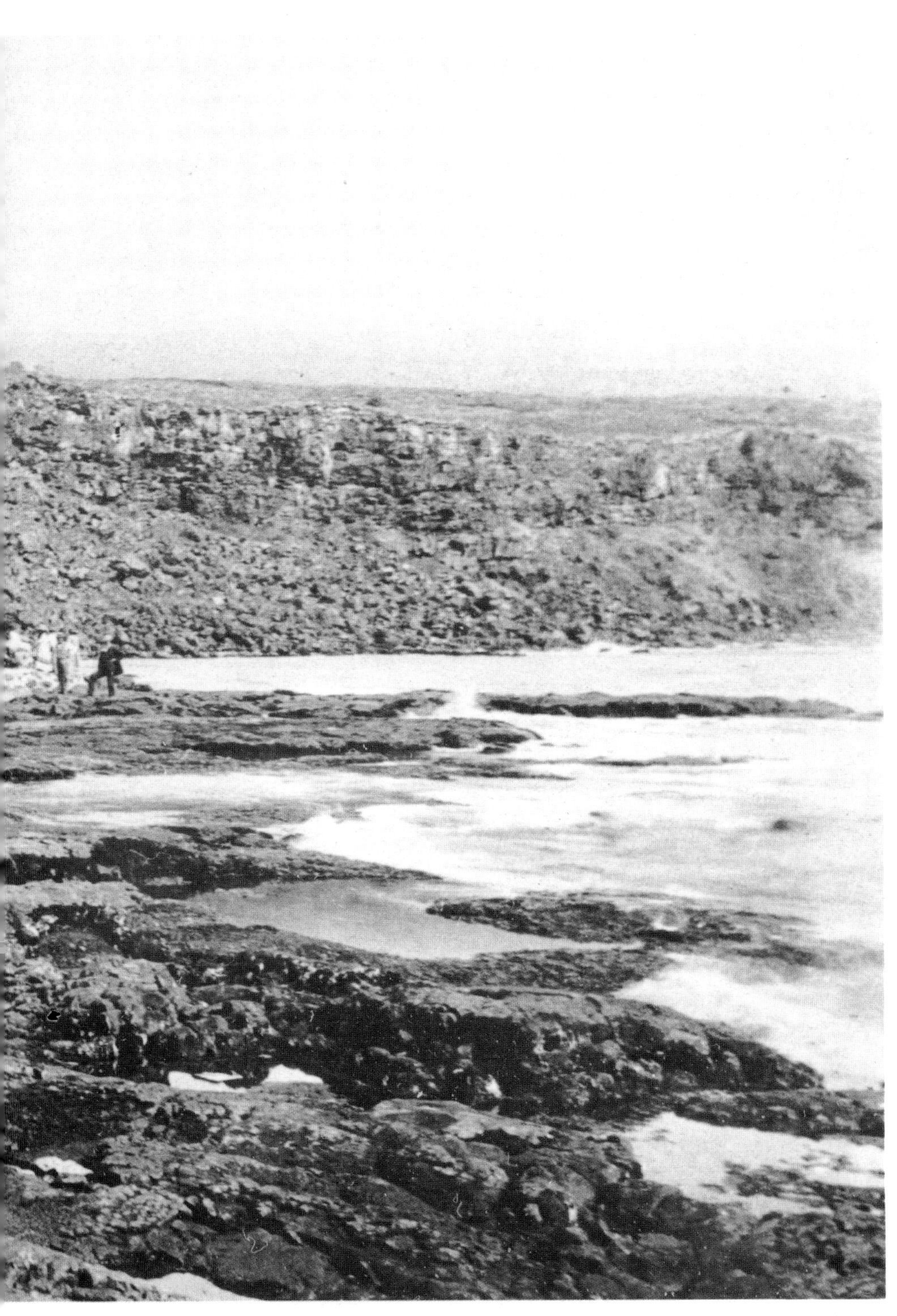

Ho'okena Landing, Kona District of Hawaii, 1800s.
J.A. Gonsalves. Hawaii State Archives.

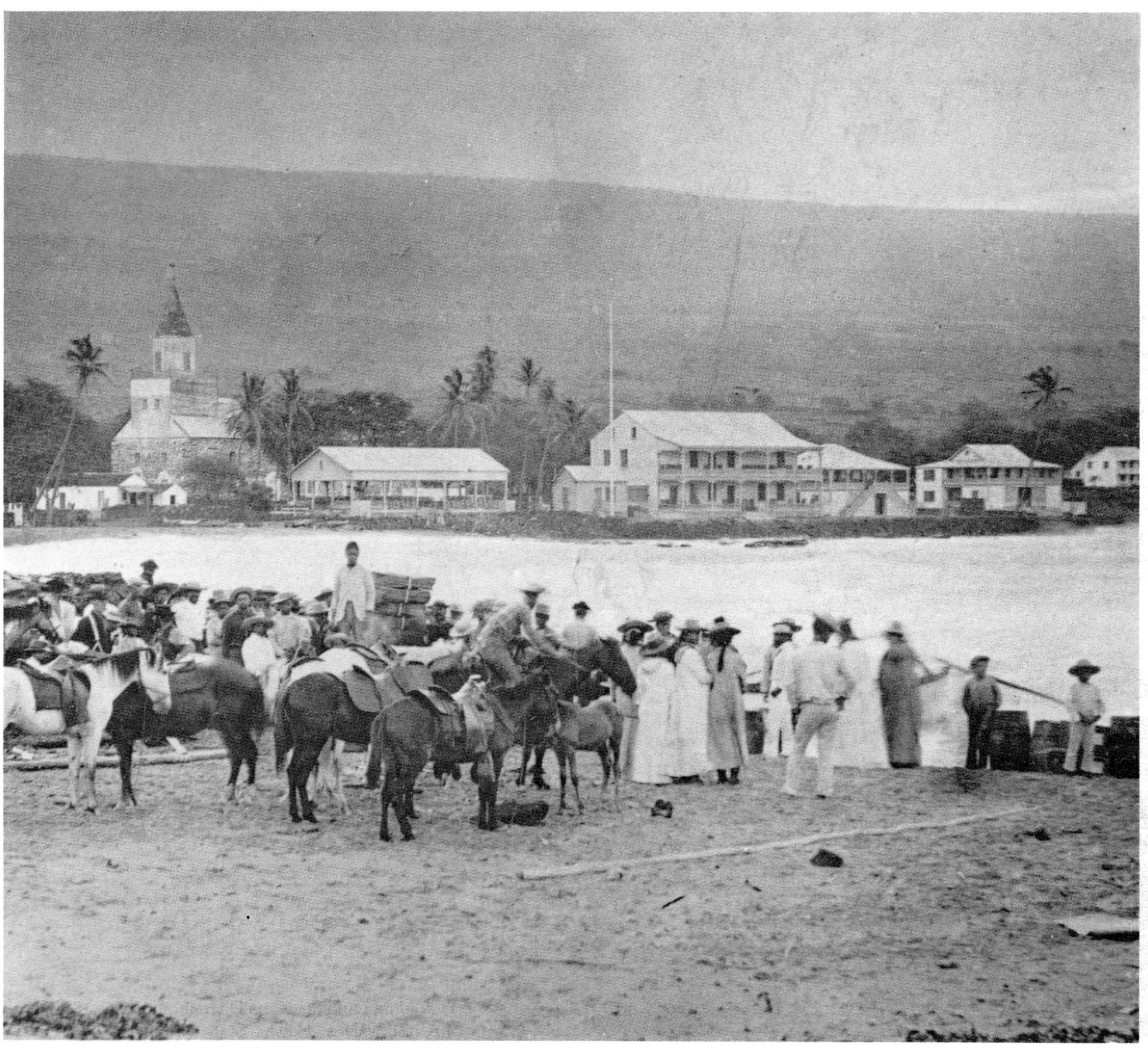

Left: Kailua, Kona on boat day, about 1880. J.A. Gonsalves. Hawaii State Archives.

Below: Volcano House around 1890. J.A. Gonsalves. Hawaii State Archives.

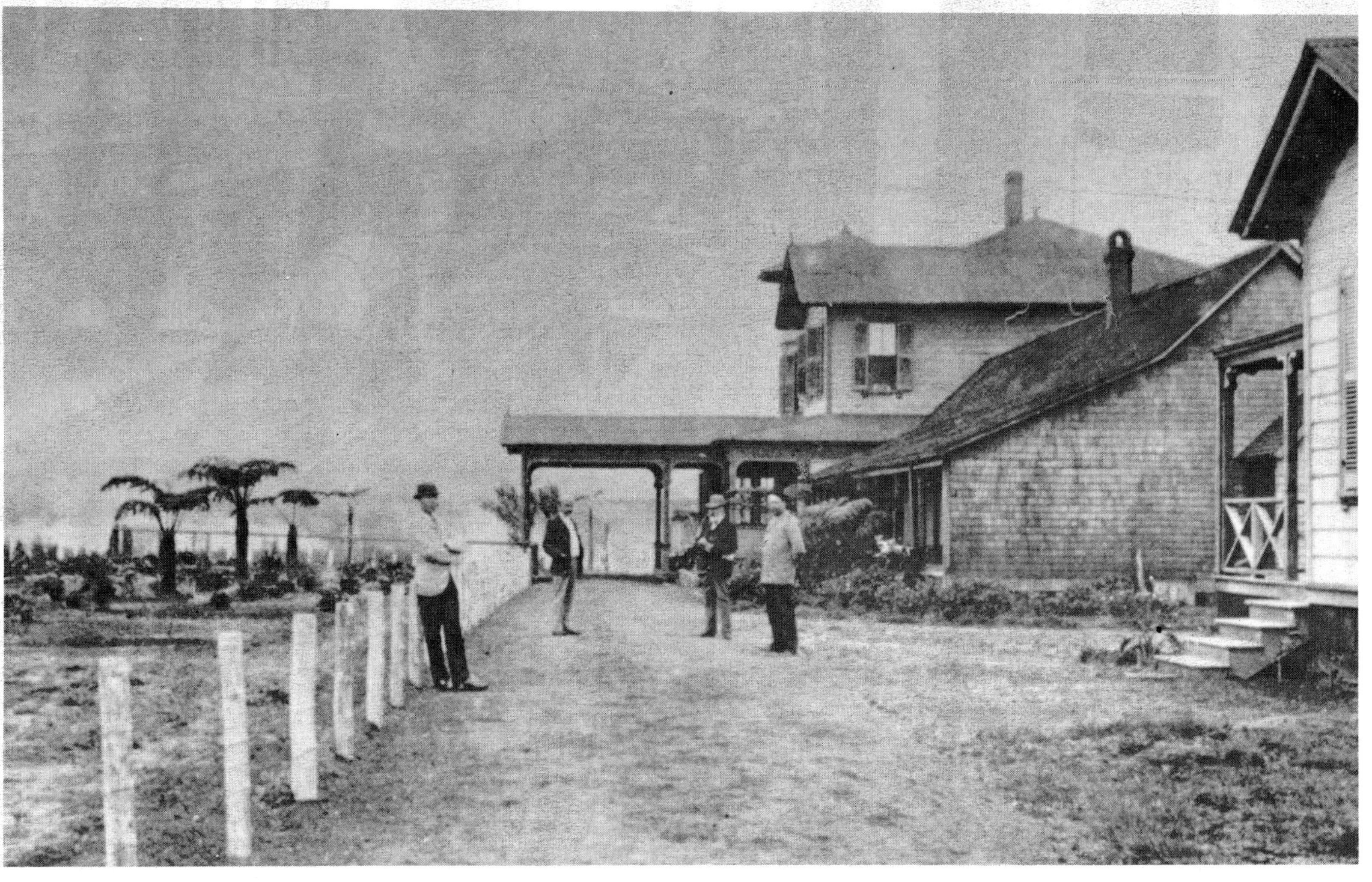

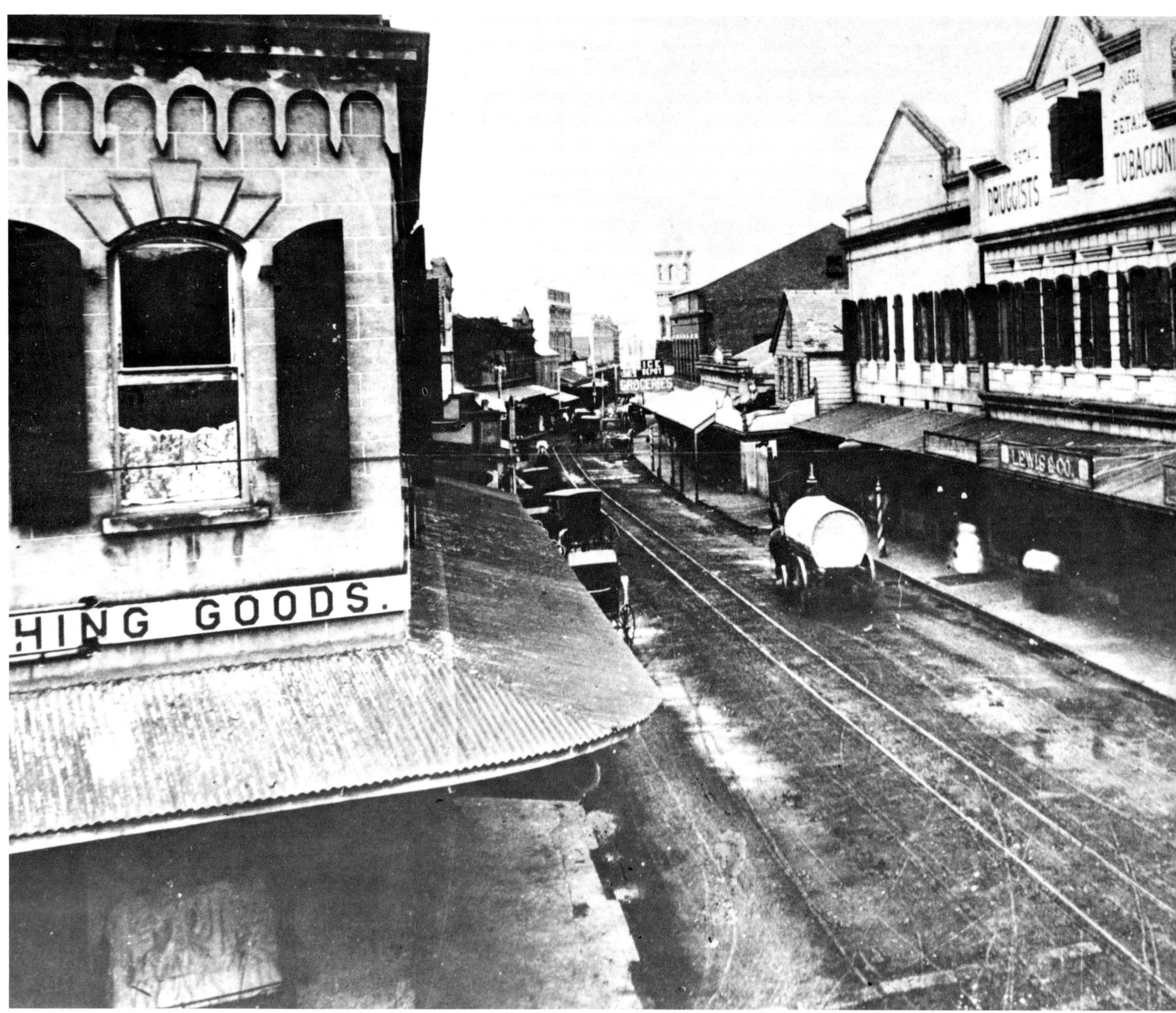
HING GOODS.
DRUGGISTS
RETAIL
TOBACCONI
ICE
GROCERIES
LEWIS & CO.

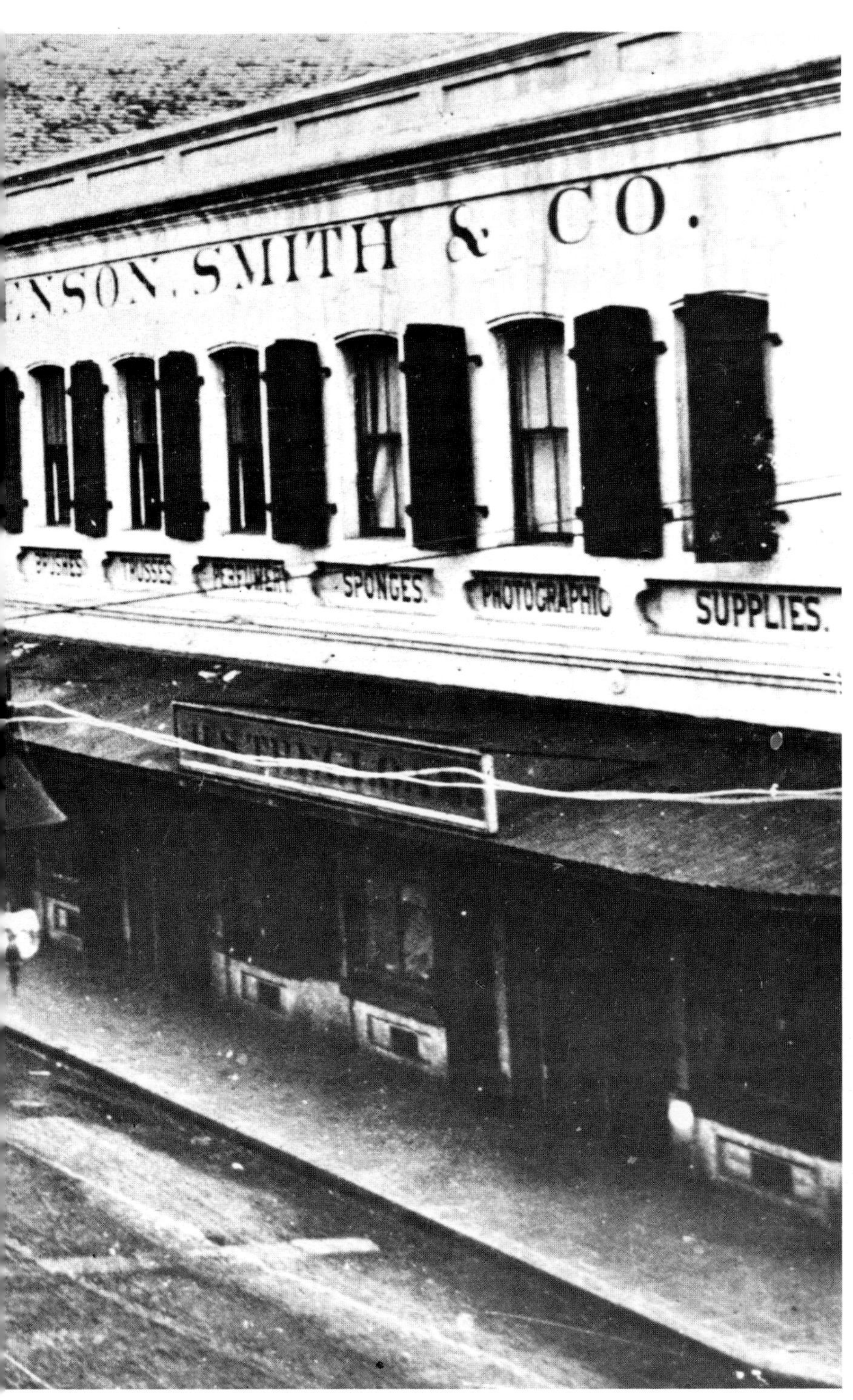

Fort Street around 1890. J.A. Gonsalves. Hawaii State Archives.

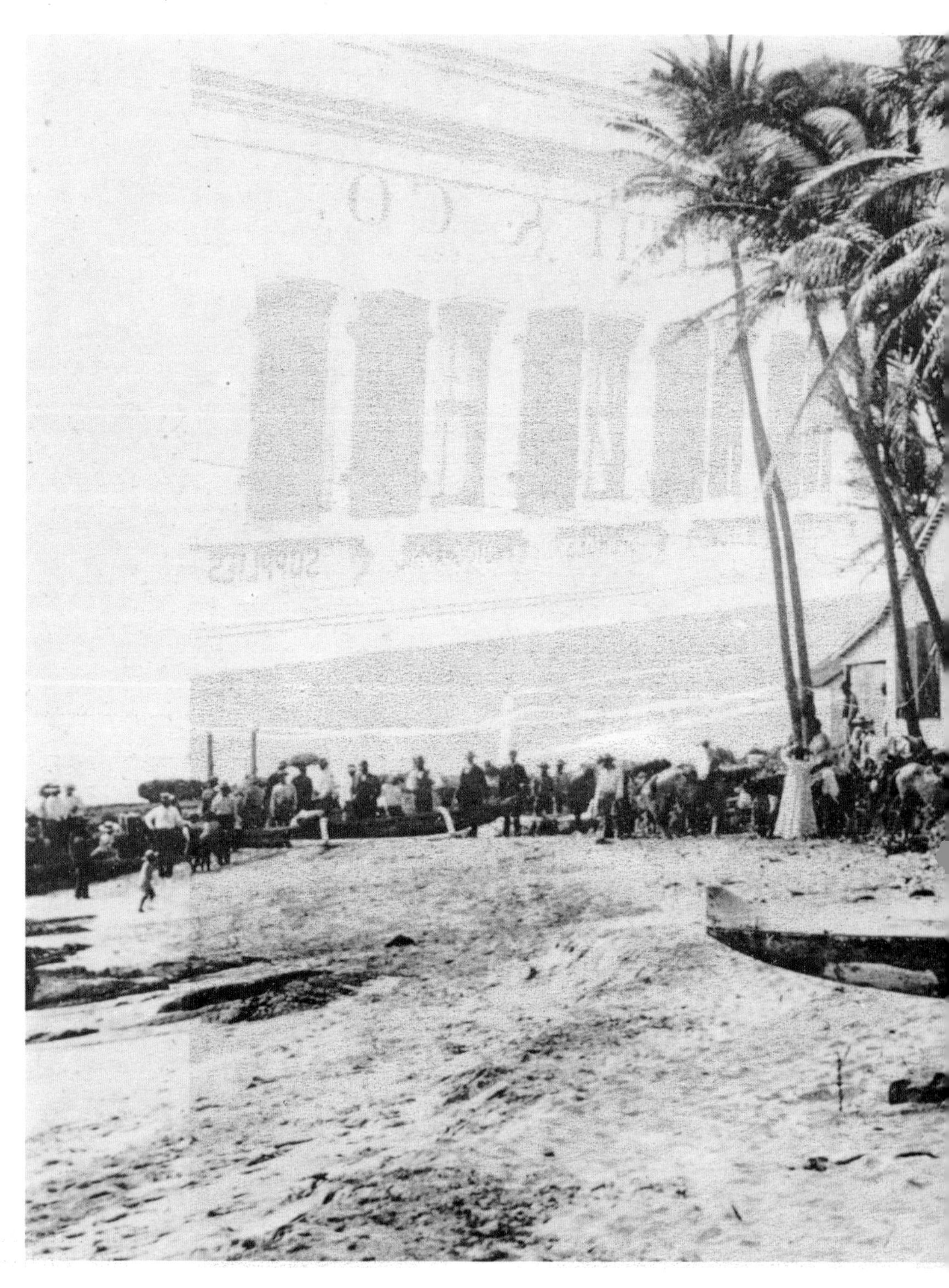

Kailua, Kona waterfront, around 1890. J.A. Gonsalves. Hawaii State Archives.

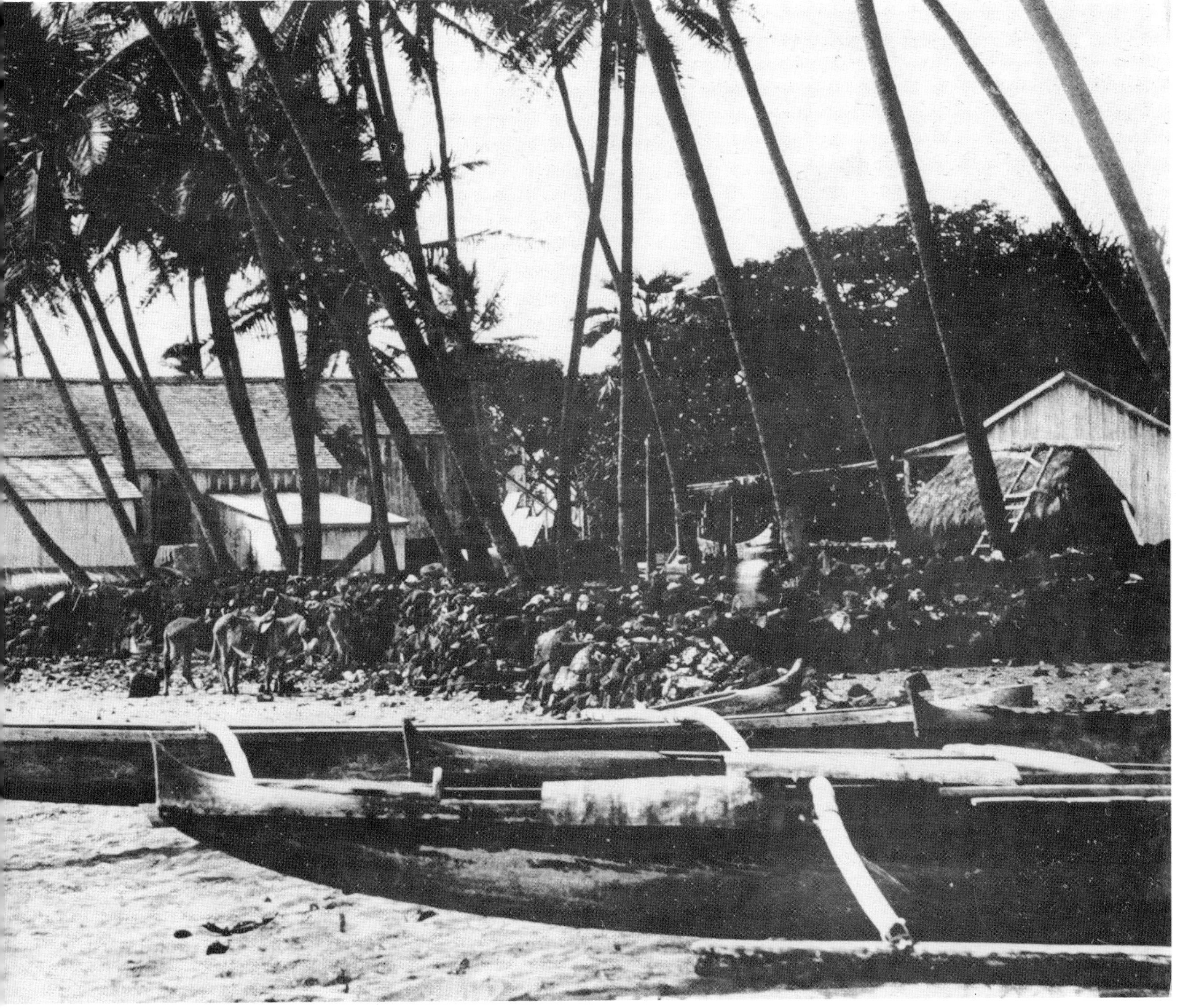

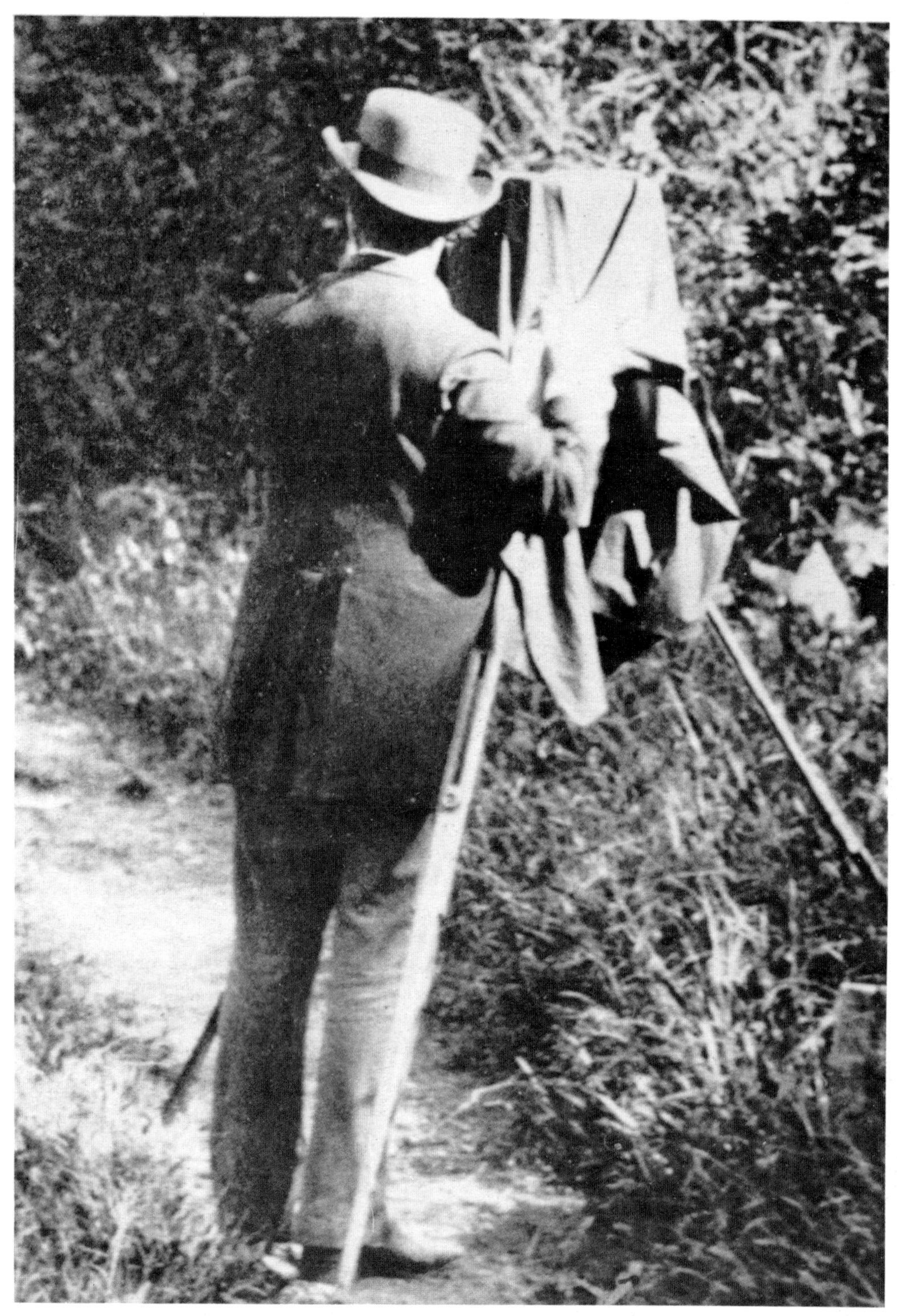

Man in picture identified as Charles Furneaux. Photographer unknown. Lyman House Memorial Museum.

Charles Furneaux

In respect to the memory of Charles Furneaux, the flags of Hilo flew at half mast on the day of his funeral and some of the social affairs that had been planned for the day were cancelled. Furneaux, according to *The Hawaii Herald* of November 14, 1913, was "one of the oldest and most respected of residents" of the area. Charles Furneaux, moreover, was remembered as a fine painter who had been forced by failing eyesight to give up painting and enter a business career. It is clear that he did very well at his new calling, for he died with holdings in many of Hilo's business corporations and with a great deal of real estate at Olaa and in the Wailoa River and Waiakea areas. Furneaux also served in pre-annexation days as American consular agent and U.S. shipping commissioner for the Port of Hilo.

Like a good many other early photographers, Furneaux came to the islands with no intention of staying. He was born in Boston in 1837, came to Hawaii as a tourist in the early 1880s, and apparently settled in the Hilo area some time around 1890.

It is possible that Furneaux at one time considered the possibility of making a career of photography for there is evidence that he was either employed by or associated with A.A. Montano at some time during the 1880s. It is just as likely, however, that Furneaux, like many other painters, considered photography a valuable aid to his painting and that he therefore asked Montano to help him acquire some photographic skill. In either case, it does not appear that he made any effort to sell his photographic work. And from the nature of the work that remains to us, it seems clear that Furneaux was mainly interested in subjects that might lend themselves to painting or that borrowed the perspective of the landscape painter. Regardless of his intentions, either his failing eyesight or his growing interest in commerce turned both painting and photography into hobbies for Charles Furneaux.

Furneaux, however, was a dedicated and accomplished amateur — among the first amateurs to come to light in Hawaii in the decades surrounding the turn of the century. In fact, during the 19th century, photography was far too expensive and cumbersome to interest most hobbiests. Perhaps for this reason, most of the photographers we have found who worked in the islands during the 19th century were professionals. With the 20th century, a number of skilled amateurs join the ranks as important contributors to the photographic record of the islands.

According to Hildreth Walker, daughter of E.N. Hitchcock, whose photographic work is represented in the next chapter, the Furneaux and Hitchcock families were well acquainted. It is even possible that Edward Hitchcock, though 30 years younger than Furneaux, shared a friendship based on their interest in photography. Certainly many of their scenic photographs are similar in style. Occasionally one even encounters a photograph by one or the other of these two amateurs that shows a second photographer tucked into the landscape. And, all too frequently, unmarked prints by one of these photographers show up in albums of views in which work by the other photographer predominates.

The largest body of Furneaux work seems now to be divided between the Bishop Museum in Honolulu and the Lyman House Memorial Museum in Hilo. But it was Hilo and its environs that provided Furneaux with his subject matter. His photographs all seem to have been made with the painter's eye. Many seem to borrow their philosophical approach from a Romantic school that allows no room for ugliness and that views even the most impoverished of surroundings as idyllic (at best) or picturesque (at worst.) In fact, Furneaux' photographs contain a languorous romantic quality that is entirely absent from his lively paintings of Kilauea volcano. Whether his subject was a sunset behind ships at anchor at Hilo Harbor, a girl resting beside a canoe, fishing nets set out to dry or the most impoverished of plantation villages, each of his scenes seems somehow placid and idyllic. It is, indeed, a long way between the contented seeming Japanese mother and child pictured by Furneaux at Wainaku Plantation village and the angry people behind a police barricade pictured in later pages in one of Frank Davey's views of Chinatown in 1900. But Furneaux' romantic view is, in its way, very much an important part of Hawaii's past.

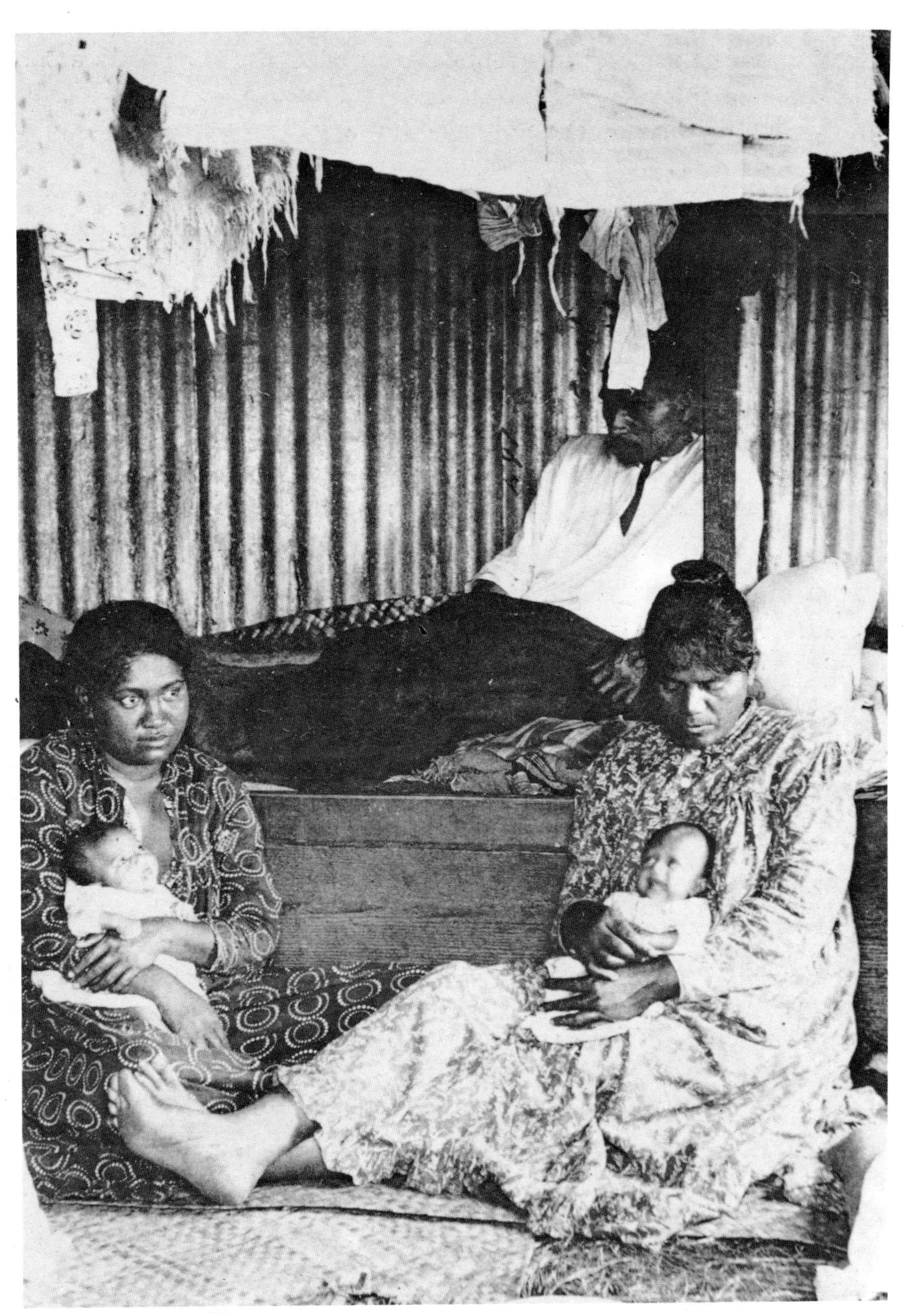

Interior of a Hawaiian hut in the Puna district, Island of Hawaii, around 1890. C. Furneaux. Lyman House Memorial Museum.

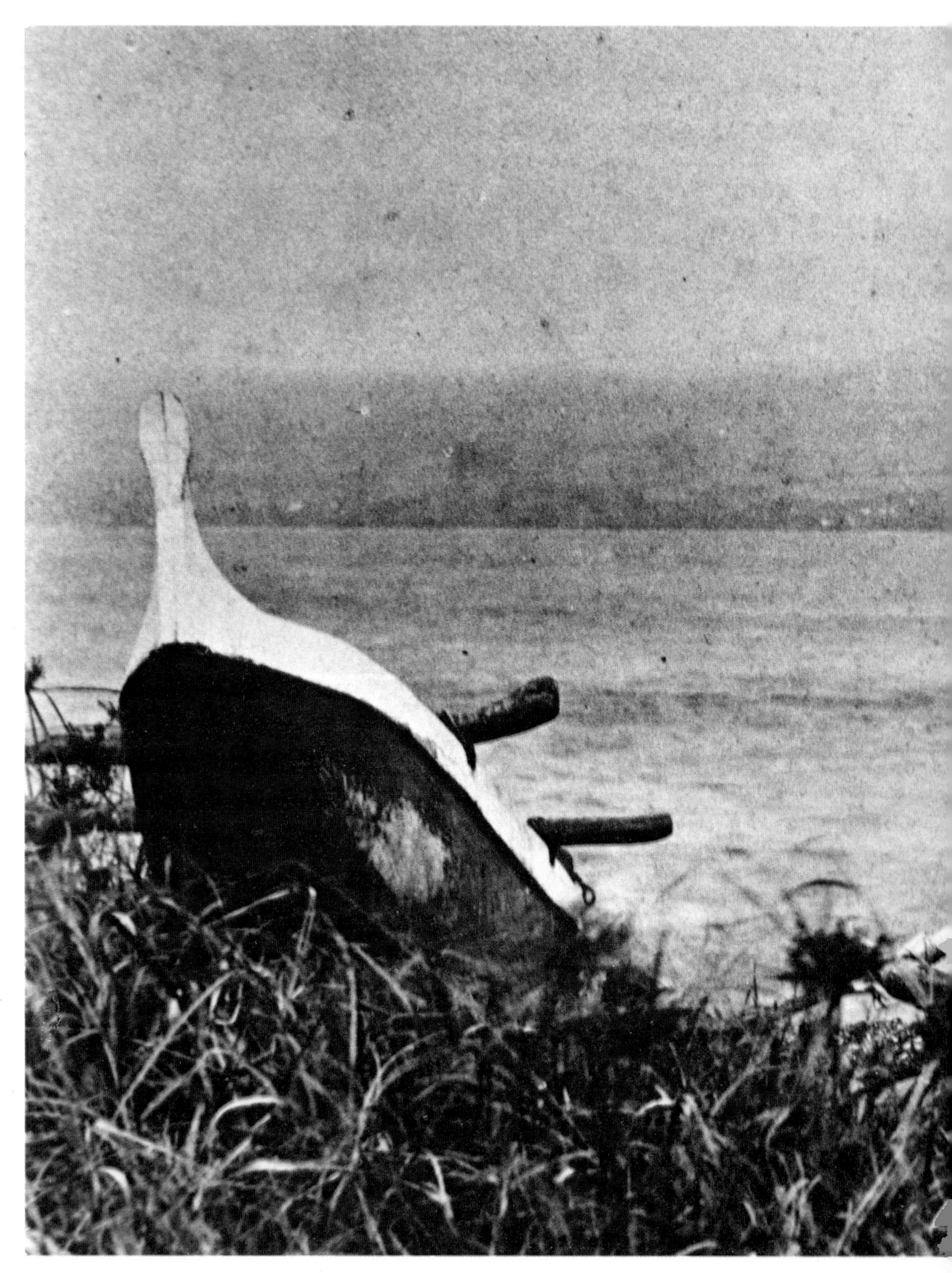

Miss Nellie Sisson Thrum at the shore of Hilo Bay, around 1890. C. Furneaux. Lyman House Memorial Museum.

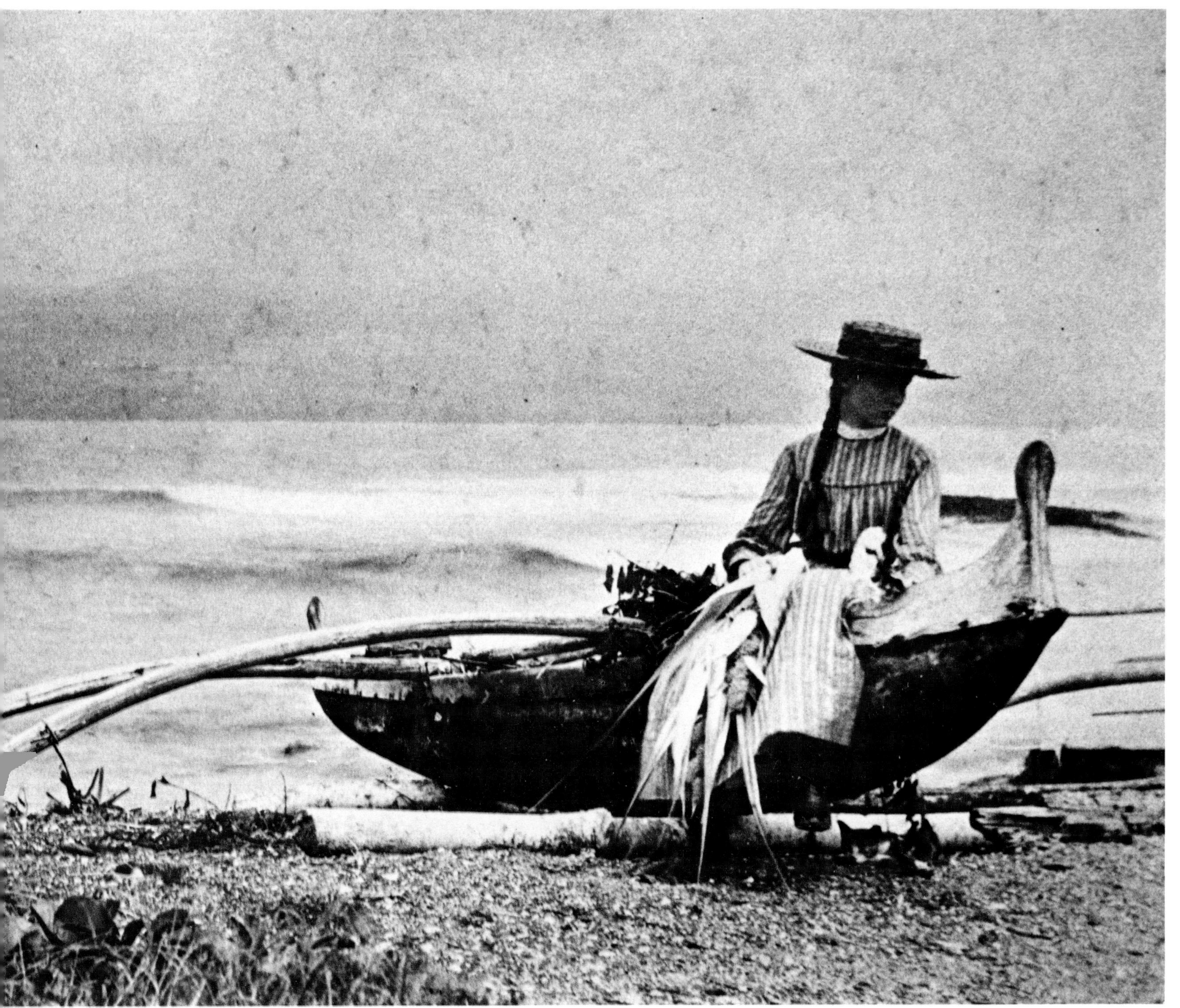

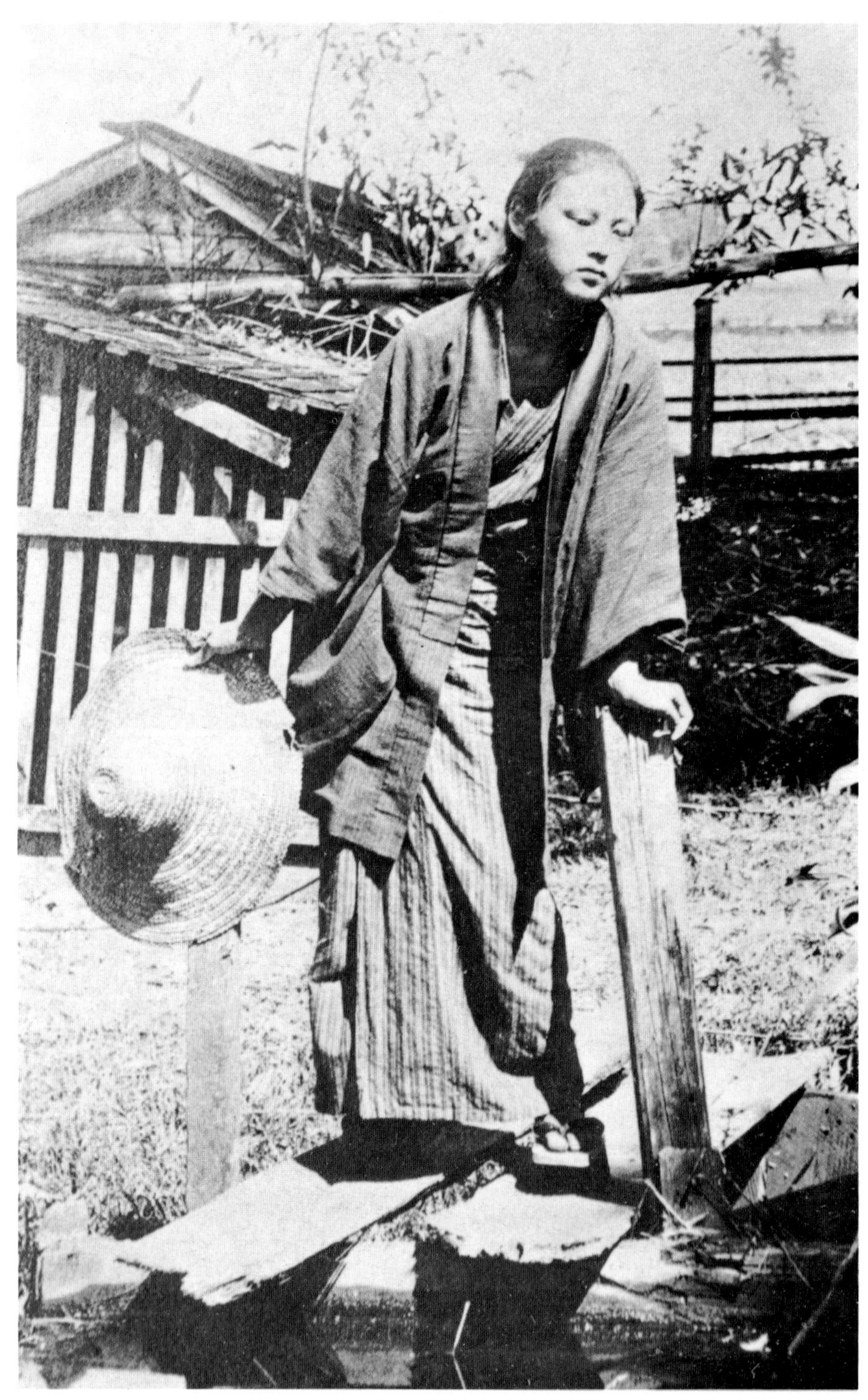

Left: Japanese girl at bridge in Wainaku plantation village outside Hilo, around 1890. C. Furneaux. Lyman House Memorial Museum.

Right: Mother and child in Japanese village at Wainaku, around 1890. C. Furneaux. Lyman House Memorial Museum.

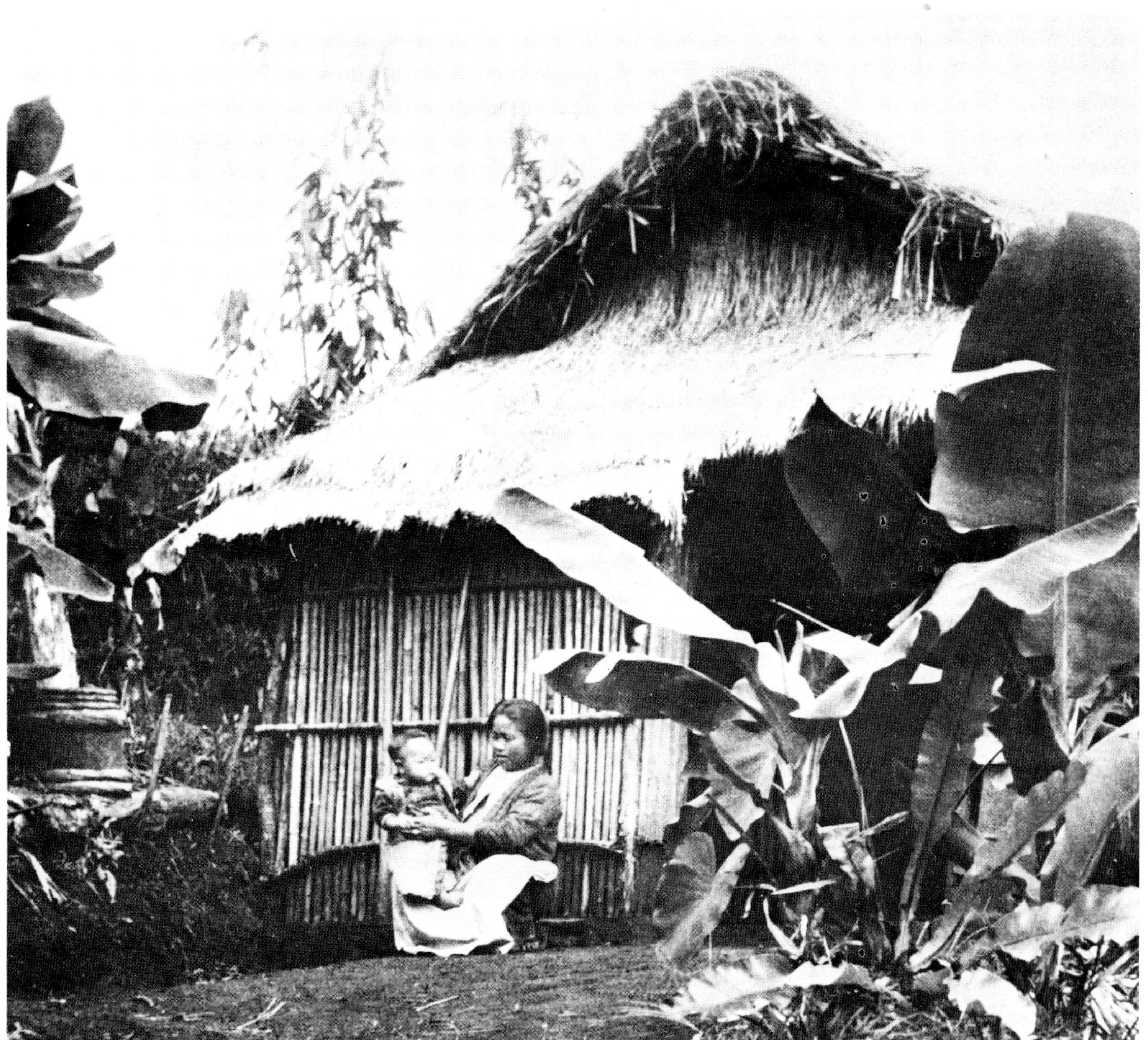

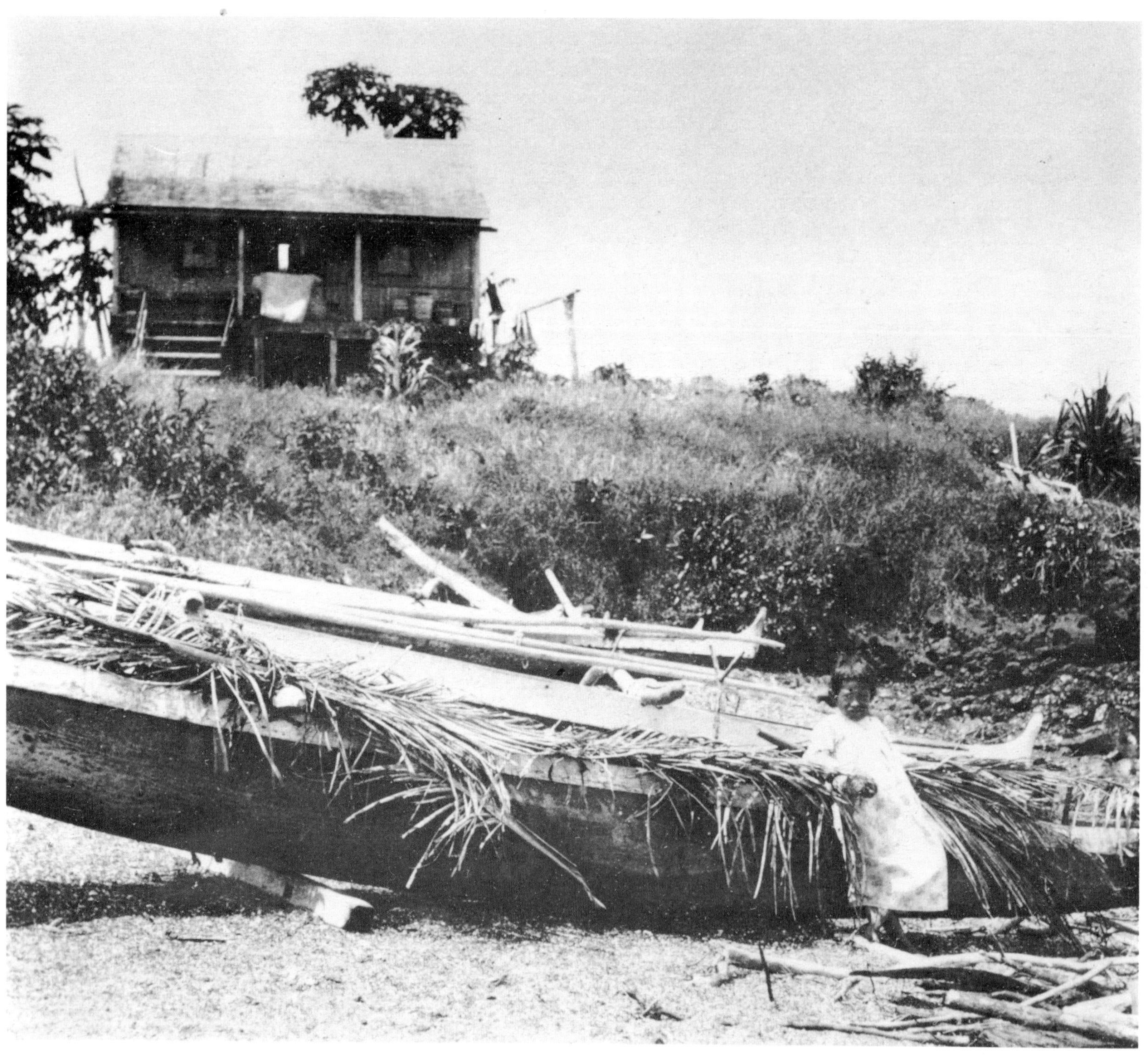

Left: Girl and canoe at Keokea Landing, Island of Hawaii, around 1890. C. Furneaux. Lyman House Memorial Museum.

Below: Hawaiians in front of hut, outskirts of Hilo around 1890. C. Furneaux. Lyman House Memorial Museum.

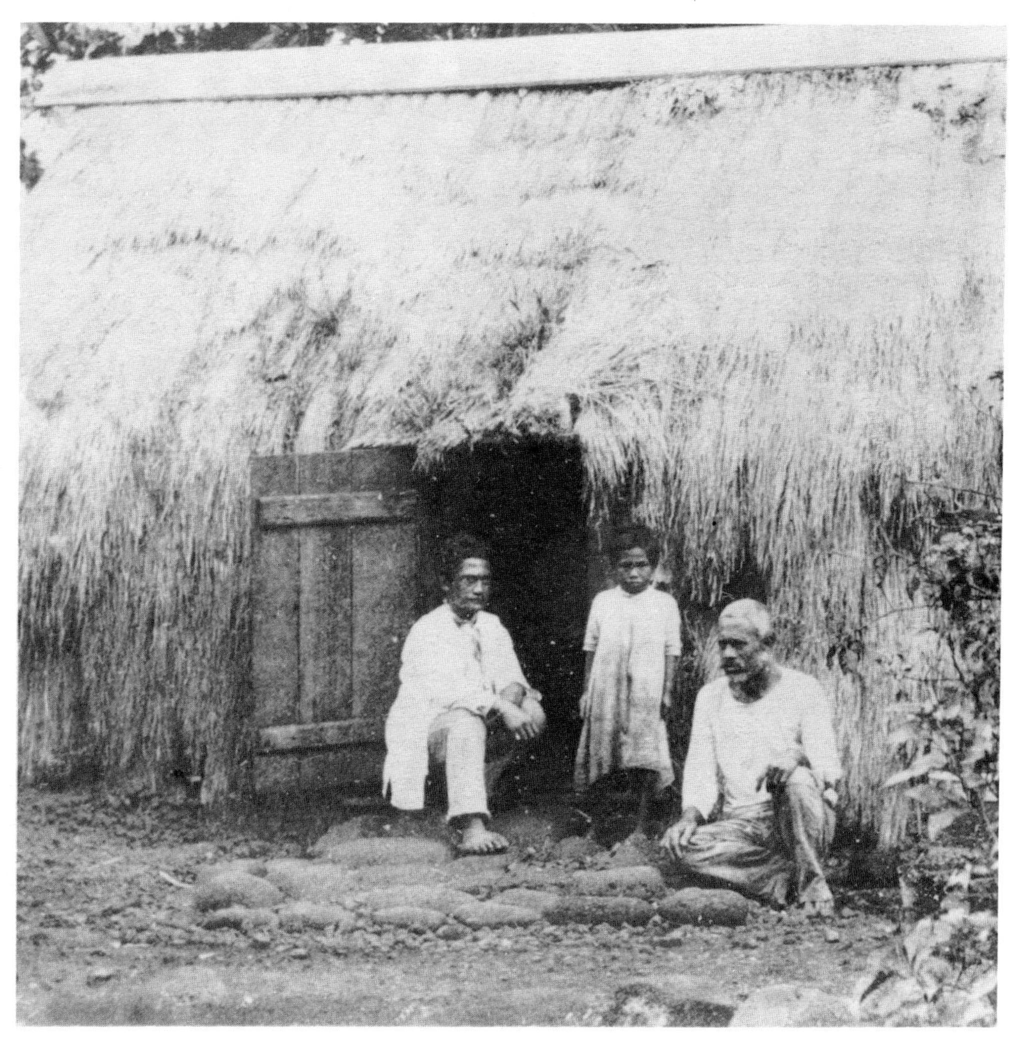

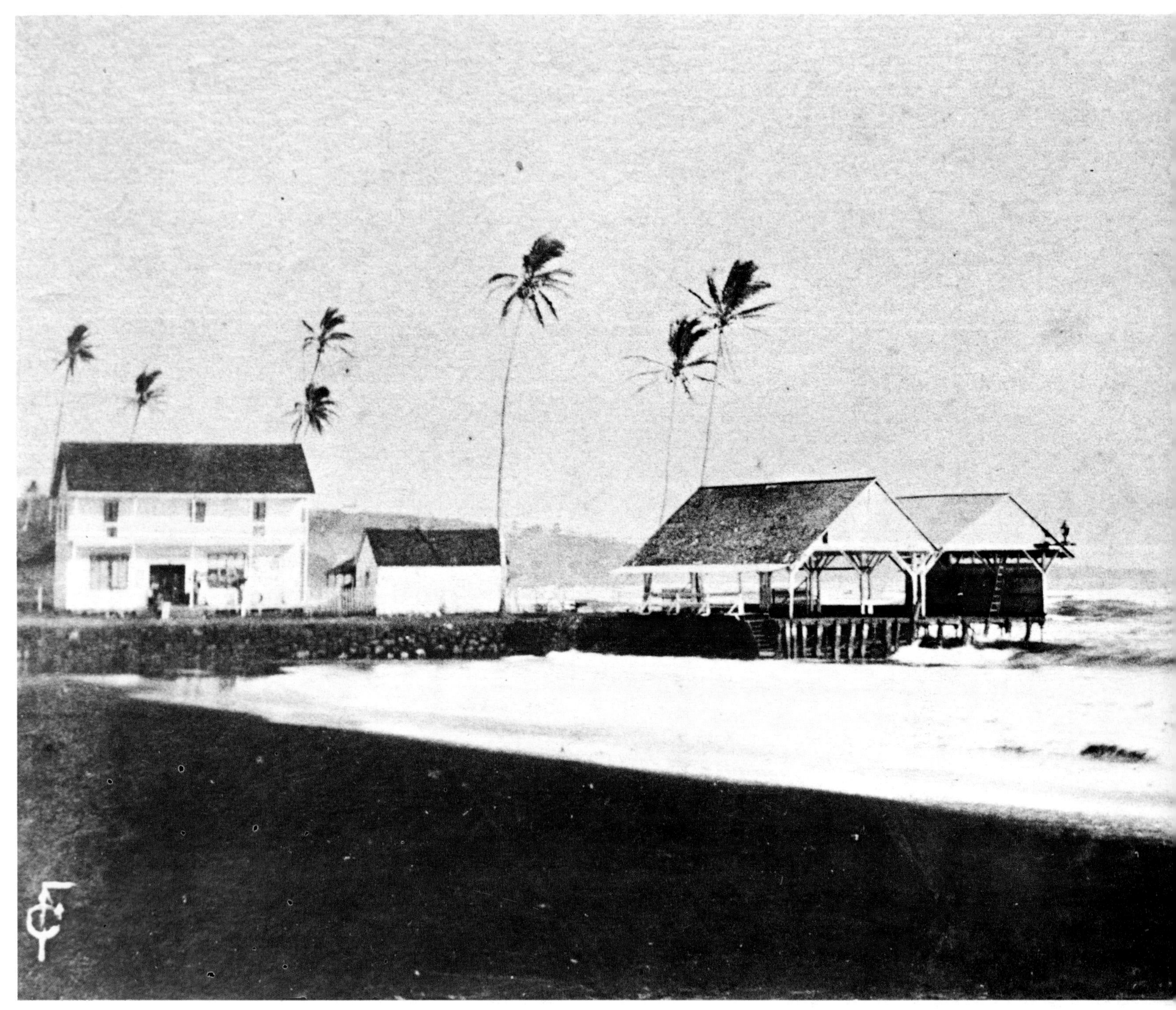

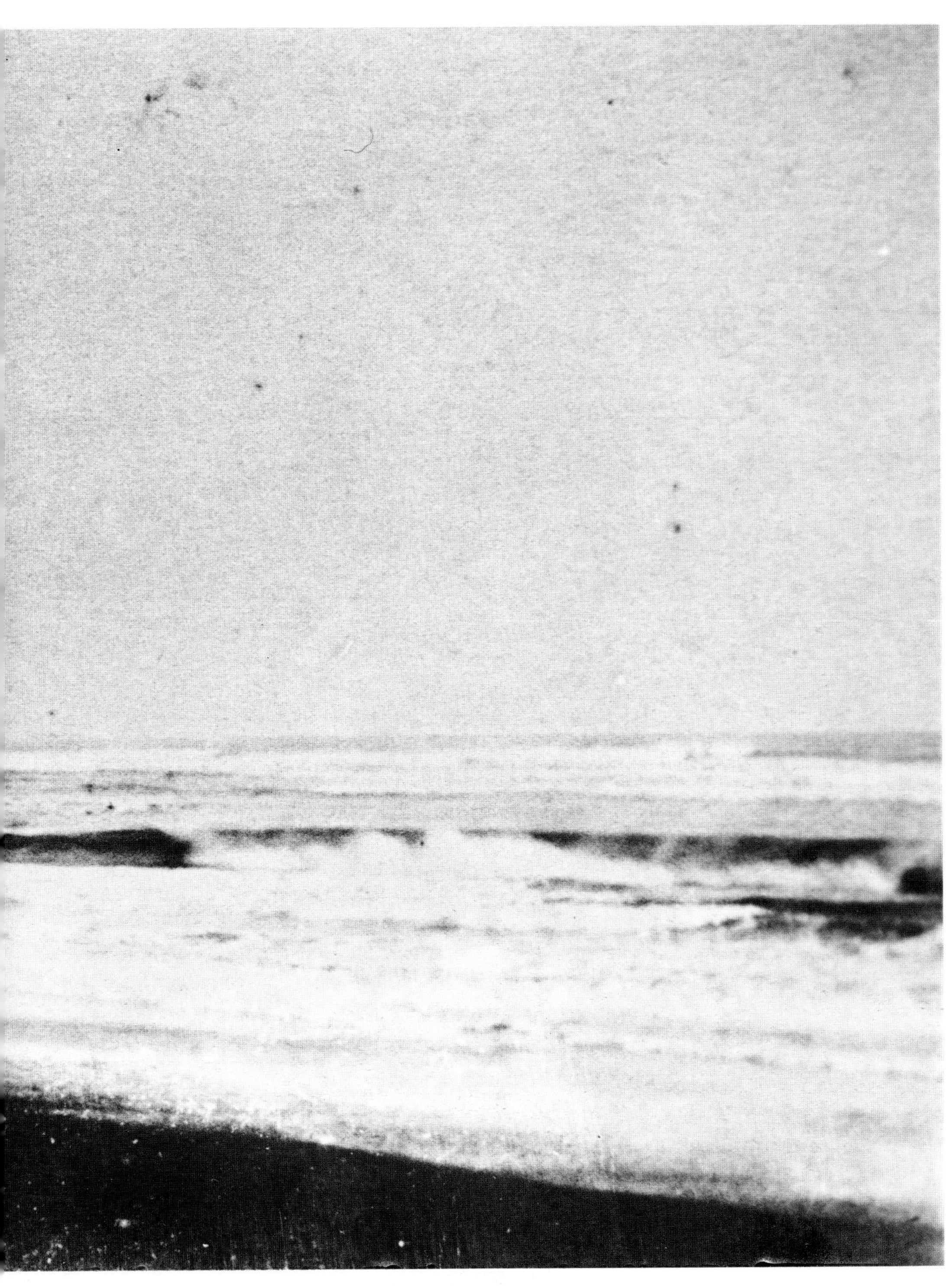

Hilo Bay landing in the 1890s. C. Furneaux. Lyman House Memorial Museum.

E. N. Hitchcock photographed at Waikiki. Photographer unknown. From the Walker Collection, Lyman House Memorial Museum.

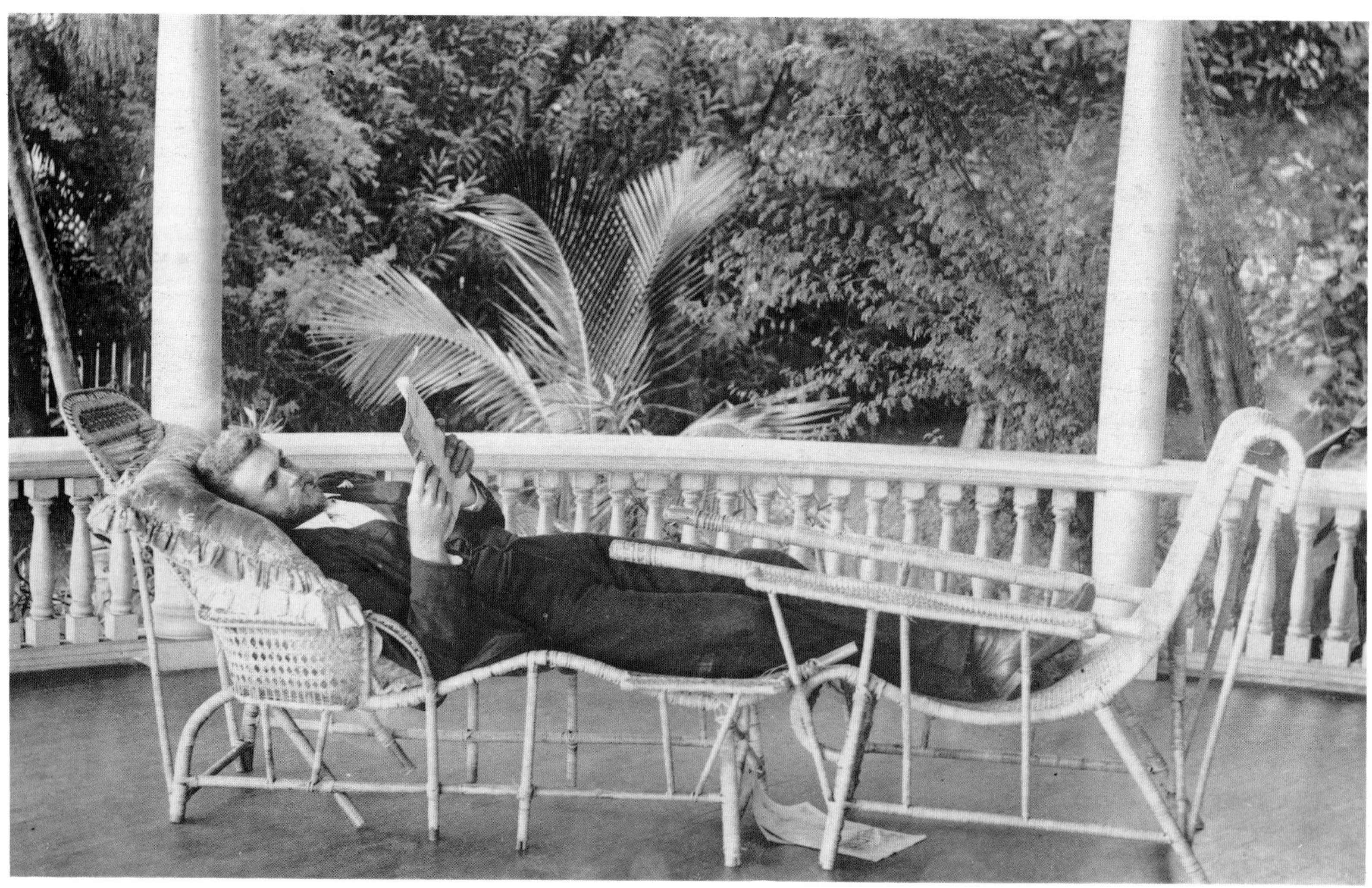

Edward N. Hitchcock

Edward Northrup Hitchcock died in 1901 at the age of 31. What is known about his photography is very limited. His daughter, Hildreth Hitchcock Walker, was less than a year old when he died. Mrs. Walker was later to relate, through stories told her by members of the family, that photography was one of her father's hobbies, along with hiking and cabinet making: Hitchcock's glass plates and prints were stored in the family home for years in a koa wood cabinet that he had made. Both cabinet and plates were treasured by the family and were kept in remarkably good condition. In 1975 the plates were donated to the Lyman House Memorial Museum by Hitchcock's grandson, Neal Walker.

Although Hitchcock did not live to become acquainted with his only child, Hildreth Walker was able to recount the flavor of the life her father led and a great deal about his family background. Hitchcock was one of only three photographers in this collection who was born in the Hawaiian Islands and the only photographer whose parents were also locally born. The Hitchcock side of the family arrived in Hawaii with the eighth company of missionaries from New England. Edward N. Hitchcock's father, Edward Griffin Hitchcock, was born in Lahaina: his parents served as missionaries on the Island of Molokai and, with the impending birth of each of their four children, Mrs. Hitchcock would travel aboard a double hulled canoe to Lahaina where some Western medical attention was available. Hitchcock's mother also came from a missionary family, the Castles, who served as missionaries on Oahu.

E.N. Hitchcock was born at Palaikau, Hawaii, on July 25, 1870, the second son and one of eight children in his family. He grew up on the Island of Hawaii and, like many of his contemporaries, was sent to a mainland college to complete his education. However, Hitchcock did not adapt well to the rugged winters of upper New York State. During both his first and second winter at Cornell University he contracted pneumonia. Doctors finally advised him to avoid further cold weather. He returned to Hawaii with only two years of college completed. Hitchcock soon began working for the newly organized telephone company on the Island of Hawaii — an area that was one of the first in the world to have fairly comprehensive phone service. Until the time of his death he was in charge of phone lines and maintenance in the area between Hilo and Olaa, through Ka'u and into Kona.

In April, 1900, Hitchcock married Claire Fassett, a young school teacher who had come to Hawaii from San Francisco. The two lived at Olaa above Glenwood, on the road to the volcano area and Ka'u. Their family home in Olaa had for years served as a half way point for people traveling between Hilo and Ka'u. Hospitality, in the form of bed and board, was always available and the Hitchcocks rarely knew how many people would appear in time for dinner.

Hitchcock apparently loved the rugged Olaa area and often trekked into the forest surrounding the family home in search of a pleasant afternoon of hiking or, as often happened, in search of one of the family cows. Family tradition holds that the forest of the area was so filled with heavy growth that hikers were required to carry cane knives. As an added precaution, a big bell hung over the front steps of the family home. When hikers had been gone for a suspiciously long time, the bell would be rung so that they could cut their way home toward the sound of the bell.

Hitchcock and his wife moved to Hilo about a year after they were married, to await the birth of their child. They had left Olaa for the same reason that Hitchcock's grandfather periodically left Molokai. Medical expertise was simply not to be found in the remote upland area. But even Hilo could not provide sufficient medical expertise for Edward N. Hitchcock. When his daughter was less than a year old, he died in Hilo, from internal bleeding that was attributed to unknown causes.

Among the approximately 200 glass plates in the Hitchcock collection are a number of family group sittings, shots of young friends on outings in the Olaa and Kilauea area, and a group of pictures of Hitchcock's wife and infant child. The collections also reflect Hitchcock's love for his home island. Predominant among the plates are scenic shots of great beauty, most taken in the Kilauea,

Hilo and Hamakua areas. In some, Hitchcock has posed family friends or local Hawaiians and plantation workers. In others he captures the natural beauty of the landscape devoid of people. But almost always there are either people or man made objects in his photographs. Hitchcock, above all, seems to have enjoyed a sense of the natural harmony between the inhabitants of the area, their dwellings and work structures, and the land. Objects of human invention, as well as men and women, seem a natural part of his landscapes.

It is quite likely that Hitchcock knew Charles Furneaux and shared with him a lively exchange on the subject of photography. Certainly the two men, though far apart in age, did work that sometimes is strikingly similar. And here and there one finds a photograph by Hitchcock where a second photographer appears in the distance. But Hitchcock's approach is less romantic than is Furneaux'. Though they often depict the same subjects: Japanese cane workers, for example, or Hawaiians resting before thatch huts, Hitchcock's people seem more firmly rooted in the real world while Furneaux' often seem to be more a part of an idyllic, painted canvas.

It is unfortunate that Hitchcock died so young. However, what remains of the work of this fine amateur is an invaluable, rich photographic record of life on the slopes of the volcano in the 1890s. The members of Hitchcock's family, who cherished his work and preserved it so carefully, deserve thanks and credit for this fine legacy.

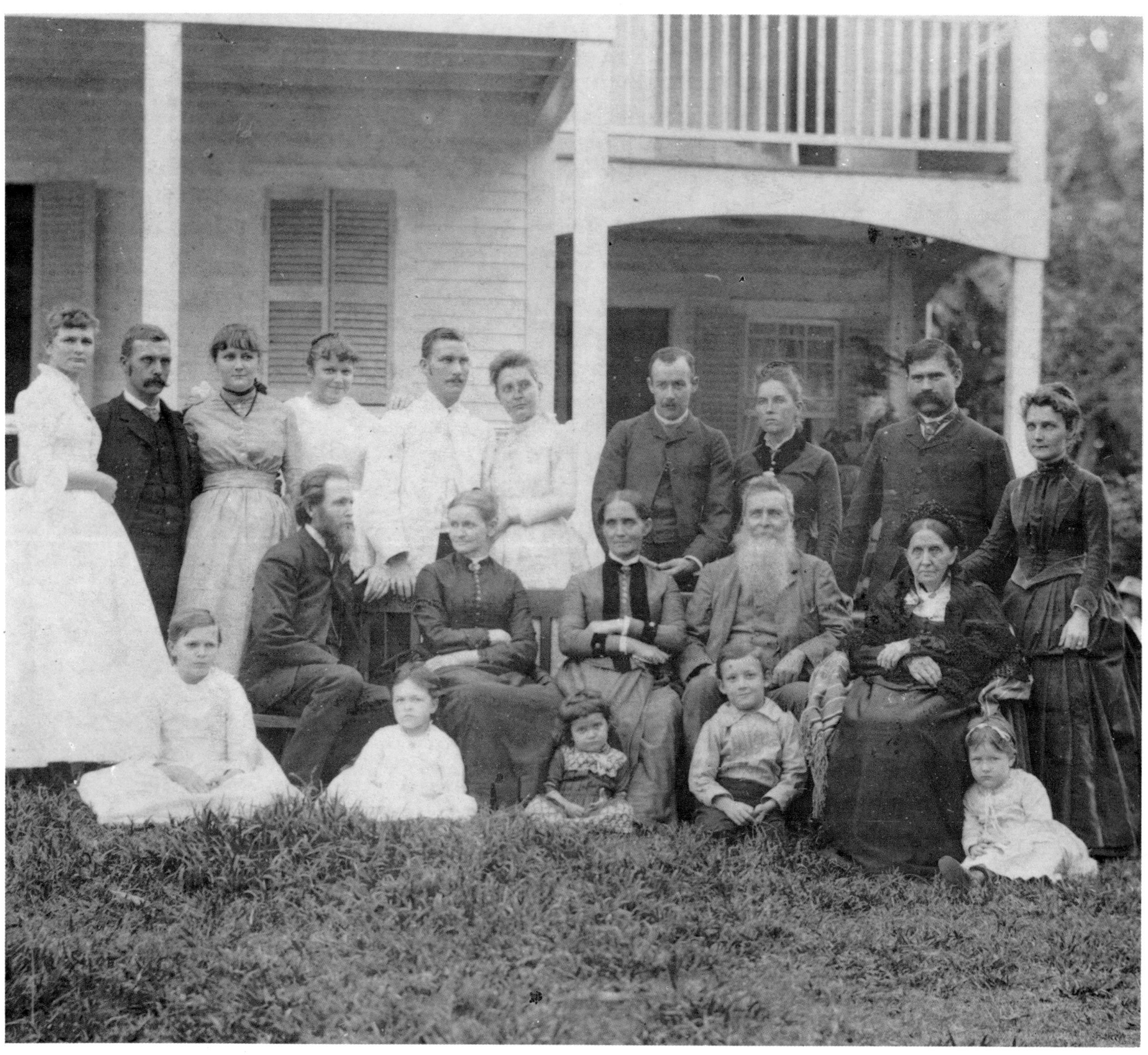

Left: The Hitchcock family about 1890. E.N. Hitchcock. Walker Collection, Lyman House Memorial Museum.

Below: A group of Hawaiians by a road in Puna, around 1895. E.N. Hitchcock. Walker Collection, Lyman House Memorial Museum.

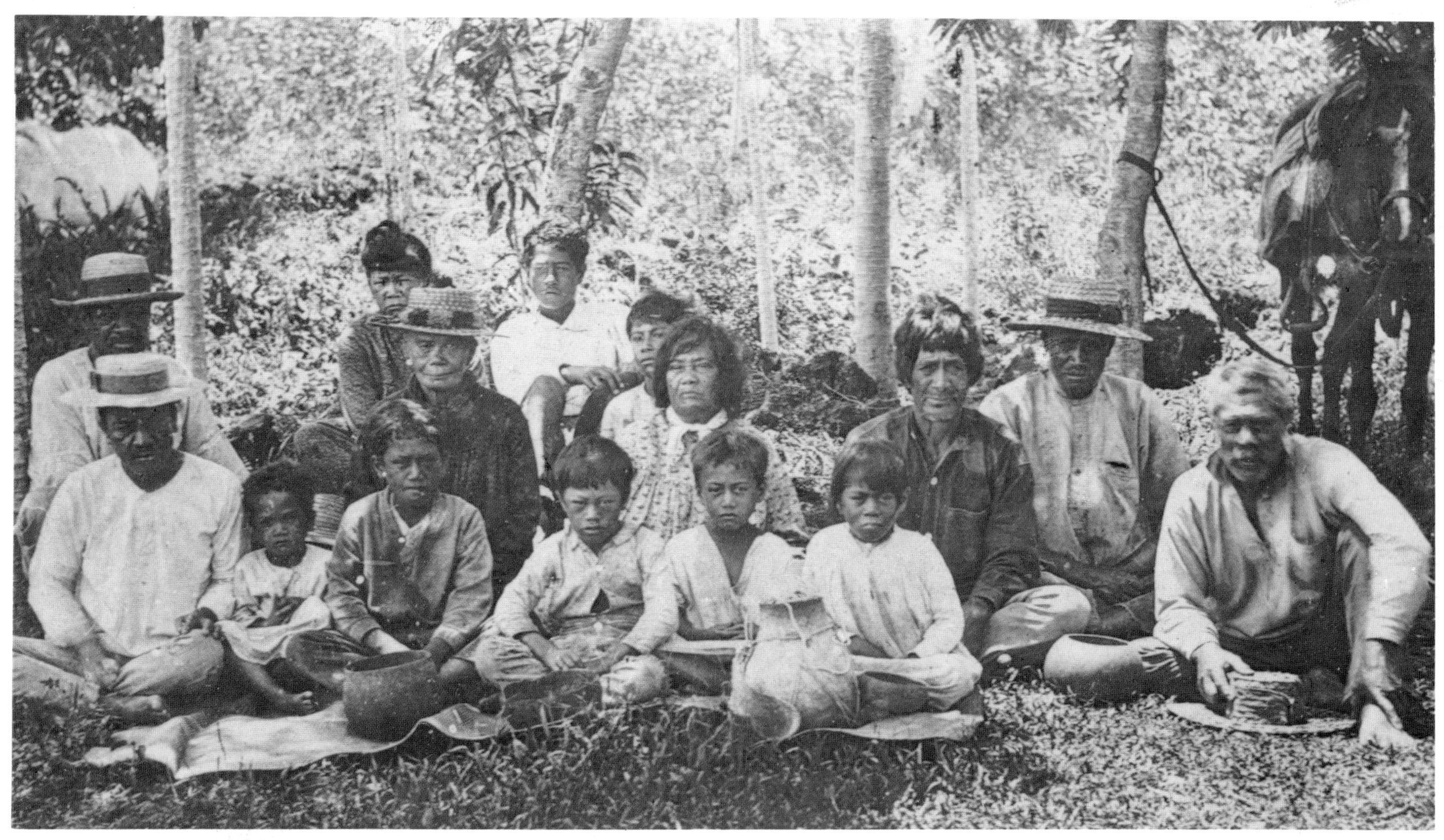

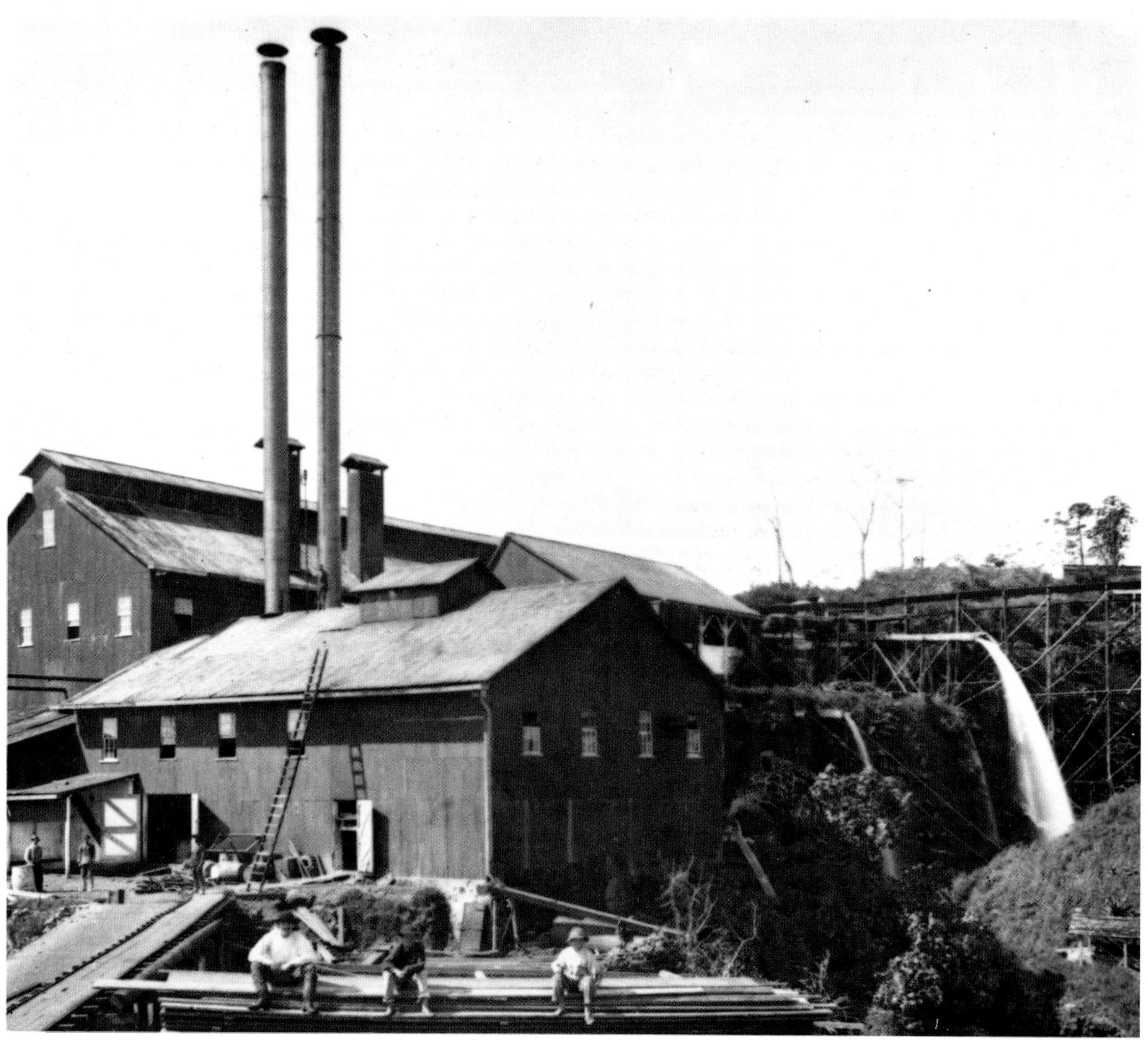

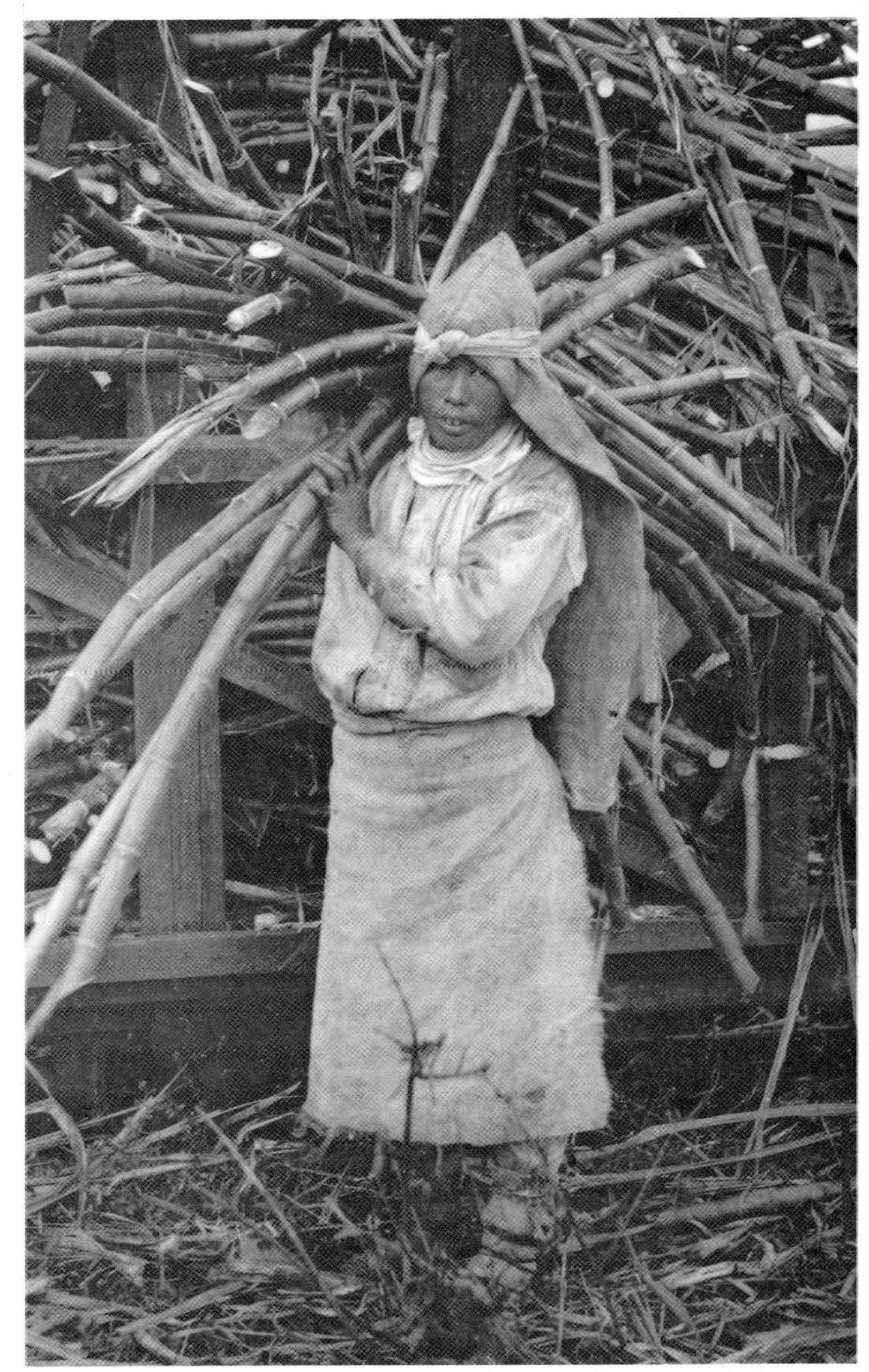

Left: The Wainaku Sugar Mill around 1890. E.N. Hitchcock. Walker Collection, Lyman House Memorial Museum.

Right: A Japanese worker with a load of cane, probably at Wainaku Plantation around 1890. E. N. Hitchcock. Walker Collection, Lyman House Memorial Museum.

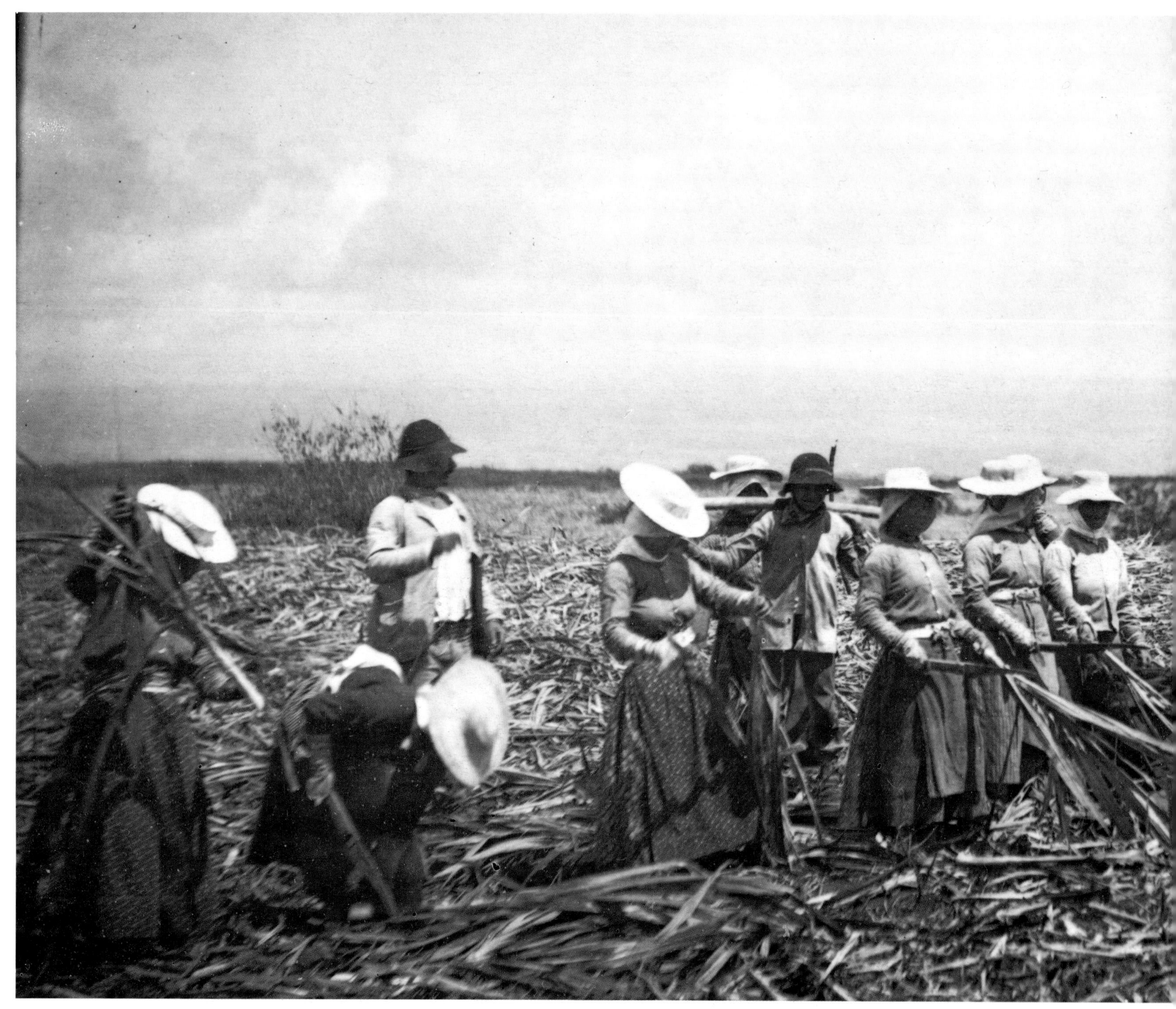

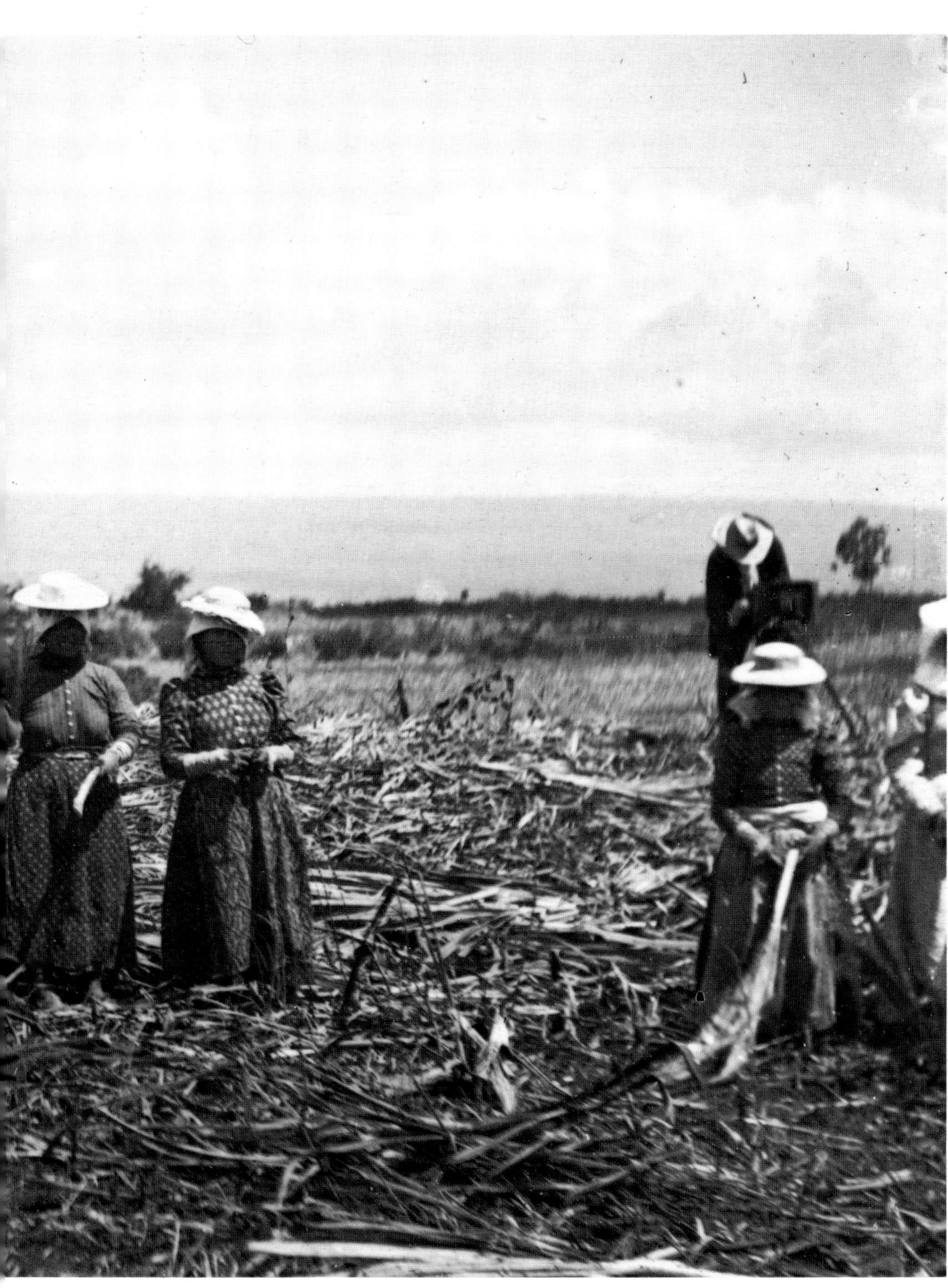

Japanese women cutting seed cane. Note second photographer in far right. About 1890. E.N. Hitchcock. Walker Collection, Lyman House Memorial Museum.

Right: Hawaiians pounding poi, about 1890. E.N. Hitchcock. Walker Collection, Lyman House Memorial Museum.

Below: Hawaiians standing before grass hut, 1890. E.N. Hitchcock. Walker Collection, Lyman House Memorial Museum.

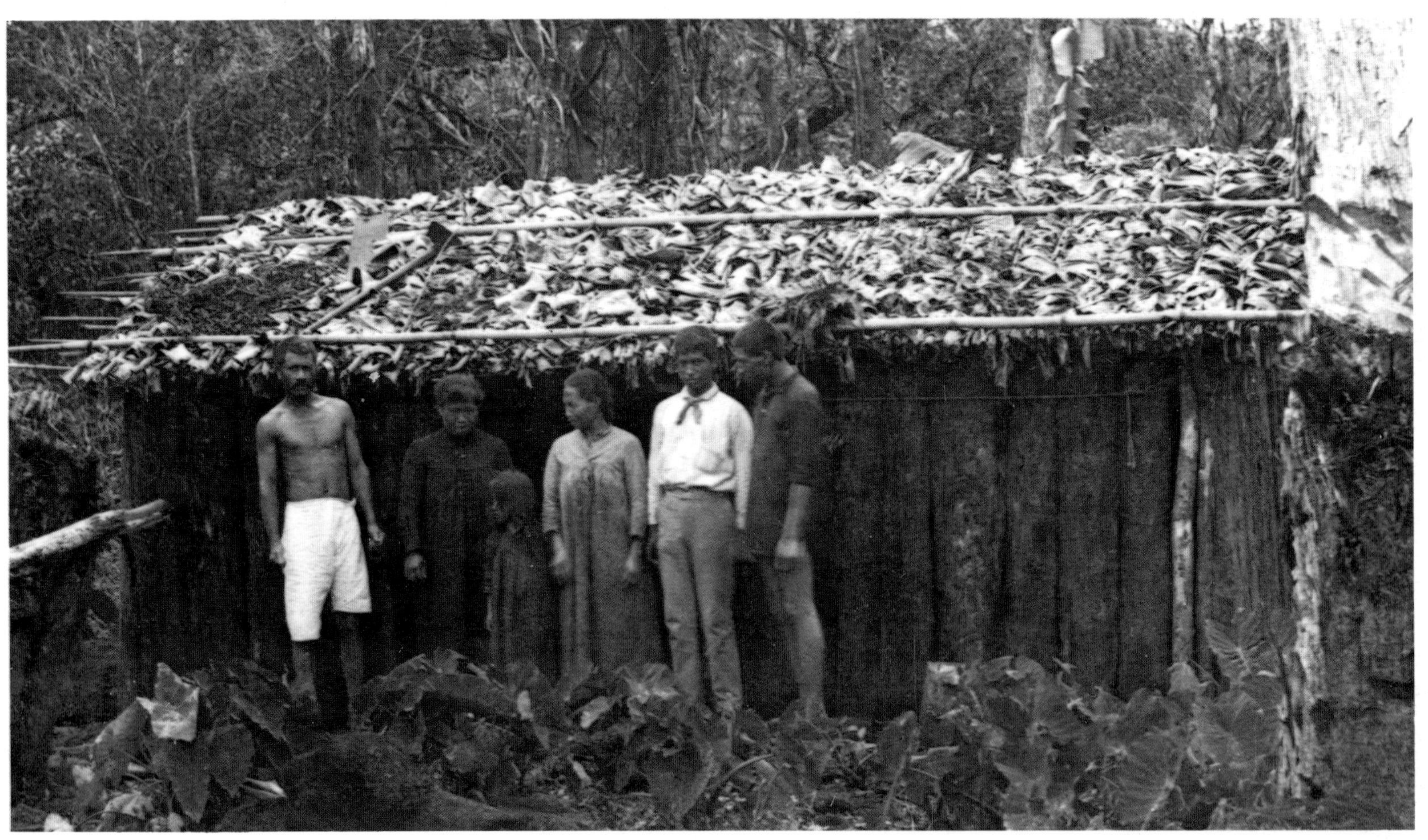

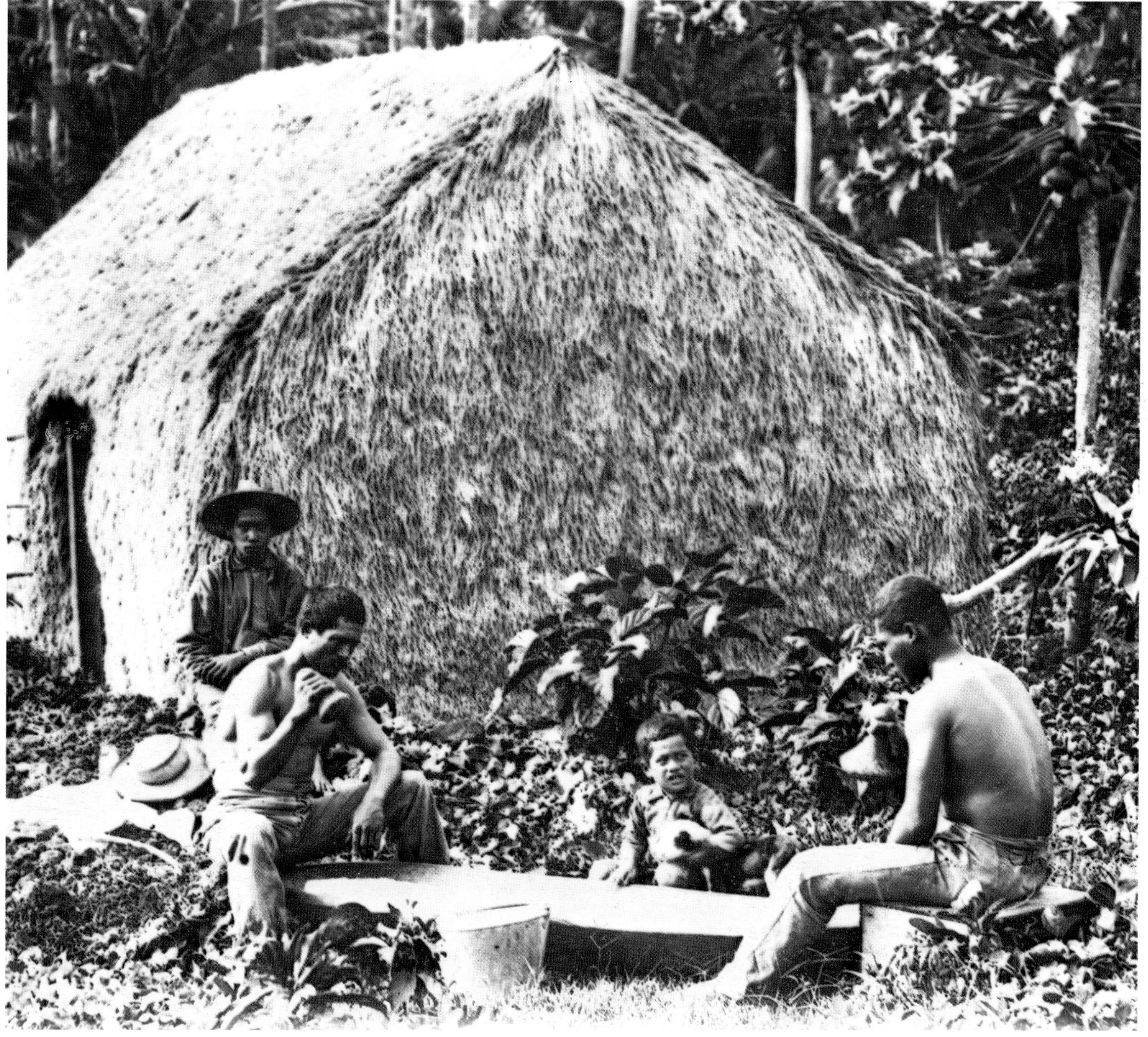

Old Hilo landing about 1890. E.N. Hitchcock. Walker Collection, Lyman House Museum.

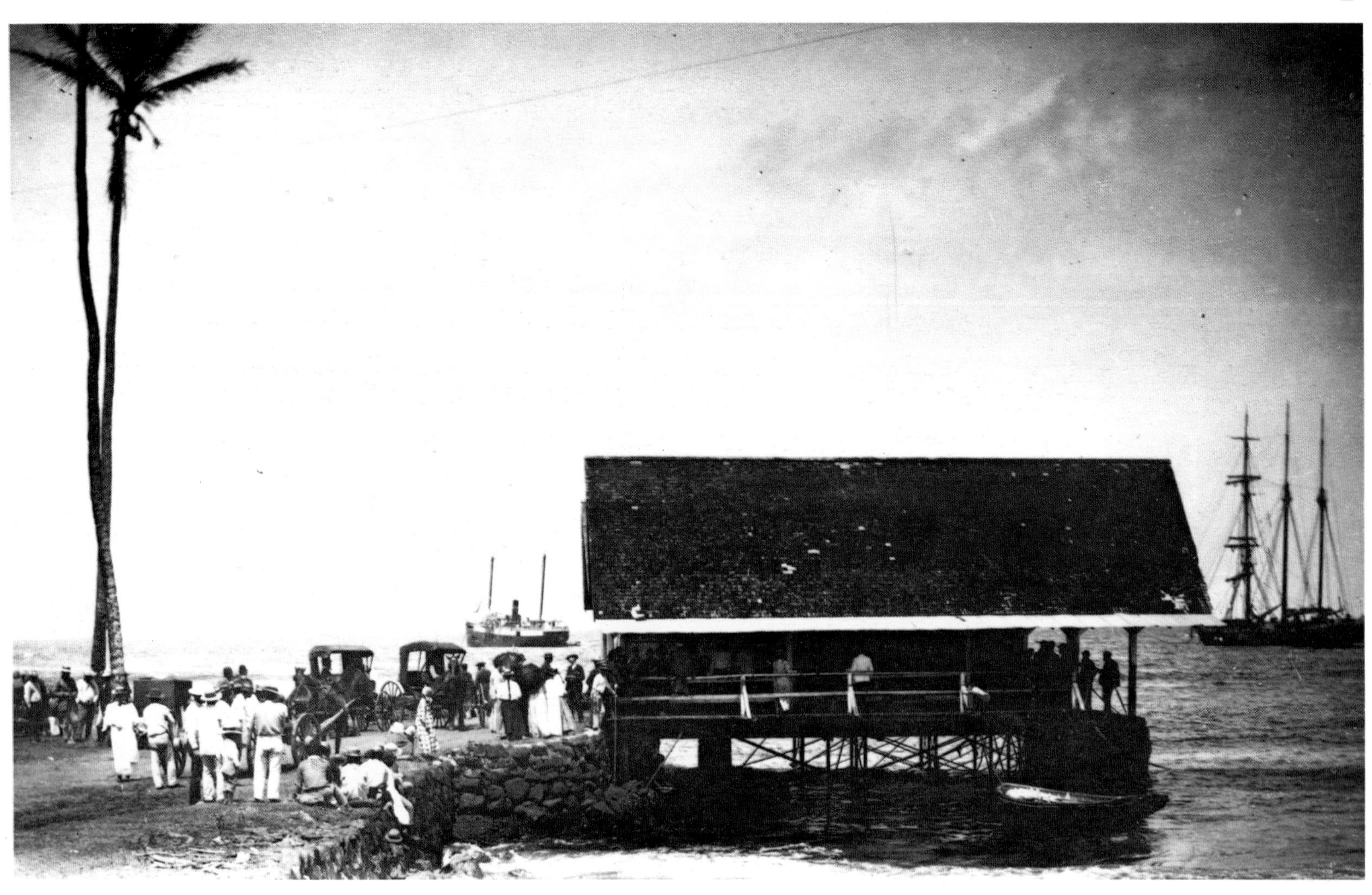

Wainuenue Street, Hilo. The American flags might indicate that the photograph was taken at the time of American annexation of the islands in 1898. E.N. Hitchcock. Walker Collection, Lyman House Memorial Museum.

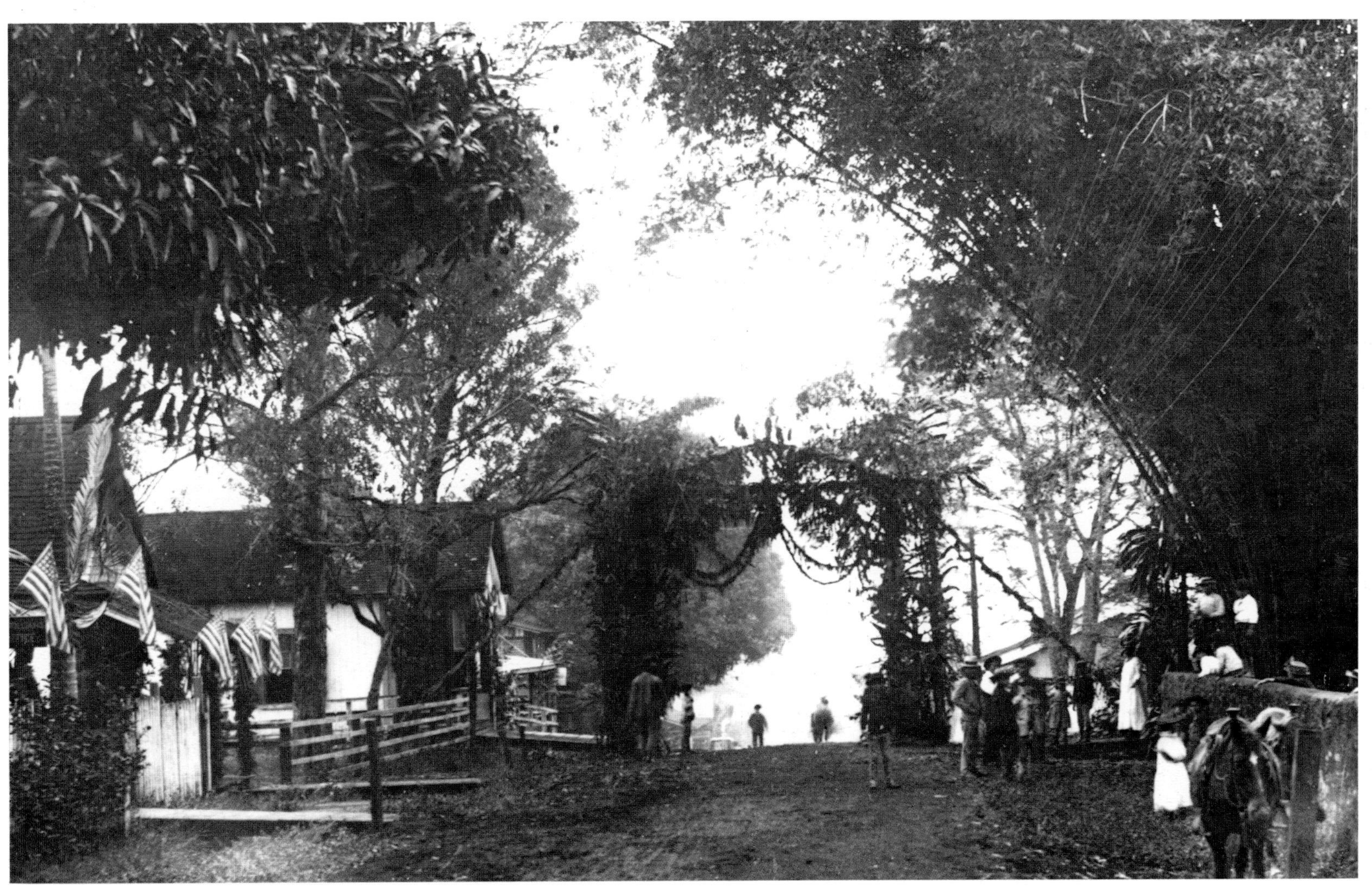

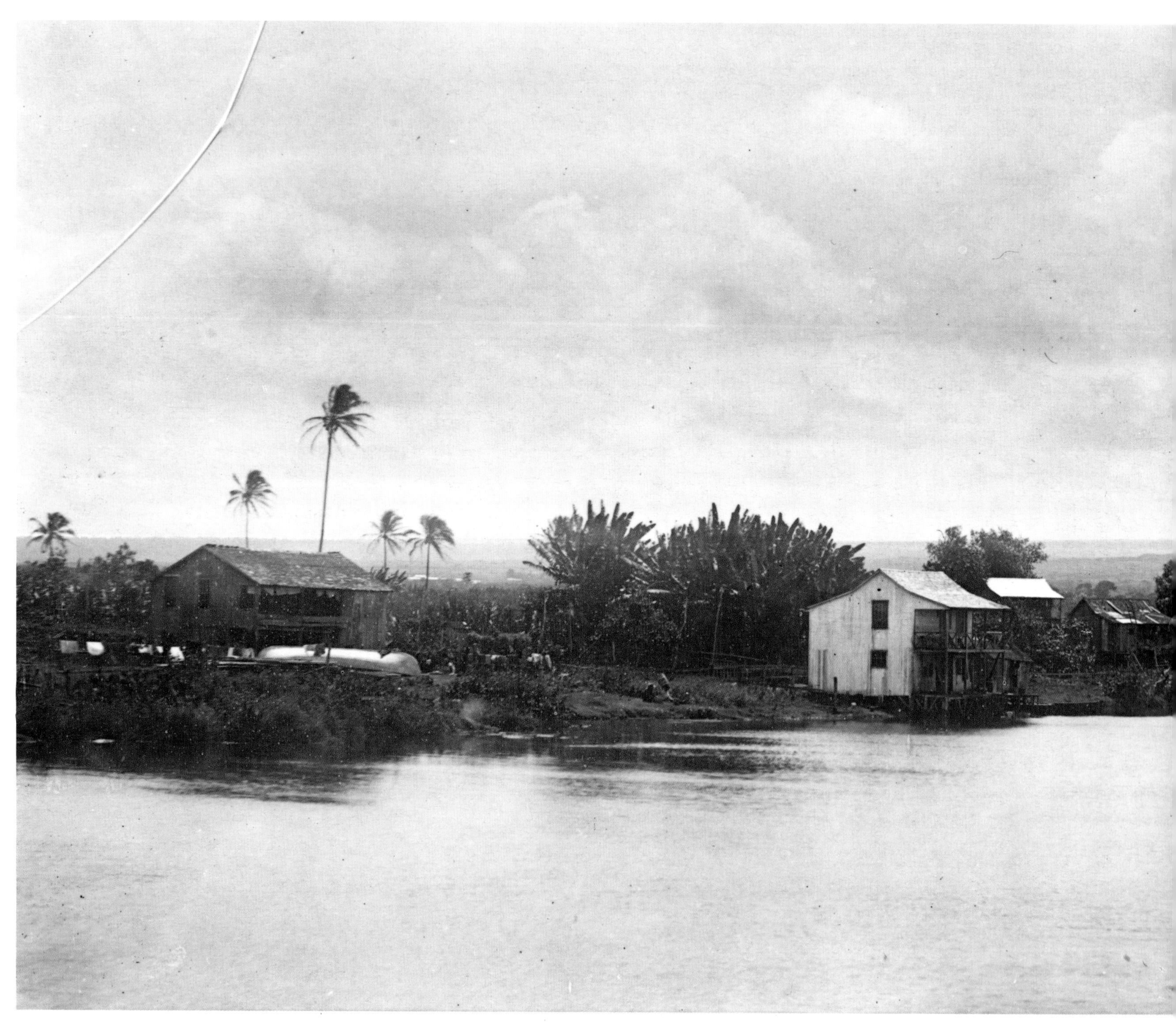

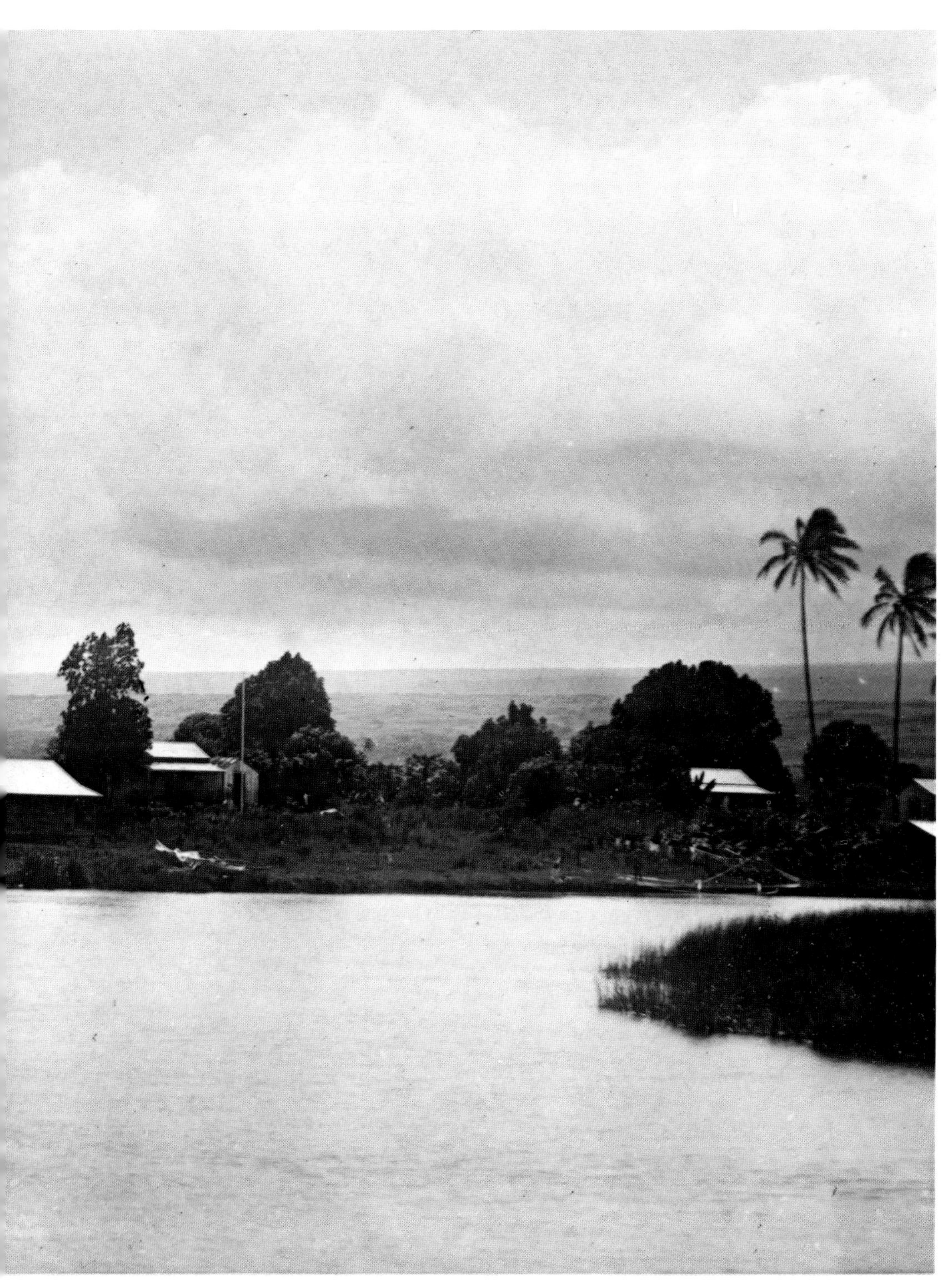

Afternoon at the Waiakea River, around 1890. E. N. Hitchcock. From the Walker Collection, Lyman House Memorial Museum.

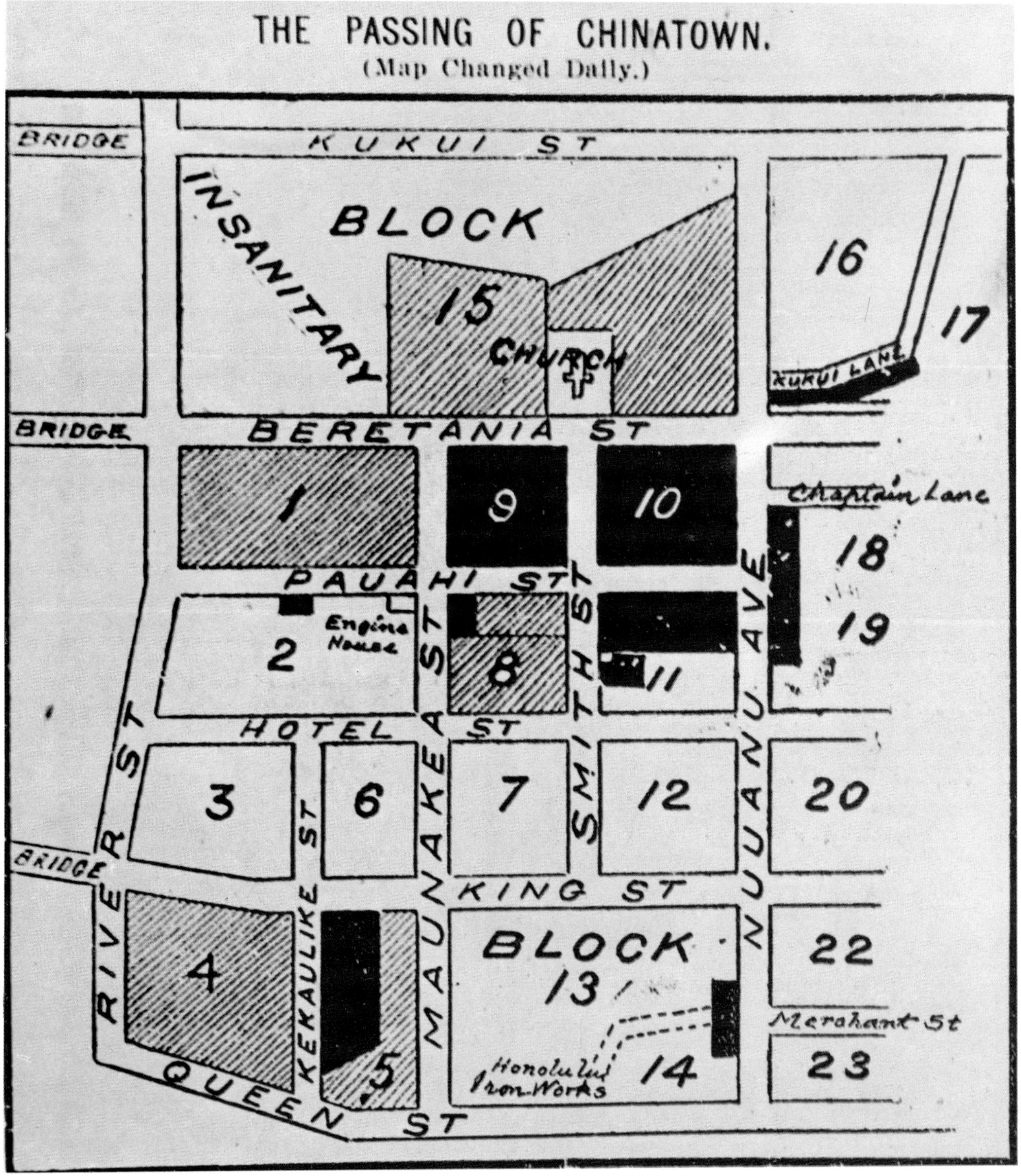

THE PASSING OF CHINATOWN.
(Map Changed Daily.)

Map is from the January 20, 1900 issue of *The Pacific Commercial Advertiser*. During the period of bubonic plague, the paper began printing maps indicating which areas of the quarantined area in Honolulu's Chinatown were scheduled for demolition. The city Board of Health had decided to burn areas of Chinatown where plague victims had been found. Hawaii State Archives.

Frank Davey

Considering the fact that he spent little more than three years in Hawaii, Frank Davey was one of the most prolific of island photographers. The record abounds with Davey photographs of papayas, mangoes and bananas, lei sellers and public buildings — all apparently taken with an eye toward the tourist market as well as the albums of local residents. In fact, his first advertisement in the September 1, 1897, issue of *The Pacific Commercial Advertiser* makes it clear that even before he opened for business Frank Davey had toured the islands and collected a considerable number of negatives of island views:

"Davey Photograph Co. Ltd. Is open for business. Portraits of every description upon the best Papers, Platinum, Iridium, Mezzo-tint, Carbon and all other papers known in Photography. Best work guaranteed at moderate prices. CABINETS from $6.00 per Dozen. Pictures made Life Size direct. Appointments made by Telephone 494. Sole proprietors of the Bas Relief and iridium processes. Large collection of recent Island views. Specimens can be seen on the ground floor, MOTT-SMITH BUILDING. COR FORT & HOTEL ST."

As was the custom, the ad was accompanied by an article in the news columns of the paper. The Davey article appeared in *The Commercial Advertiser* issue of August 30, 1897: "New Departure, Davey Photograph Co. Open for Business Today" read the headline. "The doors of the Davey Photographic Company will be thrown open to the public this morning. Frank Davey, the President of the Company, is one of the best-known photographers on the Pacific Coast, having been chief operator for Tabors for the past 10 years. Before that he was with Wallery of Paris and Vander-Weyde of London.

"Besides being a photographer, Mr. Davey is a cartoonist of note in London, and his scrap-book contains many interesting newspaper reproductions of his pencil work. In selecting the Mott-Smith building for his new operations Mr. Davey secured one of the best in the city for light effects. The rooms were arranged according to his directions, and the detail is perfect. The reception room is on the first floor near Fort Street. Here a clerk will take the orders and arrange for the sittings of the customers. This room contains some sample portraits by Mr. Davey and albums of Island views.

"Admission to the operating rooms is by stair or electric elevator to the third floor. Like the reception room, the hall and rooms are exquisitely furnished and carpeted and the walls hung with paintings by some of America's celebrated artists. One room, fitted with stationary wash-stand, dressing case, etc., is provided for ladies, and a smaller one for gentlemen. A wardrobe contains various costumes for ladies and children who desire something out of the usual order, and who do not wish to go to the expense of having clothing made for the purpose. Among the cameras in the establishment is one for making life-size photographs direct. Besides the ordinary photographs Mr. Davey will make bas-relief mezzotint and iridium effects, which are superior to any other made. These are exclusive with Mr. Davey, and are made in San Francisco only by Tabor.

"During his experience as a photographer he has made pictures of Lady Randolph Churchill, Sir Edwin Arnold, Sir George Trevelyan, Whitelaw Reid, Prince Joseph of Batenberg, Cornelius Vanderbilt, Chauncey Depew, Gen. Lew Wallace, Thomas Nast, Mill Nye, Rajah of Rampur, W.Q. Judge and hundreds of others. He has copies of each in an album in the gallery with the autograph of the sitter on each. Mr. Davey has made photographs of a number of local people and in each case the likeness is excellent."

So Frank Davey began his short Honolulu career, obviously catering to the tastes and wishes of the elite. And for a time it would appear that he was indeed *the* photographer to see in Honolulu. However, it is not for his portraits of the elegant that Davey should be remembered. Nor even for his prolific, but for the most part prosaic, island views. For Frank Davey managed to take a most remarkable series of news photographs that record the destruction of Chinatown during the plague and fire of 1900.

It is possible that Davey was covering the plague and fire in some official capacity. He may have been on assignment from the territorial Board of Health: we know that large areas of Chinatown were quarantined at one time or another and that only persons with official passes were allowed in and out of the infected area. While not all Honolulu doctors agreed with Board of Health procedures, it is also clear that there was great pressure to disinfect and burn plague stricken areas as a means of preventing the spread of the disease. Davey could have been assigned by the Board of Health to record conditions in Chinatown so that officials could document the need for some of the property destruction that was ordered in the area.

It is also possible that Davey gained permission to enter the area in order to take photographs for *The Pacific Commercial Advertiser.* At least one woodcut print of the Chinatown area under national guard protection did appear in the *Advertiser* pages during the quarantine period — a print that appears to have been copied directly from a Davey photograph. And after the Chinatown fire in January, 1900, two Davey photographs of the devastated area appear. While the engraving techniques for newspaper use of photography were already available at the turn of the century, newspapers around the world were quite slow to adopt them. *The Advertiser*, like most newspapers, used photography mainly as a means of gaining images to be copied as woodcuts for print use or, occasionally in magazine supplement sections. Indeed, *The Advertiser* of January 1, 1900, has a supplement on Honolulu homes in which a number of photographs appear. But despite the availability of both the techniques and the photographs, news photography appears in the paper only rarely during the plague and Chinatown fire.

It is also possible that Davey took photographs of the quarantine area and fire on speculation. Indeed, one week after the Chinatown fire, he ran an advertisement in *The Commercial Advertiser* announcing that he had on sale views of the quarantine area and the fire. In any event, it seems clear that Davey had access to the quarantine area and that he took advantage of his freedom of movement to photograph the activities inside that area during the plague months.

From the time officials first publicly acknowledged the possibility of plague in Honolulu in mid-November, 1899, there was a great deal of debate over how to handle the situtation. The Board of Health began by imposing a quarantine on the area where plague victims had been found — an area even then called Chinatown, where immigrant Japanese and Chinese, as well as a number of poor Hawaiians, lived in extremely crowded conditions. National guardsmen were sent to block off the area and to help in the cleaning and disinfecting of structures and streets. Old clothing, rubbish and sometimes useful household goods were piled in the streets and burned. Unpainted buildings were whitewashed in the belief that the procedure served to disinfect them, and streets were doused with unslaked lye.

While here and there a doctor objected to the extreme measures that were being used and pointed out that they had little to do with the mechanism through which the bubonic plague infected human beings, the public as a whole and most of the medical community seemed convinced that the extreme measures were necessary. *The Advertiser*, in fact, reported that many well to do families and several hotels had been inconvenienced by the plague and had been forced to get along without their servants who lived in the infested area and had been placed under military quarantine.

By mid-December, the quarantine of Chinatown was lifted and newspapers proclaimed that the plague scare had passed. But only a week later, more plague deaths occurred and a second, far stricter quarantine was imposed. Residents in the stricken area were moved to a large detention center that was set up in Kakaako. Later, a second center was opened in Kalihi and a third near Kawaiahao Church. Squads of volunteers were recruited from among the residents to clean and bury old cesspools, build new ones, and collect and burn trash. In January, *The Advertiser* began reporting the burning of whole blocks of buildings in the infected area. Soon the paper began printing a daily map, showing which blocks were scheduled to be destroyed. And occasionally, an editorial voice was heard on the question of wholesale destruction: while the burning was necessary, the voice speculated, it was also expensive. And someone was going to have to cope with large numbers of displaced persons when it was over.

Life inside the quarantined area did, however, take on a semblance of order. Sanitary stations were set up where plague workers could wash themselves and change their clothing before returning to the detention camp. Kitchens were organized to feed the thousands of persons detained in the quarantined area and games were even organized to interest the children.

But on January 20, 1900, the gradual destruction of Chinatown became a rout. The controlled burning of infected blocks became the out of control destruction of an entire community.

On the morning of January 20, the fire department set about the deliberate burning of the Waikiki part of block 15, adjoining Kaumakapili Church. Until that time, the burning of various blocks in the quarantined area had gone about uneventfully. But on the 20th, a wind whipped down from the Pali and hot coals from the burning area ignited the church itself and then spread to surrounding blocks that were not yet scheduled for demolition. The fire burned out of control for most of the day and rapidly engulfed 30 acres of Chinatown, from Kukui Street to the harbor. In the aftermath of the plague and fire, the citizens of Honolulu had to cope with enormous problems. While few people had actually died of the plague, thousands of people had been displaced and the inventories of numerous small businesses had been destroyed along with blocks of business and residential buildings.

But Frank Davey was not around to record the reconstruction of the Chinatown area. In 1901 Frank Davey sold his elaborate studio to Rice and Perkins and ended his short career as an island photographer. He returned to California and established himself in San Jose, where he remained in business for many years. Since the technology available to reproduce news photographs was not widely used in Hawaii at the time, Davey's images of the disaster that destroyed Chinatown have remained relatively unknown. Yet, of all Davey's work in the Hawaiian Islands, these photographs are his most important contribution to our understanding of the past.

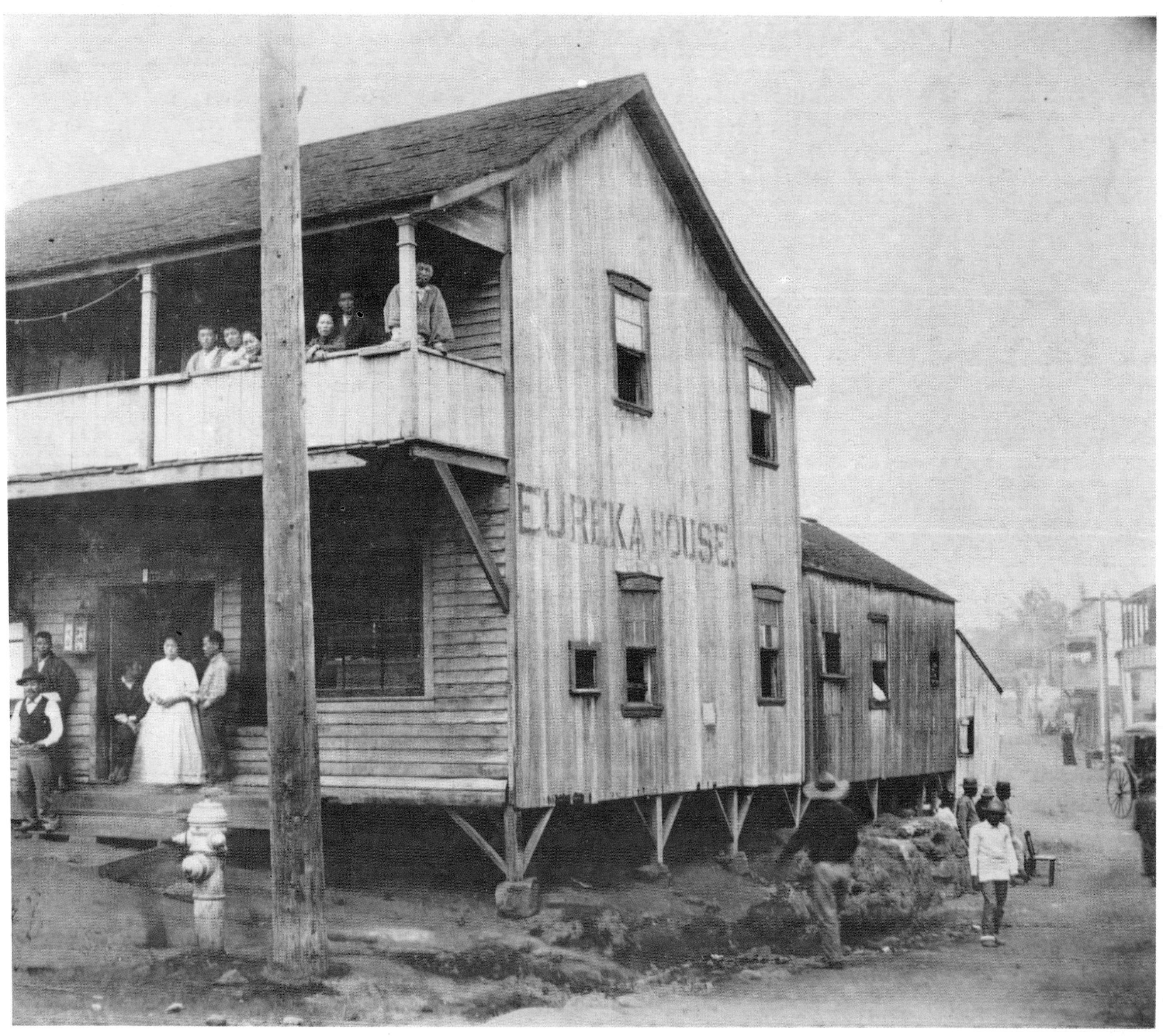
EUREKA HOUSE

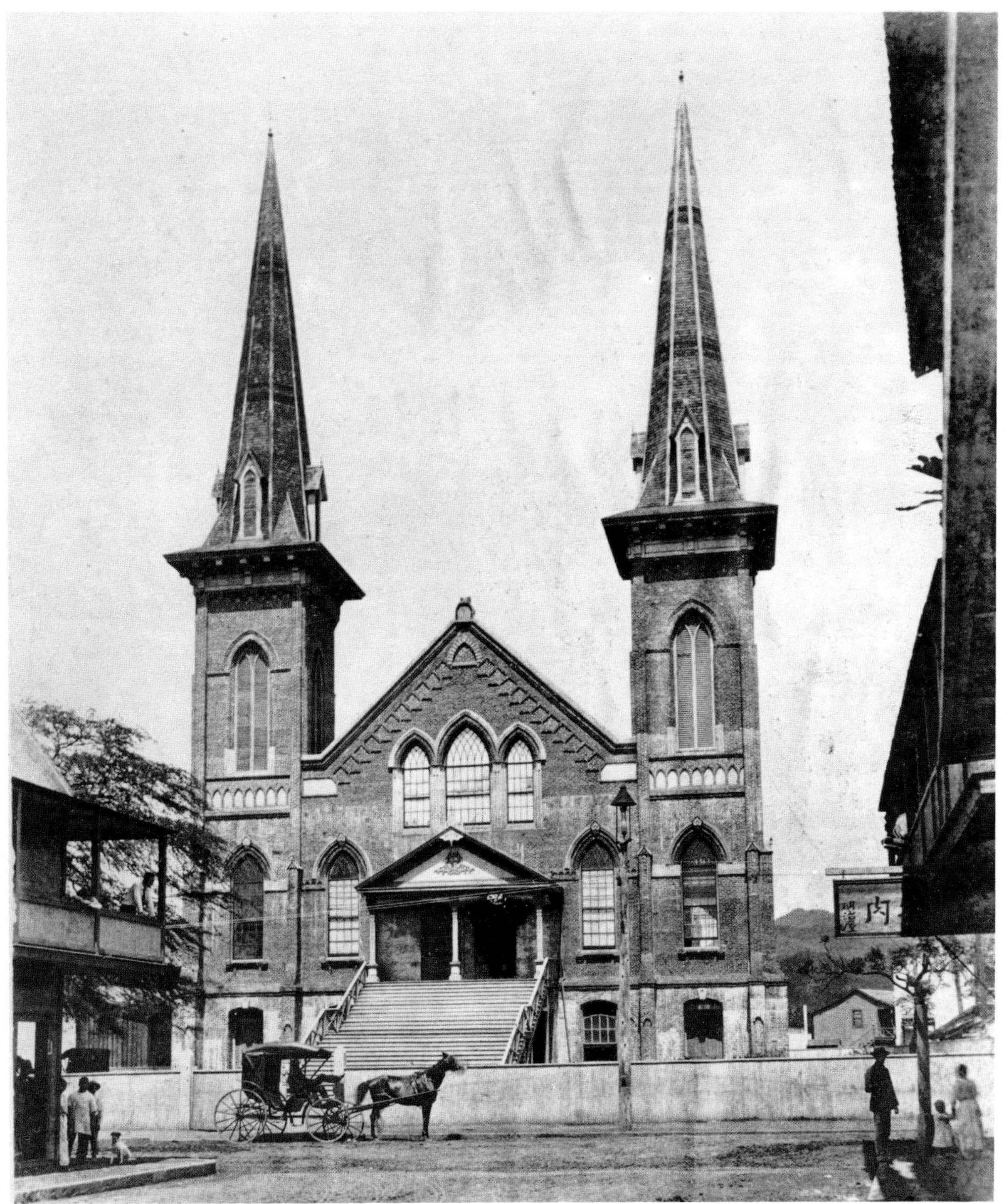

Left: A rooming house in the Chinatown area before the quarantine and fire, around November, 1899. F. Davey. Hawaii State Archives.

Right: Kaumakapili Church on the mauka side of Beretania Street, photographed from Smith Street in 1899, before it was destroyed in the great Chinatown fire of January 20, 1900. Photo by F. Davey from the Hawaii State Archives.

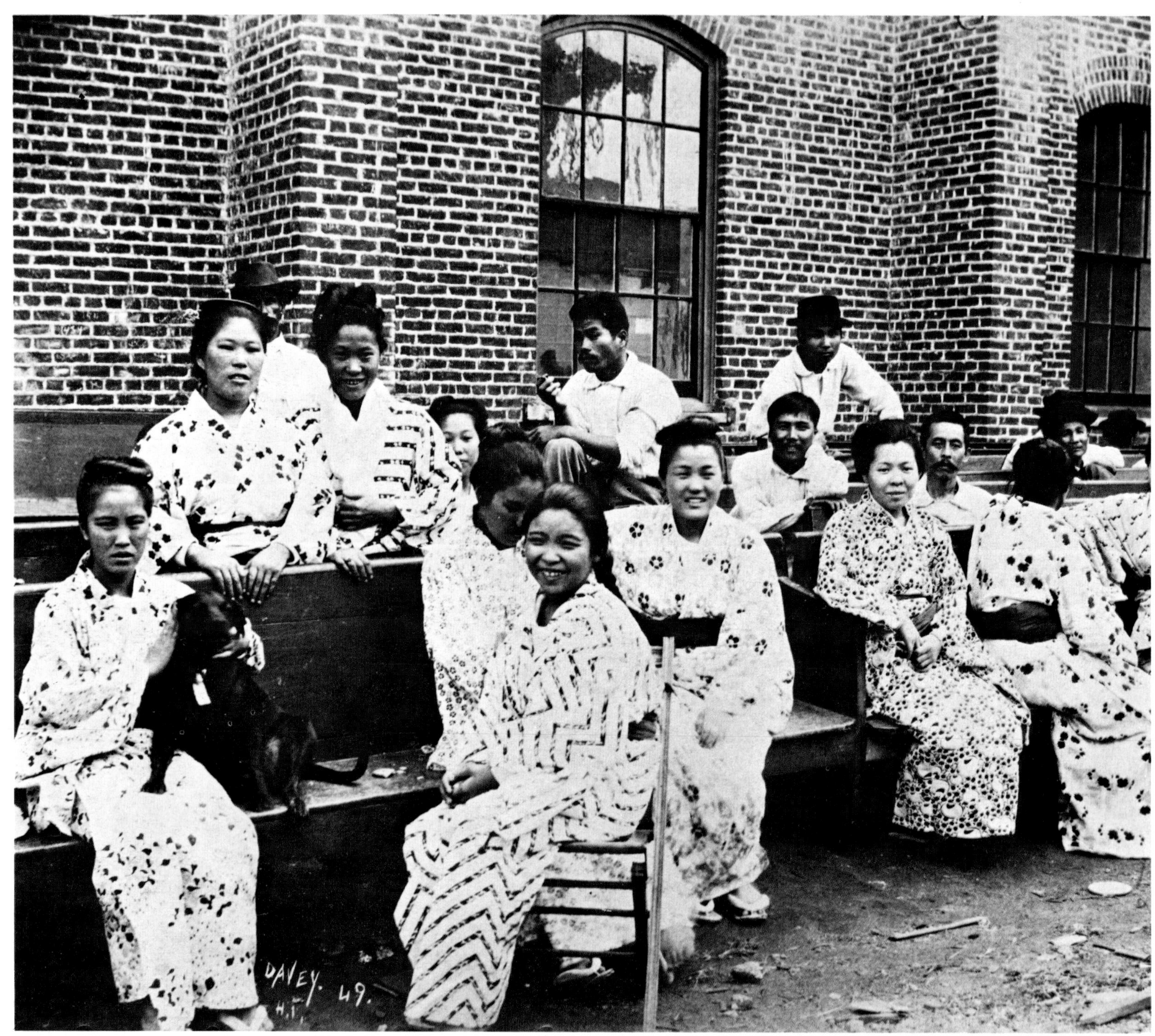
DAVEY. 49.
H.T.

Left: Japanese women gathered outside Kaumakapili Church during early days of the quarantine, possibly while disinfecting operations were carried out. F. Davey, 1900. Hawaii State Archives.

Below: National guardsmen marching into quarantined area, which was under martial law during the bubonic plague epidemic of 1899-1900. F. Davey. Hawaii State Archives.

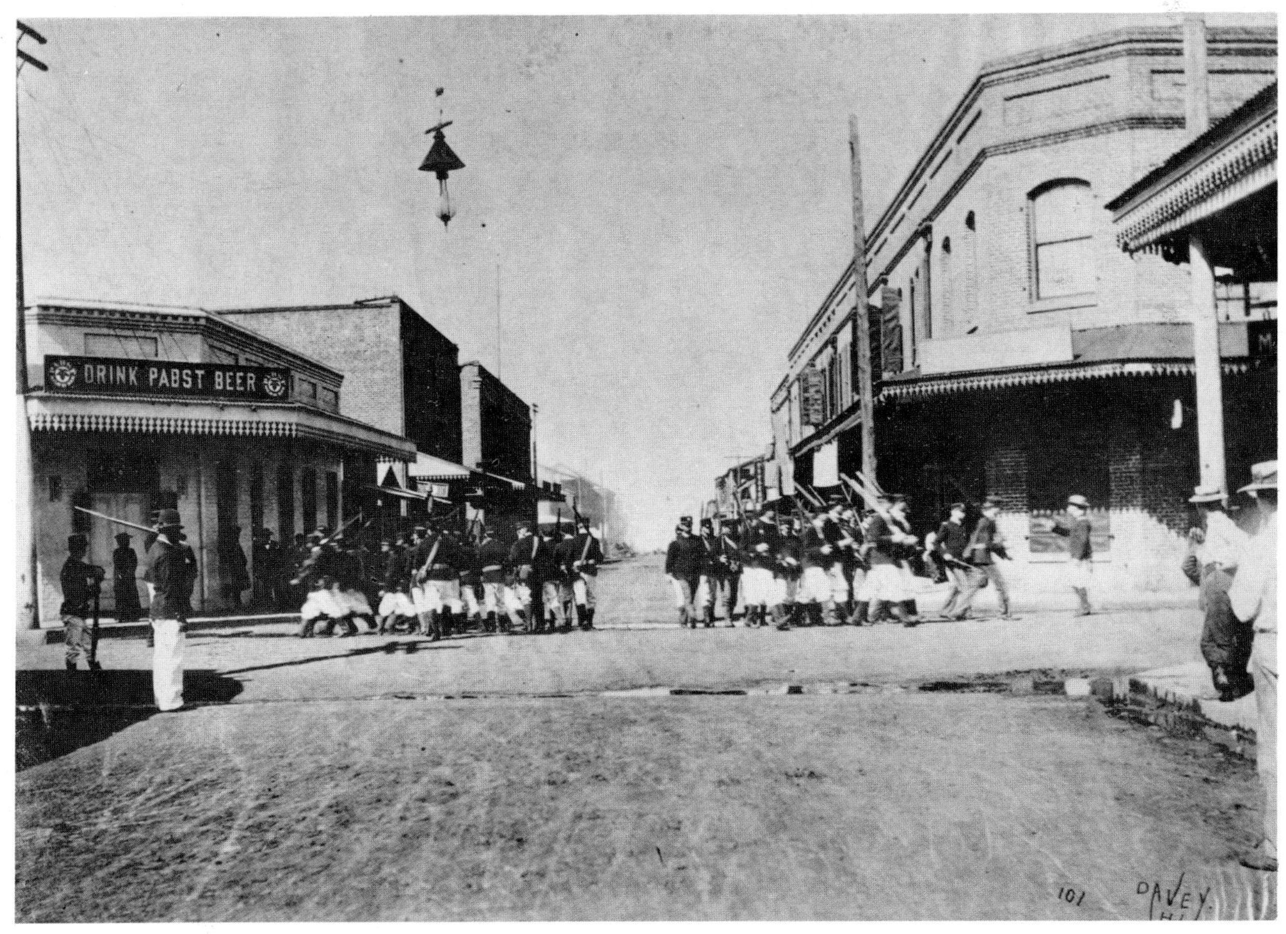

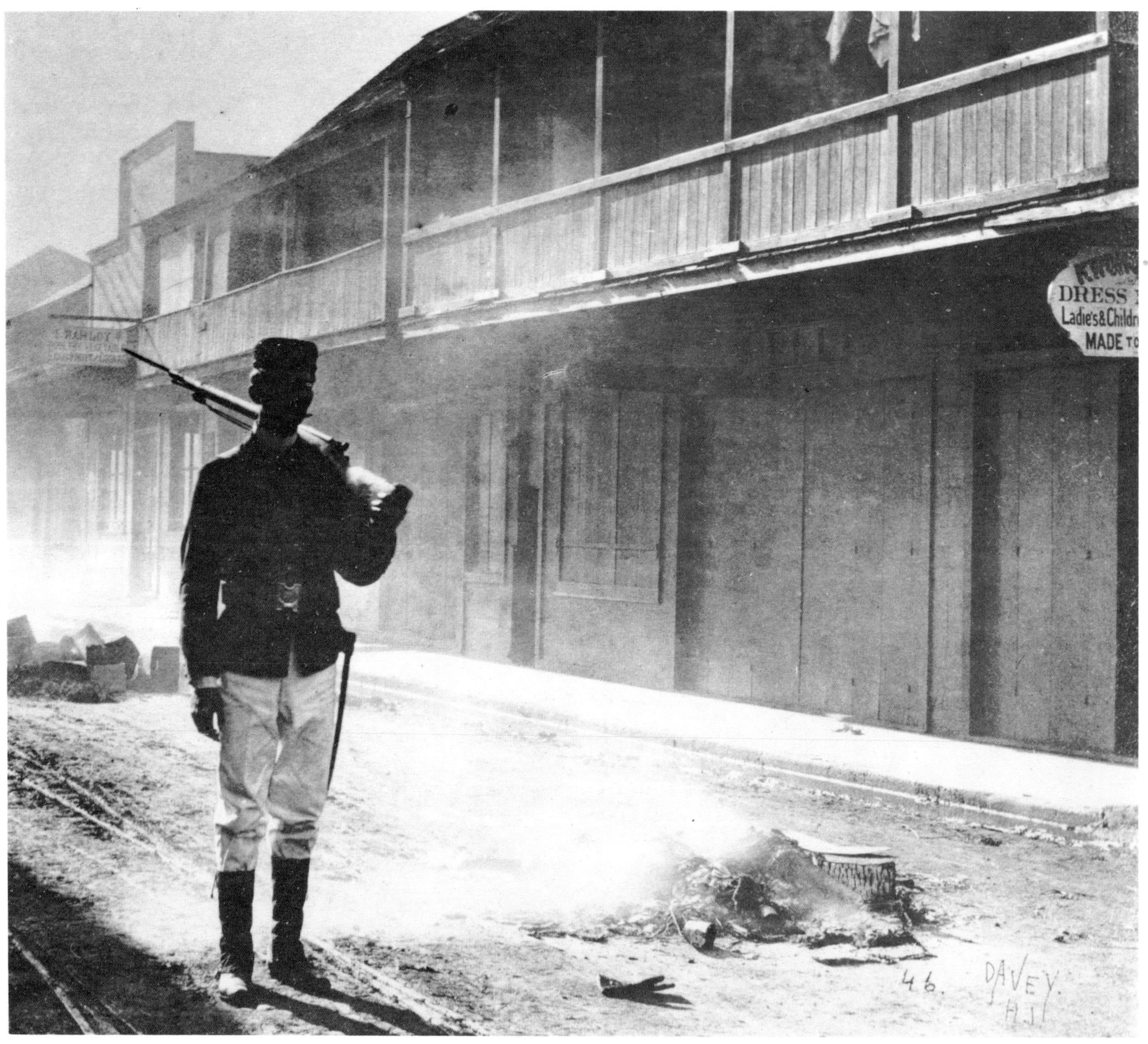
DRESS
Ladie's & Childr
MADE TO
46.
DAVEY
H.I.

Left: Guardsman in quarantine area. Piles of household goods from houses where plague victims had been found were burned in the streets. Chinatown, Honolulu, January 1900. F. Davey. Hawaii State Archives.

Below: Controlled fires were set in Chinatown in January, 1900 to demolish blocks in which plague victims had been found. F. Davey. Hawaii State Archives.

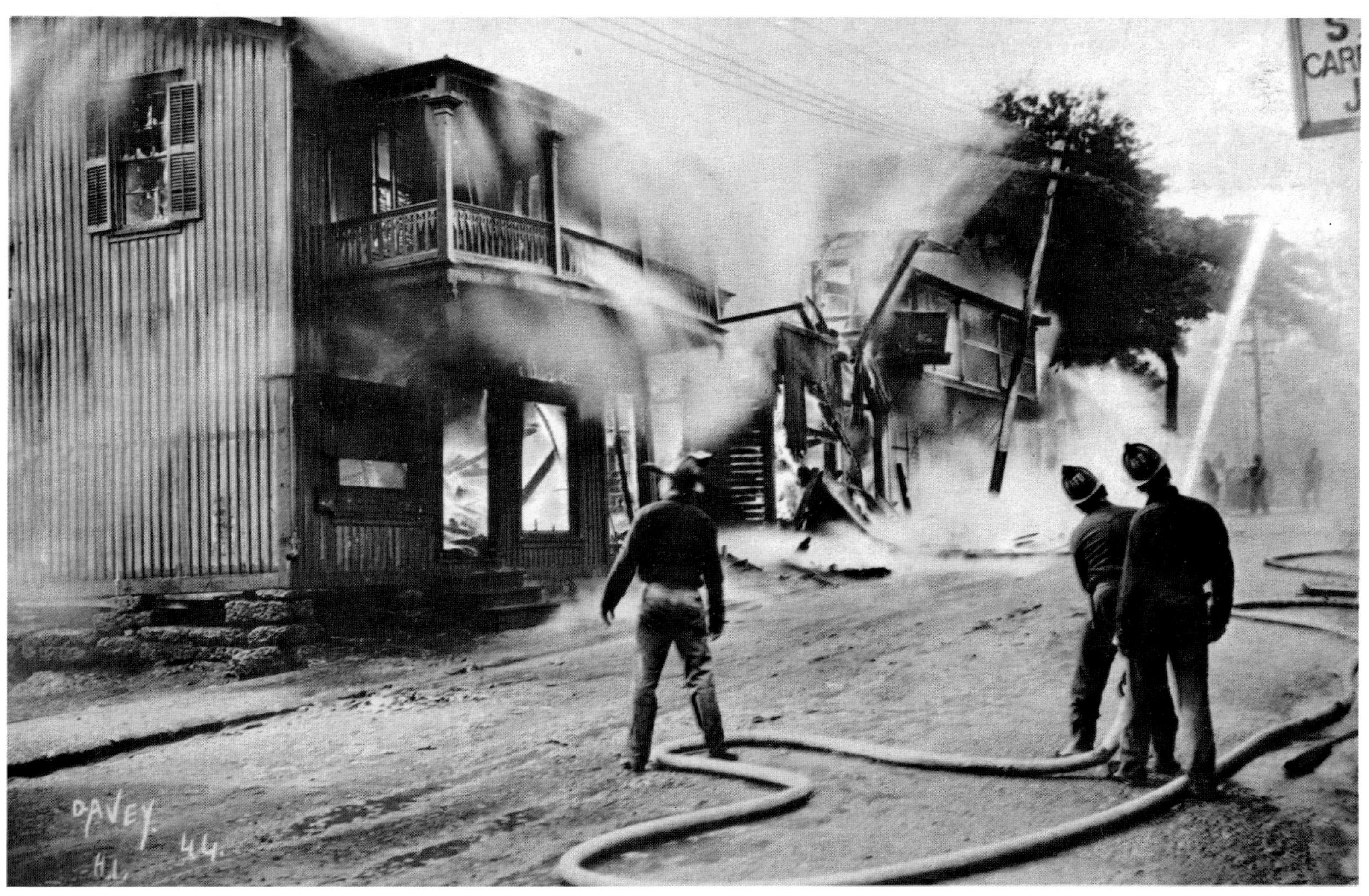

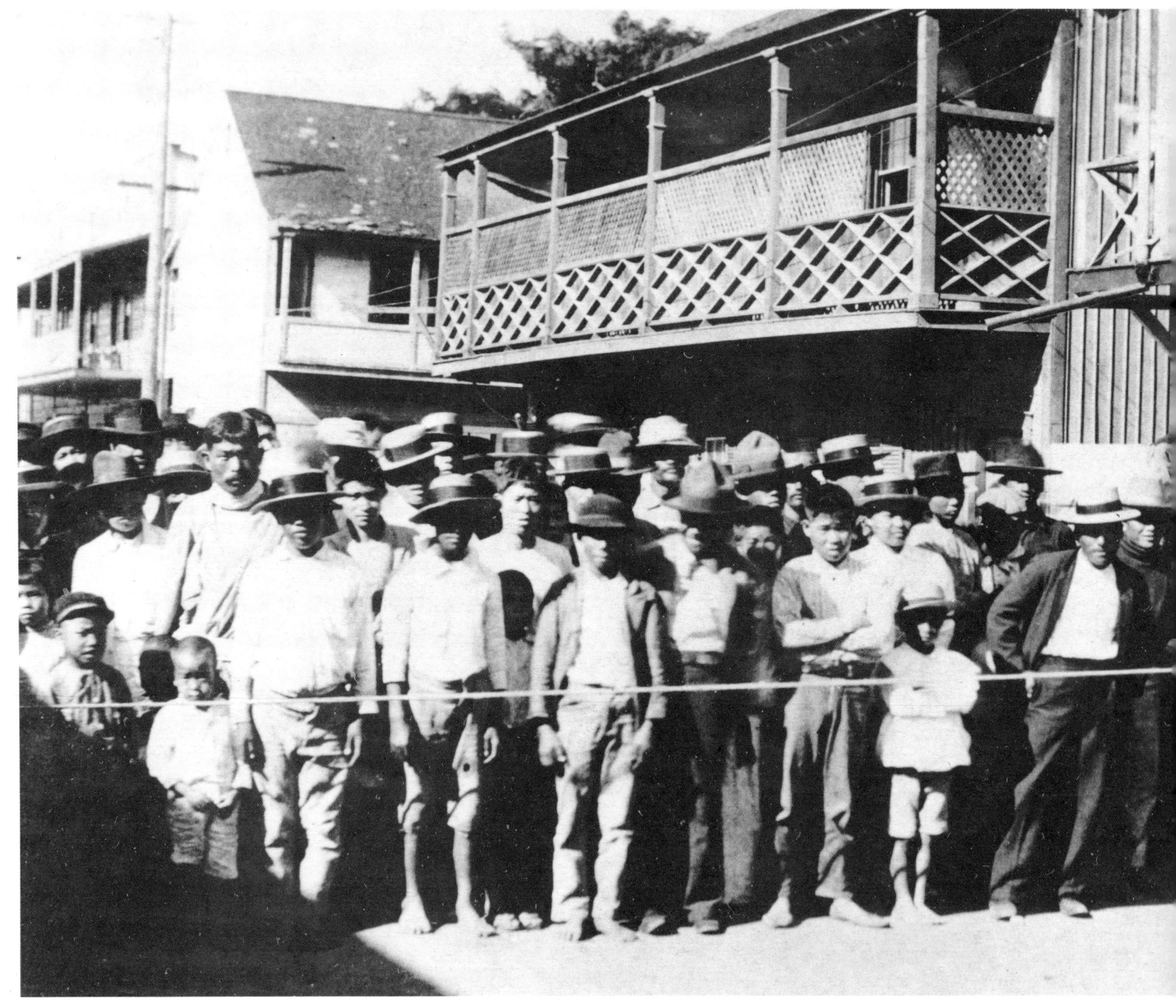

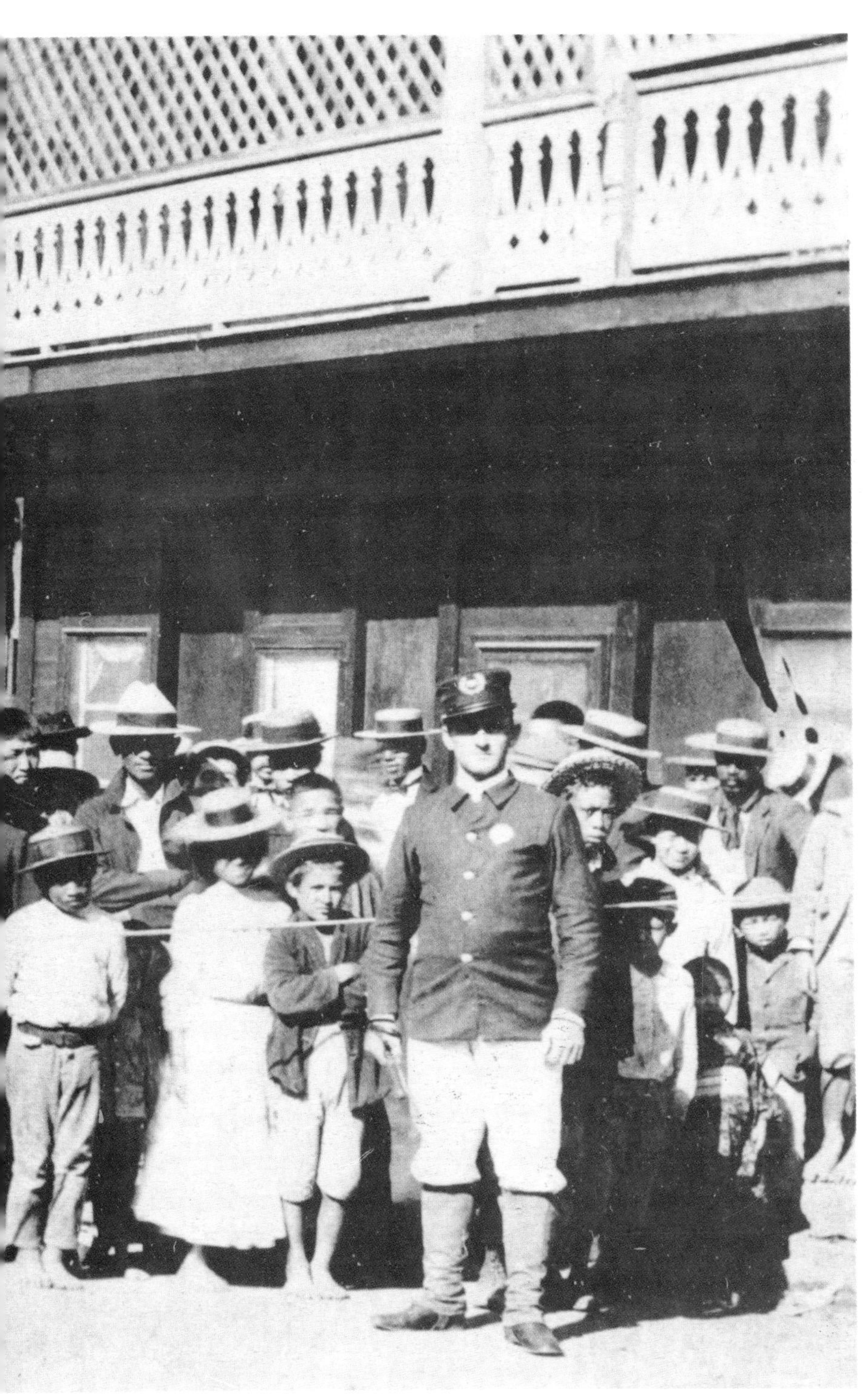

A guardsman at the entrance to the quarantined area. Residents within the area were prohibited from leaving for any reason during the quarantine. January, 1900. F. Davey. Hawaii State Archives.

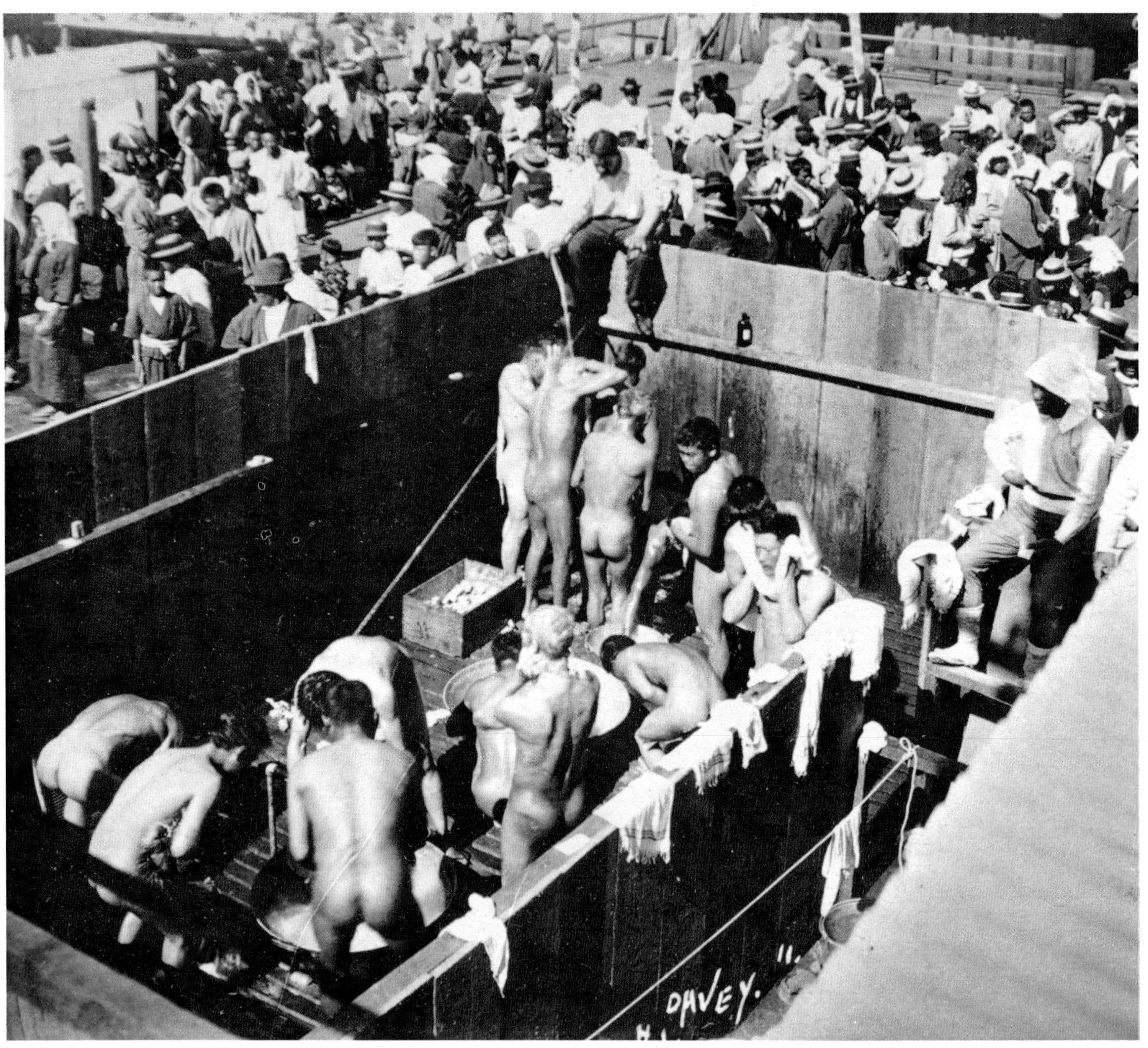
DAVEY.

Left: A sanitary station at one of the detention camps. Volunteers from among Chinatown residents were organized into crews to clean and disinfect buildings in the quarantine area. Residents were housed in several detention camps set up in Kakaako, Kalihi, and near Kawaiahao Church. F. Davey. Hawaii State Archives.

Below: Children participating in a sumo tournament organized at one of the detention camps in 1900. F. Davey. Hawaii State Archives.

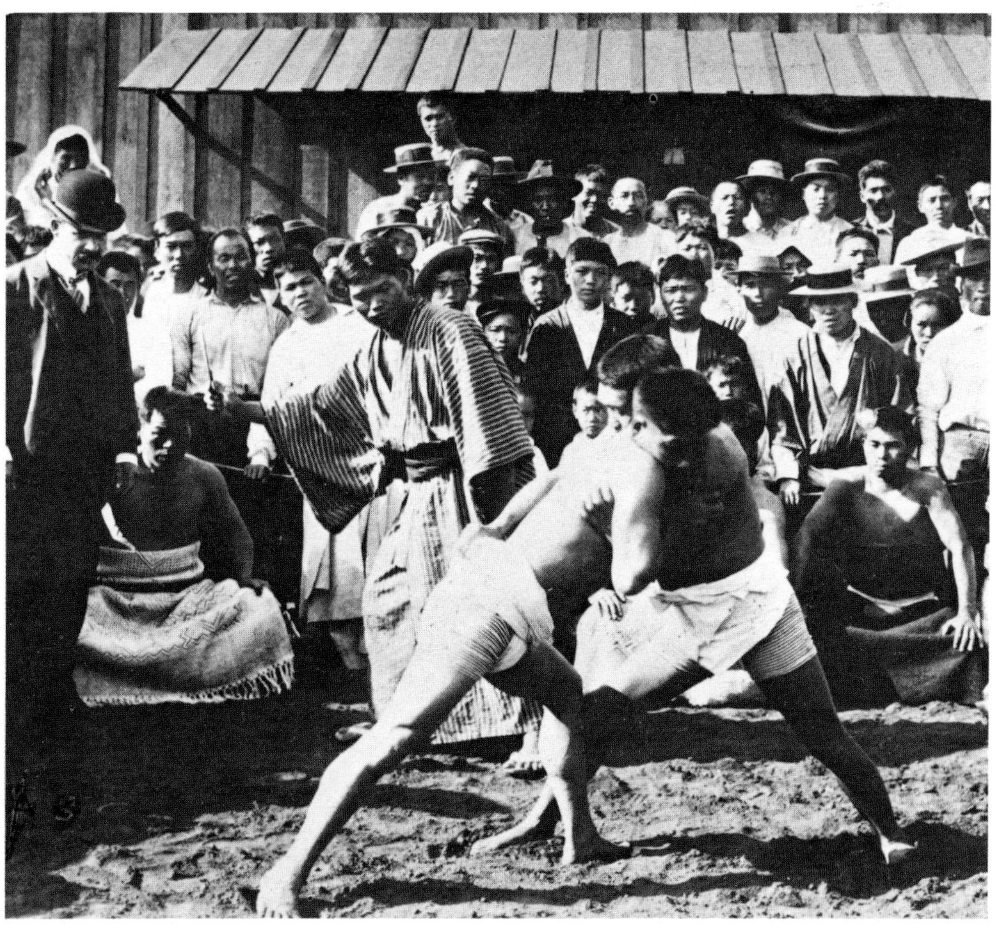

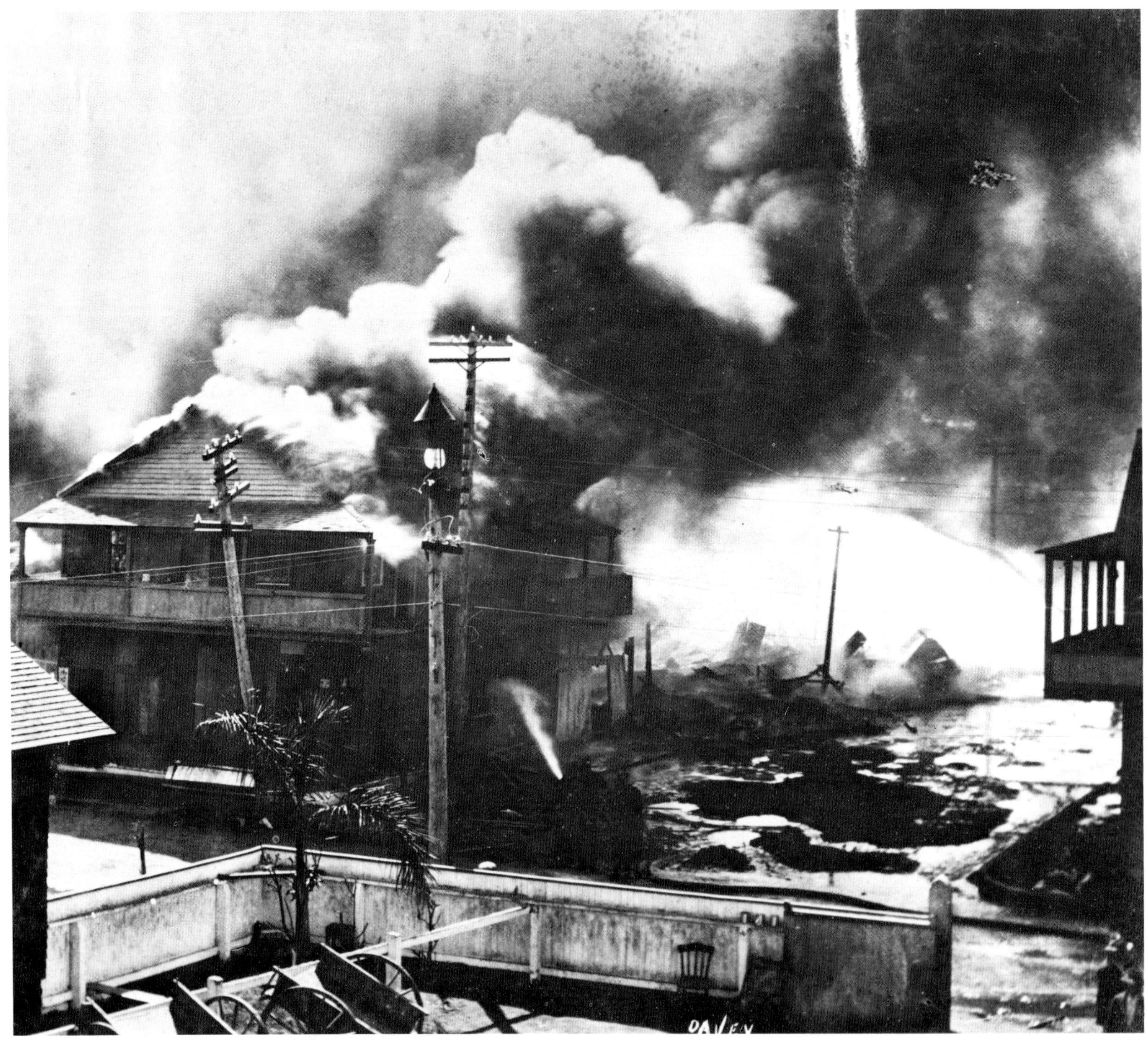

Left: On January 20, 1900, a large area at the Diamond Head side of the Kaumakapili Church was scheduled for controlled burning. Winds from the direction of the Pali whipped the fire out of control and before the day was out, thirty acres of the old Chinatown had been destroyed. F. Davey. Hawaii State Archives.

Below: Descriptions of the January 20th, 1900 Chinatown fire indicate that many buildings such as this one, grew so hot they exploded into flames. F. Davey. Hawaii State Archives.

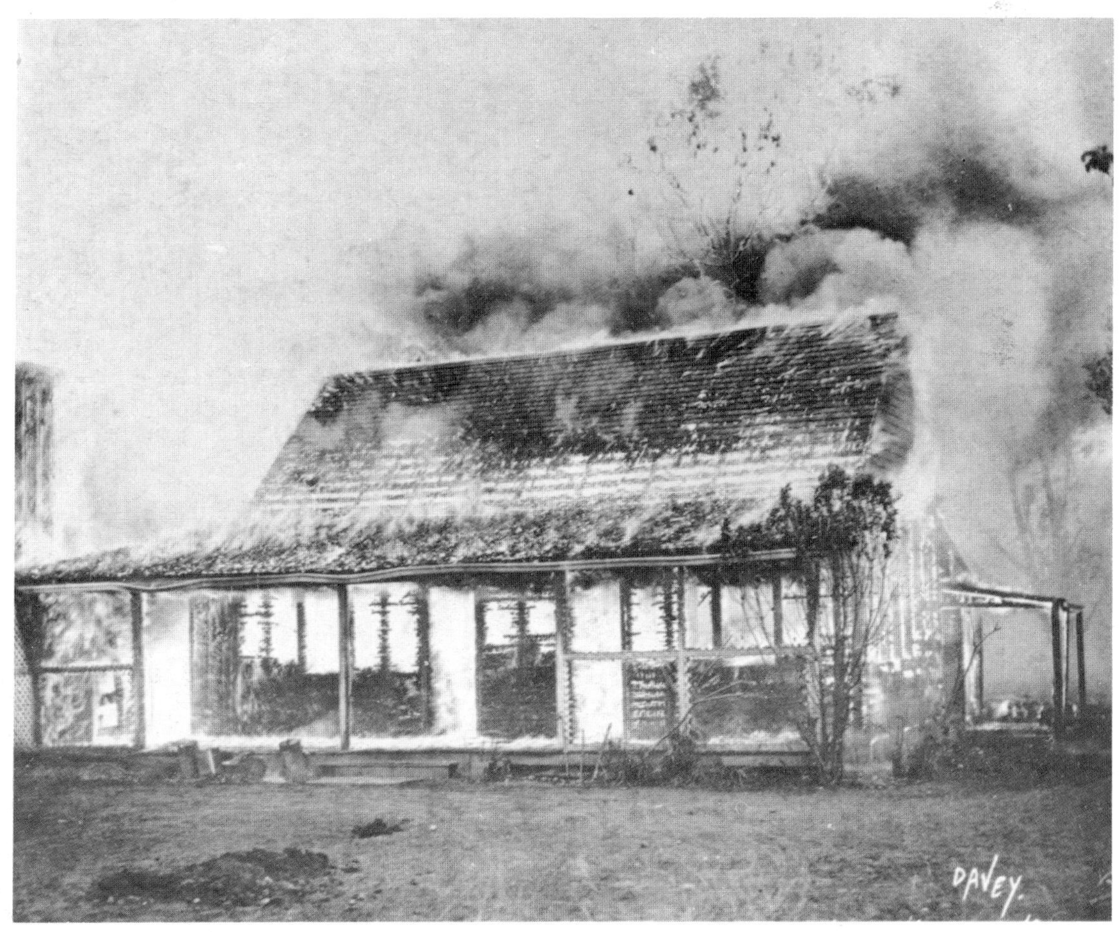

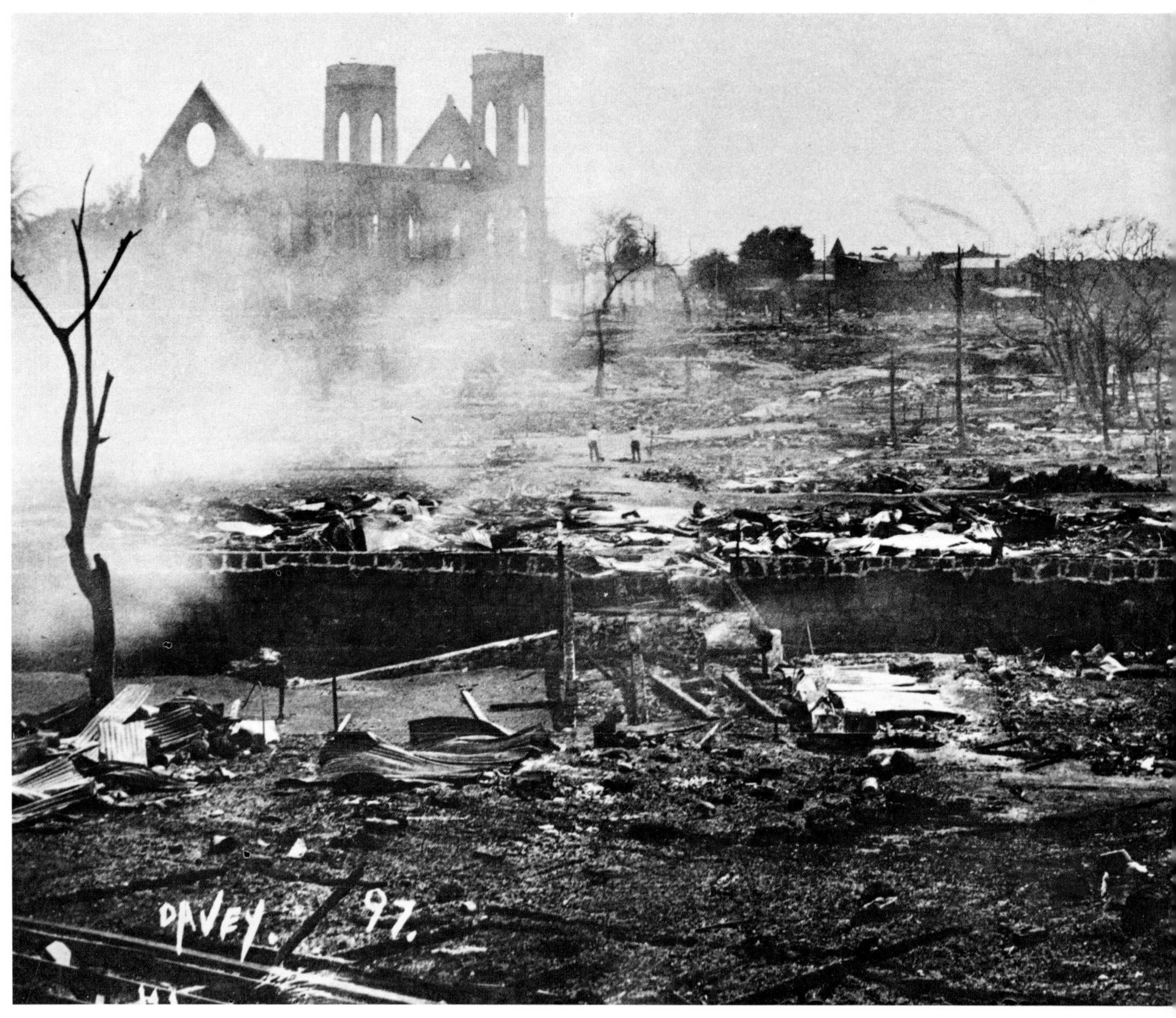
DAVEY. / 97.

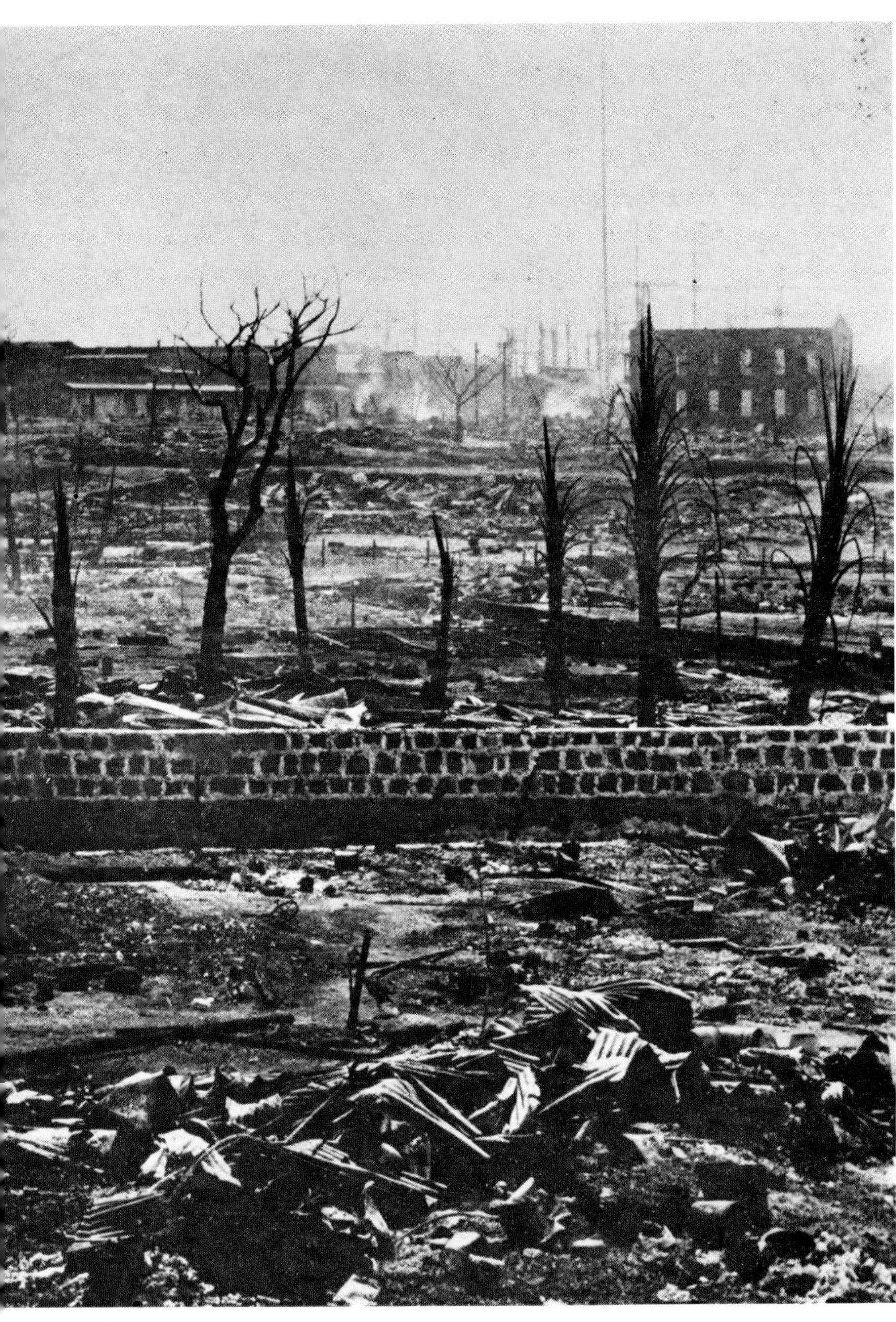

One of the first buildings burned when the fire went out of control was Kaumakapili Church. The remaining walls loom up through the smoke in the ruins. F. Davey. Hawaii State Archives.

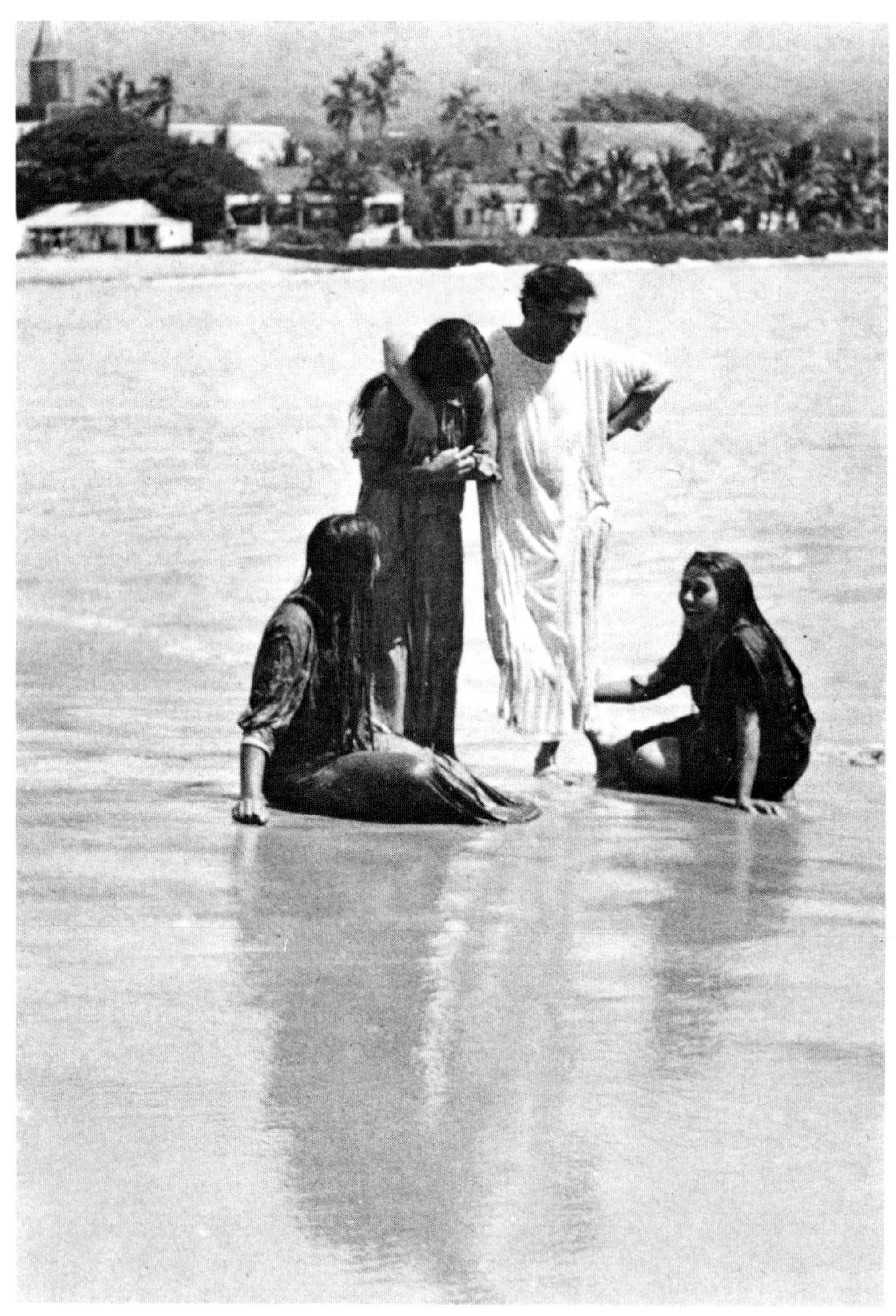

On the beach at Kona about 1908. L.C. Child.

L. C. Child

L.C. Child was born in Montana in 1887. Twenty years later the Hawaiian islands became his permanent home. His first year in Hawaii was spent in Honolulu where he worked for the Theo H. Davies Company. In 1908, he moved to Kailua, Kona, and began a career with Amfac, then called Hackfeld and Company, that was to last until his retirement.

On that first voyage to Kona, Child carried one of the early Kodak postcard cameras which he quickly put to use in shooting scenes of his new home island. His film was then packaged and shipped to Honolulu on the old inter-island steamer, the *Mauna Loa*, for at that time there were no commercial facilities on the Island of Hawaii that could handle film development for the amateur. There is some evidence that the Kodak camera was already quite popular, even in such relatively remote areas as the Big Island. At least one Hitchcock photograph in the Lyman House Museum collection shows a group of young men and women on an outing, posed against a large tree fern. Easily half of the people in the photograph are carrying early Kodak cameras. Yet, few early snapshot collections have come to light in Hawaii. Of the early amateurs, only the work of such photographers as Hitchcock and Furneaux, who worked with far more elaborate equipment and who developed their own plates, seems to have surfaced. The Child collection of snapshots has, by good fortune, been retained in print form in scrapbooks put together by L.C. Child and his wife during the early days of their marriage.

In 1971, while looking through these old views, an 84 year old L.C. Child recalled many memories of old time Kona. Many of the snapshots were of buildings that no longer exist. Child pointed to a four bedroom guest cottage that once stood beside Hulihee Palace. The cottage was the site of poker games when visiting lawyers came to town for circuit court sessions in the early days of the century. Another photo showed the Kaholoa Coffee Mill, and another the King Kalakaua boathouse, both landmarks that have long since vanished. And, with a great deal of pride, Child turned to a snapshot of the old family Buick, the car that took him to many of the places his Kodak camera recorded. It was, Child recalled, one of only two cars in Kona during the years before World War I.

Child's interest in his photographic hobby waned after his marriage in 1913. But, unlike far too many amateurs, he did not discard his work during any later effort at tidiness. It remains today a charming record of early Kona and of several other Big Island sites. And it has a value that goes beyond its use as a vehicle for stirring personal memories. Child's use of the Kodak postcard camera serves as a demonstration of the fact that good photography need not depend on elaborate professional equipment. The views that Child was able to capture with his simple camera and with commercial developing and printing are striking in tone and detail. And L.C. Child, while he may have been an amateur and while his interest in photography was short lived, did demonstrate a remarkable eye for composition that has helped give his photographs lasting charm.

The old family Buick, about 1908. It was one of two automobiles in the Kona District in the early years of the 20th century. L.C. Child.

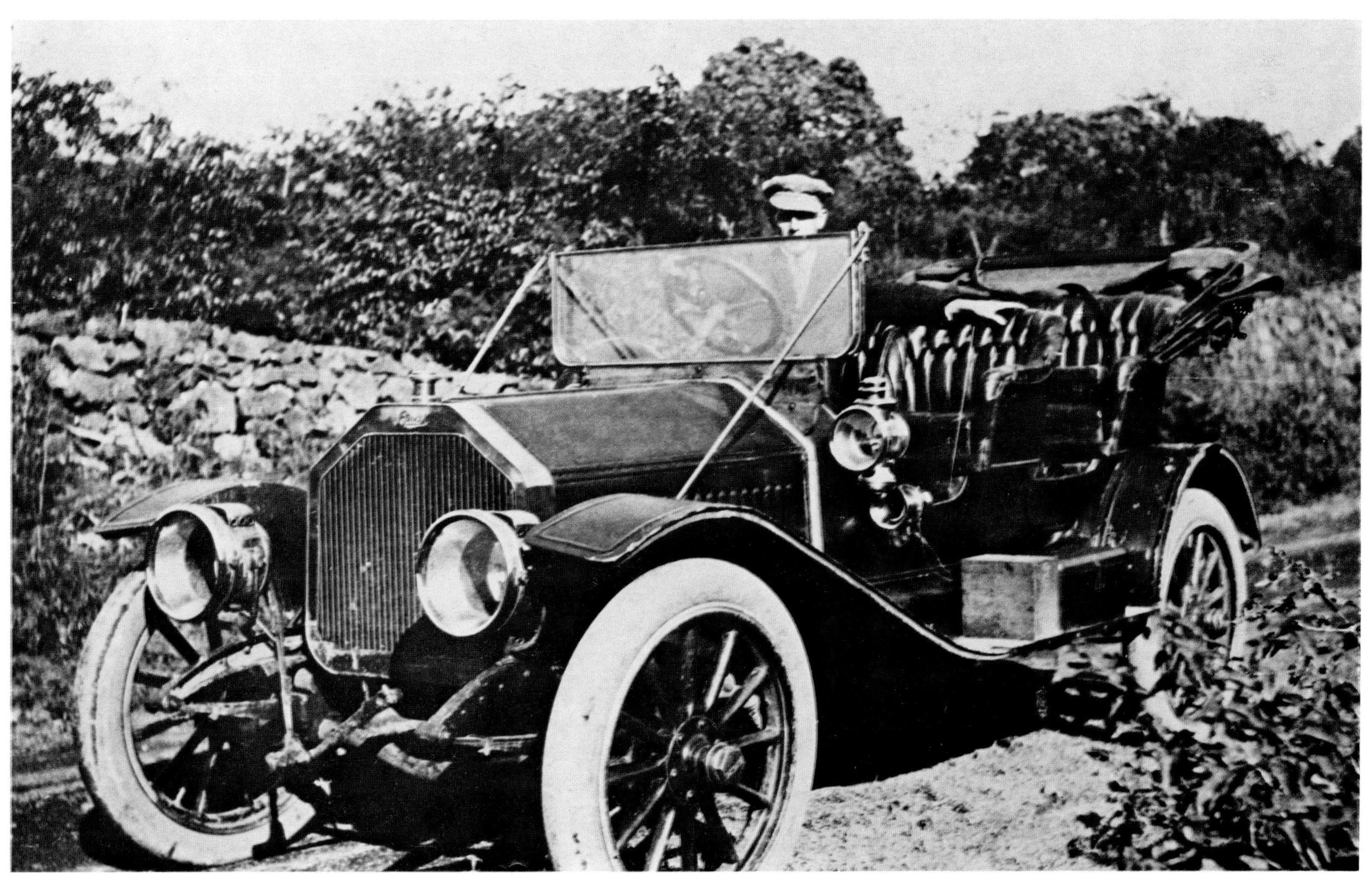

Right: Looking south along the Kailua waterfront from the wharf area in about 1908. L.C. Child.

Below: The Kalakaua boathouse in about 1908. Site is presently occupied by the King Kamehameha Hotel. L.C. Child.

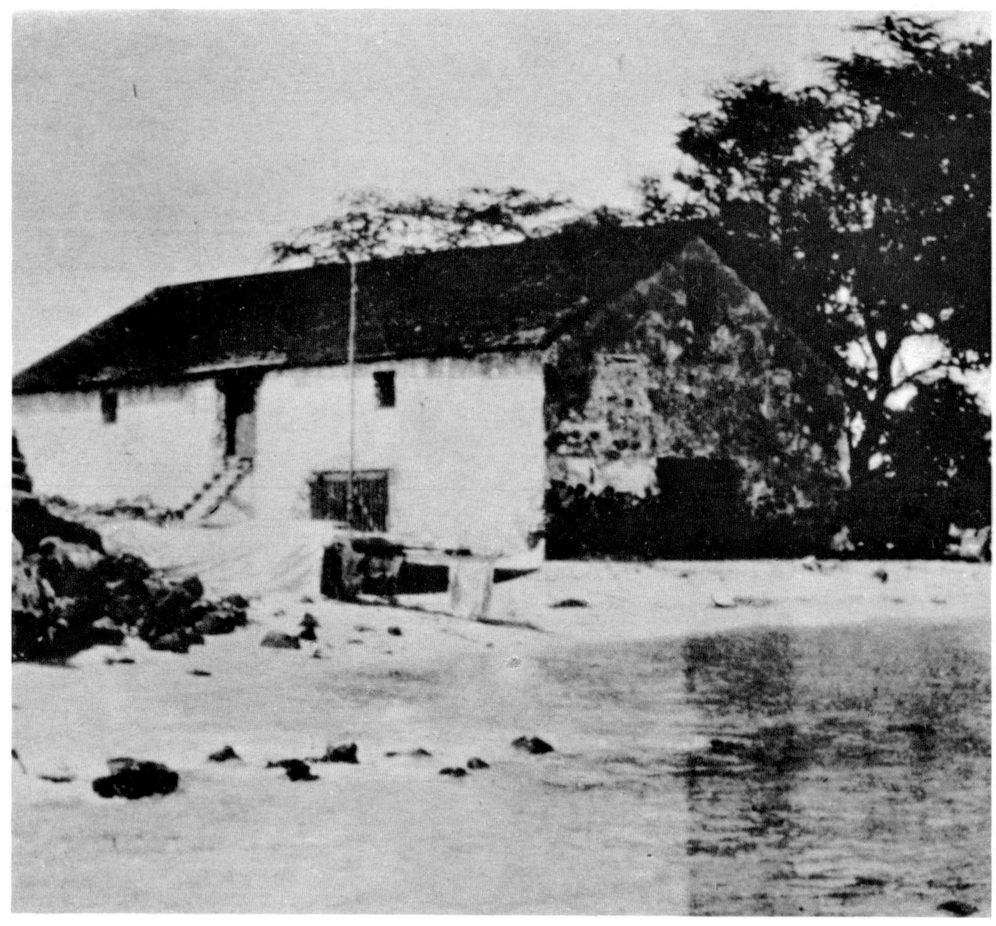

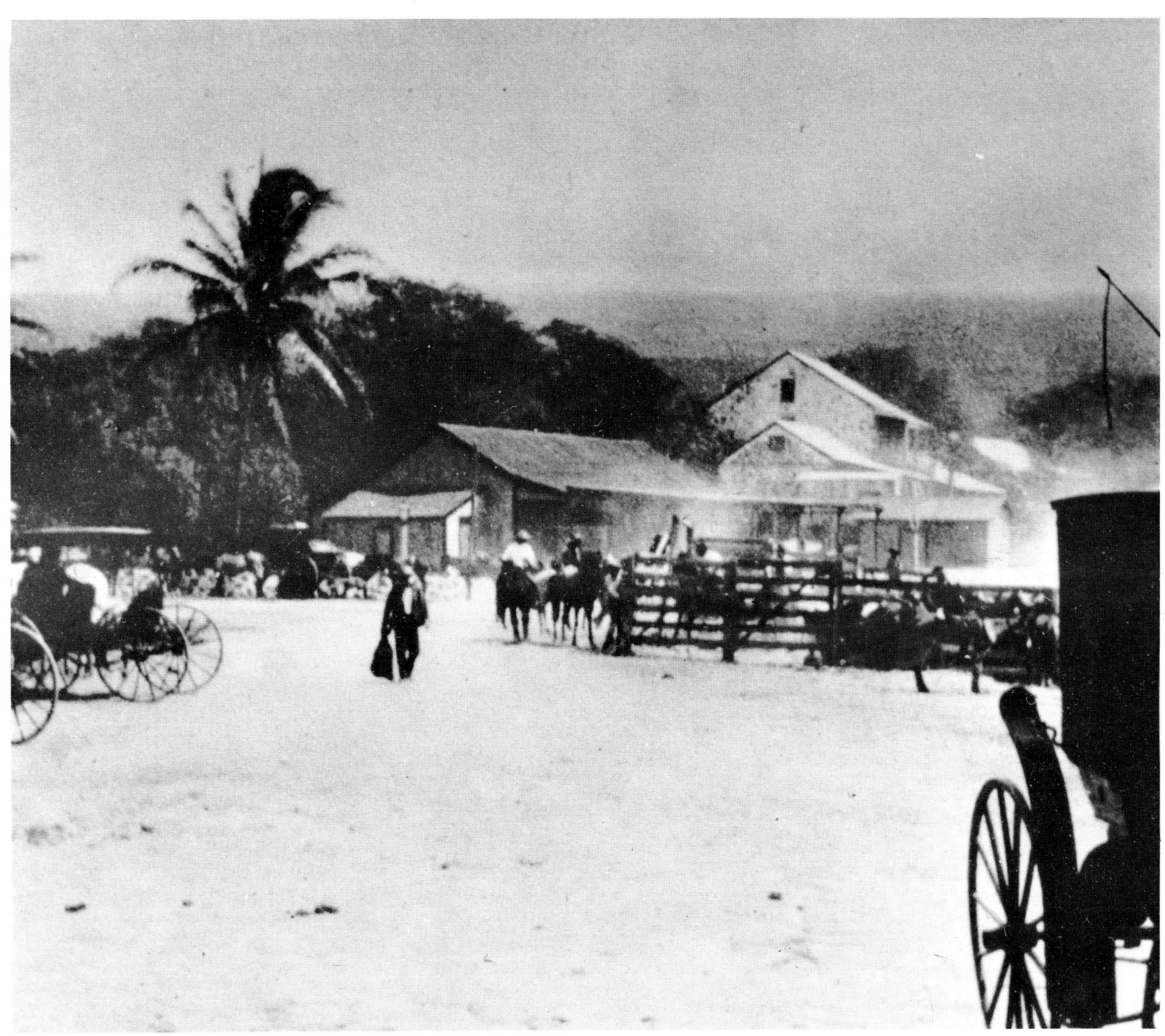

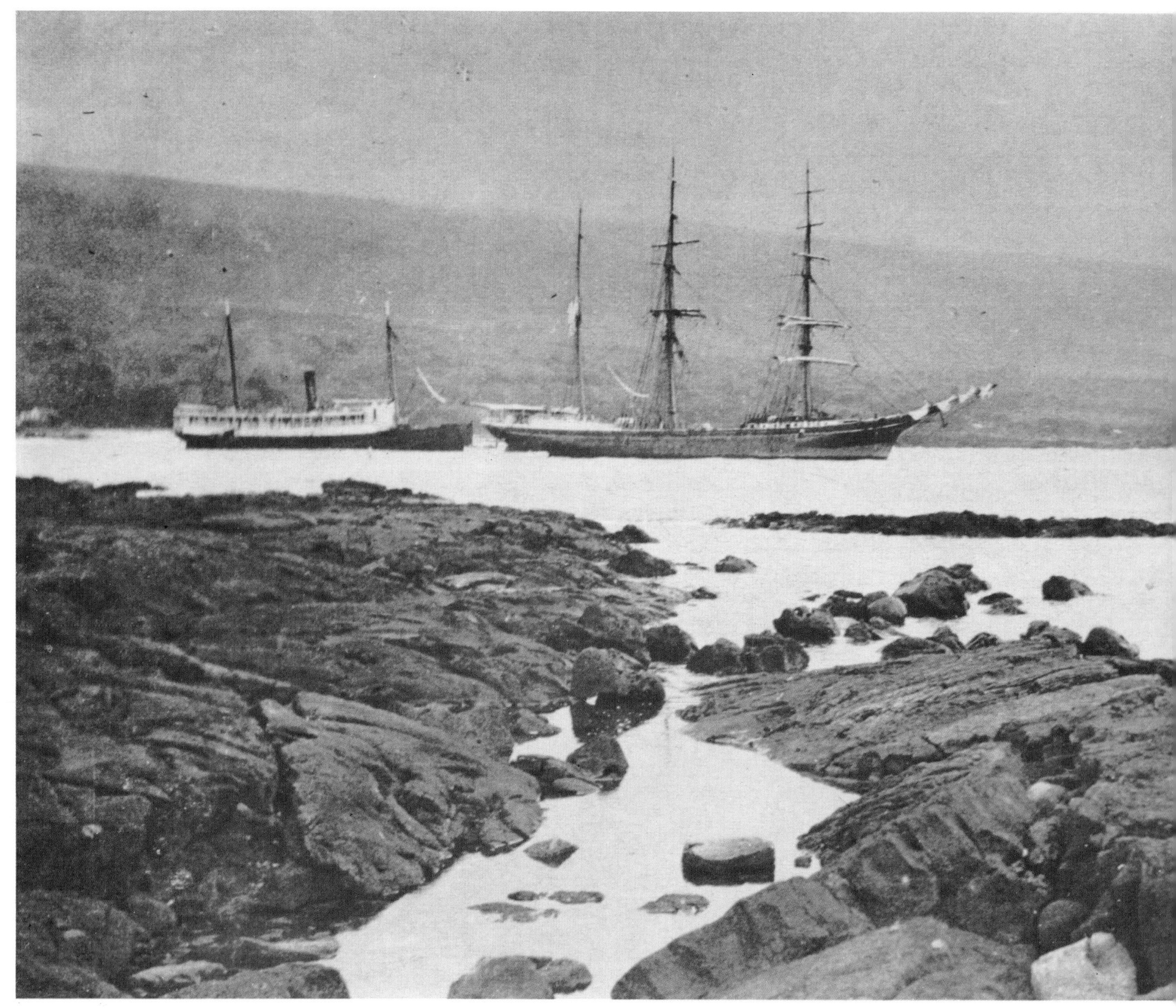

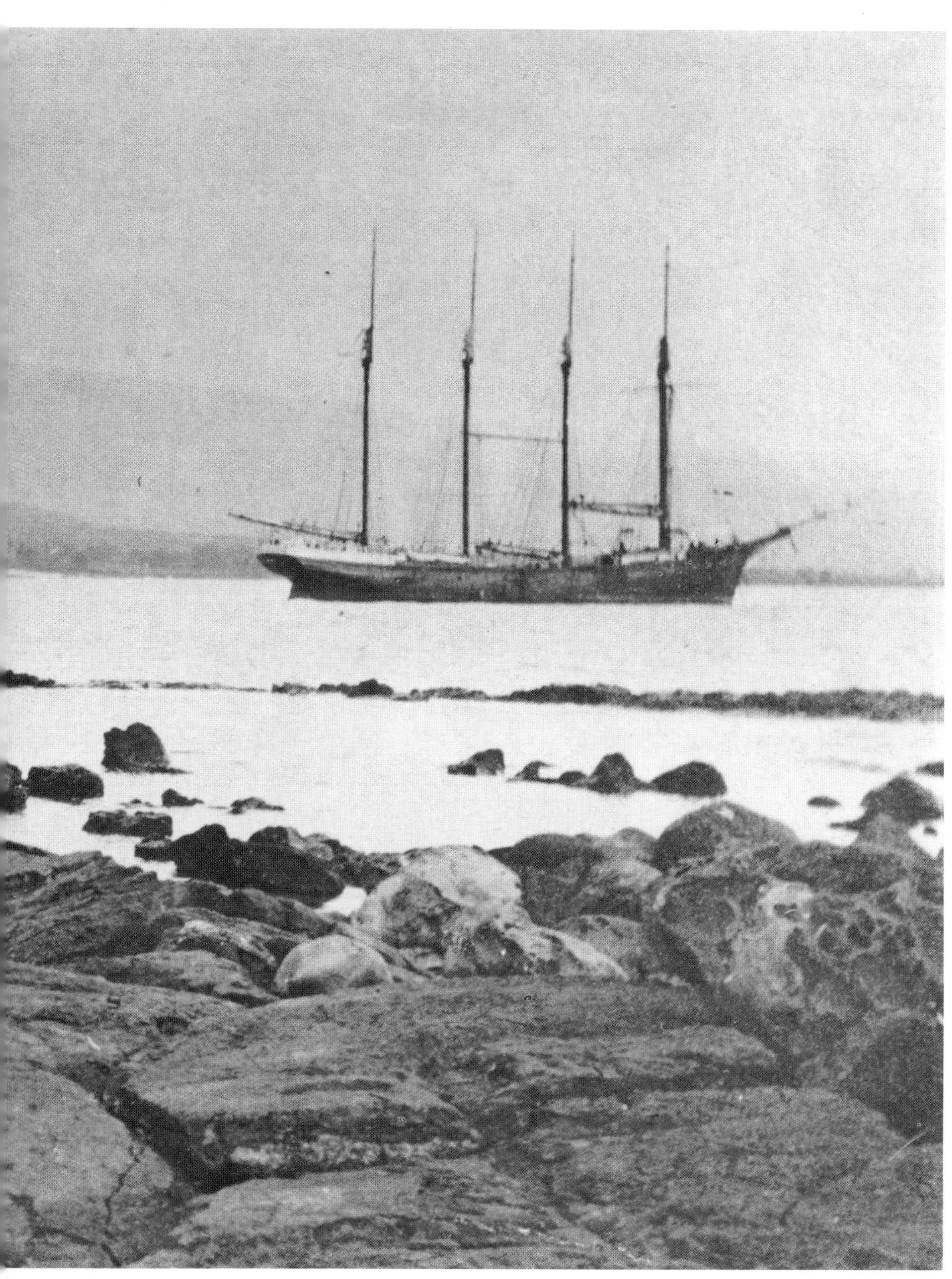

Three ships at Kailua in 1908. The steamer is the inter-island passenger ship, the Mauna Loa. L.C. Child.

Right: The Kahaloa Coffee Company, about 1908. The company was later bought out by the Captain Cook Coffee Company, which has gone out of business. L.C. Child.

Below: Coffee drying platform at the Kahaloa Coffee Company, about 1908. L.C. Child.

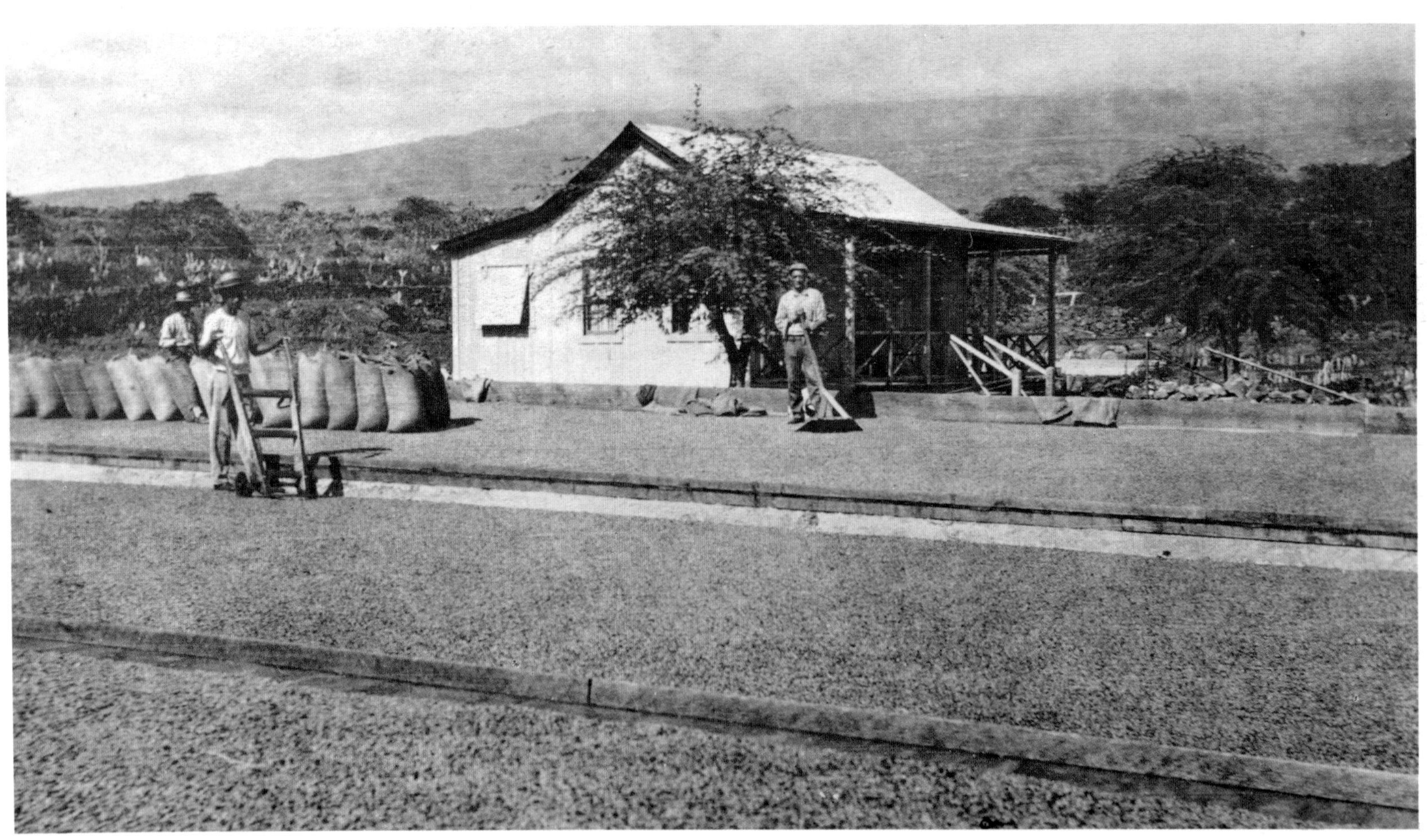

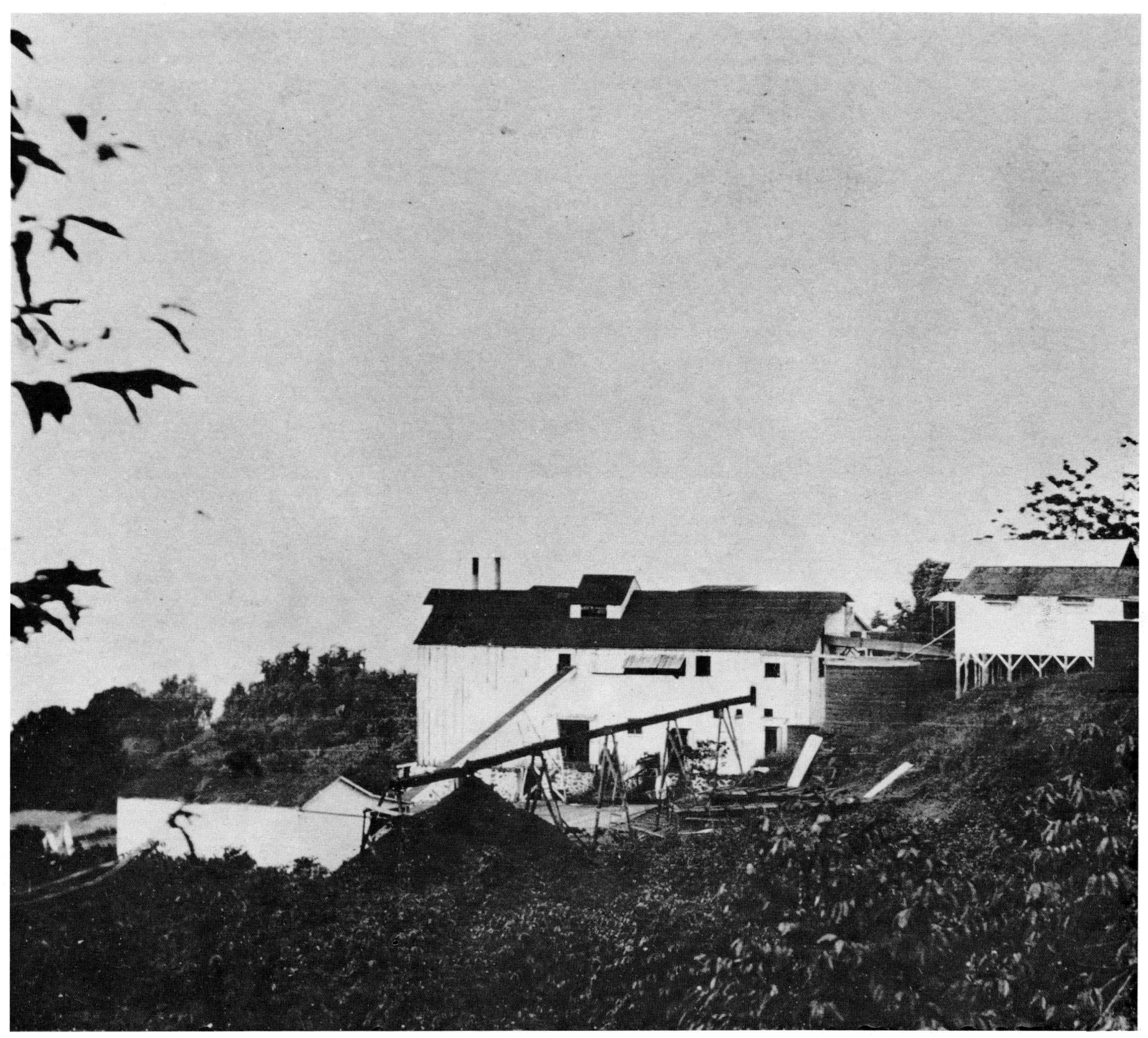

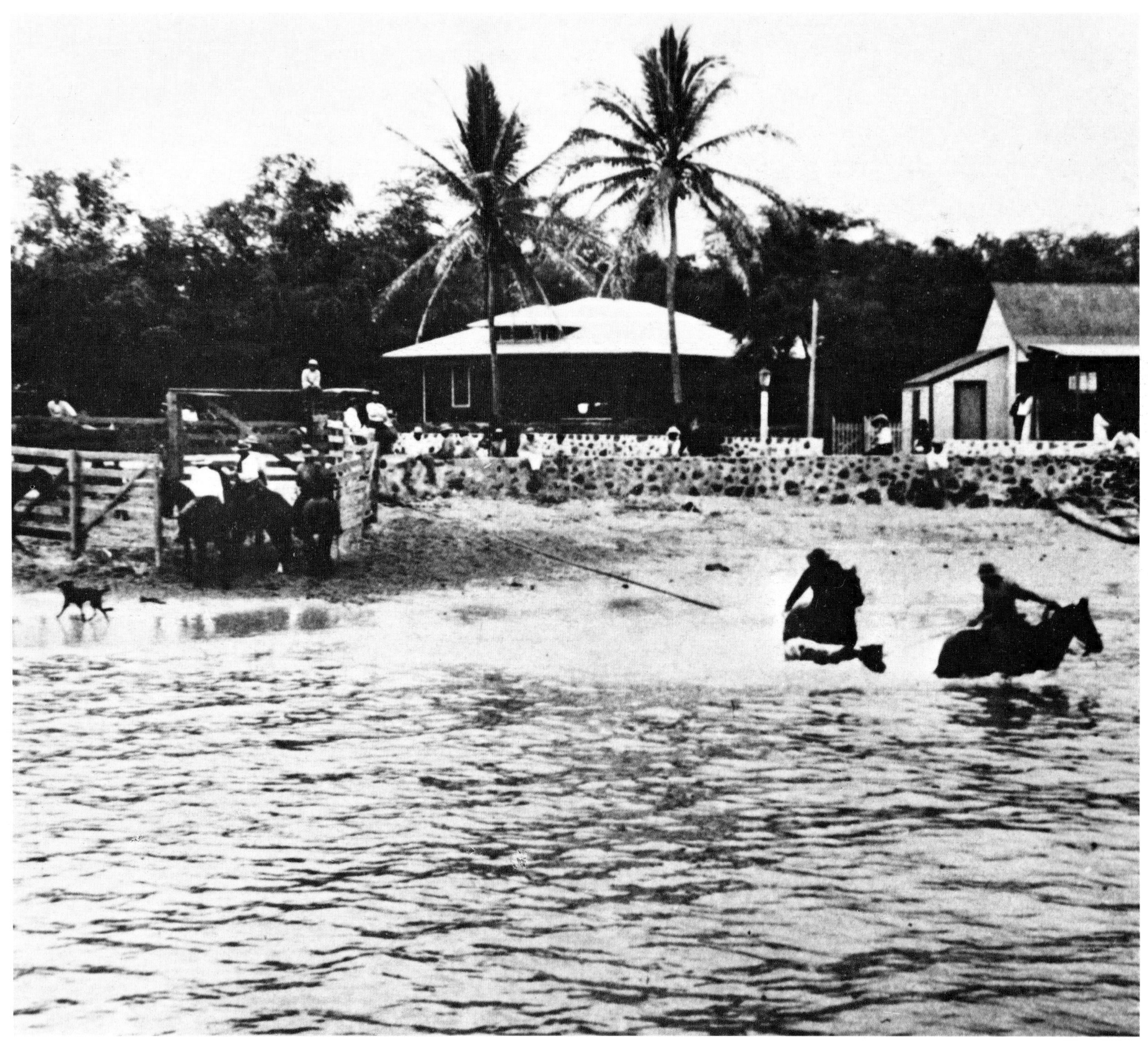

Left: Loading cattle at Kailua around 1900. Cattle had to be roped and forced to swim through the shallow water to boats waiting where there was sufficient draft. L.C. Child.

Below: People awaiting ceremonies to dedicate a new archway at Mokuaikaua Church in Kailua, Kona around 1908. L.C. Child.

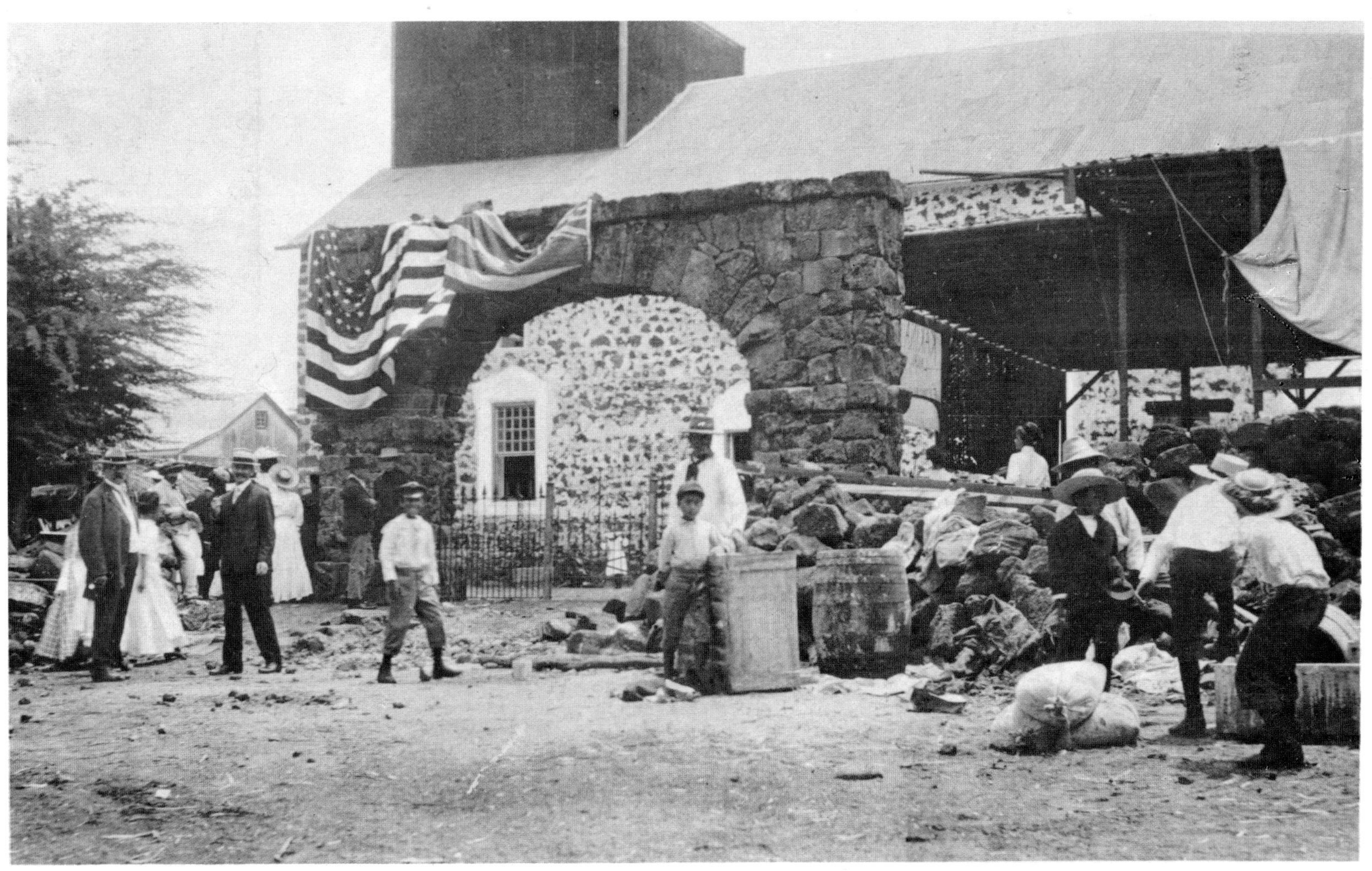

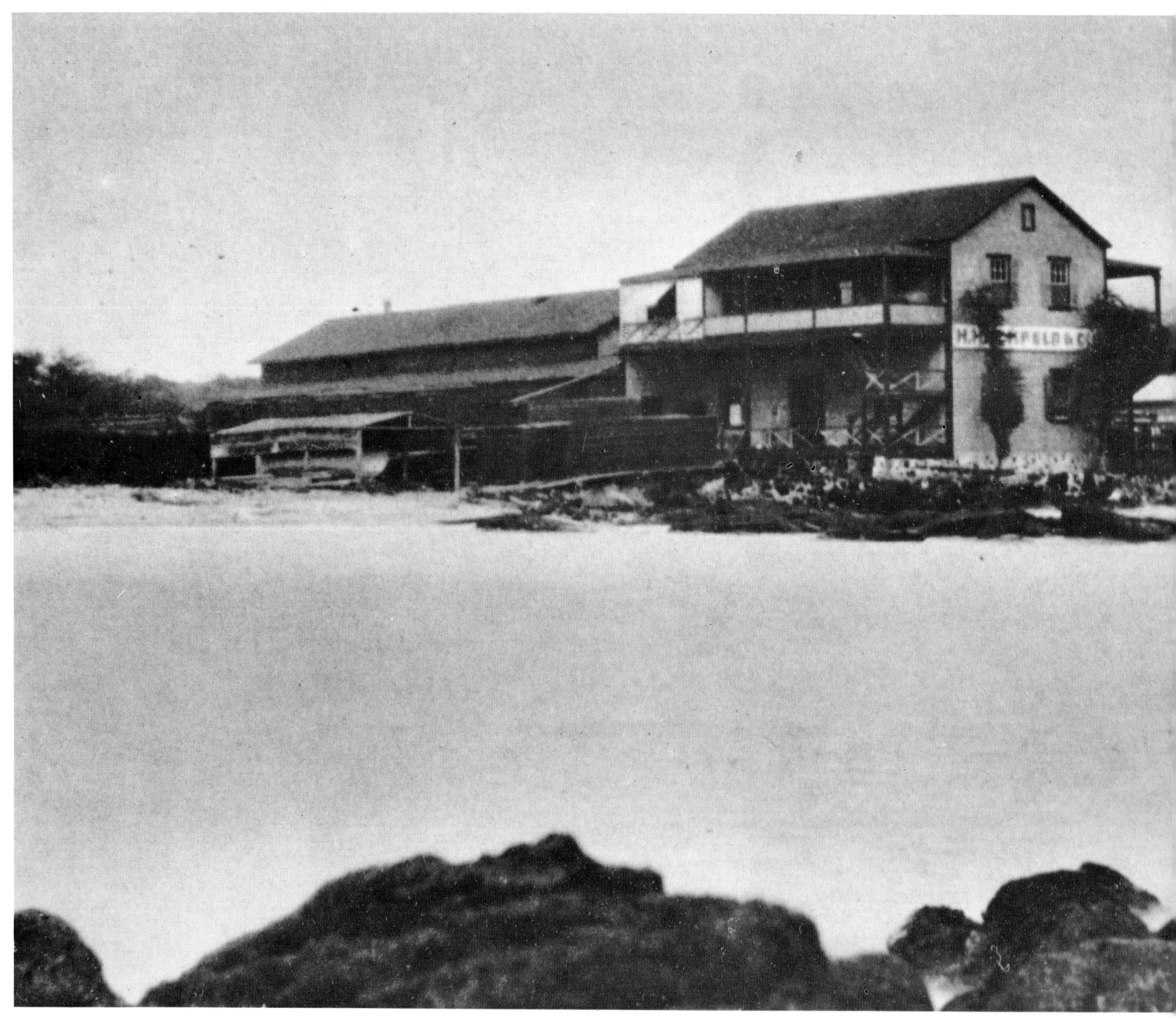

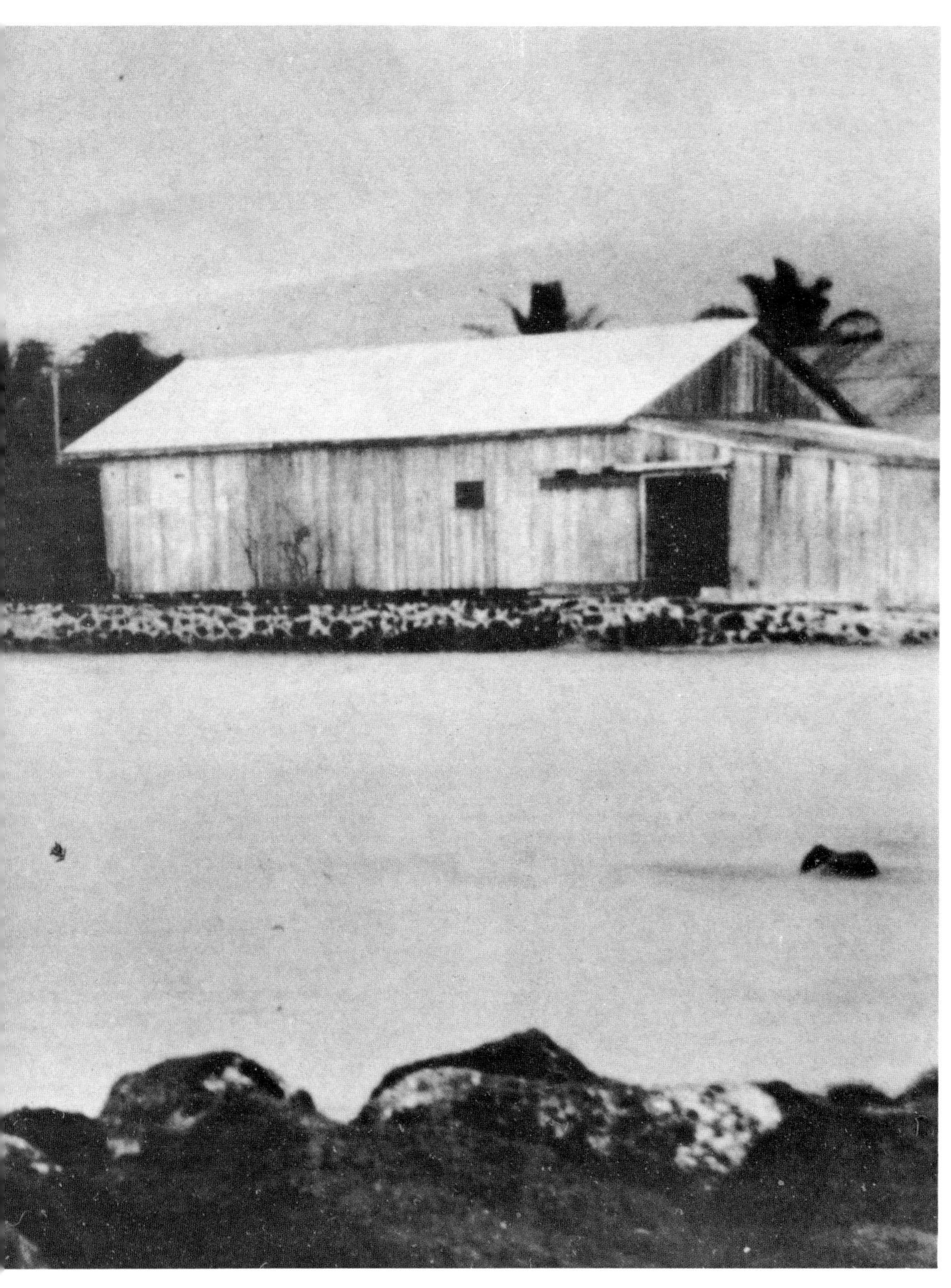

The old Hackfeld and Company building in Kailua, Kona, about 1908. L.C. Child.

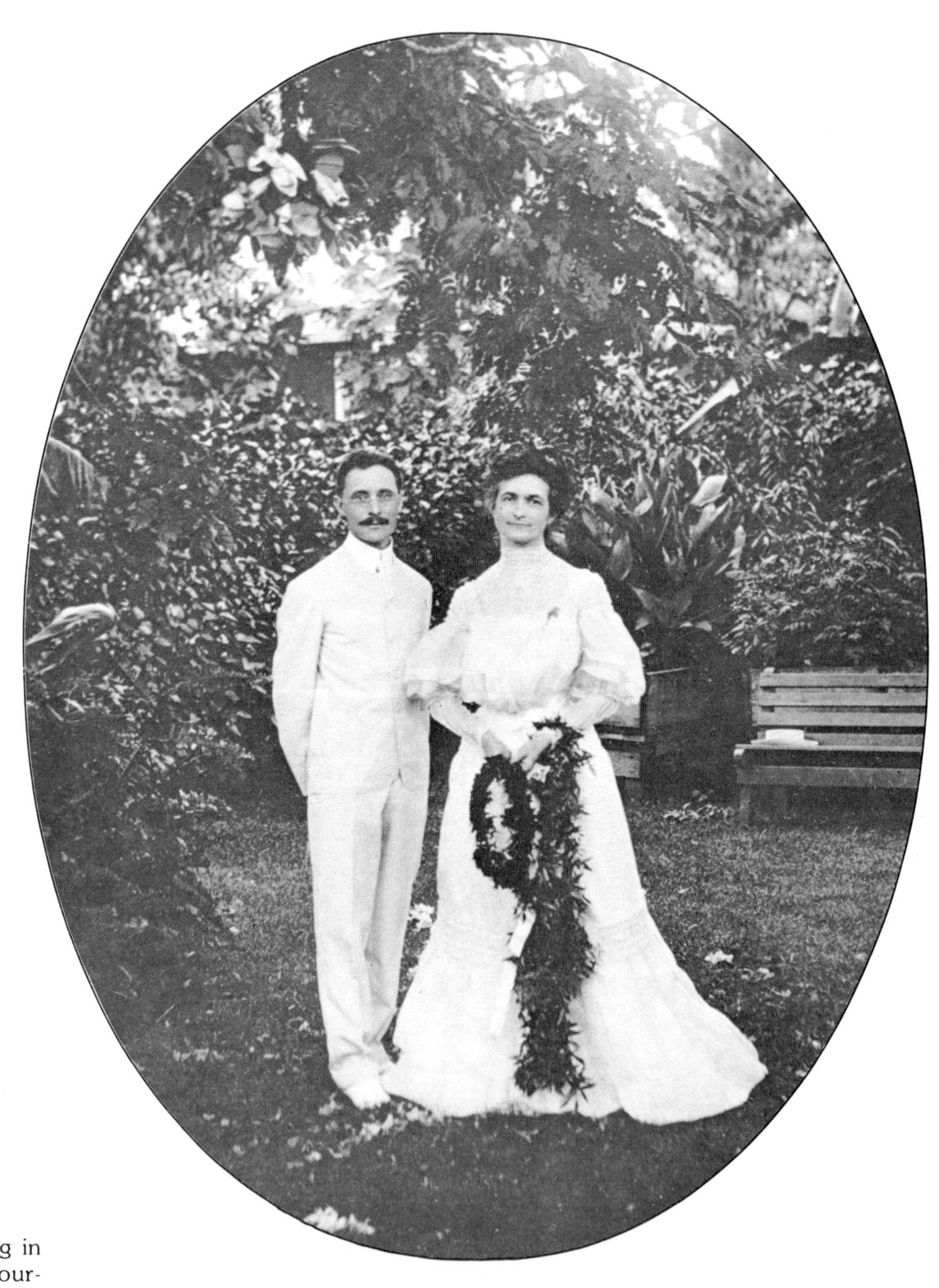

Mr. and Mrs. A.R. Gurrey, at their wedding in 1903. Photographer unknown. Photograph courtesy of Mrs. Roger Williams.

Caroline H. Gurrey

" 'The Boy and the Lobster', a photographic study by Miss Caroline Haskins of Honolulu has been pronounced the finest specimen of art photography in the Hawaiian Islands." The pronouncement came from one W. K. Vickery, a visiting art critic who had come to the islands in 1902 to exhibit, and hopefully to sell, a collection of European paintings. Vickery went on to claim of the photographer: "She is a true artist, and so some of her studies are valuable from the art standpoint. She certainly has a bright future."

That assessment of the photographic genius of Caroline Haskins Gurrey was reported on the front page of *The Pacific Commercial Advertiser* on March 25, 1902. Since that time, Mr. Vickery, who *The Advertiser* claimed "probably ranks third in the United States of art connoisseurs", has faded from memory. But, far more unfortunate, the artistry of Caroline Gurrey is little known and difficult to view today. In fact, so poorly was the memory of Gurrey's fine work preserved, that in the 1930s, when Ray Jerome Baker was attempting to trace early photographers, he reported only the following about Caroline Haskins Gurrey: "The names of two women occur in the years 1902 and 1903, Mrs. Ball and Miss C. Haskins. They did not become well established and after one or two years the names fail to appear." It is hard to believe that Baker's statement was the result of any serious effort to trace the Haskins name. It is more likely that it simply did not occur to him that in those early days a woman, working as a professional photographer, might have made a serious contribution to the art, and that he therefore did not bother to investigate his leads carefully. But the few examples of her work that Baker might have come across must surely have been arresting.

Further exploration would have revealed that some of her finest work had already been carefully preserved.

It is unfortunately true, nonetheless, that the work of Caroline Gurrey is not easy to come by. Her glass negative plates were all destroyed in a flood several years after her death in 1927. And the techniques of developing and printing she used — techniques that emphasize rather than reduce the effect of the soft focus lenses she used and leave her original prints with a tranquil and dreamlike quality — make reproduction from the prints difficult and rarely completely satisfying. Nonetheless, even in such reproductions, the quality of her genius as a photographer is obvious, as is her sincere interest in the people who served as subjects for her portraits.

Caroline Haskins Gurrey was born in California in the late 1870s. At the turn of the century, following two years at the University of California at Berkeley, she came to the Hawaiian Islands and began to establish her reputation as a portrait photographer. Photography was no idle hobby for her. It provided her income both before and after her marriage to art dealer A.R. Gurrey in 1903. Mr. Gurrey ran a small and perpetually struggling art shop in downtown Honolulu and it was Caroline Gurrey who remained, through her portraiture, the main provider for her family.

But Gurrey was always a commercial photographer with a difference. She would not be hurried. Often she spent an entire day on a single sitting. Unlike most of the commercial photographers in the islands she would not allow anyone else to do her developing and printing. And she personally destroyed any prints that did not meet her exacting standards. Each of her finished portraits was an original in the truest sense of the word as it applies to photography: an instant in time that captures the special qualities of the individuals who were her subjects.

Gurrey often made use of sunlight streaming into her work area. She often spent hours setting subjects at ease and distracting them from self-conscious observation of the camera and the photographer at work. Her portrait of two elderly Honolulu women is a good example of both these techniques, with sunlight providing fine back lighting and a table covered with old photographs providing the distraction. And, as the article in *The Commercial Advertiser* pointed out, her study of a young Hawaiian boy holding a lobster also serves as an illustration of her technique. Here the lobster served to totally distract her subject from the camera: "The boy is a young Hawaiian, well known on the waterfront, being one of the small army which dives for nickels and dimes thrown into the harbor from the decks of incoming passenger vessels. He is a pleasant faced little chap and has a good figure. Miss Haskins says the posing of the boy with a lobster in his hands was done with the object of having his attention so attracted by the wriggling of the crustacean, that he would forget himself for the nonce, and thus render him unconscious of the presence of the camera."

Gurrey's commercial work was often done in the homes of her subjects or in her own pleasant studio. The studio was located behind her home, a lovely Victorian structure that still stands on the slope of the Manoa valley and features wide, breezy verandas, shaded by large trees and carefully cultivated tropical vines.

Gurrey was well paid for her portraits of Honolulu's wealthy citizens but her interest in photography as an art went beyond the pursuit of such paying jobs. Over the years she remained fascinated by Hawaii's mixed race children. Time and again she would find a child with a particularly interesting face and convince the parents to allow the child to pose for her. Inevitably, the child would arrive at her studio dressed "mainland style", complete with tightly fitted dress or shirt, tie and jacket and even shoes. To appease parents and child, Gurrey would photograph the child in the unfamiliar and uncomfortable clothing so that she could present the proud family with a traditional portrait. It is unfortunate that none of those portraits have yet been located for it would be fascinating to compare them to the work she did to satisfy herself. For, once the formal sitting was out of the way, Gurrey would gradually work to gain the child's confidence and, with the child's mainland clothing wheedled off, would photograph each child in the simplicity of draped fabric and bare skin.

In some of these portraits a common object or activity of Hawaiian culture plays its natural role: plumeria blossoms to be strung into a flower lei, lauhala fronds or coconut fronds to be woven into a mat, or perhaps just a wooden calabash. But, in all of the portraits, the real subject is the beauty of mixed race and pure Hawaiian children and young people.

Her portraits of Hawaiian children gained Gurrey an invitation to display her work at the San Francisco Exhibition of 1915. And it was due to that exhibition that at least some of her fine work remains available today. One set of her "Hawaiian Types" series is now housed in the archives of the Library of Congress in Washington, D.C. and a second set can be found in the Academy of Arts in Honolulu. They reveal a remarkable woman who maintained a persistent interest in people and in her art.

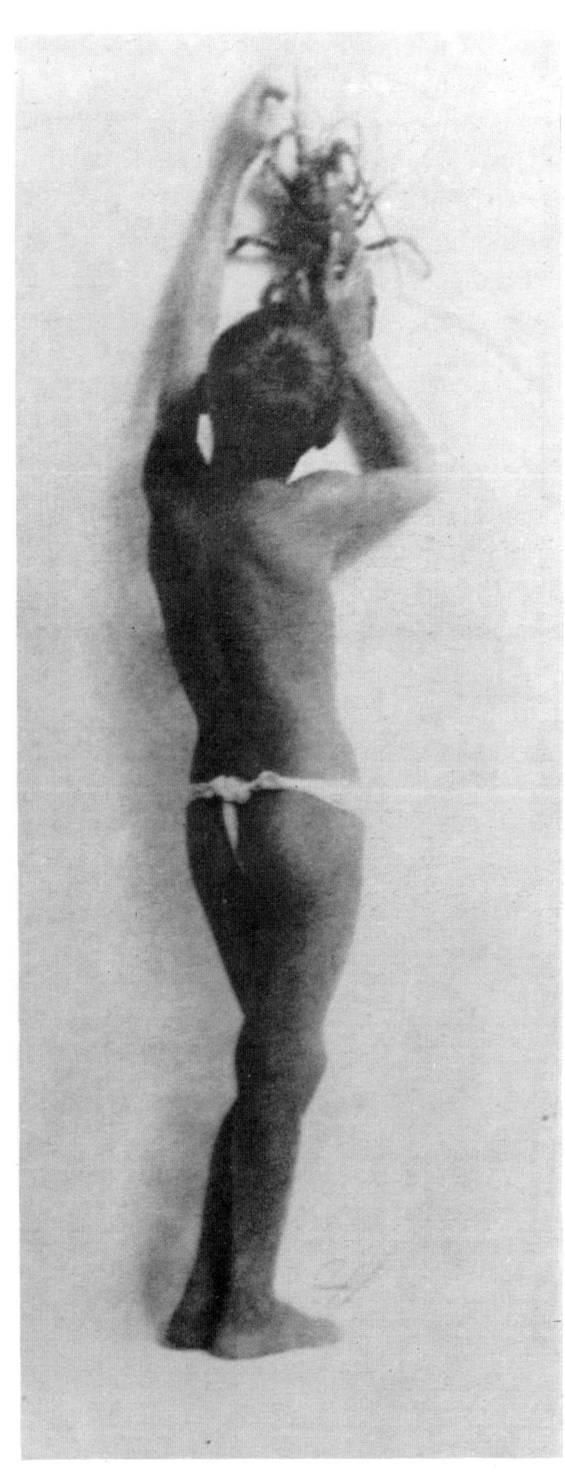

The Lobster Boy. Photograph was praised by a mainland art critic in 1902. C. Gurrey. Honolulu Academy of Arts.

The "operating room" of Gurrey's studio on Manoa Road in Honolulu, about 1915. Photograph courtesy of Mrs. Roger Williams.

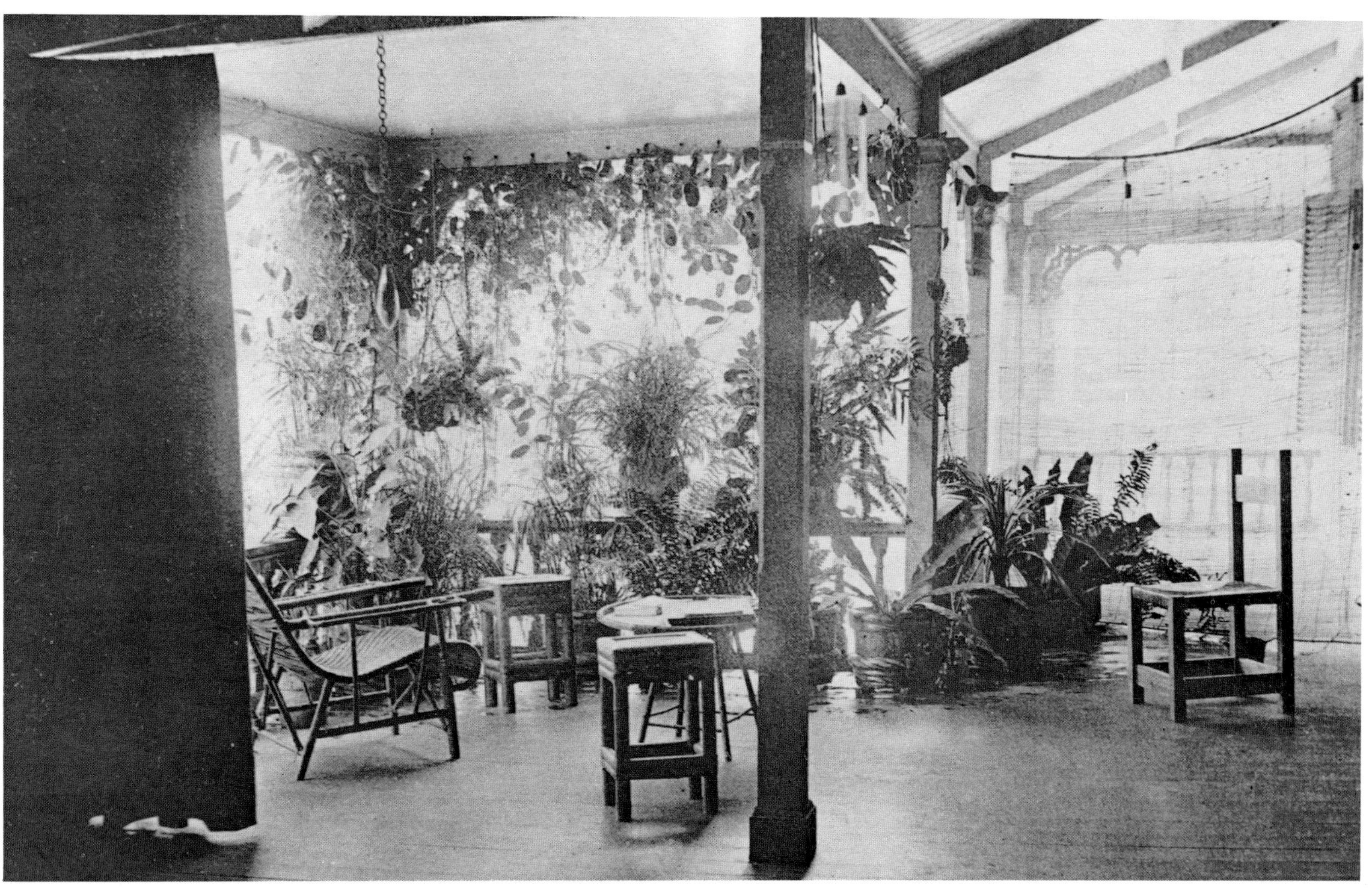

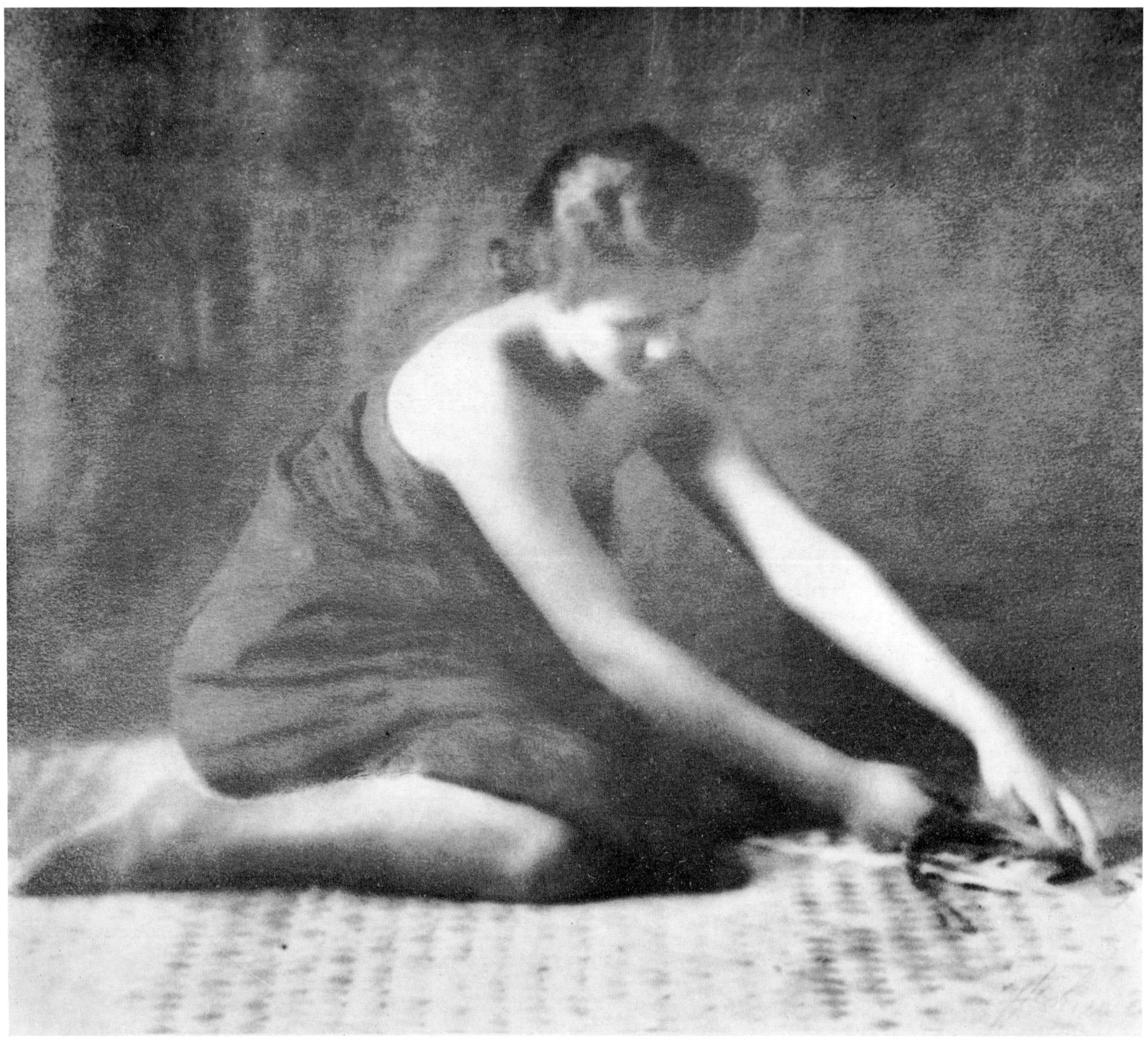

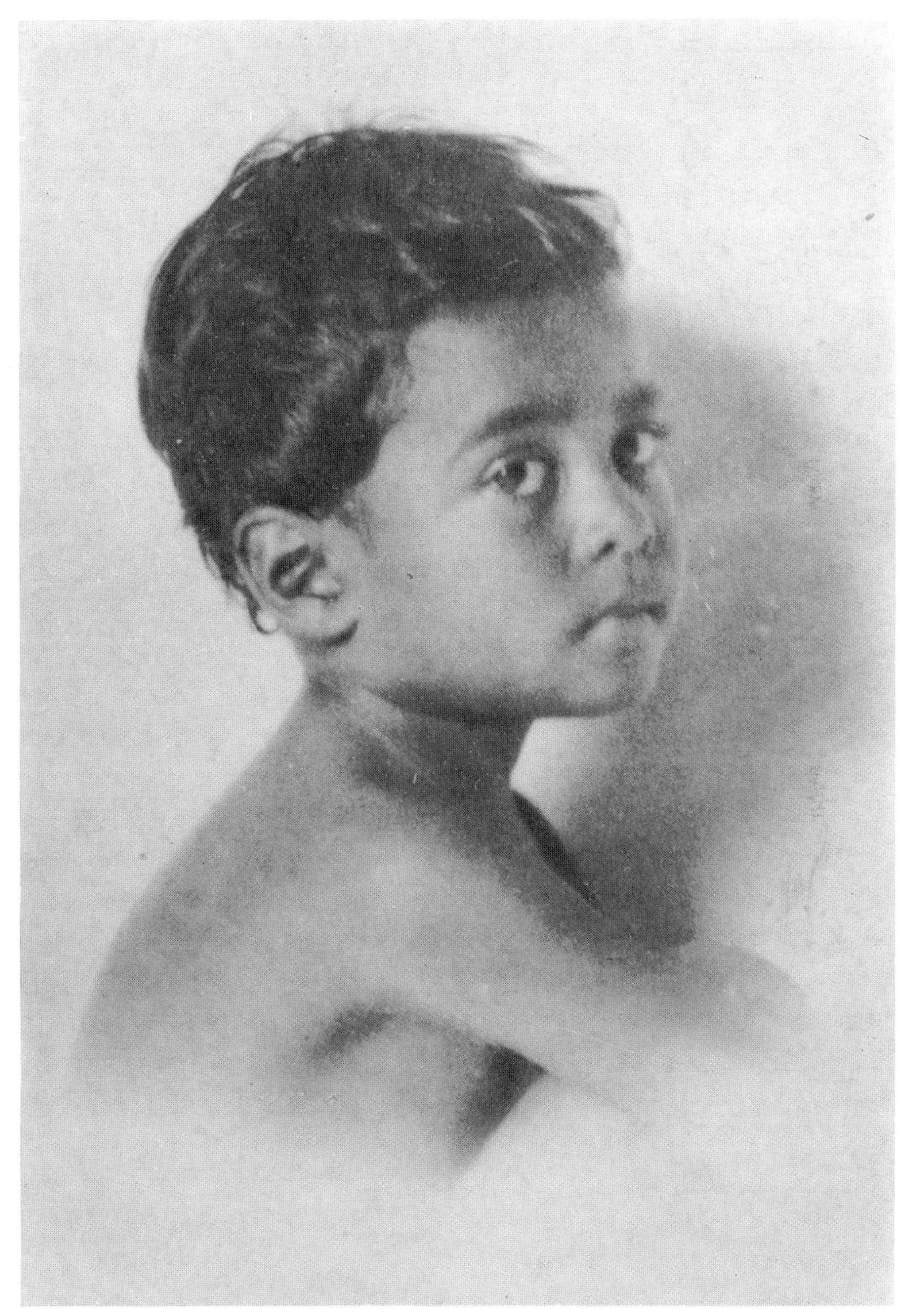

Left: The Mat Weaver, a Tahitian-Hawaiian woman, about 1905. C. Gurrey. From Honolulu Academy of Arts.

Right: Hawaiian boy, about 1905. Photographed by C. Gurrey. Honolulu Academy of Arts.

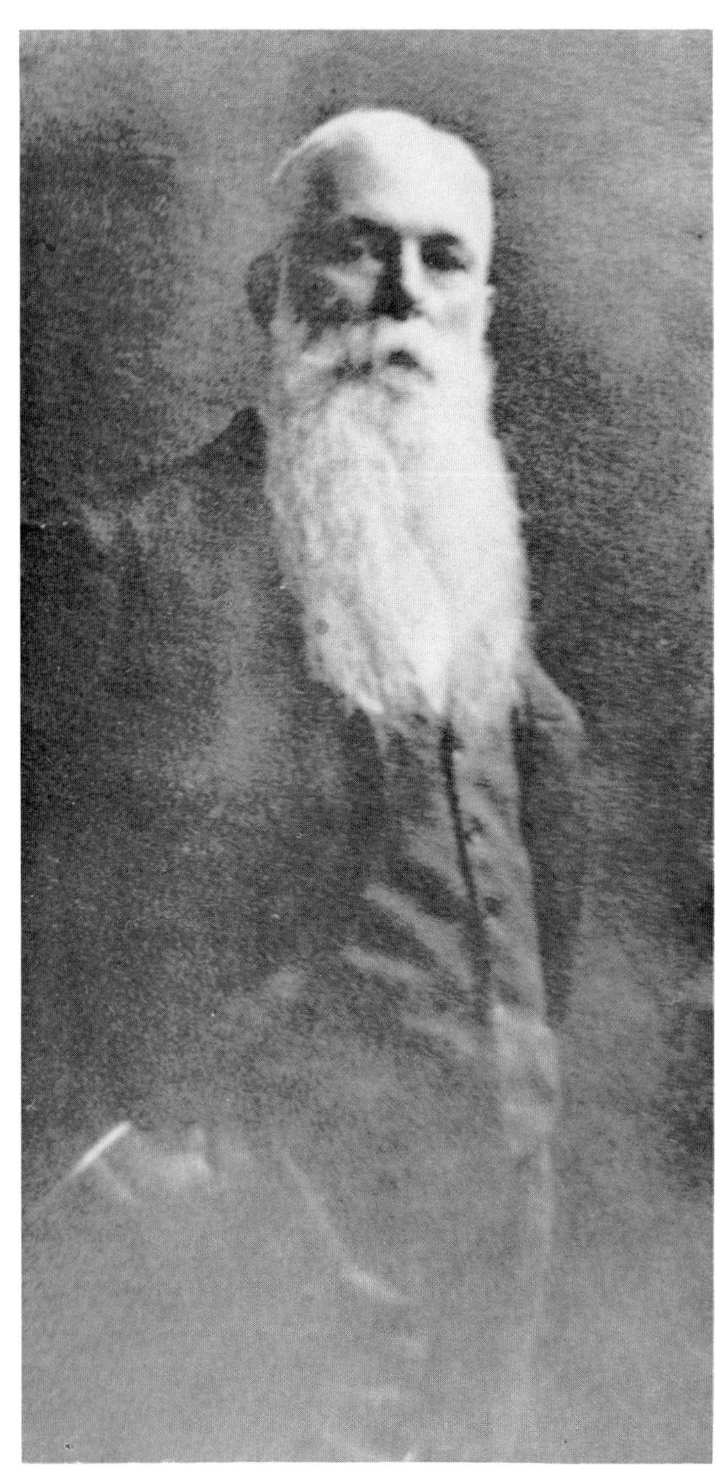

Sanford B. Dole, about 1900. C. Gurrey. Hawaii State Archives.

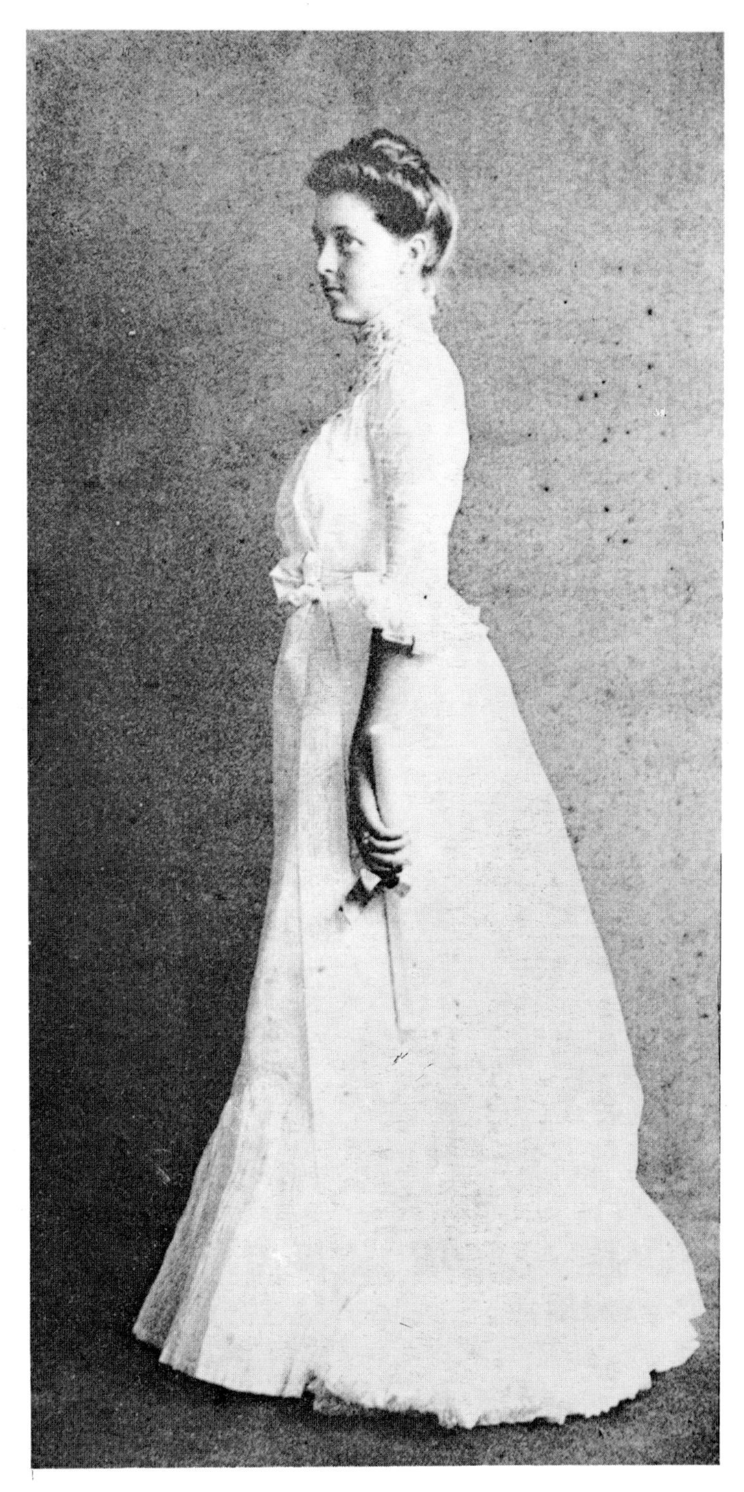

Ethel Damon, about 1900. C. Gurrey. Courtesy of Lyman Bond.

Right: Violetta. A Spanish-Hawaiian child, stringing plumeria blossoms, about 1905. C. Gurrey. Honolulu Academy of Arts.

Below: Girl with a calabash. C. Gurrey. Honolulu Academy of Arts.

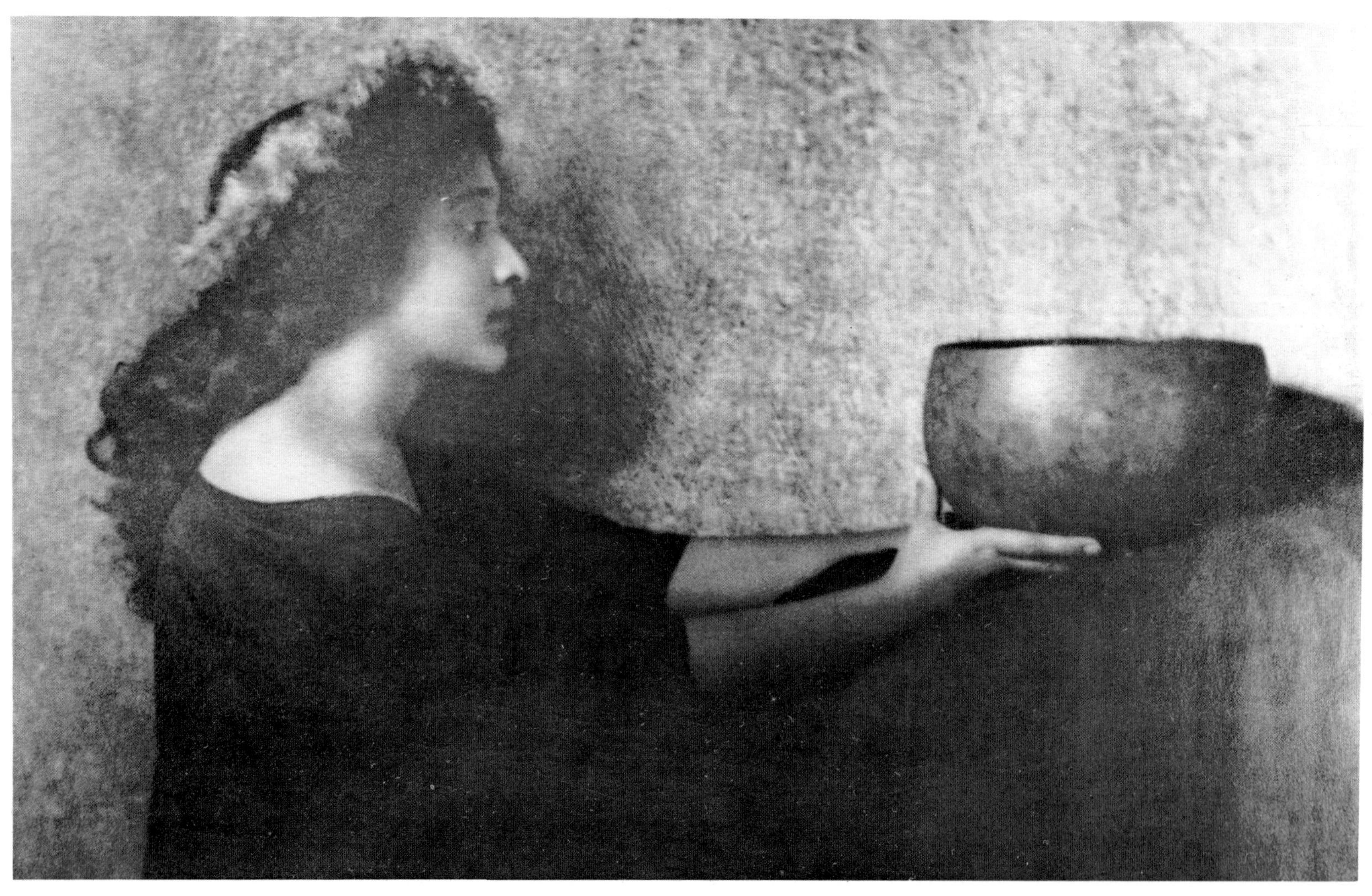

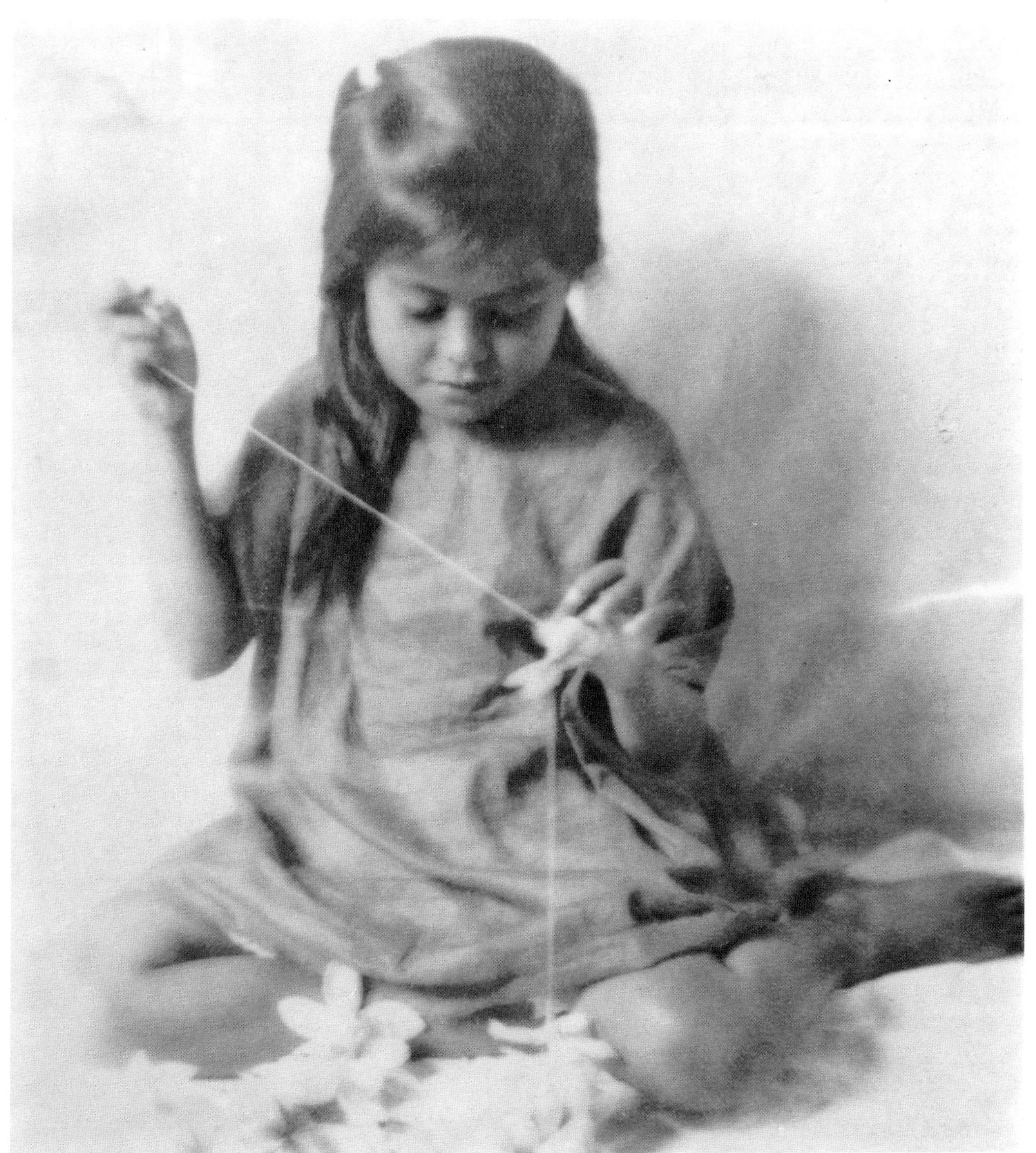

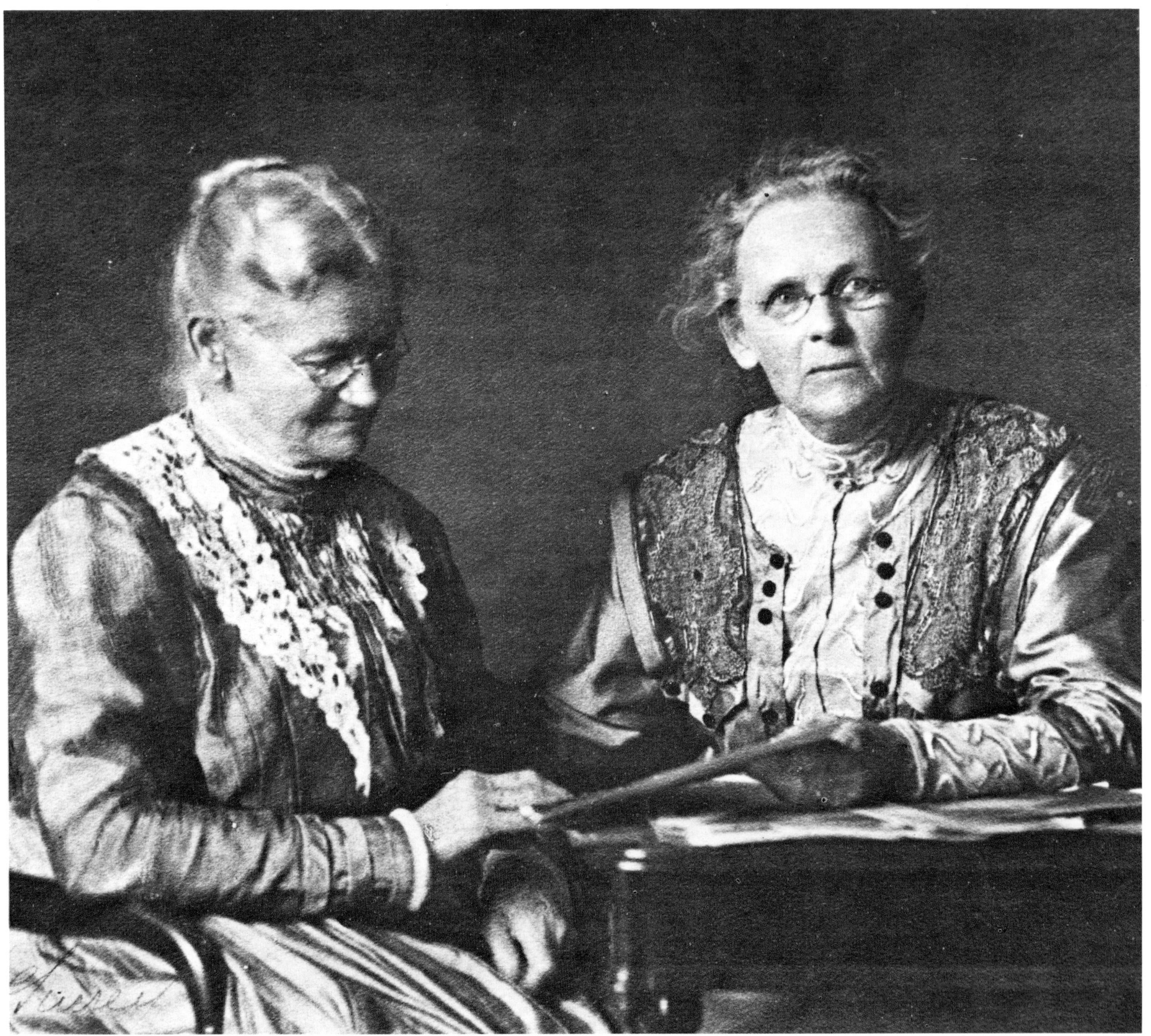

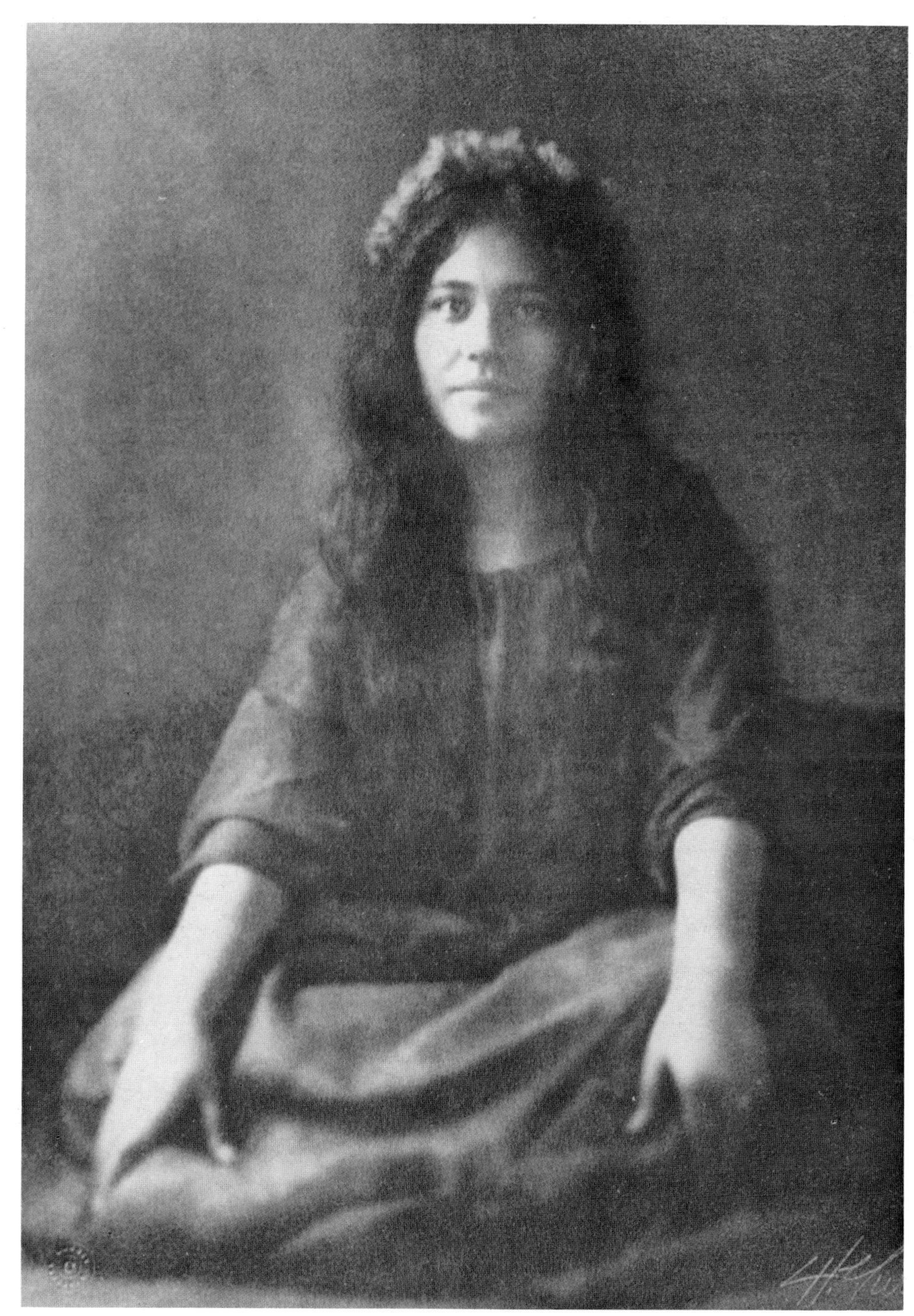

Left: Two Honolulu ladies looking through photographs, about 1905. C. Gurrey. Hawaii State Archives.

Right: A French-Hawaiian woman in a photograph titled "Repose." About 1905. C. Gurrey. Honolulu Academy of Arts.

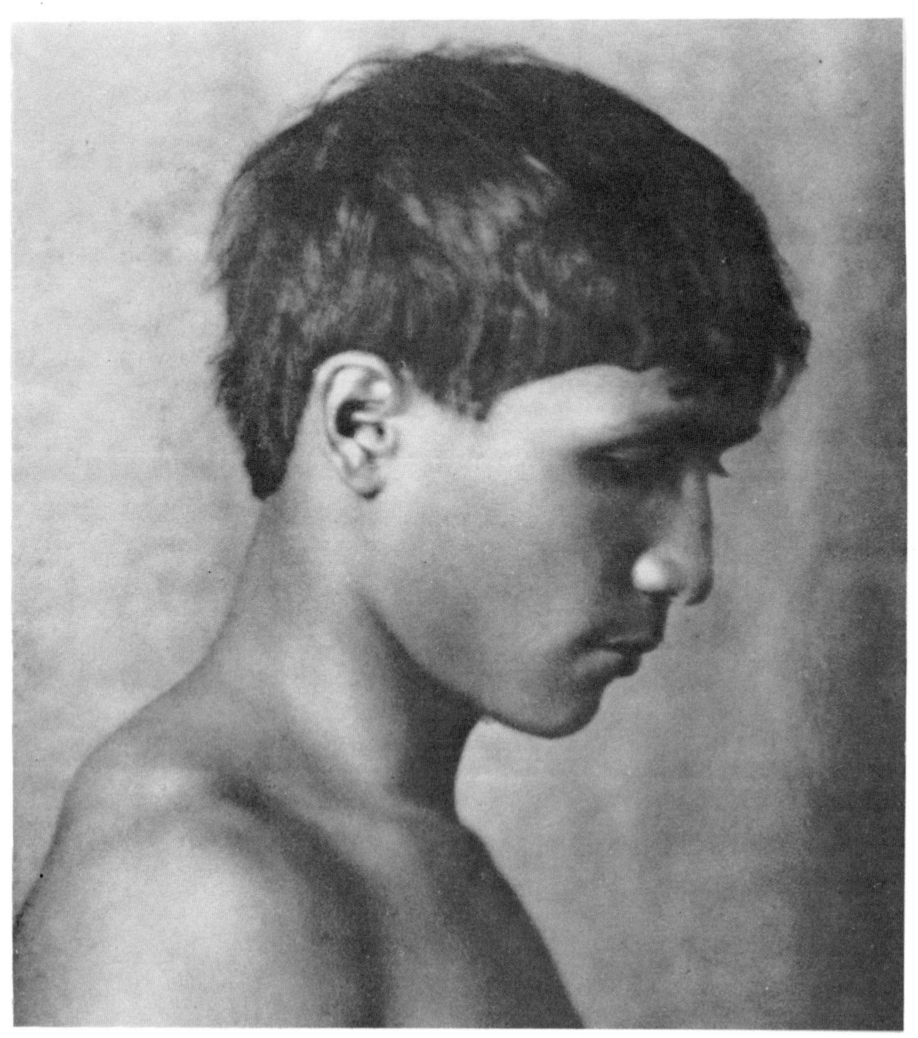

Above: Young man of pure Hawaiian background, about 1905. C. Gurrey. Honolulu Academy of Arts.

Right: Young woman of French-Portuguese-Hawaiian ancestry, about 1905. C. Gurrey. Honolulu Academy of Arts.

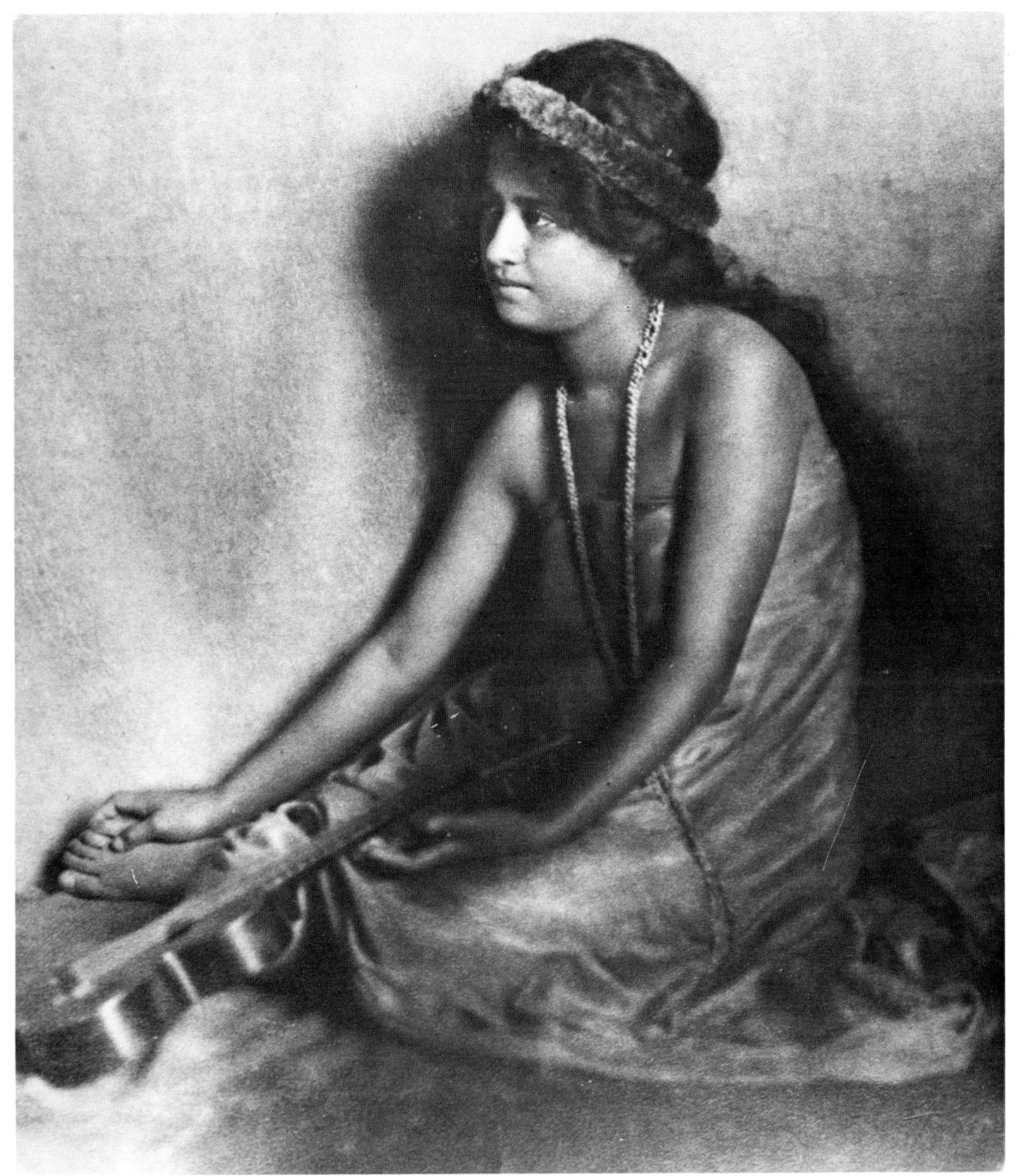

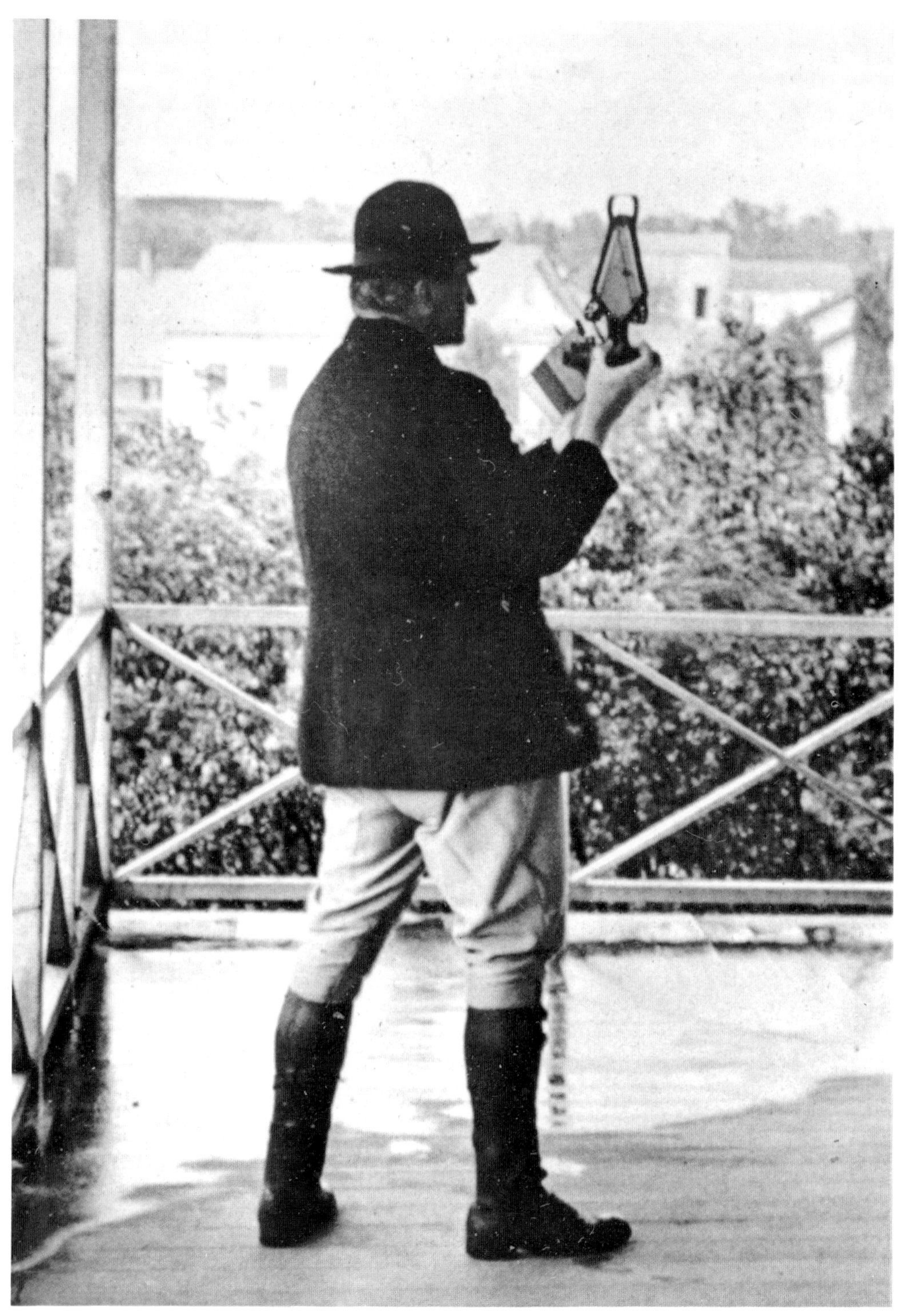

Thomas A. Jaggar taking measurements on the porch of the Hawaii Volcano Observatory, 1916. Photographer unknown. Hawaii Volcano Observatory.

Thomas A. Jaggar

In 1909, Thomas A. Jaggar was a professor of geology at Harvard University. During the summer of that year he passed through Hawaii on his way to Japan, where he toured various seismic stations and observed the considerable progress the Japanese had made in seismic and volcanic observation. But it was Hawaii that most impressed Jaggar on that trip. He left the islands convinced that the Kilauea Volcano was the most logical place in the world to build a permanent observatory for the specific purpose of studying volcanic activity and the chemistry of volcanoes. And, before he left, he had placed the seeds of interest in such a project in the minds of a number of local businessmen. Those seeds grew into the Volcano Research Association, a group of Honolulu businessmen and corporations that, by 1911, agreed to put up some funds for carrying out Jaggar's idea.

In the interim, Jaggar had left Harvard and became a professor at the Massachusetts Institute of Technology and director of the Whitney Museum and Whitney Fund at M.I.T. The museum and fund had been started for the specific purpose of studying earthquakes by a couple who had lost a son in an earthquake. By 1911, Jaggar had convinced the board of the Whitney Fund to sponsor an observatory at Kilauea and the Volcano Research Association had agreed to match Whitney funds. Jaggar obtained leave from his M.I.T. job and arrived in Hawaii in January, 1912. By that time an observation shack had already been built at the edge of Halemaumau crater and Jaggar began working to raise funds from Hilo merchants for a permanent observatory building.

From the time of his initial notion about a permanent observatory in 1909, until his retirement as observatory director in 1940, Jaggar led a remarkably fruitful double life. He was by training a geologist but by calling a kind of super-salesman who kept the volcano observatory going by force of his own ability to spellbind audiences and convince businessmen, foundations and government agencies to pick up the tab for the observatory's scientific activities. His salesmanship was unfailing until the depression years. When Whitney funds for the observatory ran out in 1917, Jaggar convinced the United States Weather Bureau to pick up his own salary as director of the observatory and much of the operating expense of the project. Again at Jaggar's urgings, the U.S. Geological Survey began paying the bills in 1924 and the observatory continued under that department until 1933, when the depression caused cutbacks in government spending that severely reduced the observatory budget. Jaggar, again using his enthusiastic salesmanship, managed to find private funding in the islands to tide the institution over until 1935, when the National Park Service took over. The observatory is now back under U.S. Geological Survey auspices and seems to be a permanently funded and valued part of the federal scientific effort. But it seems clear that Jaggar, who spent half of his time as director building financial support for the project, was responsible for keeping it afloat during its initial three decades.

Jaggar's scientific efforts seem to have been marked by the same energy and enthusiasm that allowed him to gain funding for the observatory. Over the years, as the effort to supply the ever-increasing need for money for the observatory grew, his scientific work continued apace. It did, however, change in tone: much of his writing, according to his associates, became keyed more toward spellbinding non-scientists with potential funding at their fingertips than toward advancing the frontiers of science. Indeed, one associate claims that in his enthusiasm, Jaggar began to write more and more "Gertrude Steinish" prose. Nonetheless, Jaggar appears to have been extremely creative in his ideas about the kinds of scientific work that could be pursued by the observatory staff. And he was himself constantly inventing new machinery for the recording of earth motion, volcanic activity and temperature. His efforts were not always successful, but they never failed in being imaginative.

One of his more spectacular failures (pictured in this selection of photographs) was the idea of drilling holes and sinking thermometors to record temperature changes below the floor of Kilauea crater. Such changes in temperature, he reasoned, could then be studied as a means of predicting changes in volcanic activity in the crater. The idea of developing some method of prediction was a good one. The flaw, however, was in the method Jaggar devised. The thermometers, sunk into the porous volcanic rock, merely recorded the temperature of steam rushing through the porous rock from the nearest steam vent.

Among Jaggars more spectacular successes was his late 1920s idea for a sea-going automobile which he hoped would help in the study of volcanoes in isolated areas such as the Aleutian Island chain. Jaggar wanted to be able to unload such a vehicle from an offshore ship, take it through the offshore waters on its own power and merely drive it on to a beach, over rough terrain and on to the desired research location. He obtained funding for his project from the National Geographic and, by 1929, his machinists had begun building a prototype. *The Honokai* (Sea Turtle) was completed by the early 1930s and residents of the south Kona area could see it on calm days making practice runs along the coast. Jaggar had nothing more in mind for the vehicle than the exploration of remote volcanoes and he did take it on one trip to Alaska under the sponsorship of the National Georgraphic. General Motors, however, developed the vehicle for the War Department and it became the "duck" of World War II memory.

Between his spellbinding lectures, his volcanic salesmanship and his scientific work, Jaggar also managed to find time to become a competent and enthusiastic photographer. In fact he viewed photography as a tool for recording the changing activity at the volcano and as a result he was meticulous about recording what he was doing with his cameras. Over the years Jaggar and his assistants filled page after page in the Kilauea Record Books with photographs of spatter cones, lava lakes and steam vents. Each photo was carefully annotated with time, place and date and with information about the cameras and lenses used.

For the most part, Jaggar limited his use of cameras to recording volcanic activity and the resultant record can give scientists working today an accurate and graphic idea of the history of the volcano over a number of years. But, being a man of boundless energy, Jaggar also turned his camera to the people and activities around him, photographing cars, people as they inspected the volcano, Volcano House, and even his own crowded workshop and machine shop.

As with everything else he did, Jaggar went about photography with all-consuming energy. He purchased and tried every new camera and lens he heard of and could acquire and he carefully recorded information about their usefulness to his work. Yet many of his best photographs, taken long after the development of celluloid films and long after the introduction of fast lenses, were taken with old equipment, on glass plates and with a lens that lacked a shutter —

he merely removed and replaced the lens cap to obtain his exposure.

Jaggar's enthusiasm for his observatory and his volcano can hardly be doubted. Indeed, among the people he left behind when he made his move to Hawaii were his wife and two children. His wife apparently did not share his enthusiasm for volcano watching or for living in the rugged Kilauea terrain. In fairness to the first Mrs. Jaggar, it must be said that Jaggar was a man of boundless ego as well as boundless energy: he was convinced of his absolute right to do whatever it was that pleased him, including moving off to a remote Pacific island and, shortly afterward, building his home below the rim of Kilauea crater, jutting out over the precipitous and sometime freshly lava covered terrain. He shared his home with his second wife, Isabelle Brown, who had been a schoolteacher in Kona and who apparently was far more enthusiastic about volcanoes than the first Mrs. Jaggar. No one in the area appears to have shared quite the same degree of enthusiasm about volcanoes: when Jaggar retired and moved from the area no one volunteered to occupy his precariously perched home.

Ironically, despite his great enthusiasm for volcanoes, Jaggar missed one of the most spectacular eruptions of Kilauea. Jaggar had been in Europe when the explosive May, 1924 eruption began. He was notified and immediately began the trip back to the islands. When he finally arrived in Honolulu he convinced officials of the Navy to provide him a plane and a pilot so that he could return to the Island of Hawaii as quickly as possible. The plane, however, made it only as far as Alenuihaha Channel. Jaggar spent the waning hours of the eruption floating about on a ditched Navy plane waiting to be rescued. Perhaps it was this frustrating immobility that led him to conceive of a sea-going automobile. Ruy Finch, one of the scientists at Kilauea at the time, did take Jaggar's equipment and attempt to record the eruption. But in his excitement he put the glass plates into the camera backward and spoiled his photographs. It remained for Tai Sing Loo, the official Pearl Harbor photographer, who happened to be on the island at that time, to capture the most spectacular photographs of the 1924 eruption.

Hawaii Volcano Observatory in 1912, shortly after the building was completed. T. A. Jaggar. Hawaii Volcano Observatory.

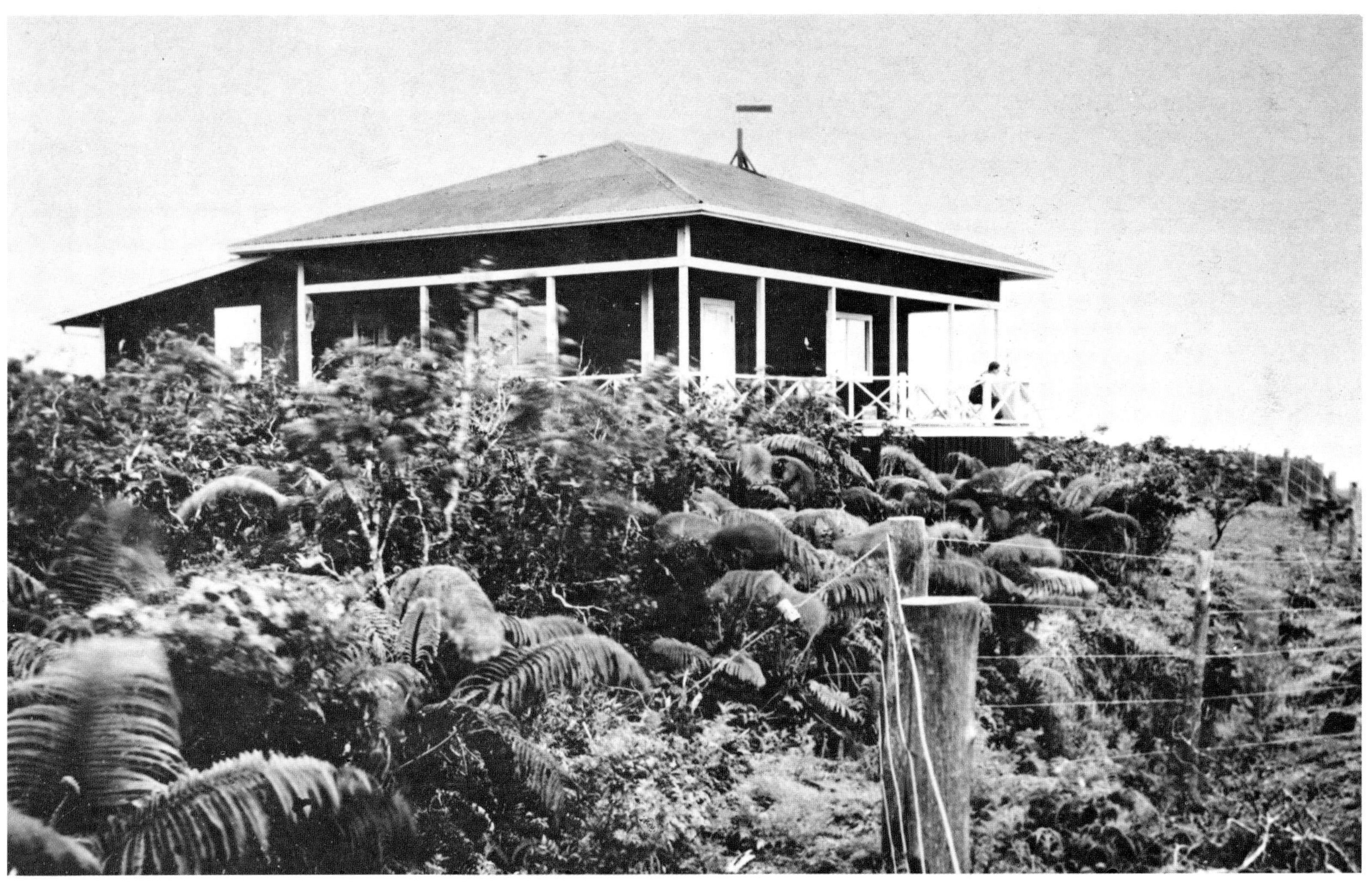

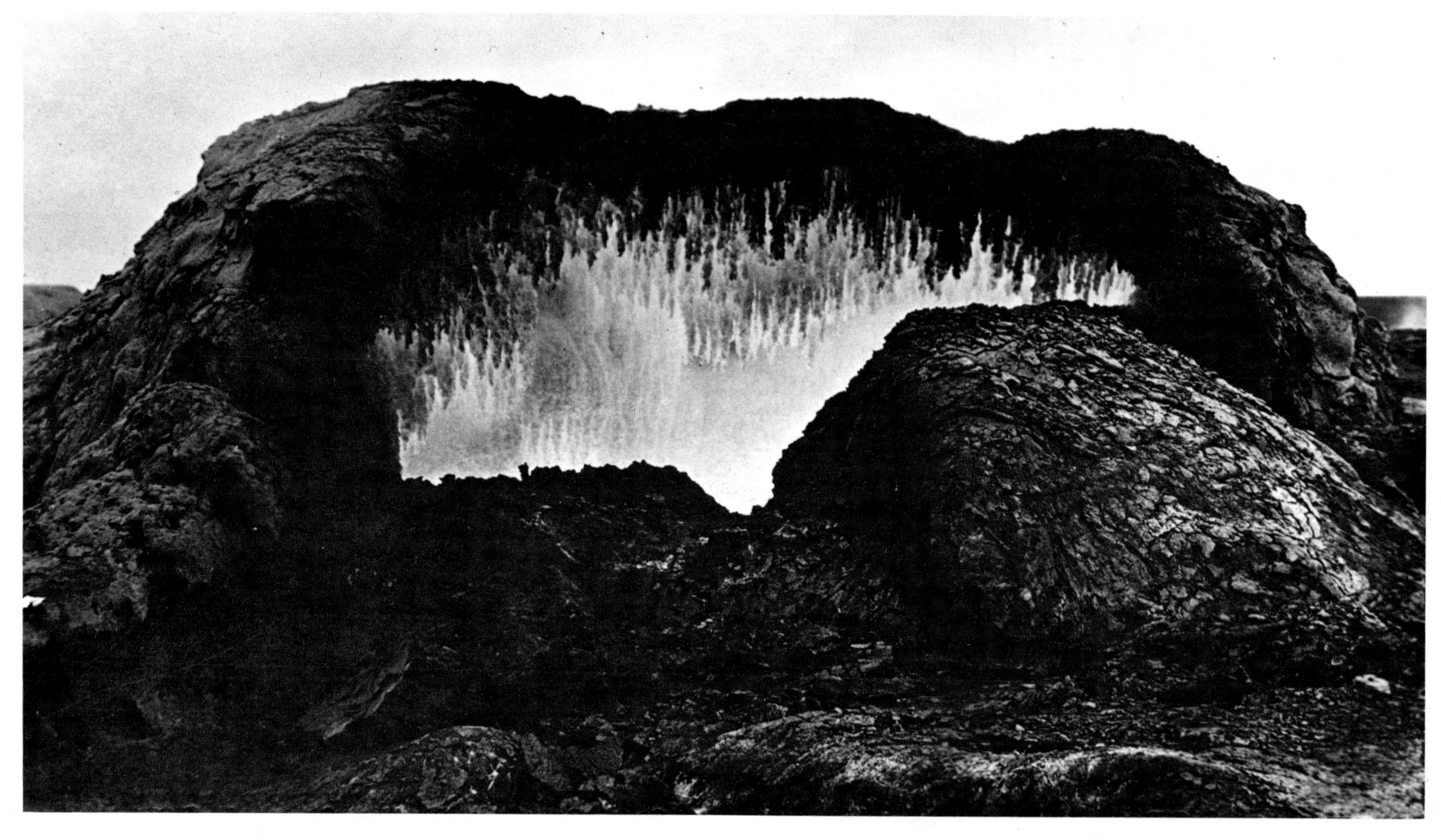

Above: A lava cone with glowing stalactites, 1921. T. A. Jaggar. Hawaii Volcano Observatory.

Right: Autos on road near Halemaumau crater, 1918. T. A. Jaggar. Hawaii Volcano Observatory.

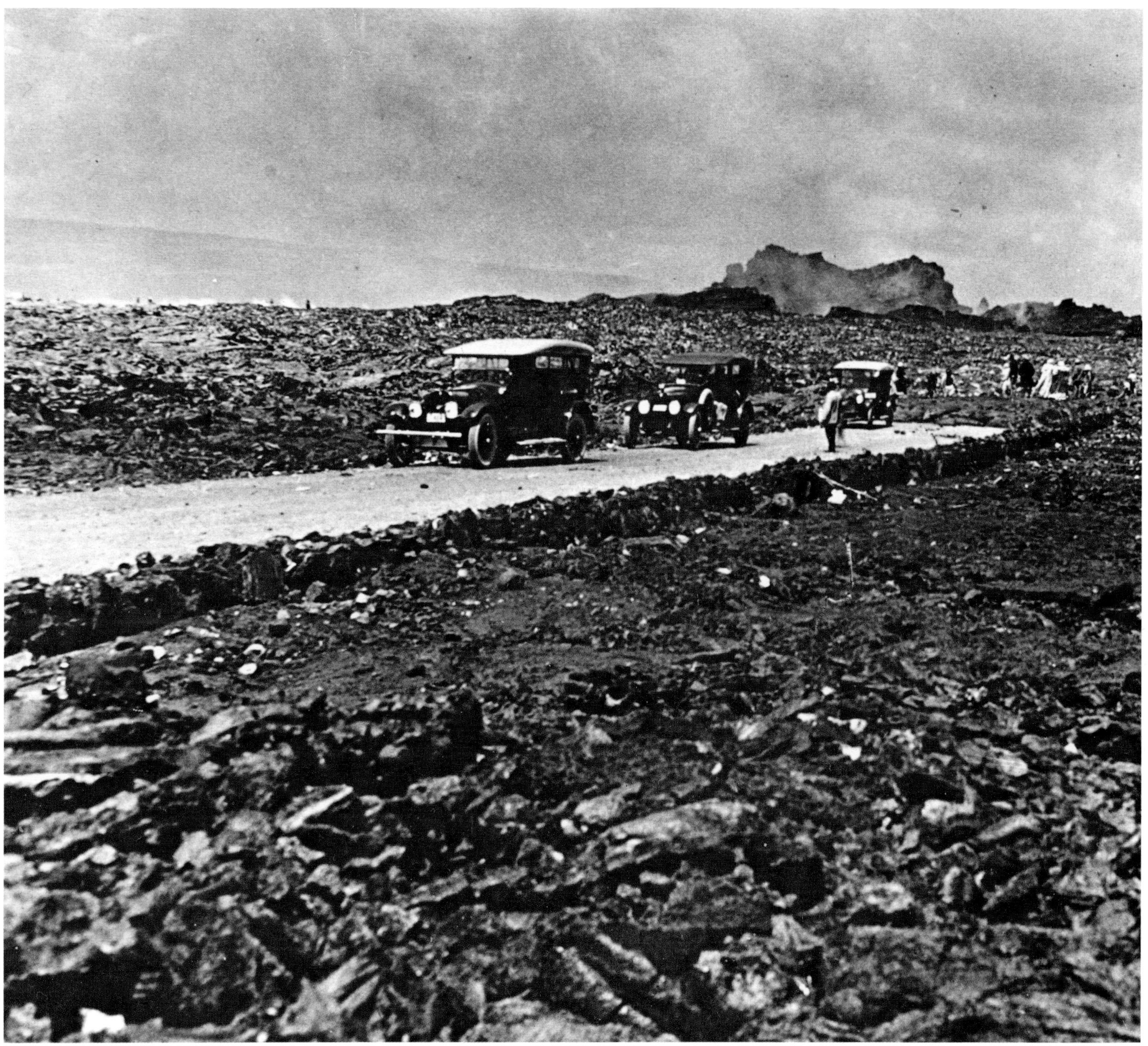

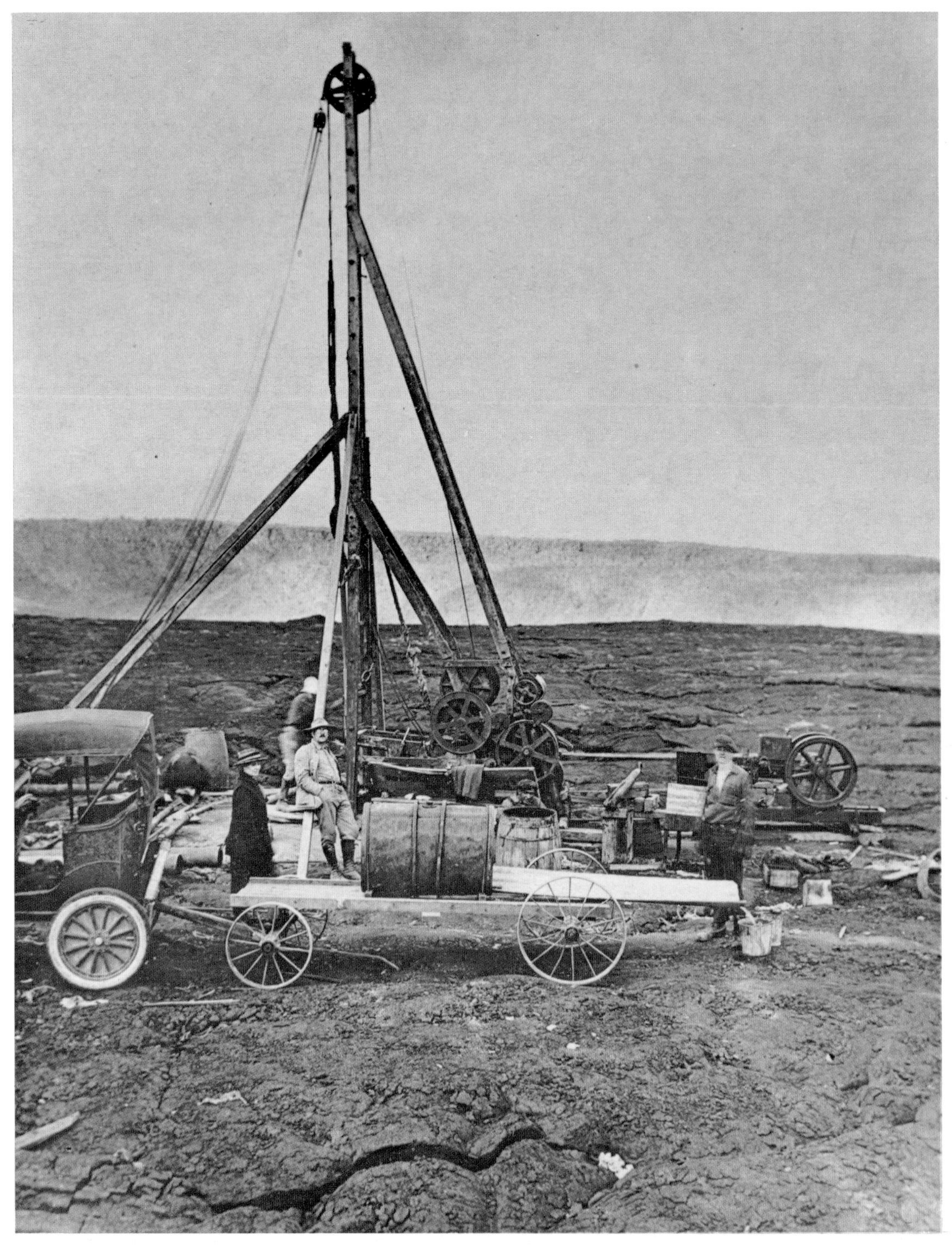

Left: Setting up drilling equipment on the floor of Kilauea Crater, July, 1921. T. A. Jaggar. Hawaii Volcano Observatory.

Below: A Ford hauling water to drill workers on the floor of Kilauea Crater, July, 1921. Photograph by T. A. Jaggar. Hawaii Volcano Observatory.

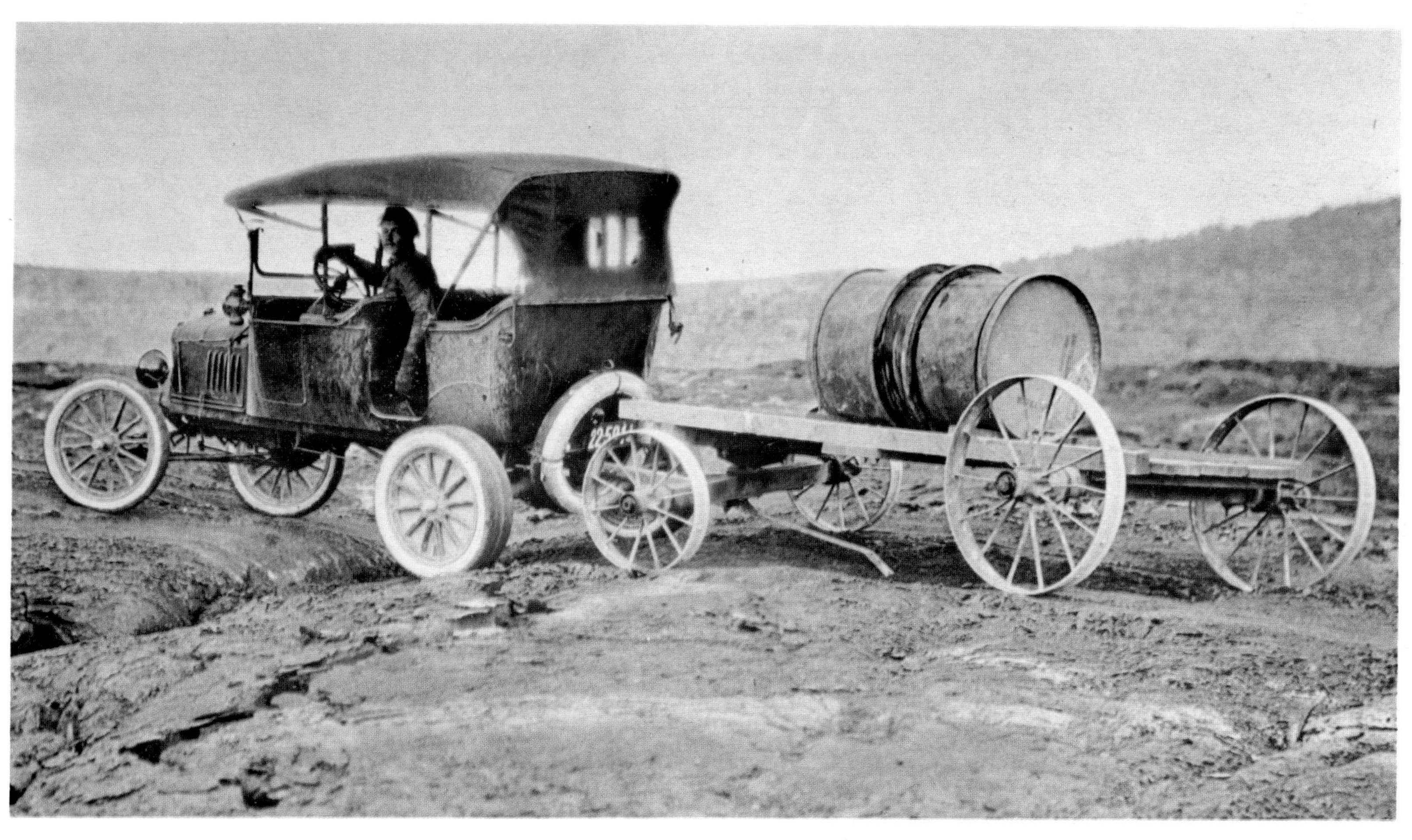

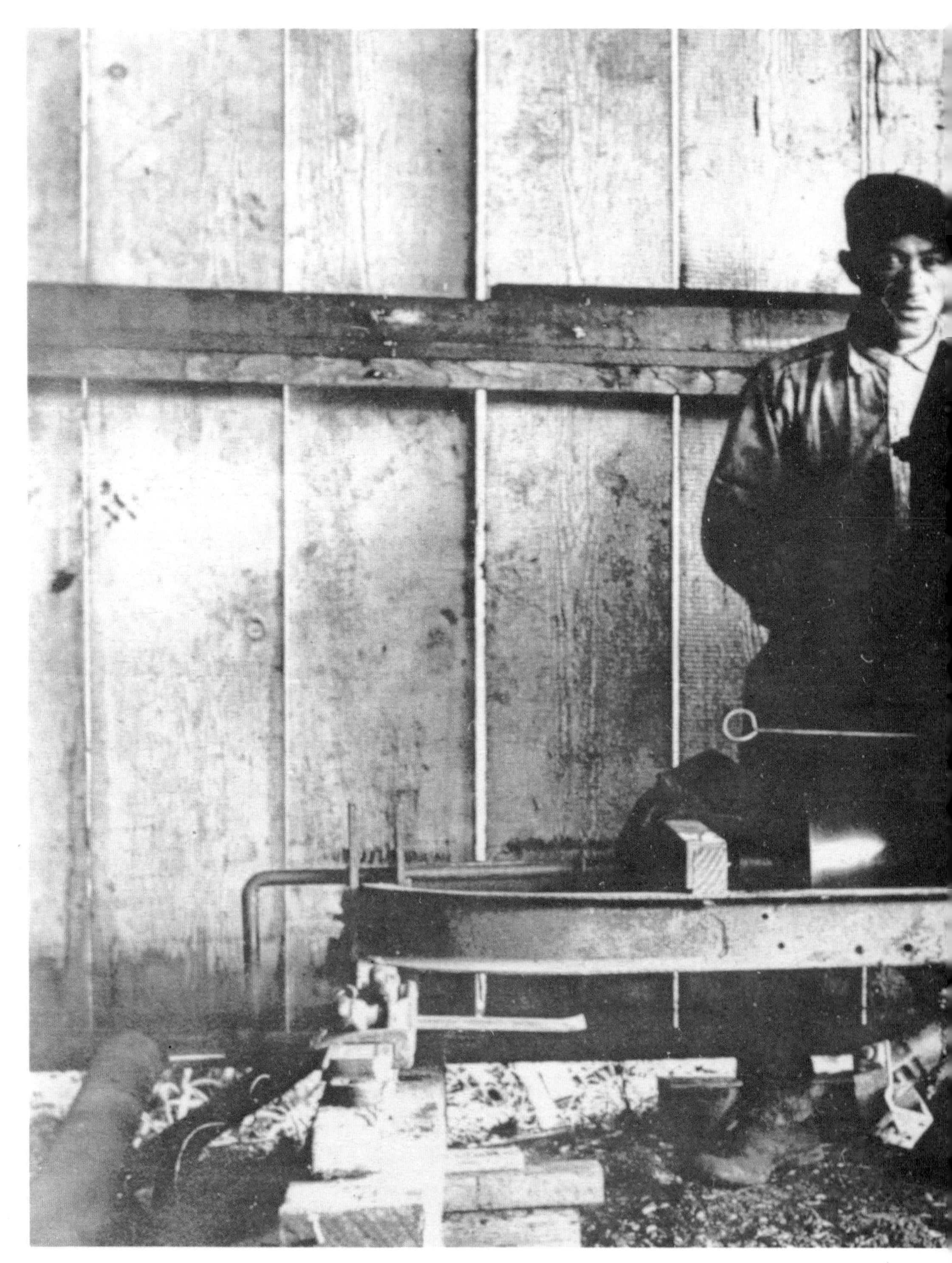

Mechanics in the machine shop, 1921. T.A. Jaggar. Hawaii Volcano Observatory.

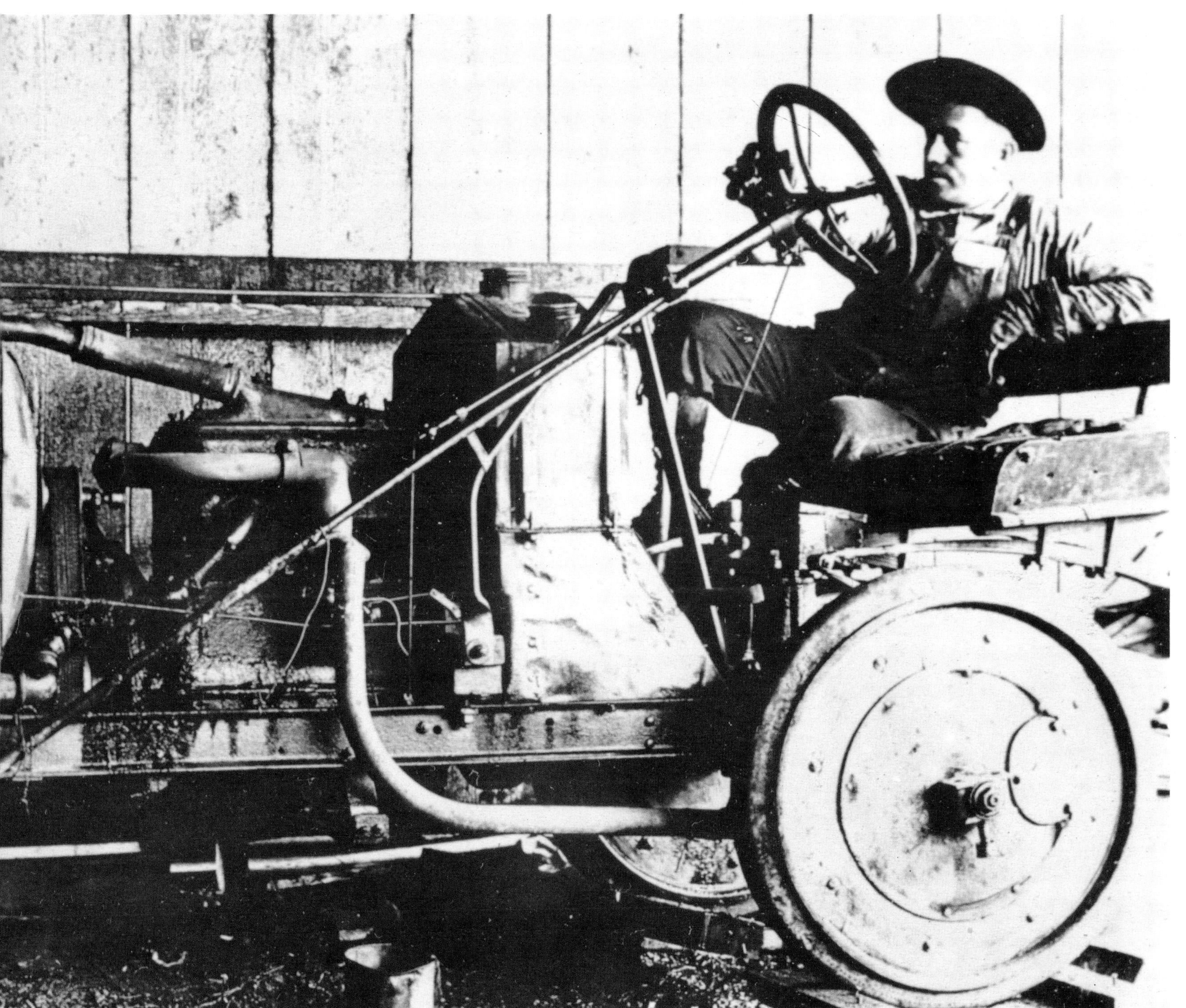

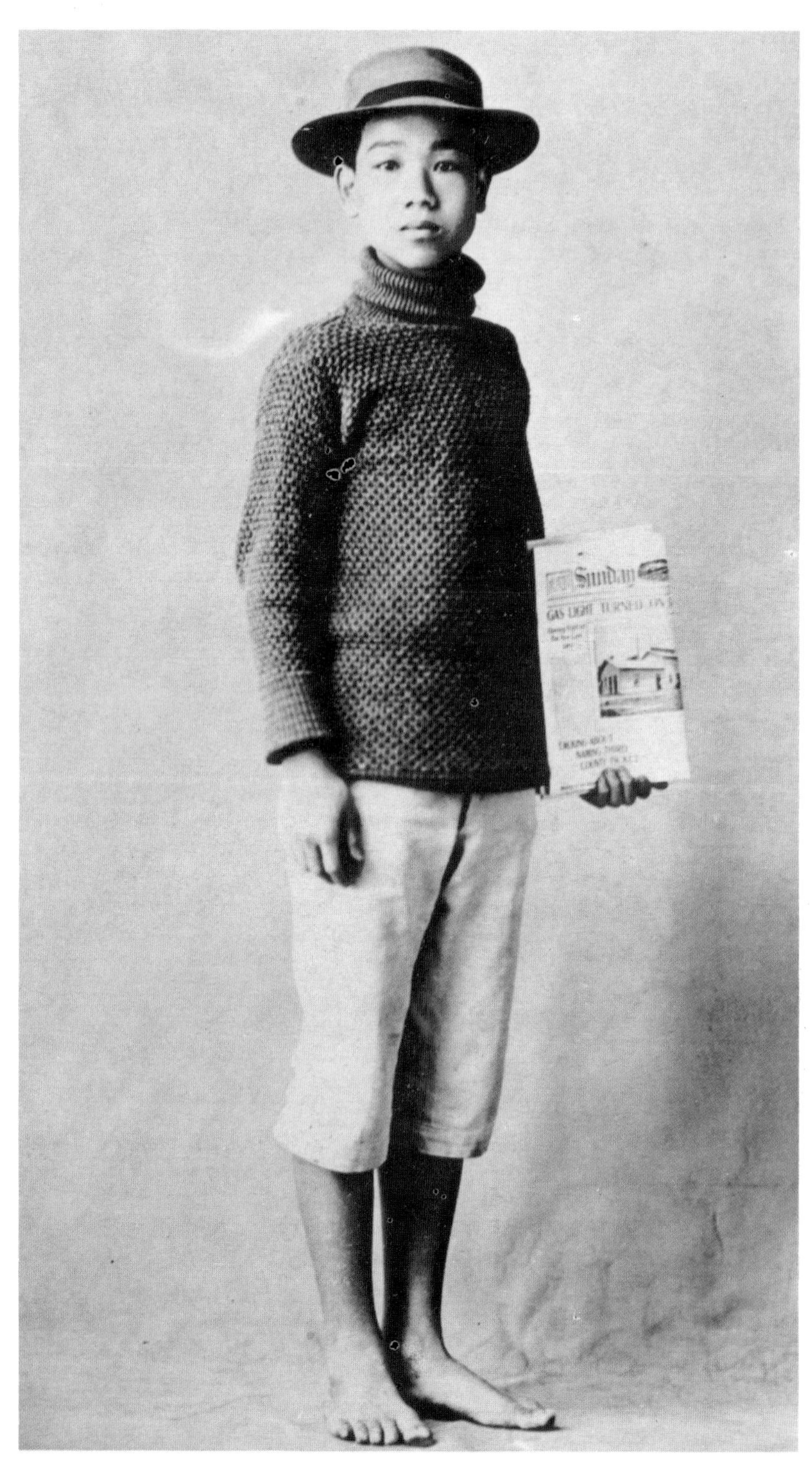

On Char, posing for his first photograph in 1904.
R. Perkins. Courtesy of On Char.

On Char

In 1904, Honolulu photographer Roscoe Perkins came to Kaiulani School to take class pictures. As he was leaving the school building, one of the students followed him and asked if he could come to the Perkins studio to learn photography. The young man had watched Perkins work and had then and there conceived the notion of becoming a professional photographer. Perkins agreed to accept the young man as an apprentice and thereby launched one of the longest, most successful careers in commercial photography in Hawaii.

The young apprentice, On Char, had come to Honolulu four years earlier from the Island of Hawaii. He was born in Kohala in February, 1889, the son of Char Loy Kui and Char Ng Shee, who had come to Hawaii from Kwangtung Province in China, to work in the sugar fields. After a few years as plantation workers, Char's parents moved to Kailua, where they worked on a tobacco farm owned by an uncle. Then they moved on to the south Kona area, where the senior Char had purchased a small coffee plantation.

In 1899, Char Loy Kui asked his son if he would like to live in Honolulu so that he could attend school and learn the grocery business at the Palama Street store of a relative. Char agreed and the trip to Honolulu was arranged— in fact, young Char arrived in Honolulu shortly after the fire that leveled Chinatown in the winter of 1900. The ruins of Kaumakapili Church and the surrounding area were still smoldering when he disembarked. If the smoking ruins were any kind of portent for Char they were a positive one, for they marked the beginning of a long and successful life as a Honolulu resident.

Char spent the first few years of the new century attending Kaiulani School and working in the Palama Street store. His spare hours were spent selling *The Commercial Advertiser* — at that time newsboys purchased papers at two for a nickel and resold them for a nickel each. And, in 1904, he began his apprenticeship in photography at the Perkins studio.

Char worked for Perkins from 1904 to 1907, first sweeping and cleaning and then helping with photo finishing and camera operation. It was in the beginning of his apprenticeship that Perkins took the photograph of Char the newsboy — the first photograph Char had ever had taken of himself. And it was also during these first years that Char, practicing his new trade, took the strikingly simple portraits of his parents that hung in an honored place in his home throughout his life.

In 1907, when he was eighteen, Char left the Perkins studio and became manager of the K.M. Henry studio. He remained in that position until 1911, the year in which he began both his marriage and his career as an independent businessman and owner of City Photo Company.

Char's early photographs record a unique phase of Chinese history in Hawaii. Through thousands of sittings, many of them formal and grave, they explore a panorama of Chinese family life. Weddings, the arrival of new offspring, business ventures, graduations and deaths were all recorded by his camera.

As the years went by the tastes of Char's clients changed. The younger generations no longer wanted photographs in the formal manner. They preferred modern poses, smiling faces and less formal settings. And Char responded to these changes as he kept abreast of developments in his profession. Shortly after World War I, he left his studio in the hands of relatives and went to New York, where he studied at the New York Institute of Photography. After his graduation, he returned to Hawaii but maintained his contacts through frequent attendance at meetings and conventions of professional photographers on the mainland.

The changes in style that were reflected in On Char's work over the years also reflect the change in taste of the people whose photographic needs he served. And he managed all the changes with great professional skill. But perhaps his most unique contribution to the history of Hawaii is his vast record of that early period when the old ways of Chinese family life had not yet completely given way to the new. Indeed, throughout his life, Char seemed to identify most strongly with the old ways. A spry and independent Char, at 86 years of age, expressed his feelings about those ways in January, 1976: "To tell you the truth," said Char, "the times have changed. The people, the times and the people are different than the old days. To me the young people who are under 40, those people are different altogether. You can see these old Chinese, anyone of 50, 60, and up. Why those people, their mind is a little different than today. Even my own children. Today we've got too much education, (they become) over smart."

In a vivid testimonial to the old ways, Char described the matchmaking process through which he met his wife, Margaret Liu. The tradition was that the name and birth date of the girl selected by a matchmaker was written down and placed under the prospective bridegroom's pillow for three consecutive nights. If, during that time, nothing untoward occurred, the match would proceed. If anything inauspicious happened, a different match would be tried. Char's wife was the fourth woman tried by the matchmakers. Such tests have gone out of style, Char said. "I don't think anybody would take a chance because they are already in love and they have already picked and don't want to change it," he explained. But in the old days such methods seemed to work well — at least they worked well for him, Char said.

That special rapport with the old ways that marked Char's life is evident in his early work. The early photographs have a quiet dignity and grace that could come only from mutual respect and shared values between the subjects and the photographer. These early works compose a remarkable record of an old culture transplanted to a new environment at the moment of change.

On Char left his photographic business in 1954, but it can hardly be said that he retired. Instead, he shifted his energies to a number of projects. Among them were a series of proposals for creating or remodeling, along traditional lines, buildings of historical and social significance to the Hawaii Chinese community. That same energy and independence remained with Char until his death on February 16, 1976. Char lived alone and spent much of his time until shortly before his death pursuing his community development projects, trying out new cameras, and talking with enthusiasm about his family of nine children, thirty three grandchildren and three great grandchildren. He was, in fact, waiting to hear about visa arrangements for a trip he planned to take to mainland China.

In 1972, Char contributed his negatives — over 90,000 of them spanning a half century of his work — to the Bernice P. Bishop Museum, an important legacy for all the people of Hawaii.

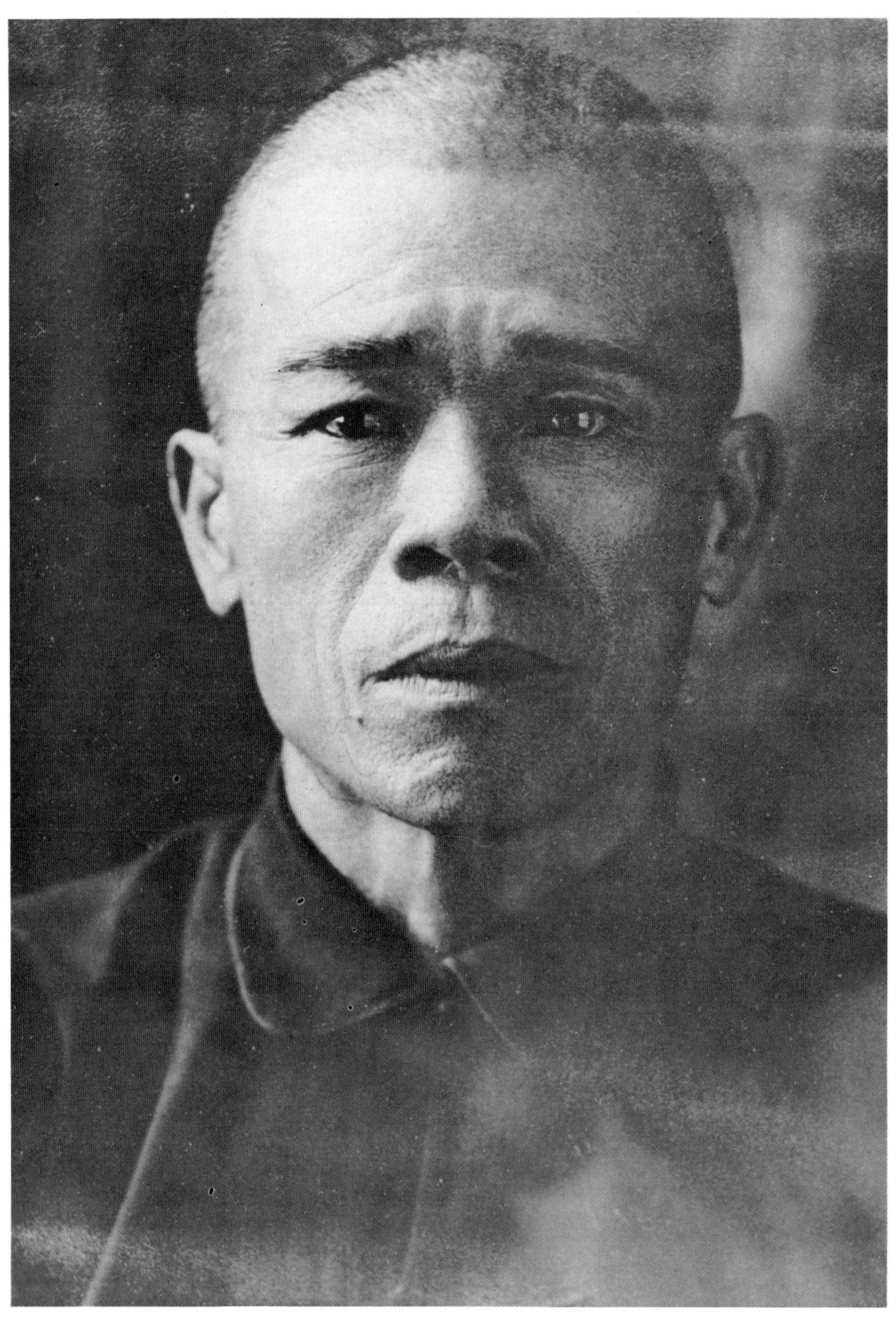

Char Loy Kui, father of On Char. Photographed by On Char when he was a young apprentice in the Honolulu studio of Roscoe Perkins in 1904. Courtesy of On Char.

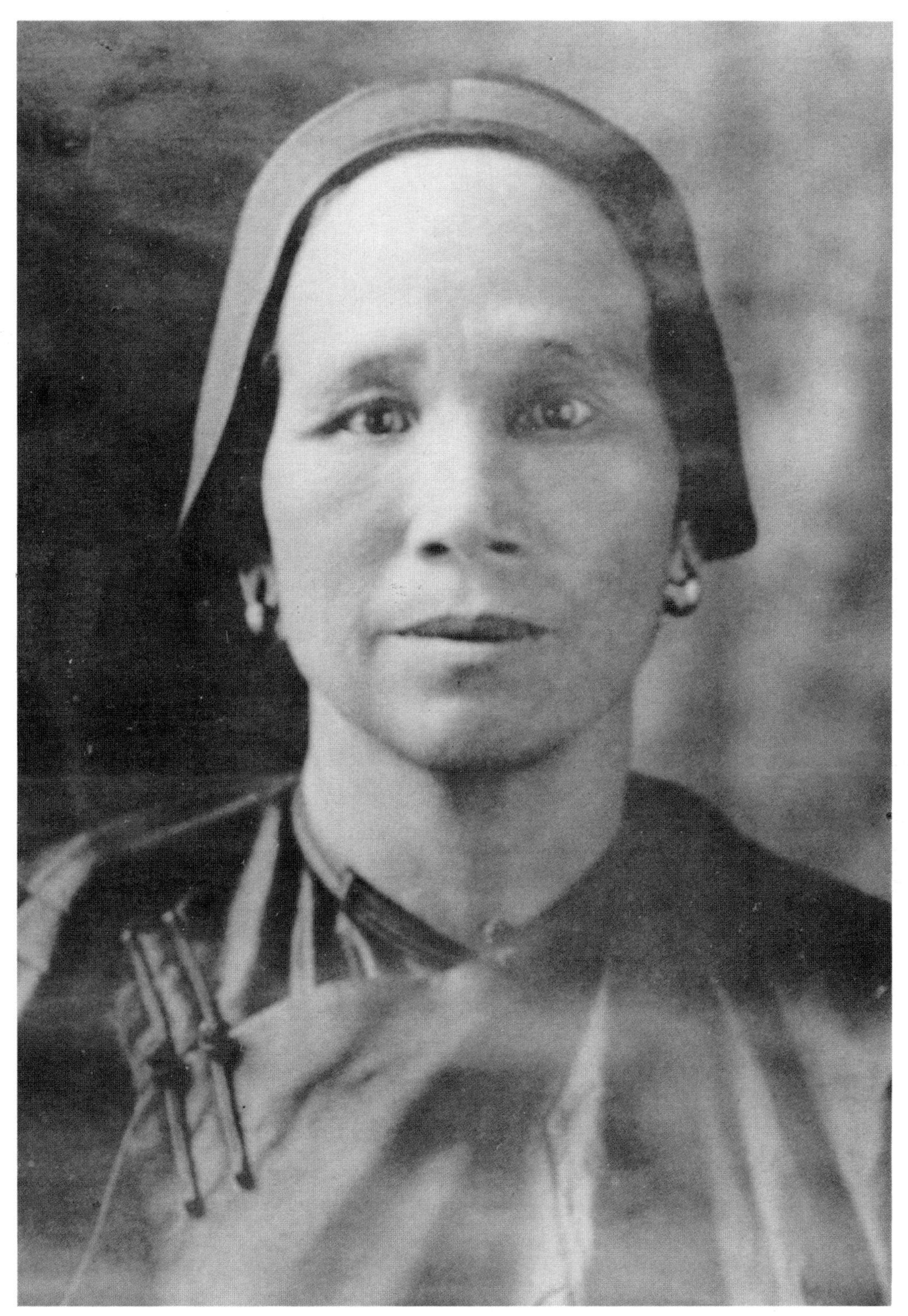

Char Ng Shee, On Char's mother, photographed in 1904. On Char kept the two portraits of his parents on the wall of his home throughout his life. Courtesy of On Char.

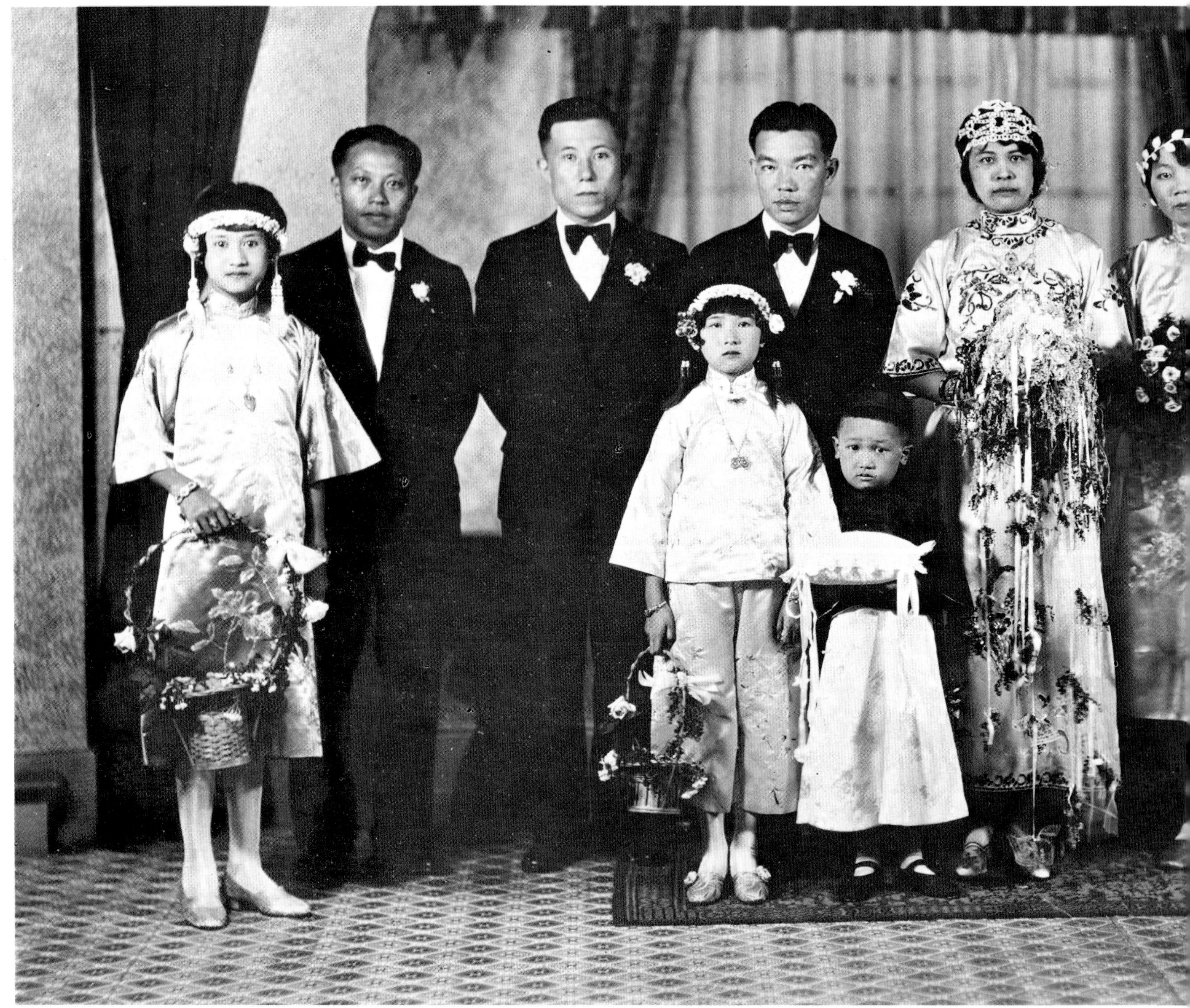

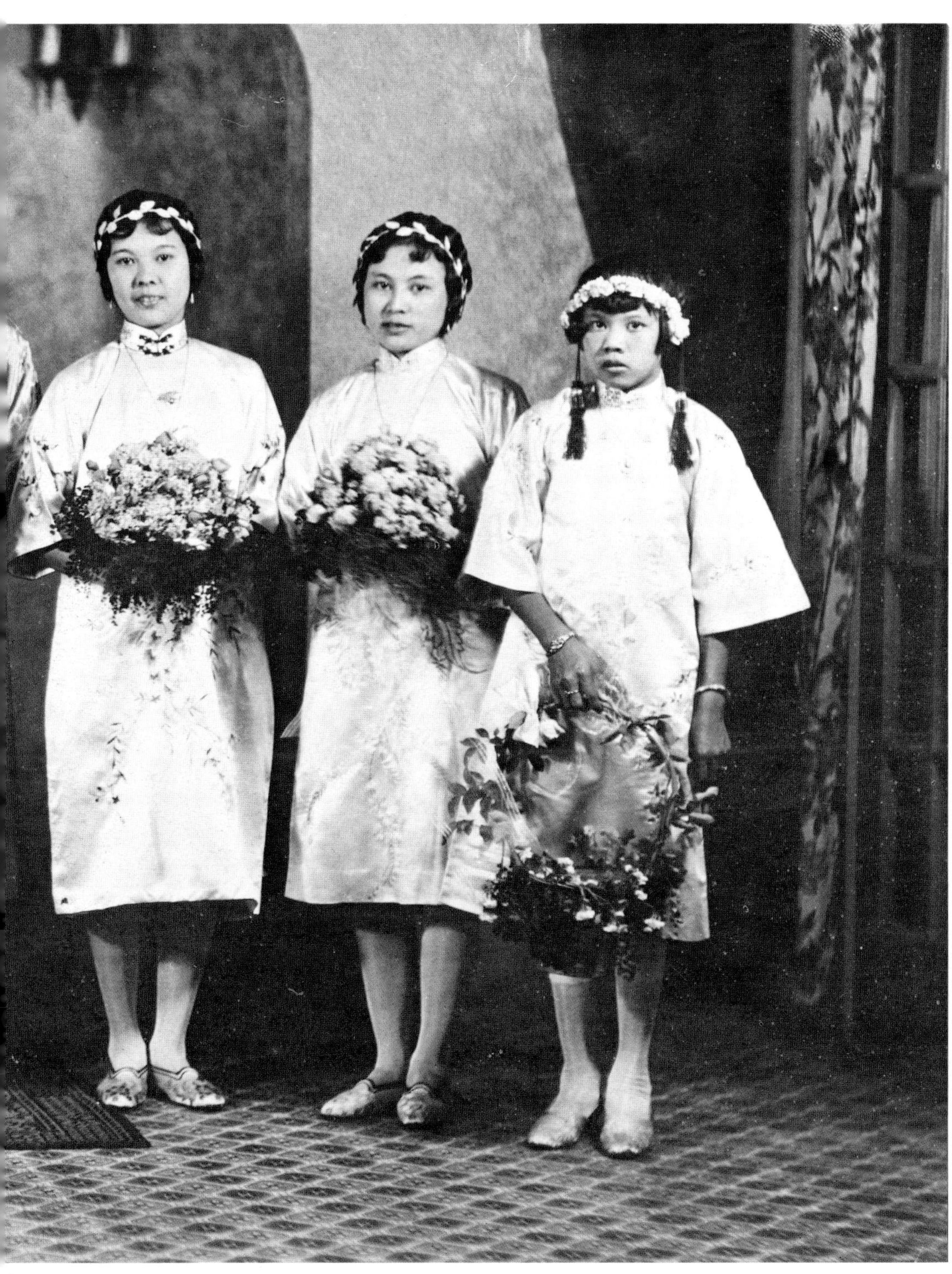

A wedding party, about 1915. On Char. Bernice P. Bishop Museum.

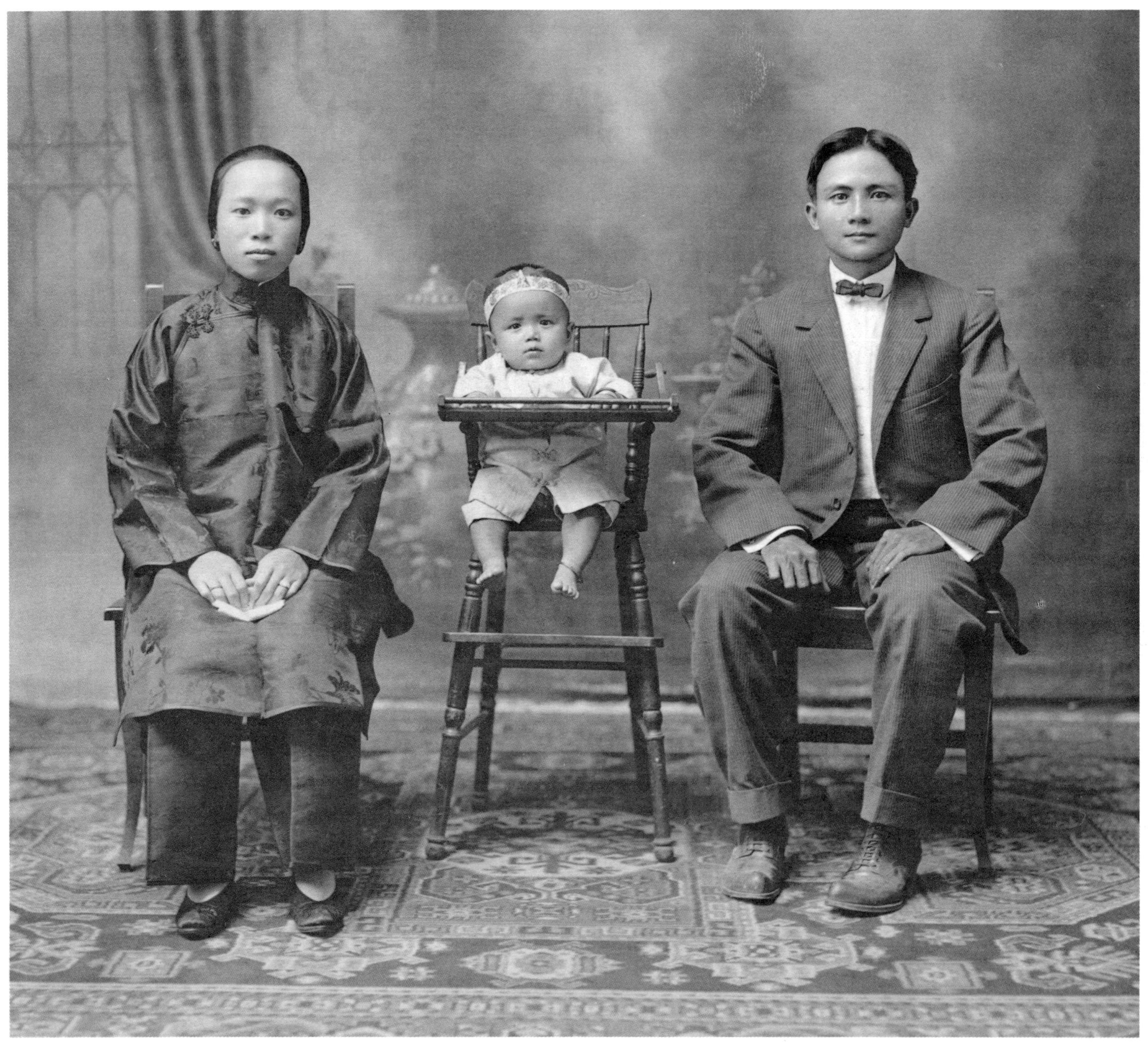

Left: A young couple pose with their first child, about 1915. On Char. Bernice P. Bishop Museum.

Below: An auspicious occasion is recorded for the family about 1915. On Char. Bernice P. Bishop Museum.

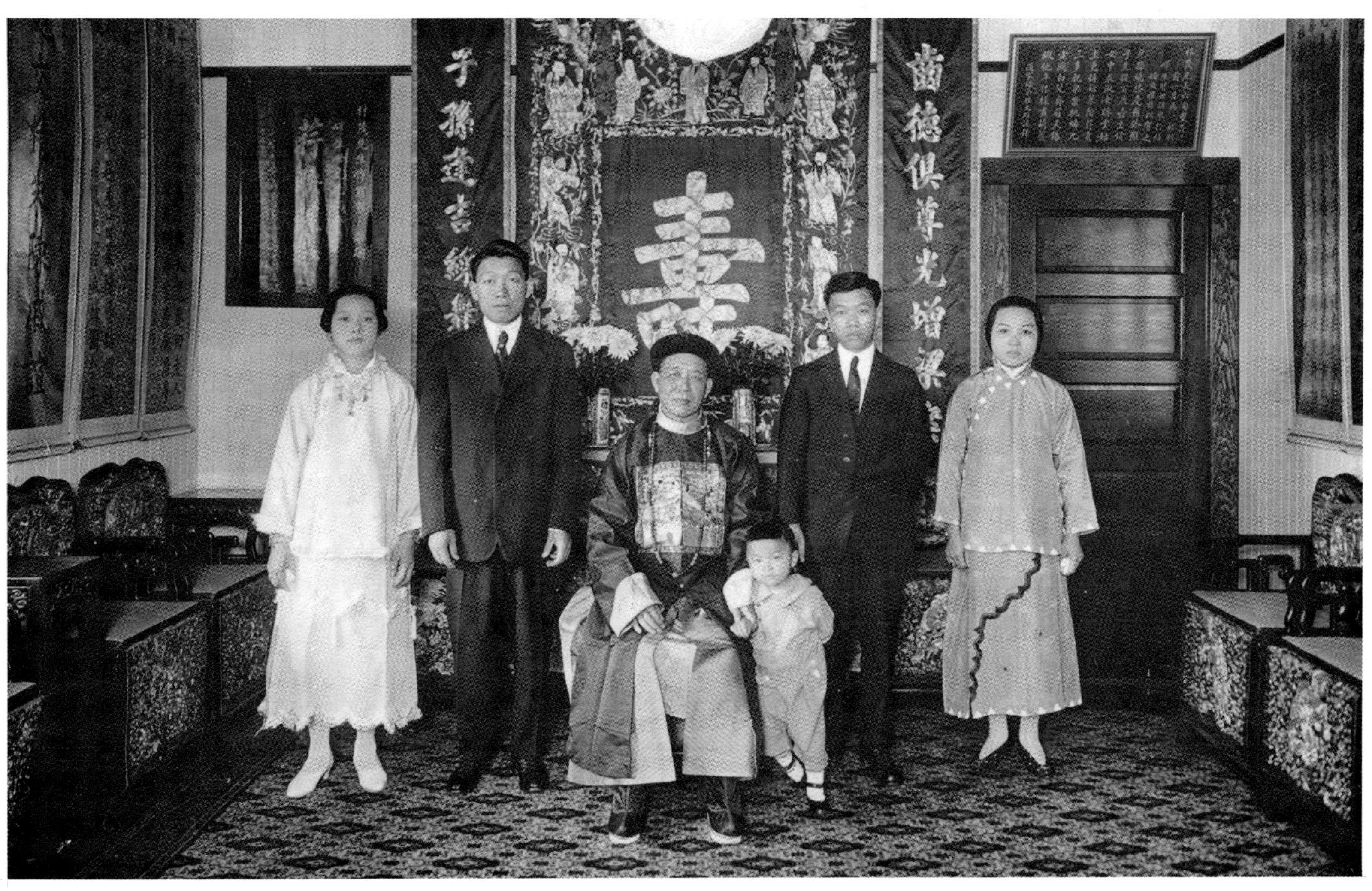

Right: Mother and three children about 1905. On Char. Bernice P. Bishop Museum.

Below: A growing family, about 1915. On Char. Bernice P. Bishop Museum.

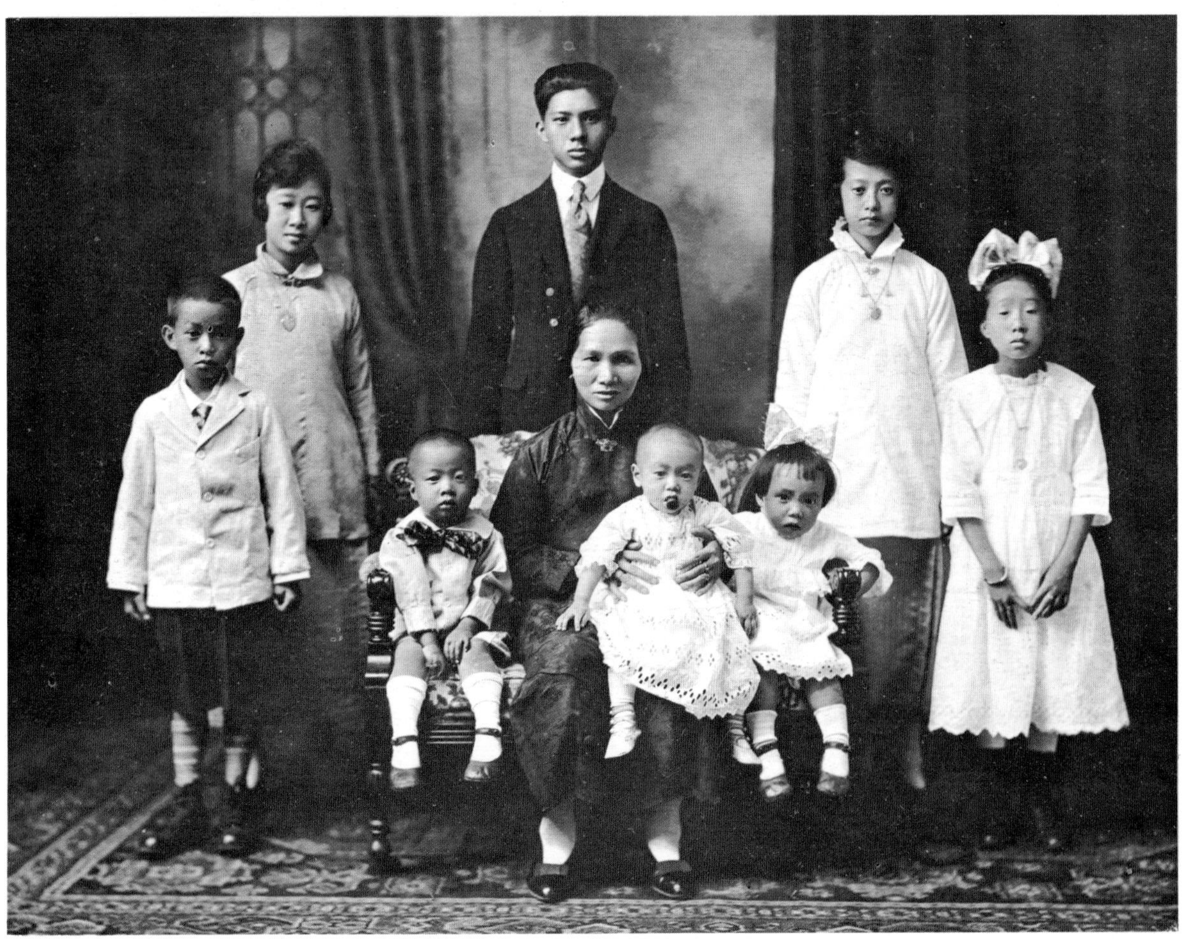

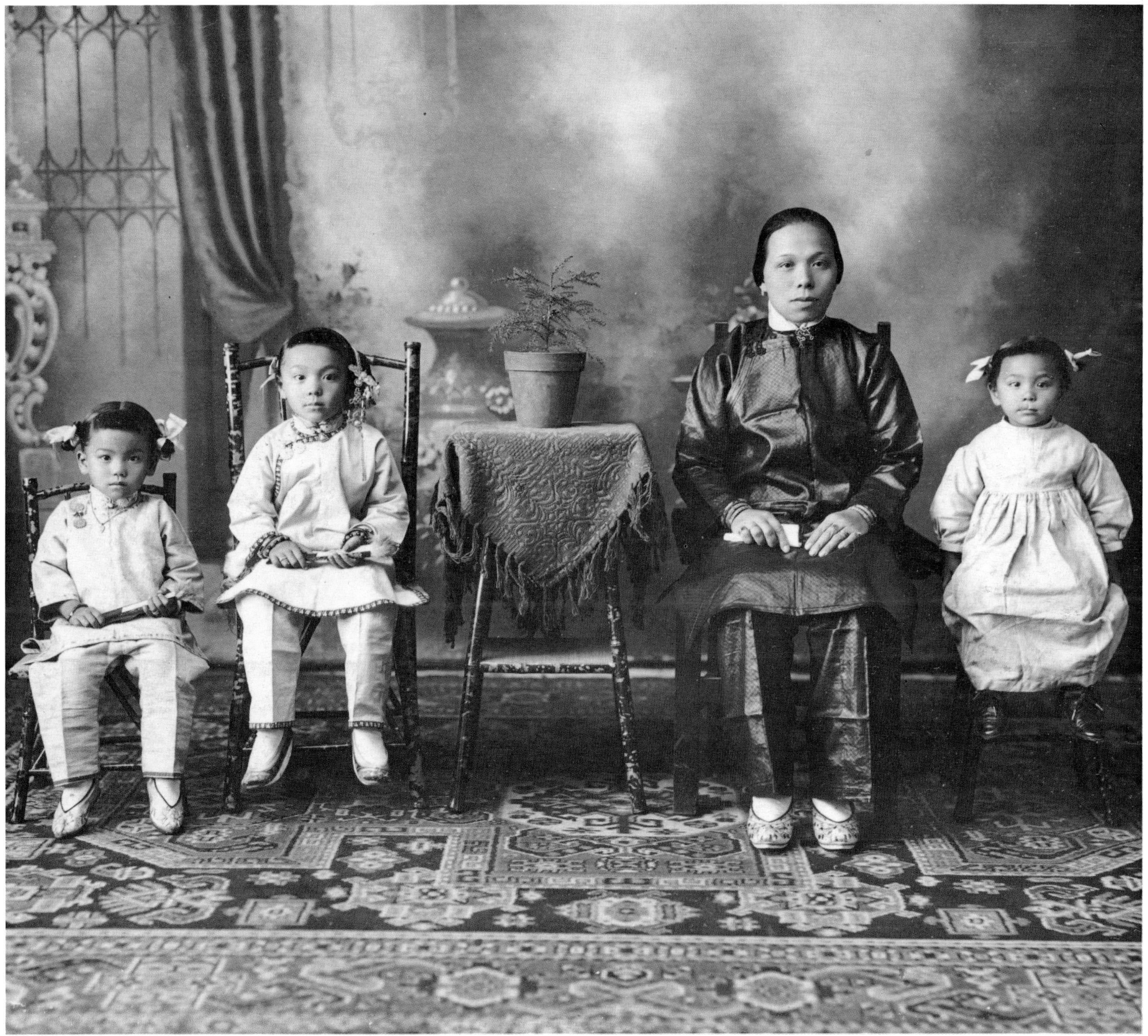

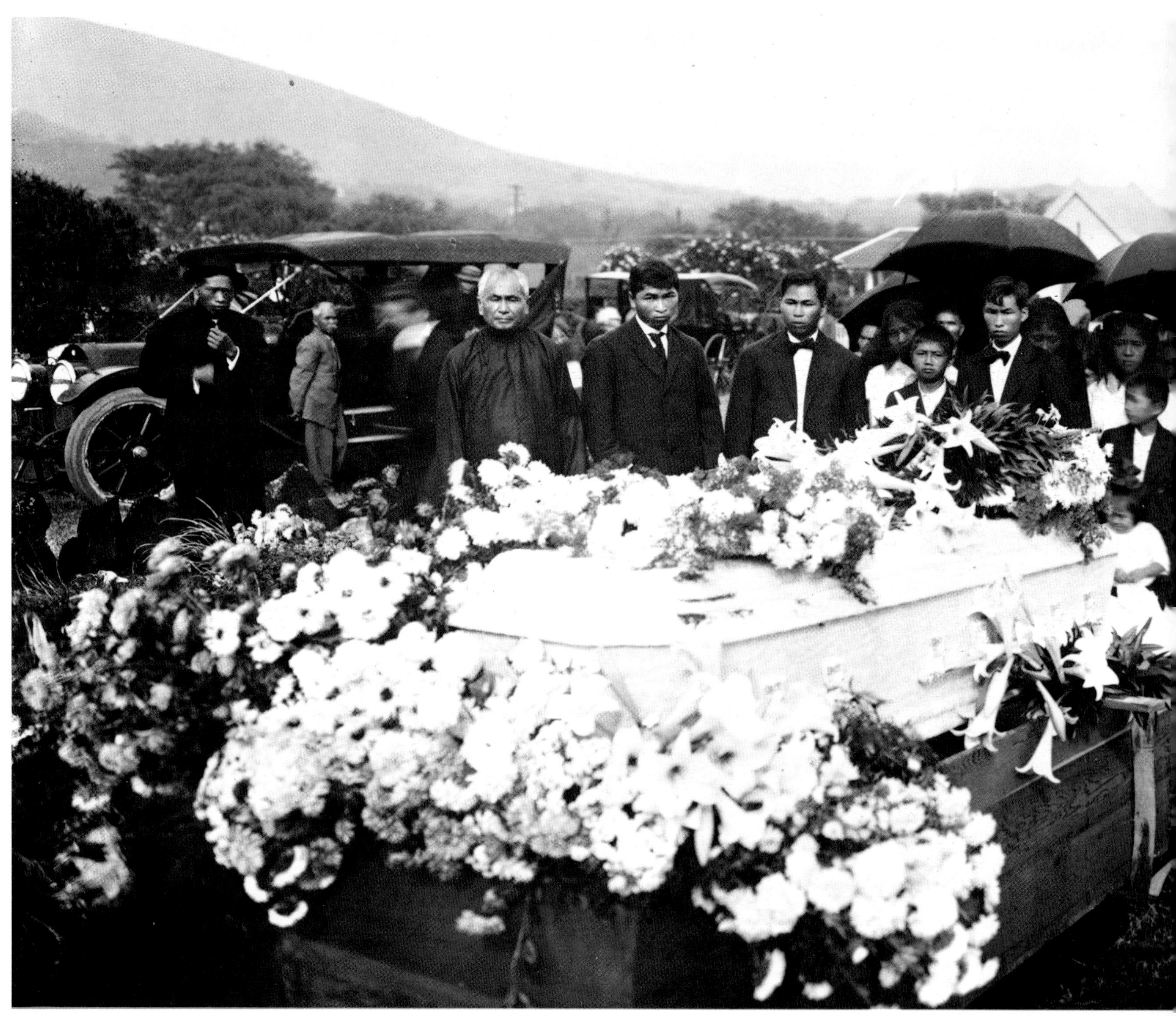

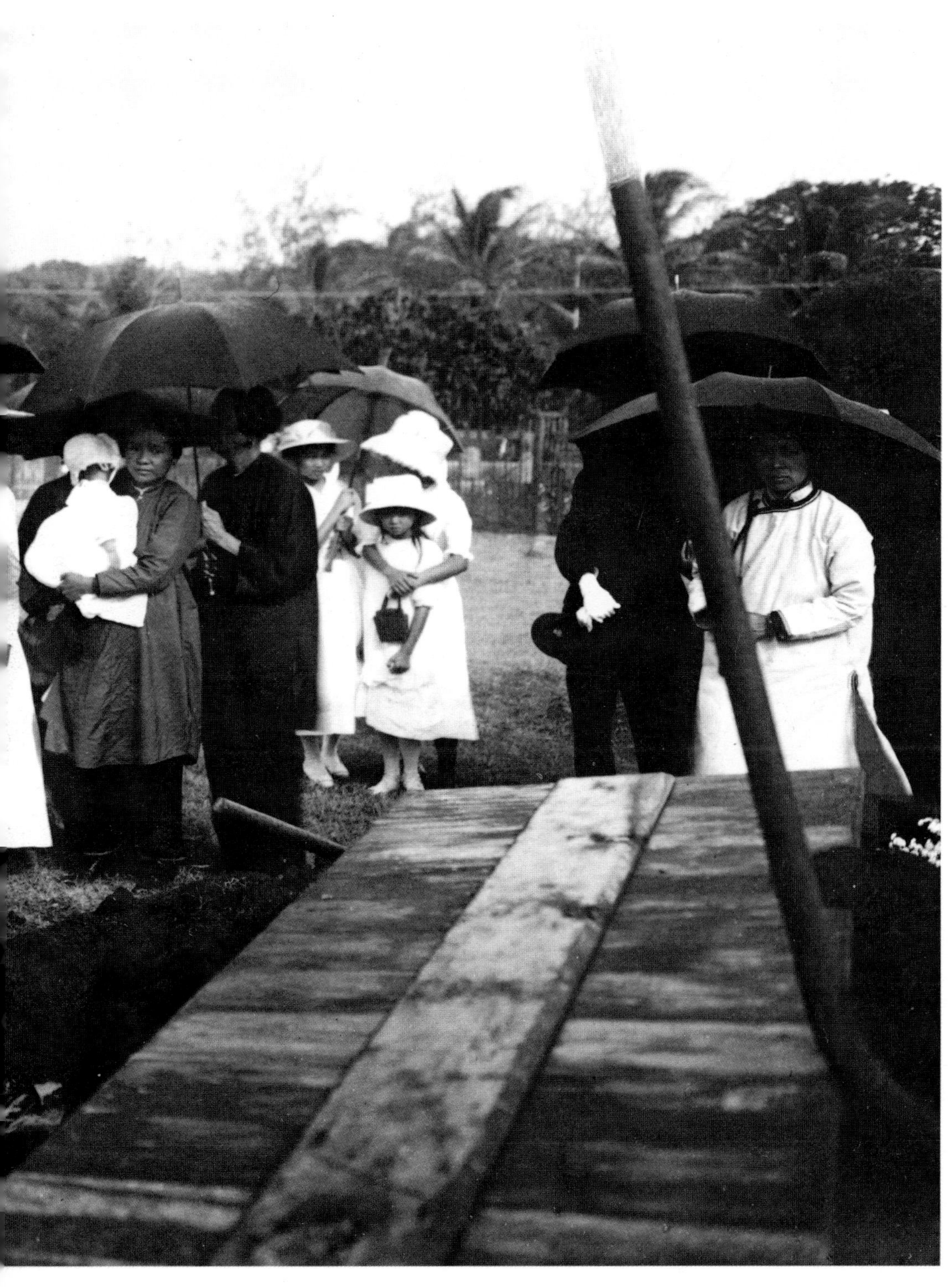

A funeral, 1915. On Char. Bernice P. Bishop Museum.

Theodore Kelsey receiving flower lei from Samantha Gibson at his 84th birthday party, August 4, 1975. Theresa Gutmanis (left) waits her turn to present lei. Photo by Richard H. Gibson. Courtesy of June Gutmanis.

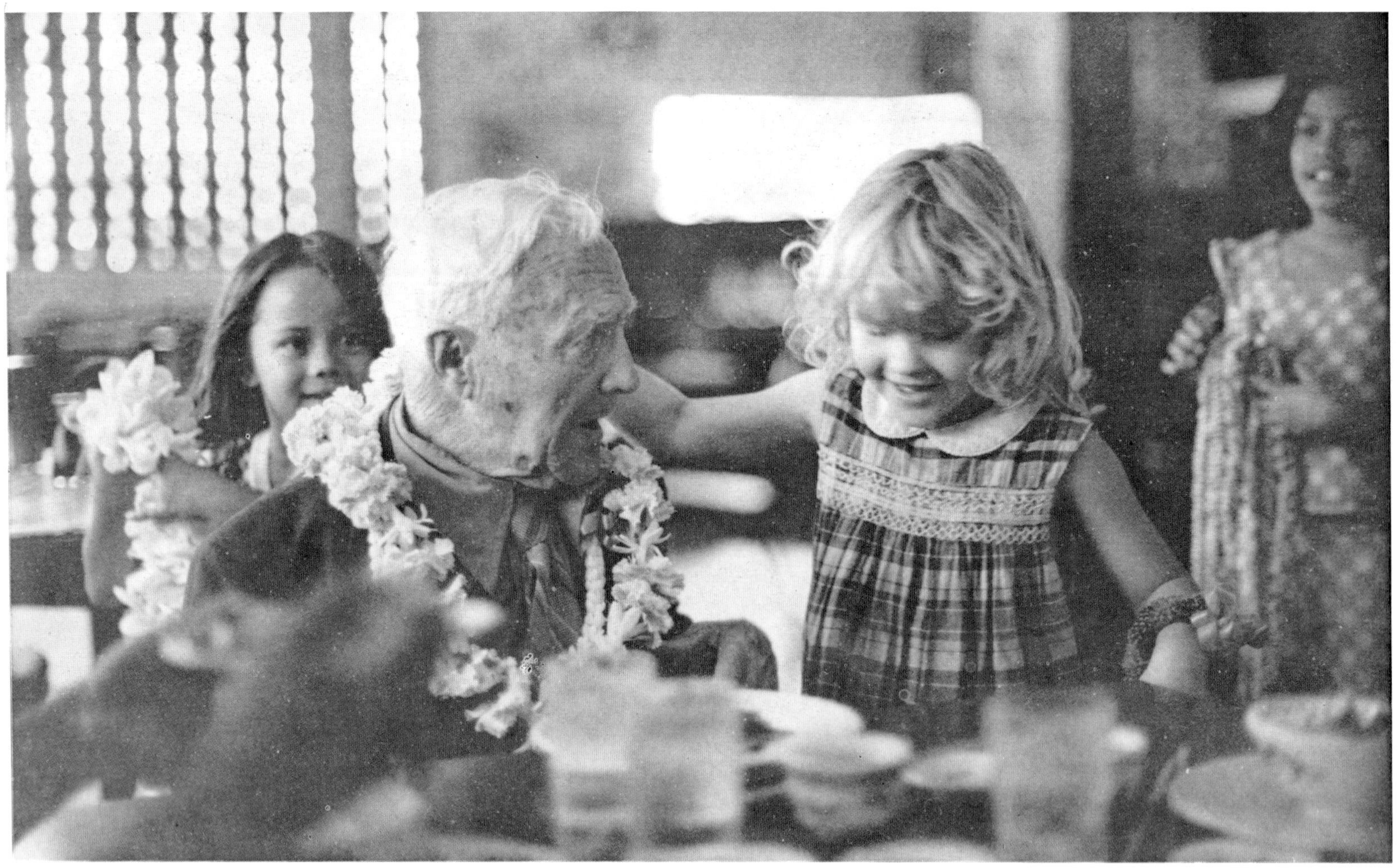

Theodore Kelsey

Theodore Kelsey arrived in the Hawaiian Islands in 1895. He was born in Seattle, Washington, four years earlier, on August 4, 1891, but he rapidly became absorbed in island life and remains, to the time of publication, actively interested in Hawaiian life, culture and language. To this day, Kelsey's letters on the proper use of Hawaiian terms still appear in the pages of Honolulu's daily papers. Much of Kelsey's youth was spent on the Island of Hawaii where his father ran various businesses in Hilo and Hamakua. In fact, it was his father who first interested Kelsey in photography and trained him in it. For a time Kelsey ran a photographic studio in offices above his father's store at the corner of Hualalai and Kilauea in Hilo. His business was, he recalls, almost exclusively in the sale of albums of island views, rather than in portrait work.

But photography was not the primary interest in Kelsey's life. When he was quite young, perhaps only eleven or twelve, Kelsey had come across a Japanese-Hawaiian-English phrase book. The book and the languages fascinated him and he began memorizing both Japanese and Hawaiian terms. Later, he recalls, he forgot the Japanese he had learned from the book. But he retained the Hawaiian along with an abiding interest in the Hawaiian culture.

When he was in his teens, Kelsey was sent to the mainland to complete his education. He stayed with family members in Cambridge, Massachusetts and then went to Nova Scotia where he graduated from the Horton Collegiate Academy. His academy work was intended to prepare Kelsey for college. In fact, Dr. Herbert Gregory, then director of the Bishop Museum, offered to pay a year's tuition for Kelsey at Yale, and offered him a museum job on his return to the islands. But, like a great many island children, Kelsey had found the climate on the mainland too harsh. He had no desire to leave Hawaii again and considered his time away during preparatory school years to be a time of exile.

Writing of the unaccepted opportunity years later, Kelsey said, "I have never been sorry, as very likely I would have missed the assistance of very helpful Hawaiian friends." And perhaps he is right, for Kelsey, with no university training, immediately launched himself into a career as an ethnographer of the Hawaiian culture, a career that gained him some professional recognition and honor from archaeologists but, more important, gained him a lifetime of close and satisfying work and friendship within the Hawaiian community.

Throughout his career, Theodore Kelsey considered his photography to be of little or no importance. His work was in the gathering, recording and understanding of the Hawaiian language and culture. Photography was at best merely a means of supporting his work in ethnography and the sale of his albums of island views made the continuation of that work possible. But Kelsey did oblige many of his Hawaiian friends by taking photographs of them and of their families with the five by seven inch view camera he ordinarily used for his album work. Many of these photographs are posed — generally on the front porch or in the yard of some modest dwelling. But all, despite being posed, have an unstudied quality thoroughly in keeping with Kelsey's attitude toward his photography. Photography simply was not important to Theodore Kelsey. His photographs, perhaps as a result, remain important.

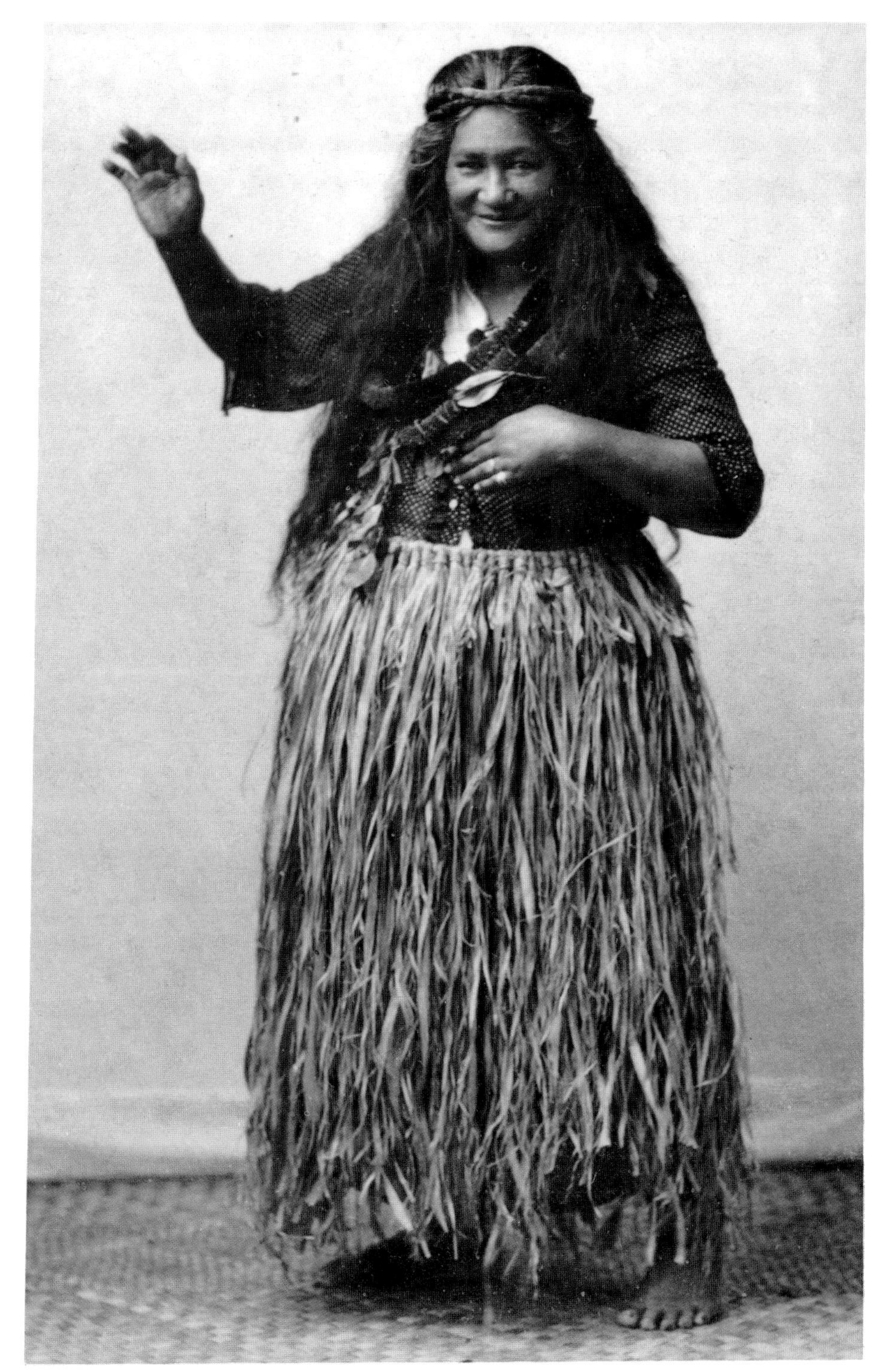

Mrs. Mary Kaoulionalani Pahio, at Hilo, Hawaii, about 1925. T. Kelsey. Hawaii Historical Society.

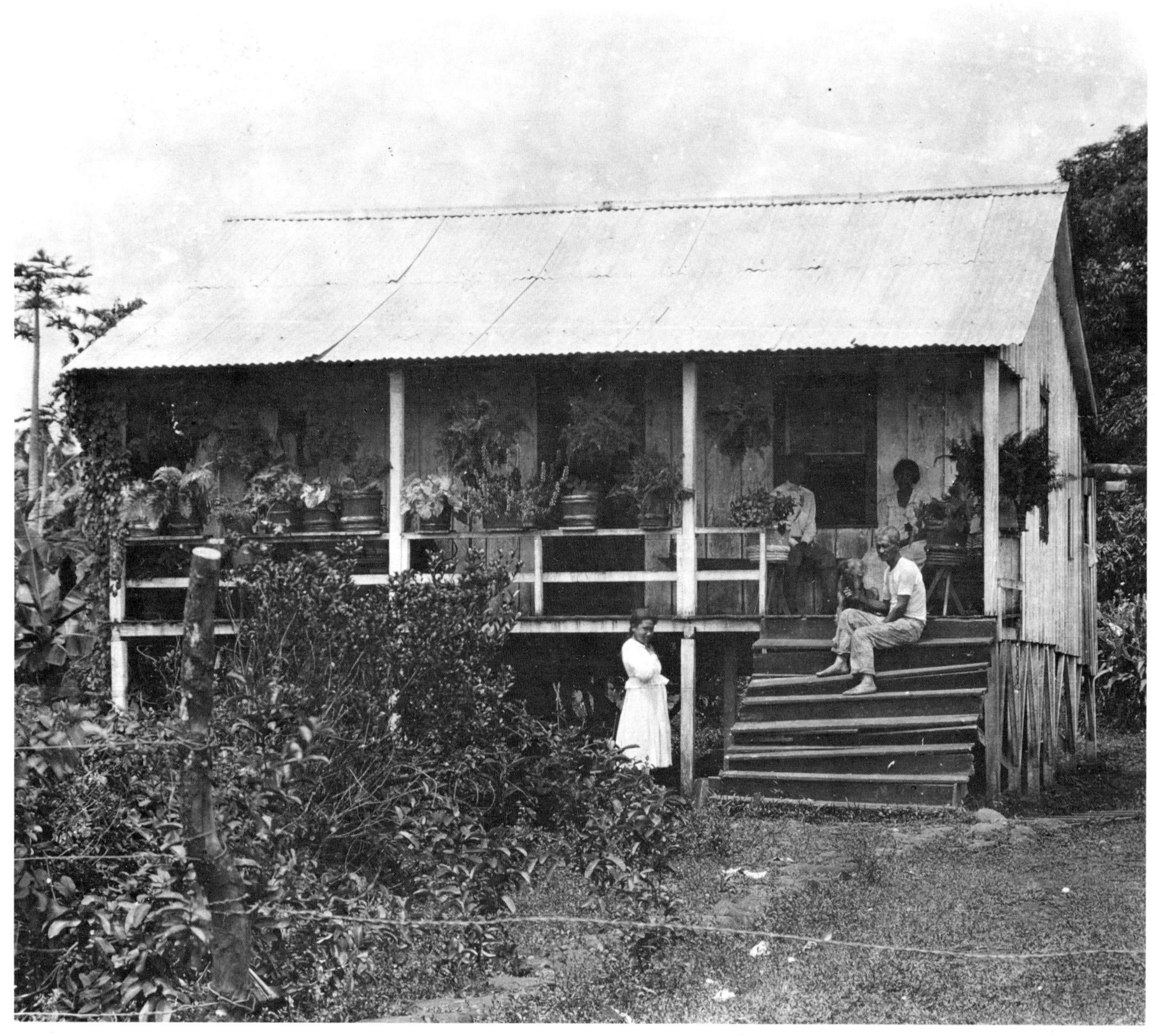

Left: Home of river guide Lameka Ahulau in Pahonua, Hilo, about 1925. T. Kelsey. Hawaiian Historical Society.

Below: Lameka Ahulau and family on front porch, 1925. T. Kelsey. Hawaiian Historical Society.

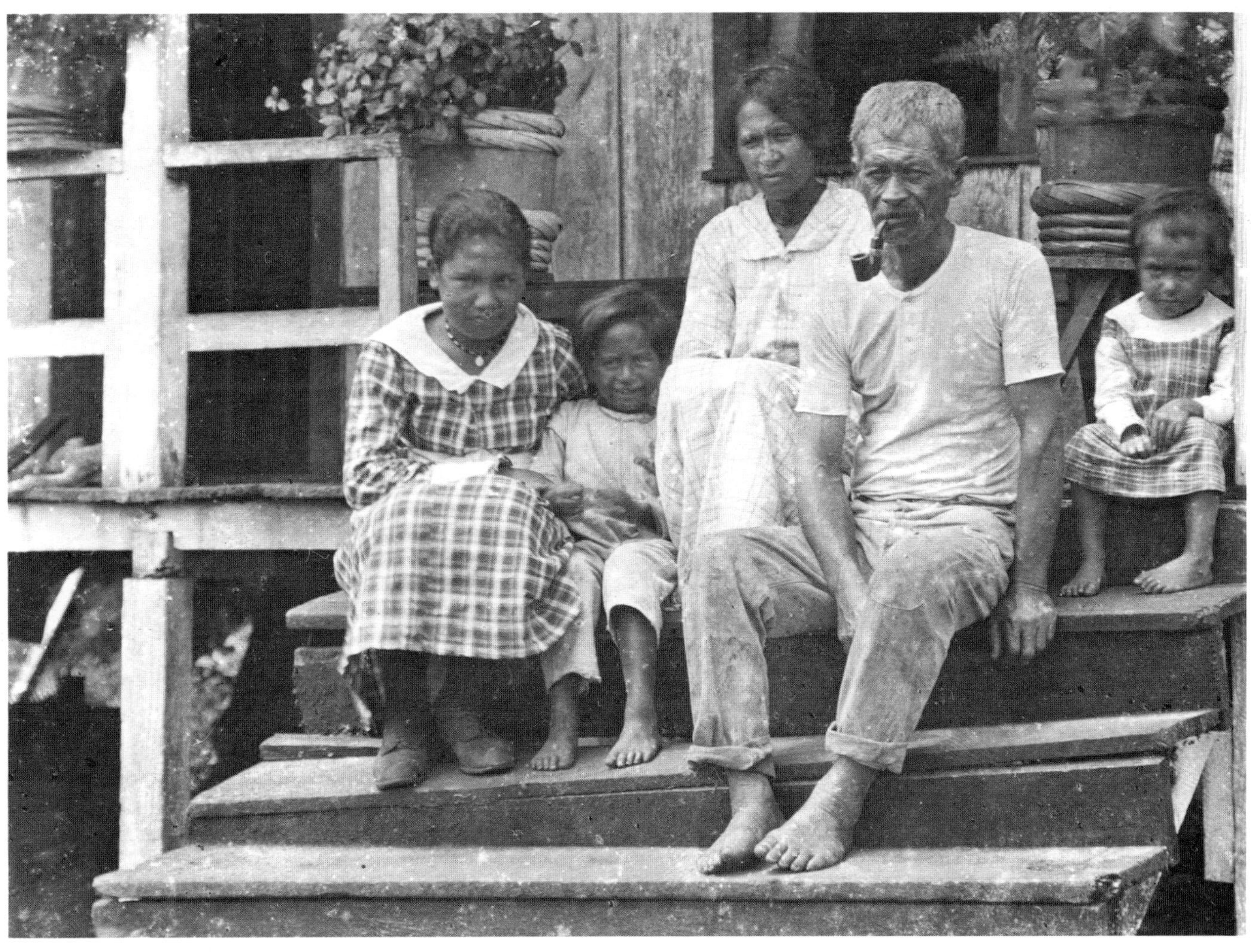

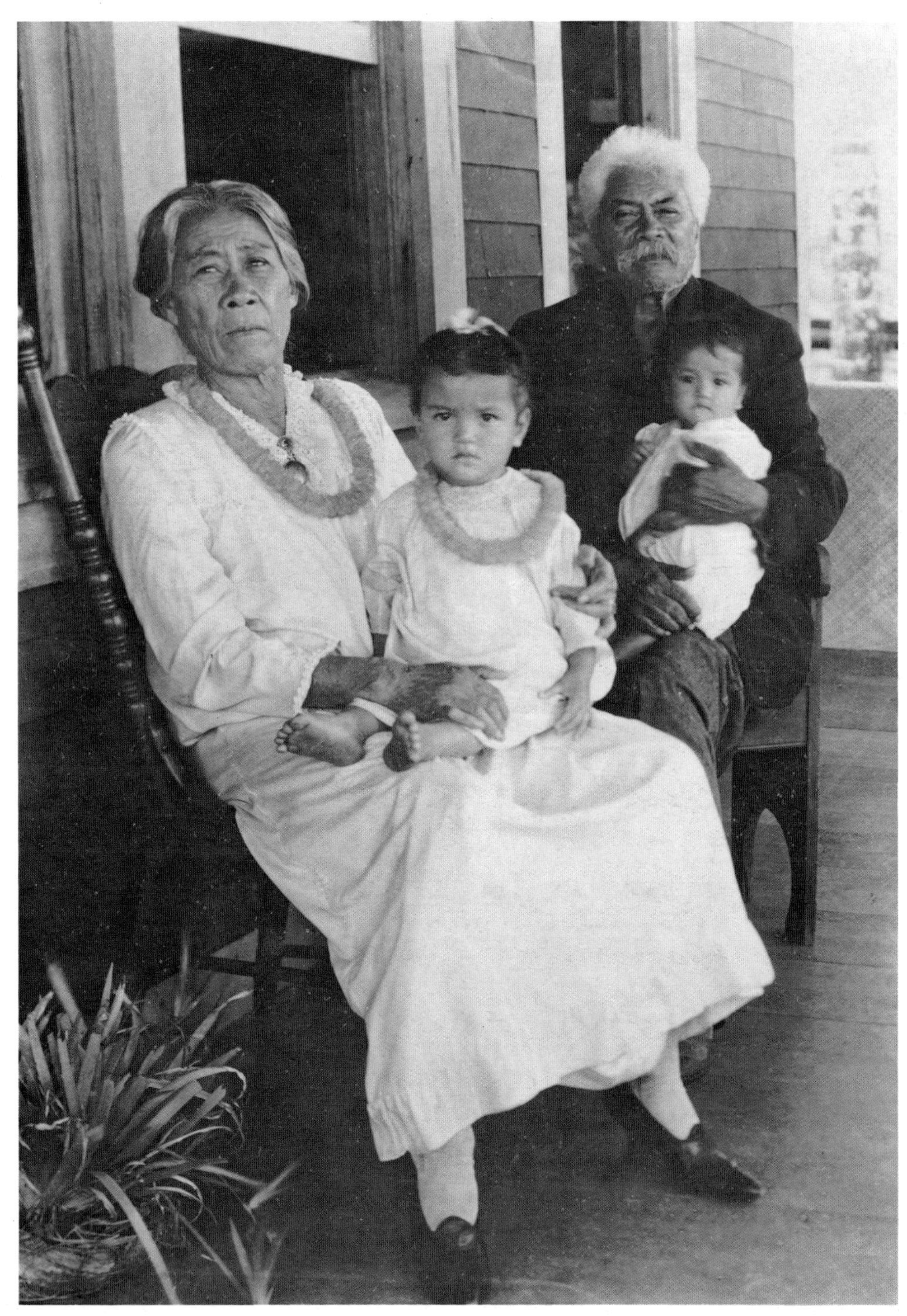

Left: Mr. and Mrs. Daniel Hoolapa and their grandchildren, Kahaluu, North Kona, 1925. T. Kelsey. Hawaiian Historical Society.

Right: A group of men on the Island of Hawaii, about 1925. Driver is Kapihe, who later became a Honolulu streetcar driver and retired to Kaimuki. T. Kelsey. Hawaiian Historical Society.

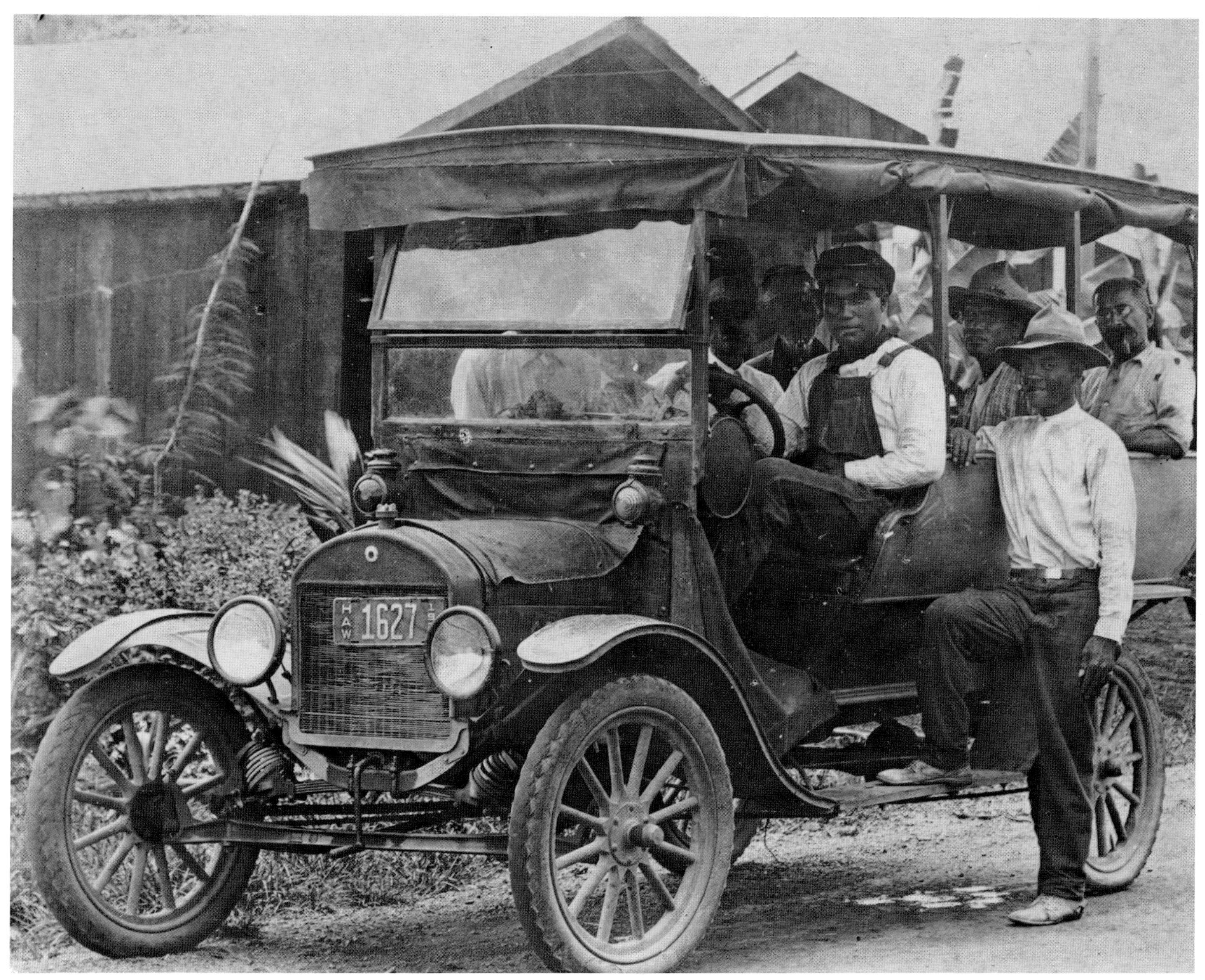
HAW 1627

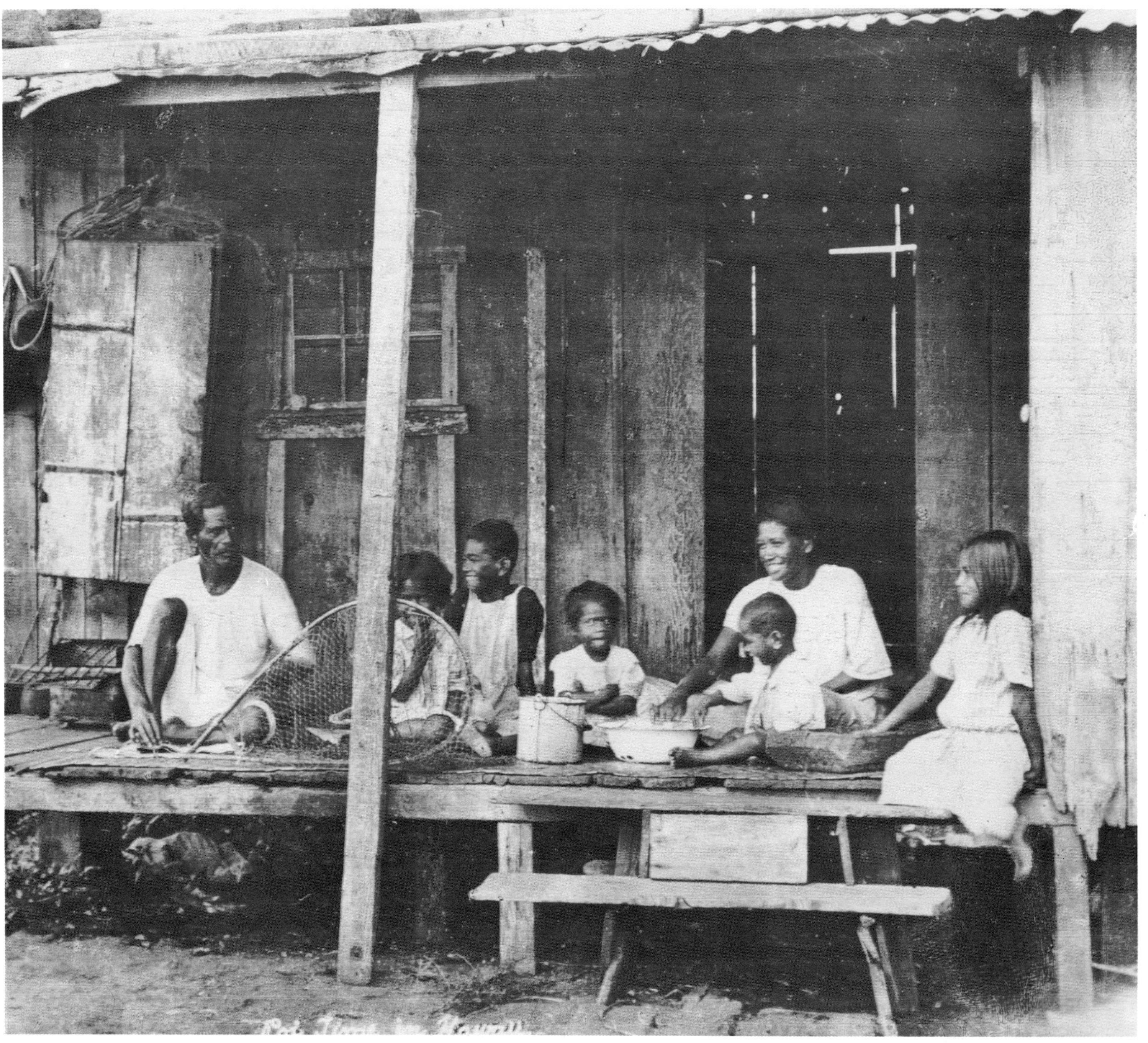

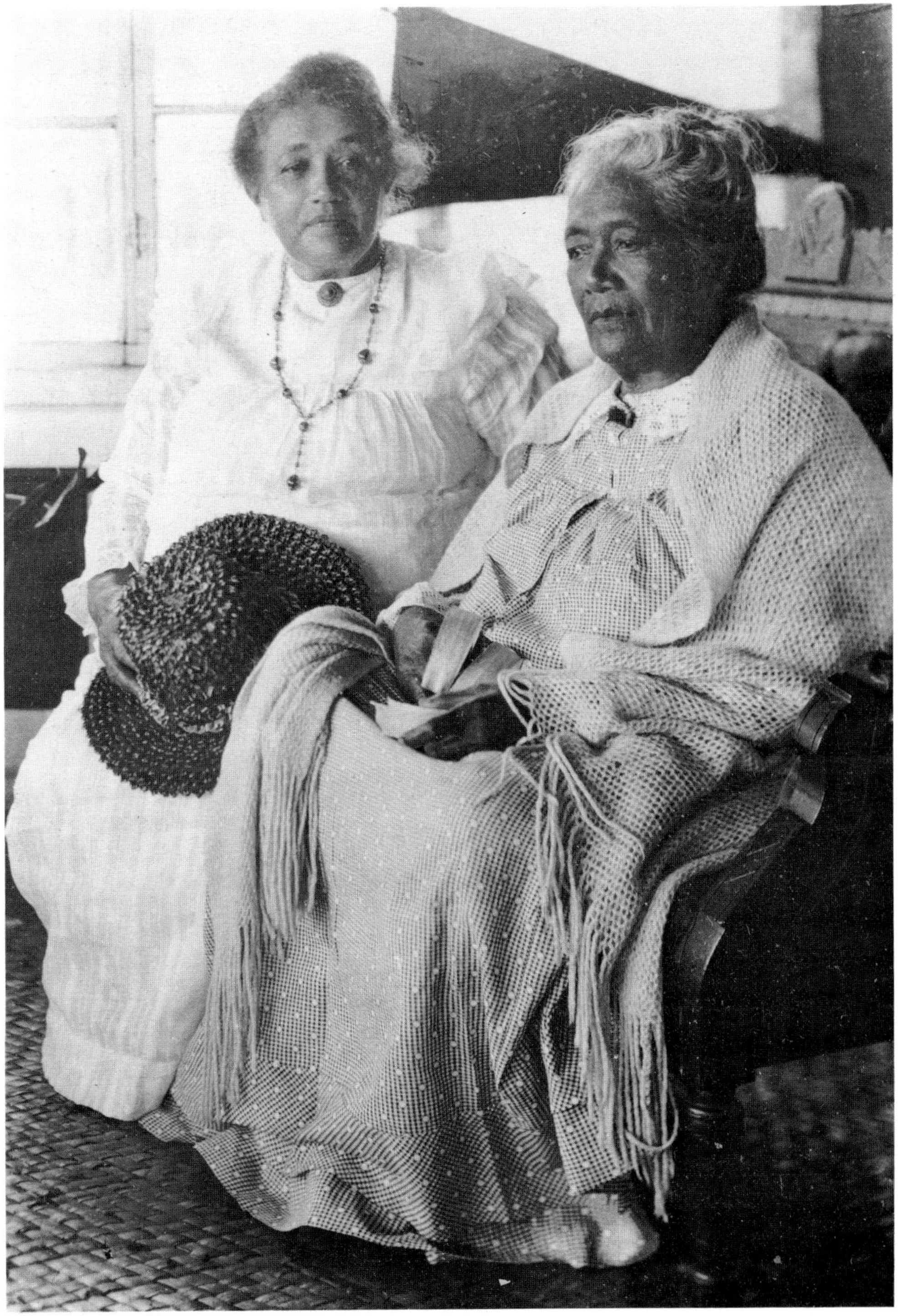

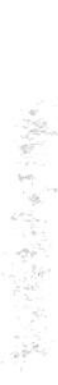

Left: David Malo and his family, at Waiuli, Keaukaha, about 1925. T. Kelsey. Hawaiian Historical Society.

Right: Mrs. Conradt and her daughter, Kukona Porter, Hilo, about 1925. T. Kelsey. Hawaiian Historical Society.

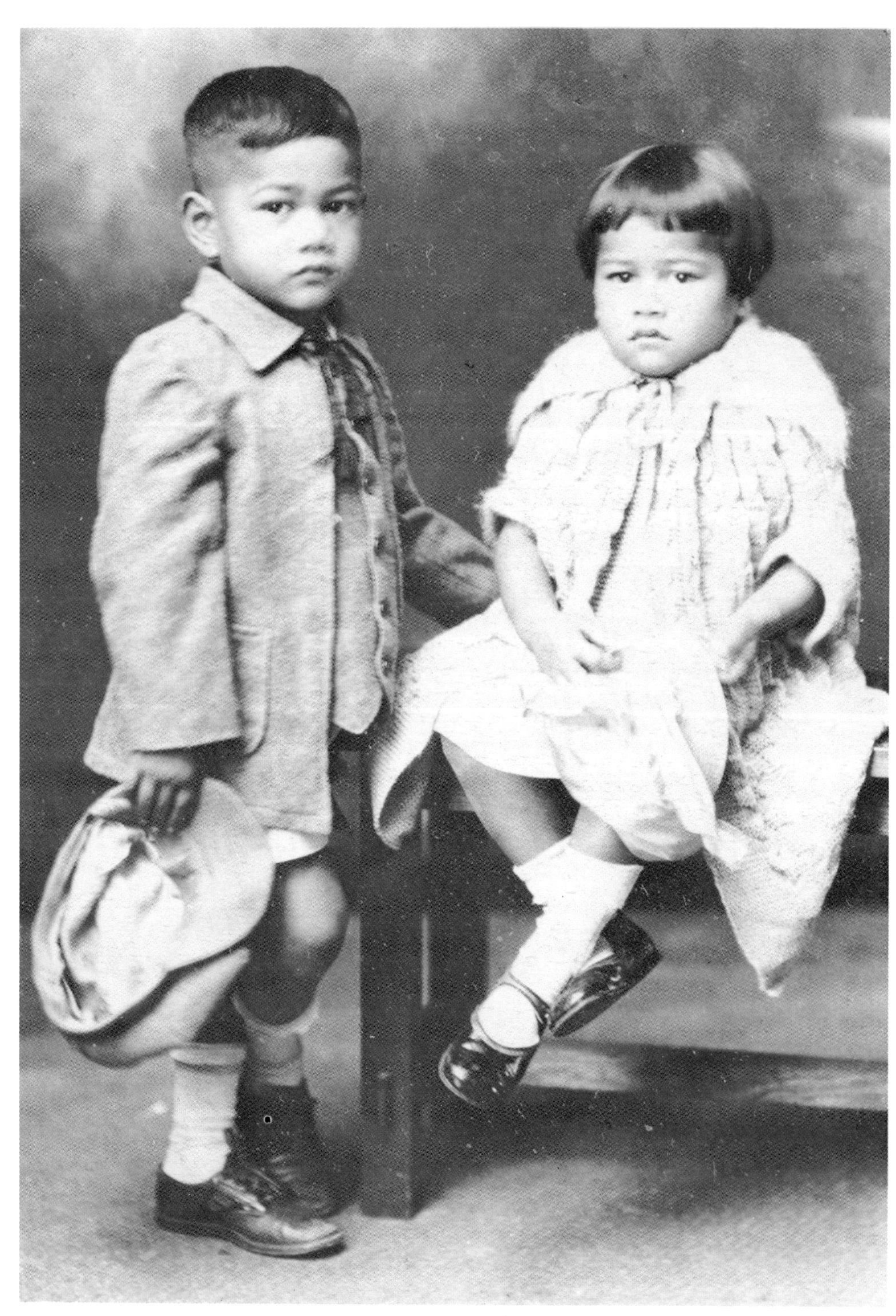

Two children, about 1925. T. Kelsey. Hawaiian Historical Society.

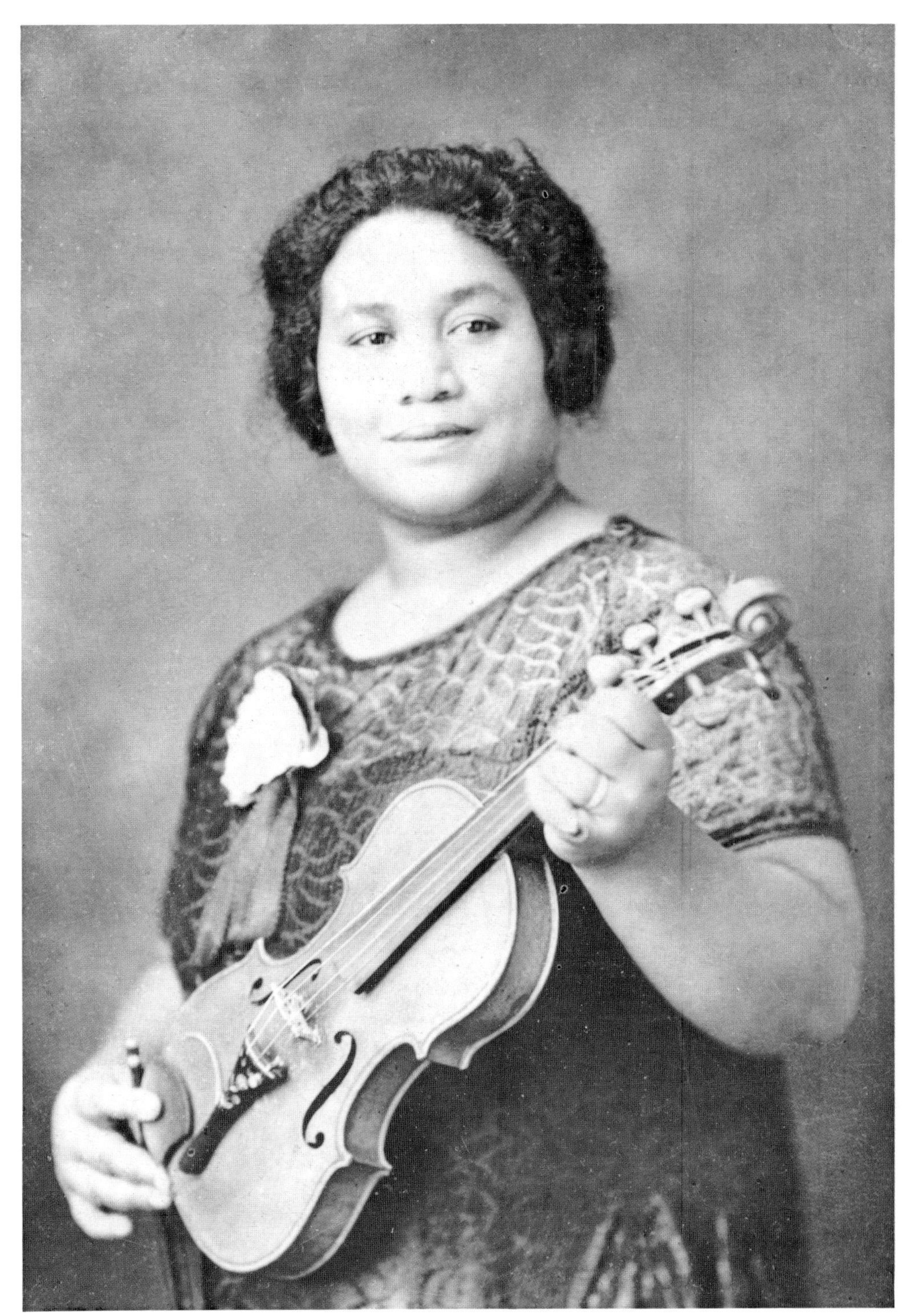

Mary Iokepa, daughter of Hilo police sergeant Philip Iokepa, 1925. T. Kelsey. Hawaiian Historical Society.

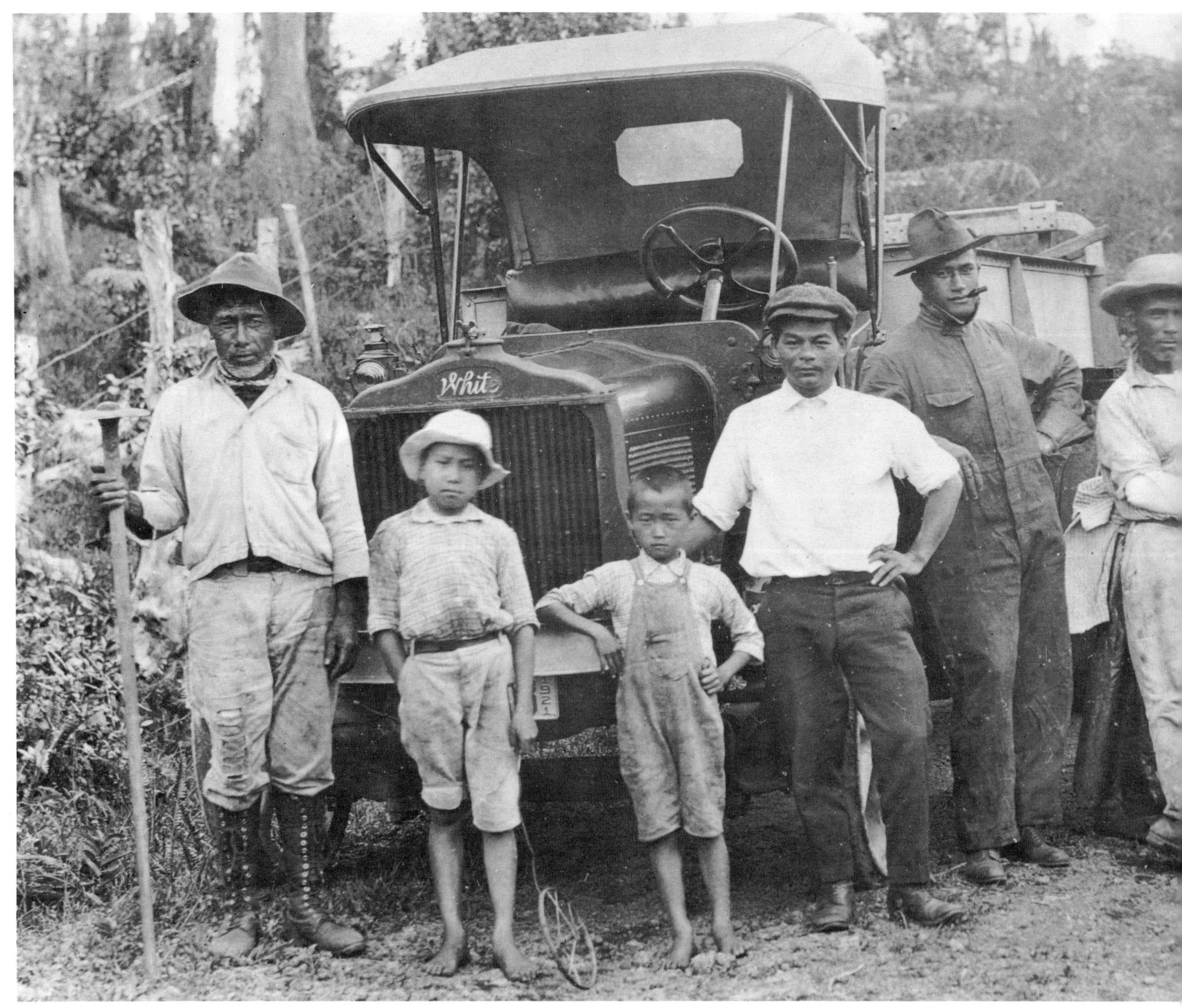
White

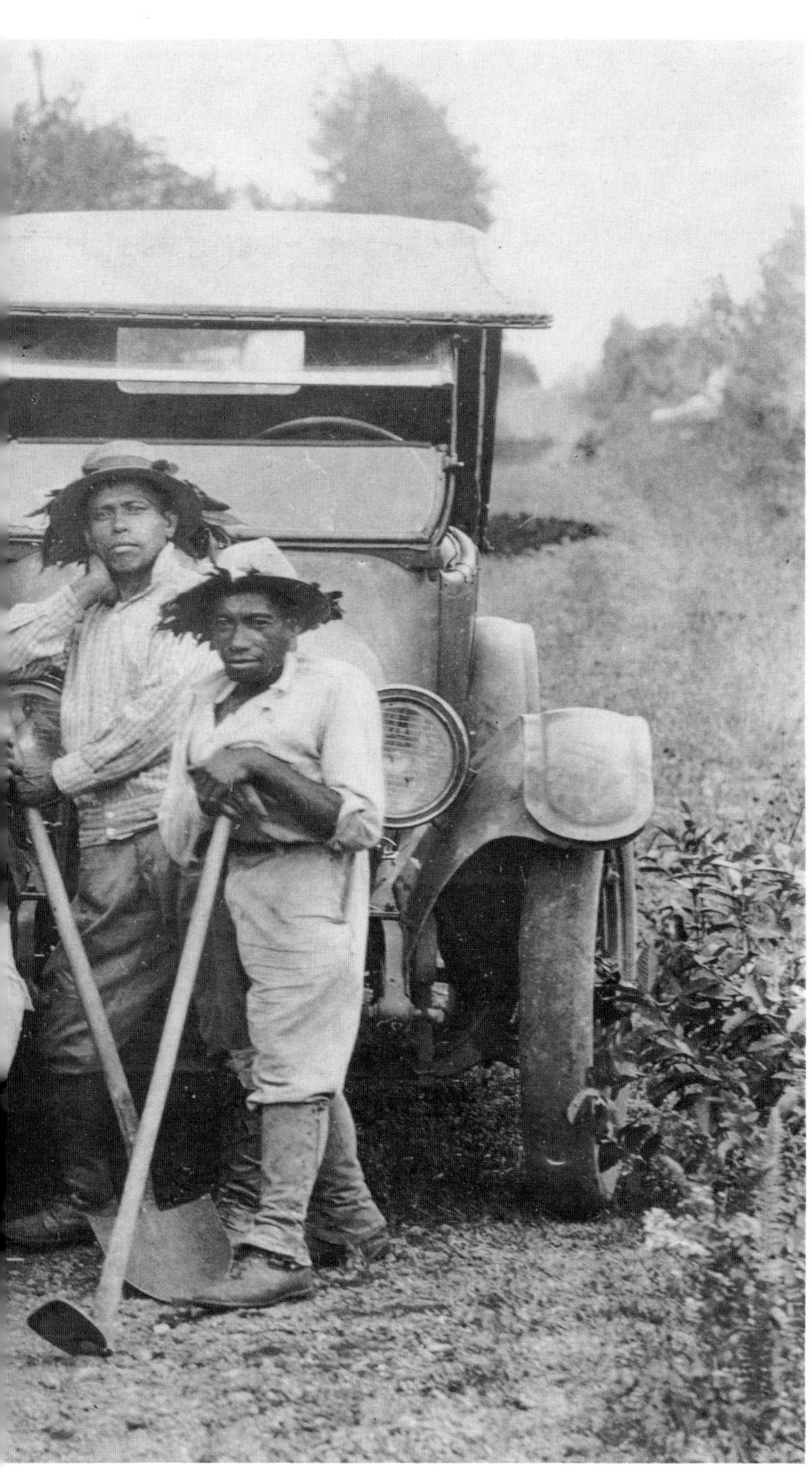

Road workers at Olaa, 1925. T. Kelsey. Hawaiian Historical Society.

Tai Sing Loo in the late 1940s. He used this motorbike to travel about Pearl Harbor. Photographer unknown. Courtesy Mrs. Tai Sing Loo.

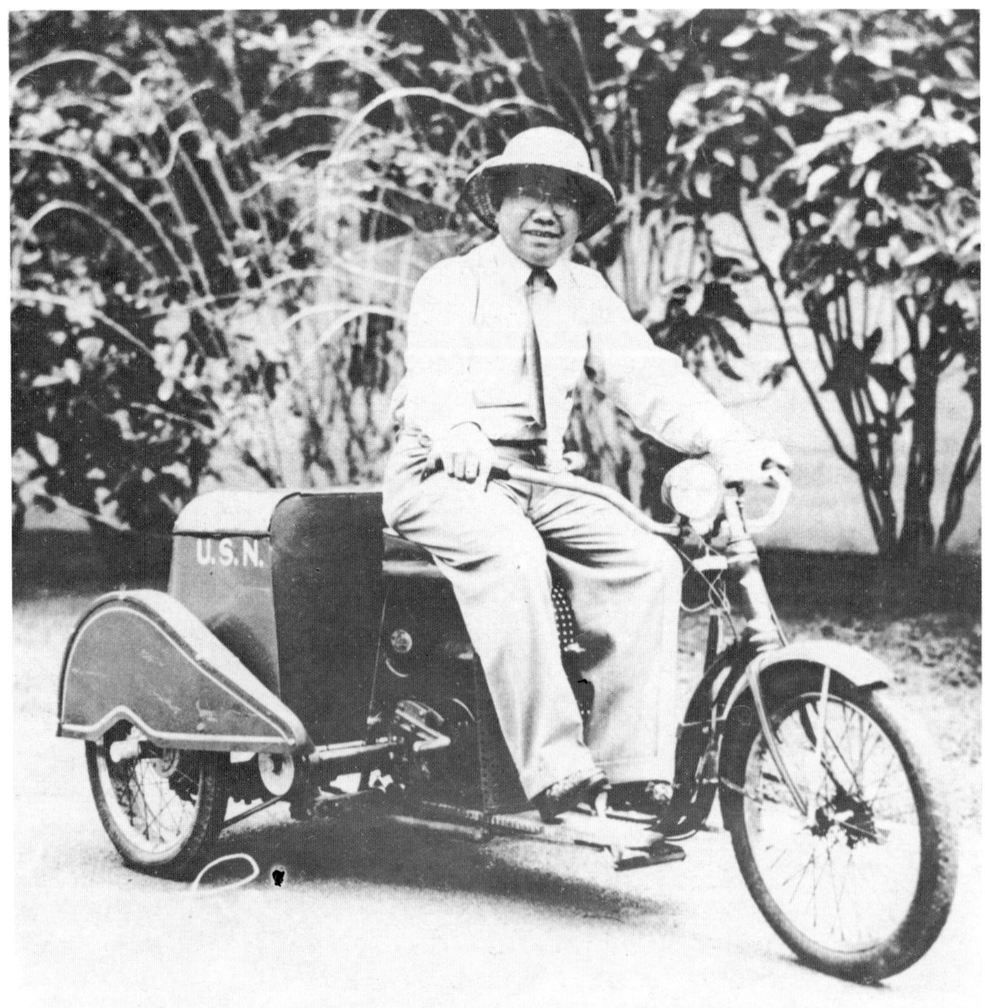

Tai Sing Loo

When the Japanese attacked Pearl Harbor on December 7, 1941, Tai Sing Loo, Pearl Harbor's official photographer, was without his camera. His instinct was to get to his studio inside Pearl Harbor as quickly as possible and begin recording the battle on film. But he never made it to his cameras. Instead, he spent the day and most of the evening organizing squads to help fight fires, directing traffic that had become snarled in the confusion, and locating and delivering food to exhausted and hungry rescue workers.

The Pearl Harbor battle topped the list of historic events during Loo's long career as official photographer of the base, but it was the only one he did not record on film. Characteristically, Loo's career is marked by the thoroughness and the energy with which he went about his work. Visiting politicians, presidents, congressional representatives, movie stars, admirals and generals all had their photographs taken by Loo, both while inspecting Pearl Harbor and while touring the volcano — a tour that seemed for many years to be a mandatory part of the visit of any notable to the islands. Workers on Pearl Harbor building projects, members of base athletic teams and ordinary seamen on parade also had their pictures taken by Tai Sing Loo. Indeed, by the time he retired from his 31 years as base photographer, Loo had left a complete record of life at the Pearl Harbor base as he had witnessed it.

Tai Sing Loo was born in Honolulu in 1886. His parents were not well off and Loo left school at the age of 12 in order to help support his family. When he was 76 years of age, Loo recorded the high points of his life and career in a written memoir. What his notes lack in formal schooling they more than make up in vividness: it is clear that Loo was a man with a zest for life and for his work. It seems appropriate then, to allow Loo's own words to speak for him, for he was a man who observed well and with humor.

Loo recalls one incident from his early working life that may strike a familiar note with many readers: "I was very lucky I was offer another job in the Cigar Store as salesman to wait on customers buy cigars and cigarettes, soda water counter. I was 14 years old, I was very short in height. I have to stand on an empty soda water box to look through the counter door. The customers are very nice to me and pleasant smile at me when I hand them the box of cigars or cigarettes. I am very curious one day I tried to learn how to smoke a Cock & Gold tip cigarette from London, sale for 10¢ each, first experience to attempt to try to smoke, I choke myself. Never again. Another temptation learn to smoke cigar sold for 50¢ each. Germany best brand. I try to patch up the small hole in it and puff one or two times, the result was I was too dizzy, my headache, since now I never touch the smoke — that teach me a good lesson of the temptation to use the evil drug, also the drinking liquor or beer and evil gambling. I thank the Lord for guidance."

Despite his youthful encounter with "the evil drug," that selling job led to a series of other selling positions and in 1908 Loo found himself on the Big Island as a "drummer of dry goods and shoes". It was while he was on Hawaii that Loo first heard the suggestion that he should take up a career in photography. It was during that same trip that volcanoes, one of Loo's lifelong photographic interests, first became an object of fascination to him. His memoir tells of this time:

"Mr. Chock Chong own the Standard Drug Store. He say I should be a photographer, very good talent and judgment of subjects. He show me many places of beautiful scenic view. Another friend, Mr. Chun, I knew him in Honolulu, one day he and I went out to the Puna district to see the sightseeing — the lava mold, tree ferns and warm spring which I take some nice picture, myself stand alongside, which I have in my collection. Suddenly an earthquake, the road crack side open, the little calf fall into the crack. I have the opportunity to take a rare picture. I mislay my negative. I have no record."

In 1909, Loo went to work for the Gurrey Art Shop in Honolulu. Gurrey, the husband of photographer Caroline Haskins Gurrey, took Loo with him that year on a buying trip to California. It was Loo's first trip outside Hawaii and he has preserved some bittersweet memories of it: "I went to have my hair cut next door to the hotel. The barber refuse me to have my hair cut, therefore I have to go up to the Chinatown to have my hair cut. So I take the slow walking to the Chinatown — it's give me the opportunity to see the famous Chinatown in San Francisco in 1906 the ruin of the earthquake destruction big area Chinatown three years ago. I am very glad to see the great area where all the homes were destroyed, still some remaining and the Fairmount Hotel still intact up the hill. The Chinatown Chinese are very surprise to see me, a small boy alone in San Francisco from Hawaii. I have a very happy enjoy the friendship which no color line. I have my hair cut at last."

Loo continued working for Gurrey until 1918. The Gurrey shop had a contract, during those years, to do all photo finishing work for the Navy Department of Public Works. In 1918, the Navy photographer left Hawaii and recommended Loo as his successor. Loo took the job and continued in it until his retirement in 1949. After a long and active retirement, he died in Honolulu in 1971.

During his career as official photographer for Pearl Harbor, Loo never gave up his interest in Madame Pele. In fact, over the years, he accompanied innumerable Navy excursions to the Big Island and arranged uncounted tours of the volcano for Navy personnel. In addition, his wife, who still occupies the long time family home in lower Manoa, reports that Loo would often rush to the Big Island at the first word of volcanic activity. The result is that among his thousands of photographs on hundreds of subjects, Loo has left an extensive and superb record of Madame Pele in action. The particular volcanic event reproduced here took place in the town of Hoopuloa in 1926. Tai Sing Loo had been sent to the Island of Hawaii by the Star Bulletin and the Inter-Island Steamship Company. He arrived in time for both spectacular photographs and a story of Madame Pele.

The story, which he claims to have heard in Hoopuloa Village two days before it was destroyed, is recorded in his memoir: "I take the first picture at Kona brighten glow over the sky when the volcano fire eruption flowing down the Maunaloa, the slow A.A. lava creeping across the road which I take the mass of the lava avalanche descending the Hoopuloa. The lady standing by the automobile watching the red hot lava down the road. 'May I tell you the strange story.' Before I'm going to tell you all 'Believe or not,' which I heard at the Hoopuloa Village two days before destruction of the lava doom. On the day, one afternoon an old lady ask the fisherman for some fish. 'Go away, our fish for sale, not to give away.' The strange old lady, dressed in white say 'Within three days Pele will destroy your fish ground.' Then she get to the Japanese driver talking along. Suddenly she disappear so the Japanese drove back to tell the tale. I have prove. The first day I was up at the Kona Road taking the lava flow across the street, the very afternoon down to the Village waiting for the grand spectacural of the molten red hot lava flow down. Second day I took a most wonderful picture of the flow between two palm trees at three o'clock in the morning, the very doom. The third day early in the morning about five o'clock the red hot molten lava destruction the village houses and water tank, then flow into the sea beach. Before seven o'clock the show all over when the Navy airplane arrival is too late."

Right: An explosion cloud at Kilauea, May, 1924. Tai Sing Loo. Hawaii Volcano Observatory.

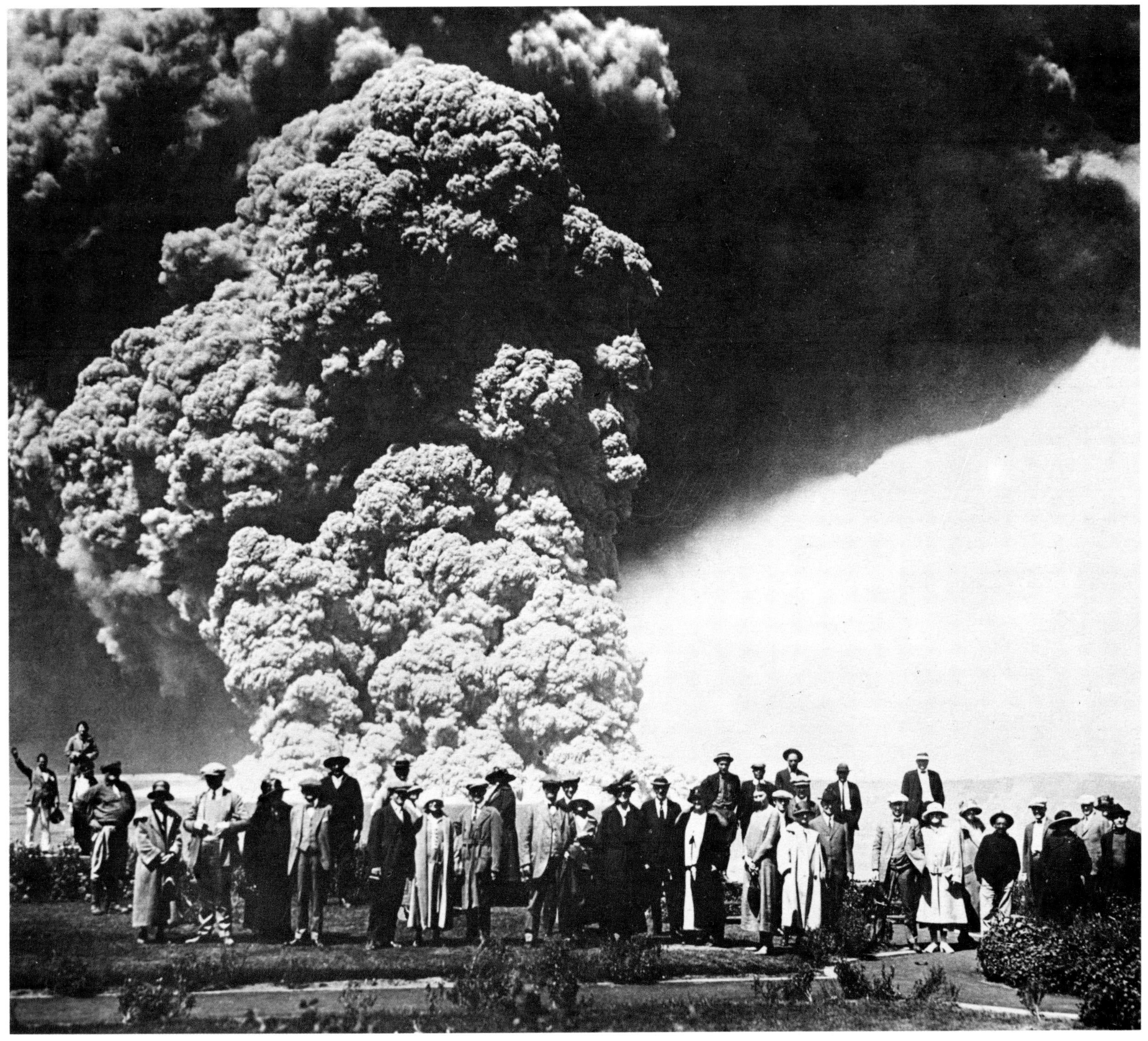

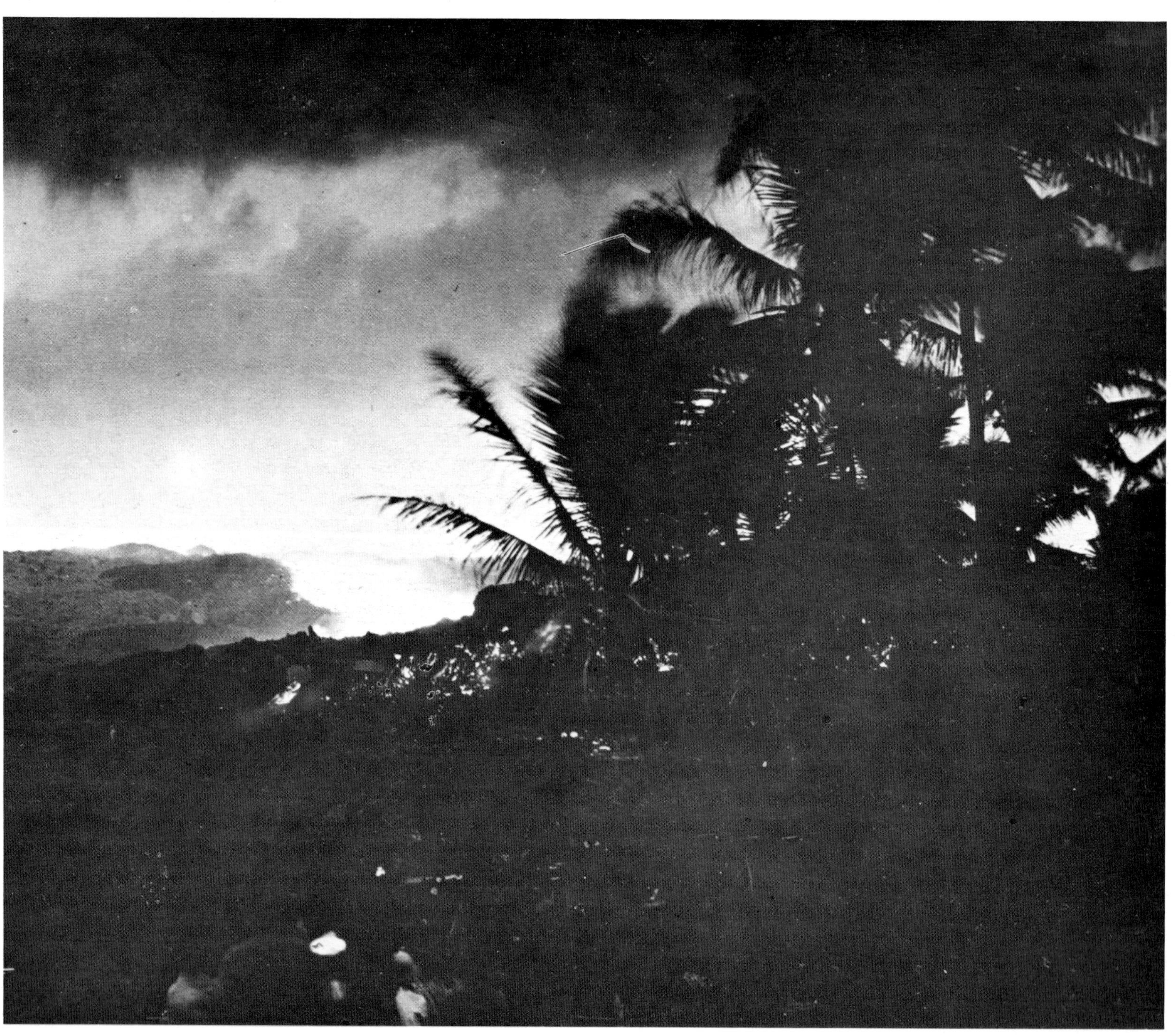

Left: Lava flow from Mauna Kea pictured at 5 a.m. on April 18, 1926, as it heads toward Hoopuloa Village. Tai Sing Loo. Hawaii State Archives.

Below: Lava begins to enter the Village of Hoopuloa, April 18, 1926. Tai Sing Loo. Hawaii State Archives.

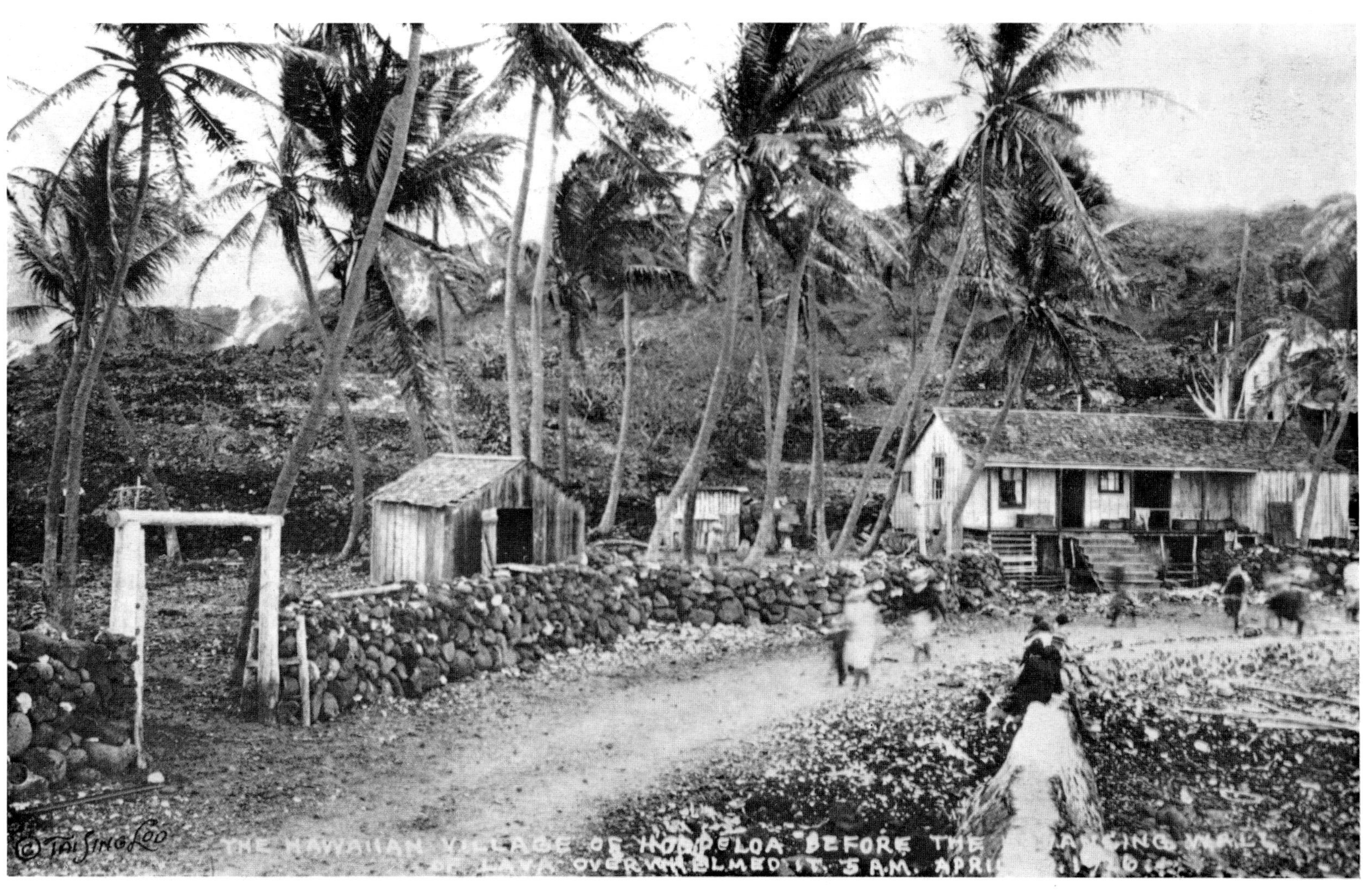

Right: Lava wall overtakes the wharf and water tanks at Hoopuloa, April 18, 1926. Tai Sing Loo. Hawaii State Archives.

Below: A pig in the middle of the road seems undisturbed by the advancing wall of a'a, Hoopuloa Village, April 18, 1926. Tai Sing Loo. Hawaii State Archives.

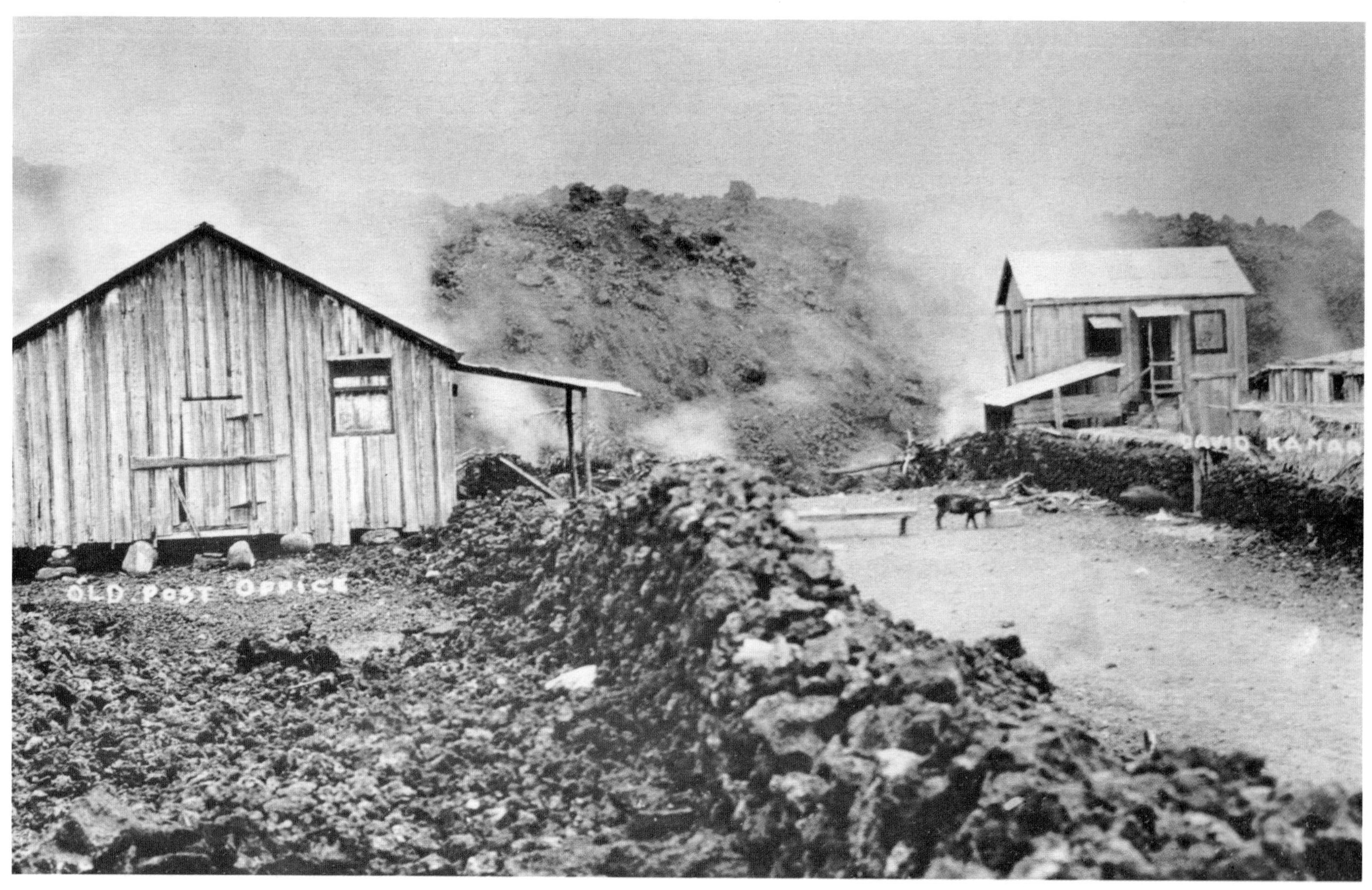

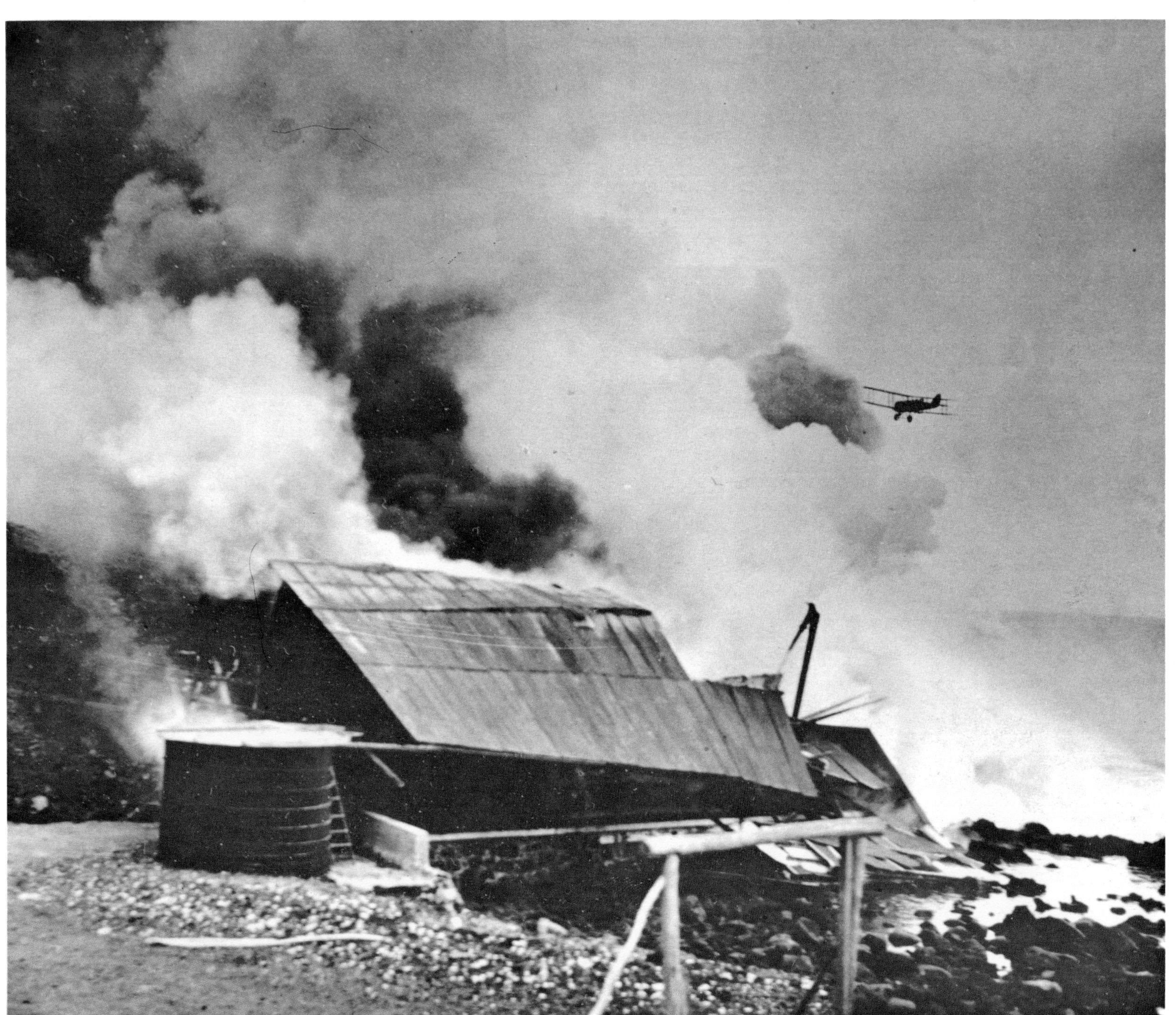

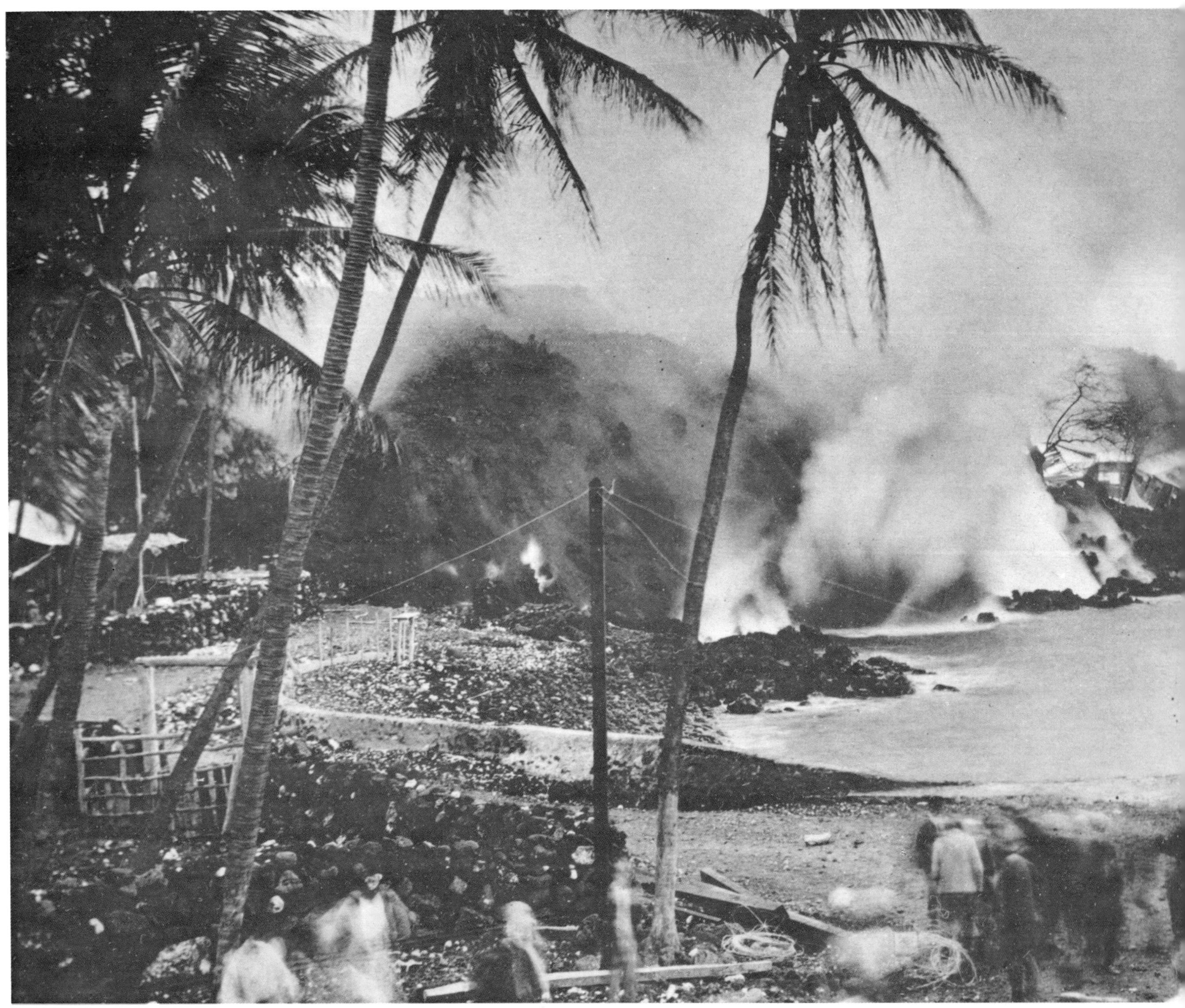

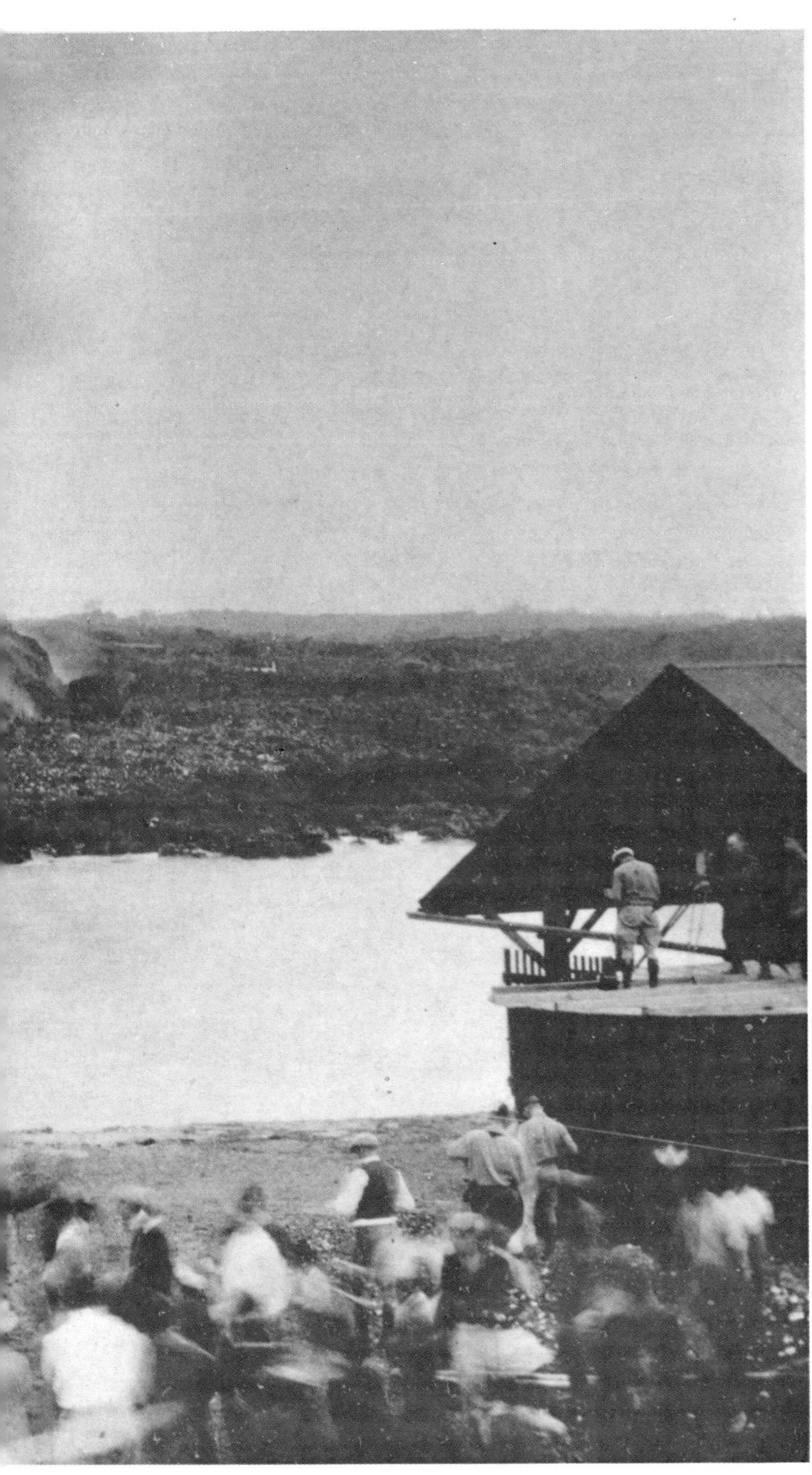

The river of molten lava going to the sea, April 19, 1926. Tai Sing Loo. Hawaii State Archives.

R. J. Baker leaning on a twin-six Packard during tour of the Island of Hawaii he conducted in 1925. R. J. Baker. Hawaii State Archives.

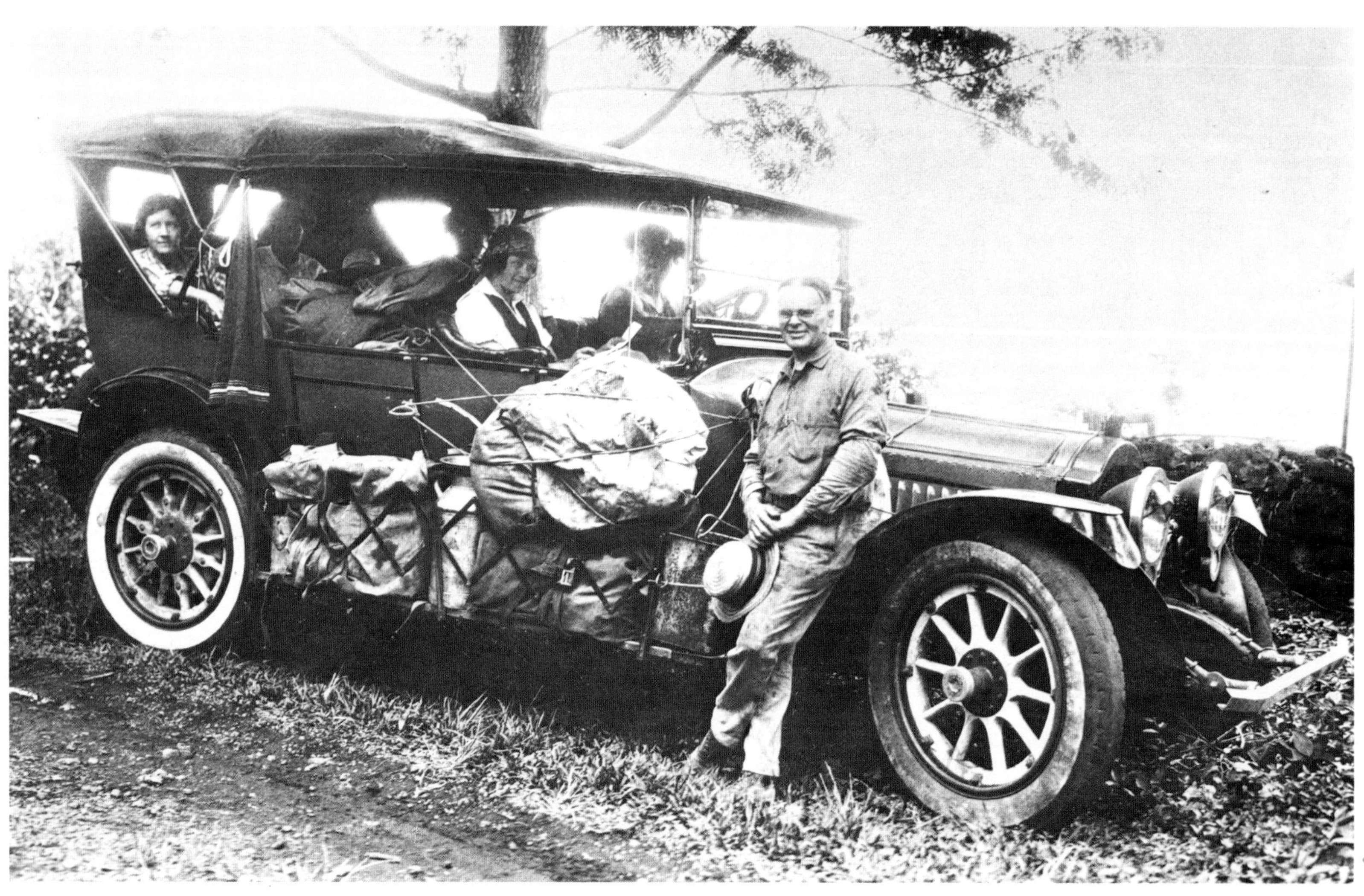

Ray Jerome Baker

When the subject of early day Hawaiian photography is raised, most people immediately think of Ray Jerome Baker. Baker's name has been inextricably tied to early photography in the islands. Many people do not even realize that a number of photographers worked in the islands before Baker and that Baker was in fact, a relatively late arrival to Hawaii. Yet, Baker's efforts in tracing the history of his predecessors in the islands is almost as valuable as his own photographic work. Baker spent much of his time during the 1930s and 1940s collecting, photographing and indentifying images of such early photographers as Stangenwald and Chase. He poured through early newspapers in an effort to trace the early photographers and learn something of their origins, their lives and their photographic techniques. He privately printed and issued over a dozen books on early Hawaii, each of them carefully cataloging places and events and the photographers who recorded them. And he left to the State Archives and to Bishop Museum numbers of fine copies of early photographs — both his own work and the work of others — all with as much information as possible about their dates, subjects, locations and photographers.

Ray Jerome Baker was born in Rockford, Illinois in 1880. His first exposure to Hawaii came in 1908, when he and his wife, who were then living in Eureka, California, came to the islands for a two week vacation. The visit, however, was extended to over four months, during which Baker took dozens of photographs of the islands. Apparently the 1908 stay was a turning point for Baker, for in 1910 he returned to Hawaii, this time to become a permanent resident and an ardent student of island life and growth.

Baker was a prolific photographer and when he was not doing his own photographic work, he kept busy copying and studying the work of earlier photographers. He traveled extensively, visiting and photographing close to 60 countries before he set aside his cameras. In the 1920s he traveled widely in the United States, lecturing on a variety of topics, and in the early 1920s he found time to attend the University of Hawaii and acquire a bachelor of arts degree. Baker also served for a time as a motion picture cameraman for Pathe News. He took the only motion pictures of the funeral of Queen Liliuokalani in 1917 and the funeral of Prince Kuhio in 1922. He was also a student of early Honolulu architecture and over the years recorded on film almost every old building in the city.

Like several of the photographers who preceded him, Baker was involved in a large share of political activity. From an early date he was a supporter of various liberal causes, both in the islands and on the mainland. An obituary notice in the October 31, 1972 issue of *The Honolulu Advertiser*, noted that he frequently wrote letters to the Honolulu press in praise of the Russian revolution. The paper also noted that Baker, who had long wished to visit Russia, made the trip in 1958, when he was 78 years old. Apparently he came back disappointed, claiming the Russian revolutionary leaders had failed to keep their promises to the Russian people.

But perhaps the most interesting story of his political activities, one that reveals the character of the man, is the story of his expulsion from the Honolulu Lions Club in 1948. The reason apparently was that he had taken a suspected communist to lunch. Baker fought his expulsion. He hired a lawyer and threatened to take the Lions Club to court: he accused the group of being "a forum for the 'full and free discussion' of their own reactionary and antisocial viewpoints." Baker was reinstated in the club under legal pressure and, satisfied that he had won his point, he then publically announced his resignation from the Lions.

In keeping with his vigorous and independent nature, Baker maintained his photographic business at 1911-1915 Kalakaua Avenue from 1918 until his retirement in 1959 at the age of 79. He died in 1972, at 91 years of age, after living for some time in the Laniolu Retirement home in Waikiki. Those who are interested in early photography in the islands owe a great debt of gratitude to R. J. Baker, a native of the midwest who became enamored of the Hawaiian Islands in 1908 and who made them his home in 1910. His work of locating, identifying and cataloging early photography in the islands has proved to be invaluable, as has his own prolific photographic record of Hawaii in the early decades of the 20th century.

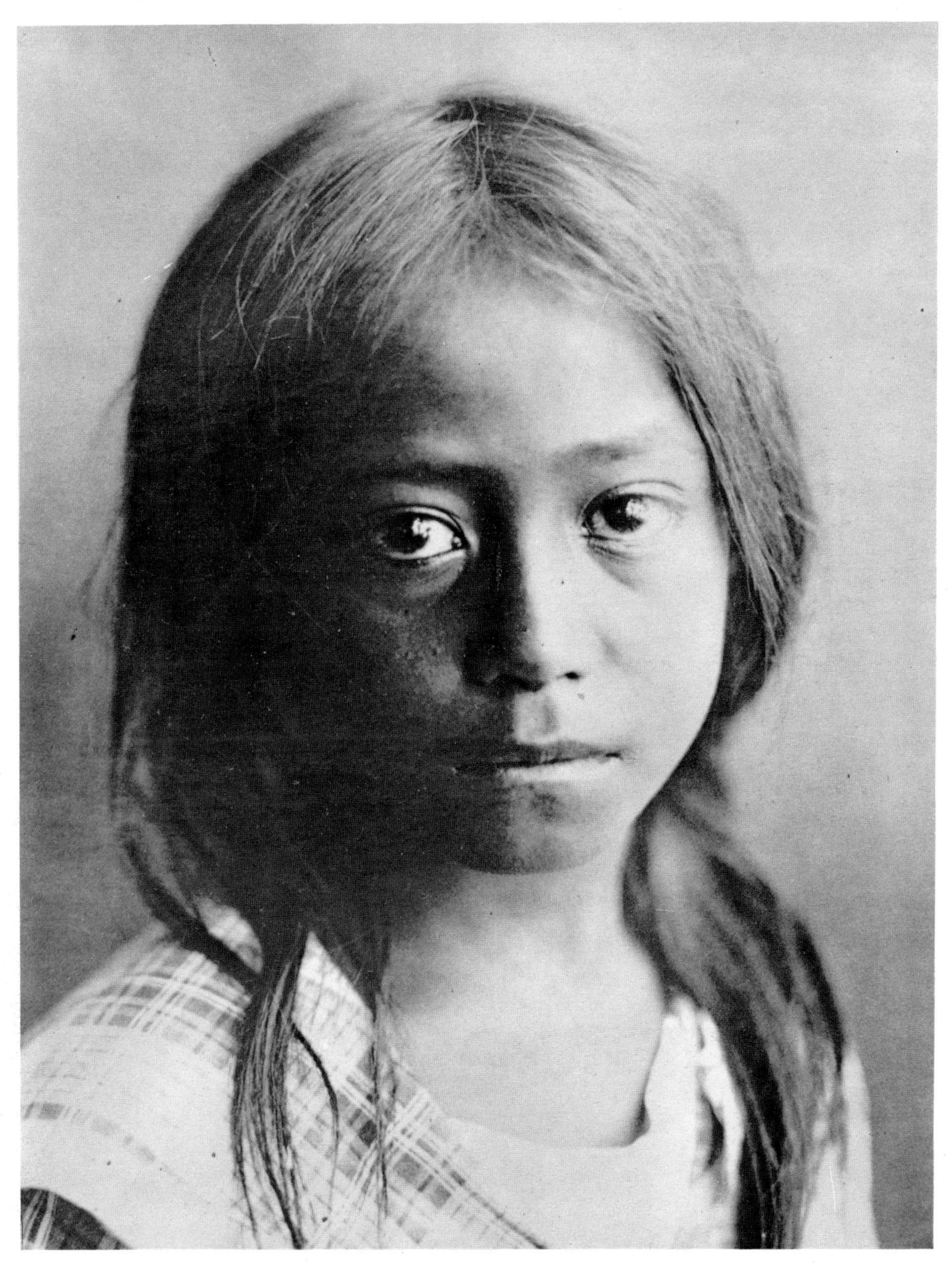

Hawaiian girl, Maui, 1912. R.J. Baker.
Hawaii State Archives.

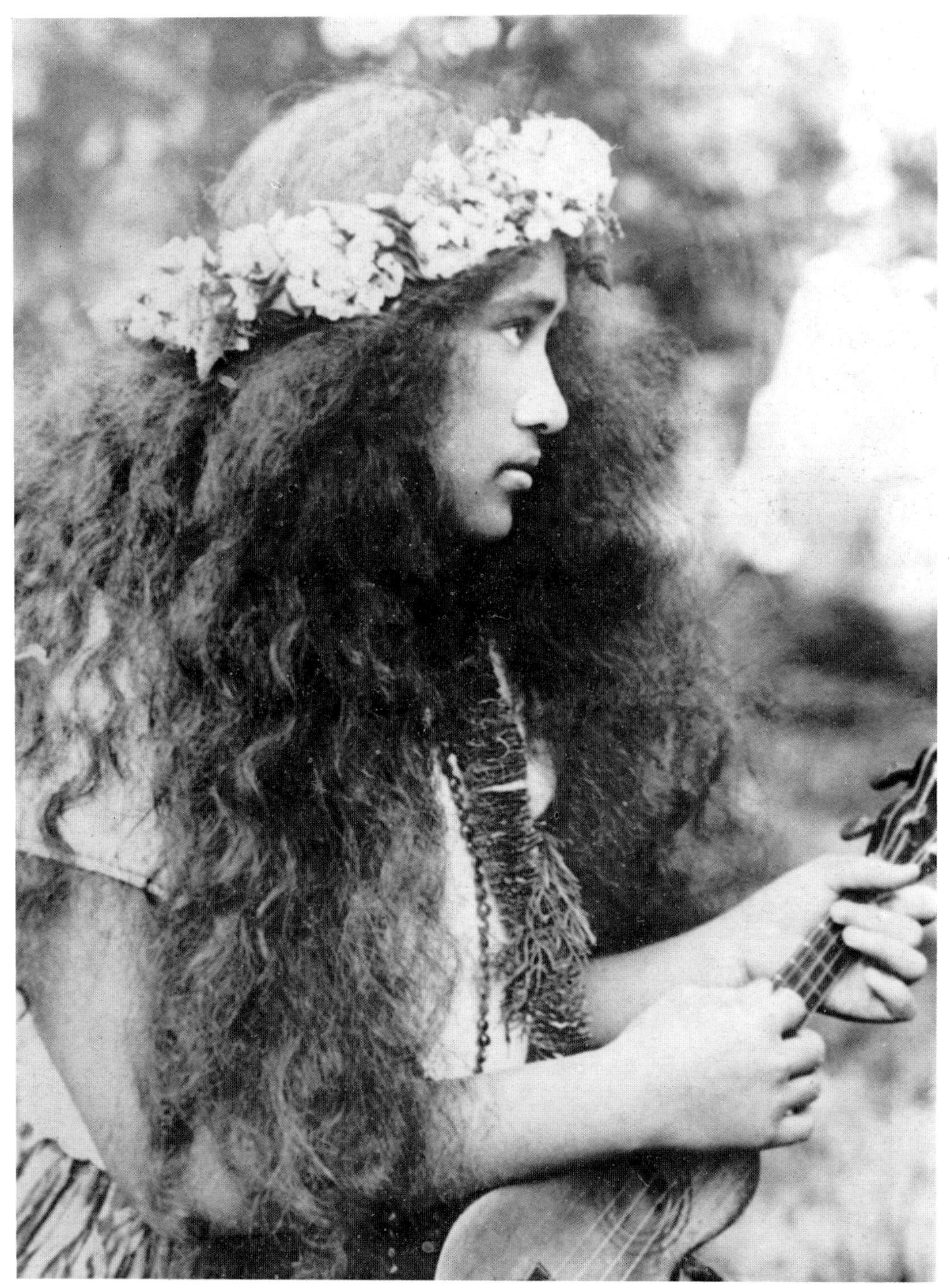

Left: A student at Kohala Seminary on the Island of Hawaii, about 1912. R. J. Baker. Hawaii State Archives.

Right: Hawaiian woman repairing fish nets at Lahaina, Maui, about 1912. R. J. Baker. Hawaii State Archives.

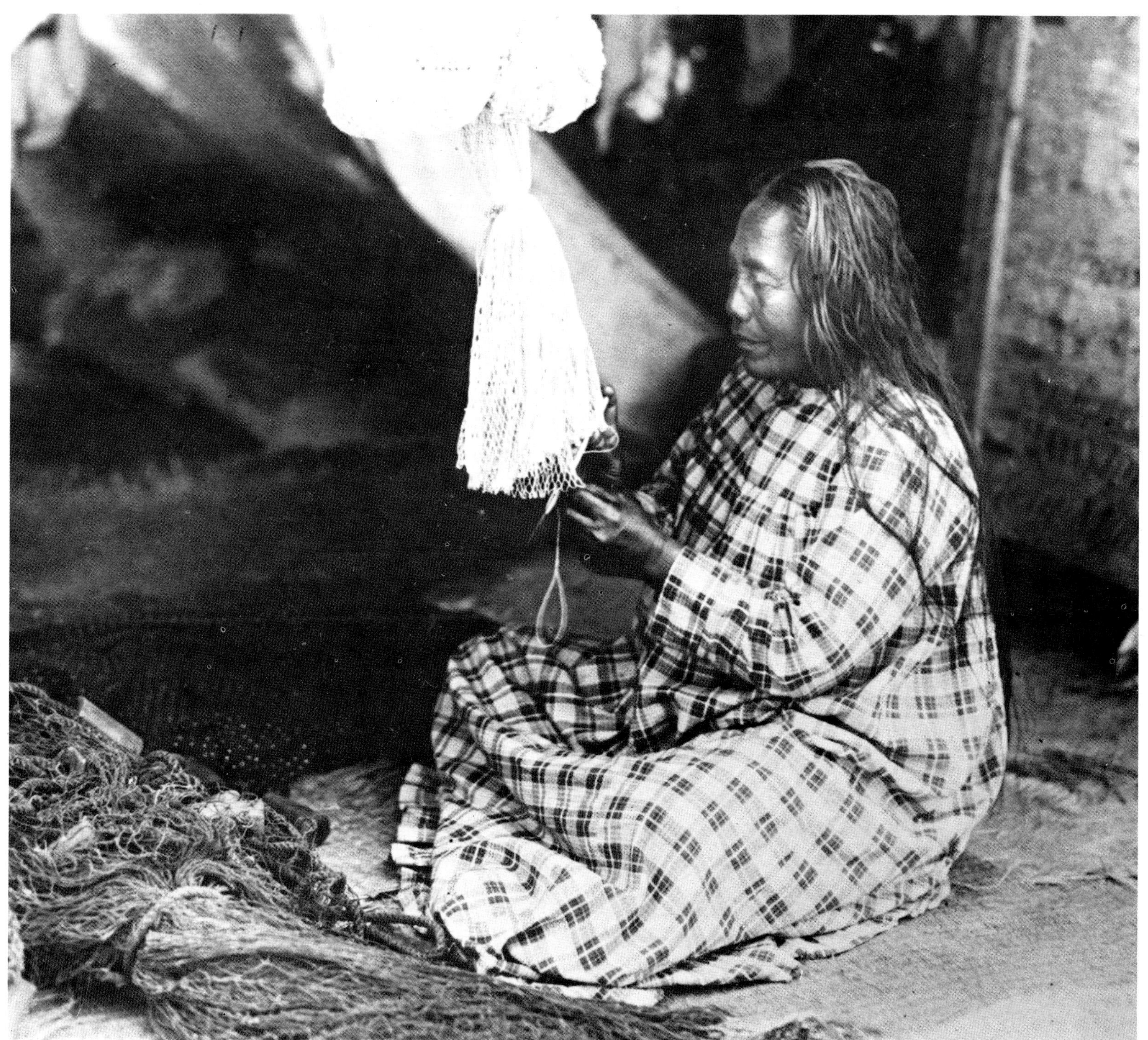

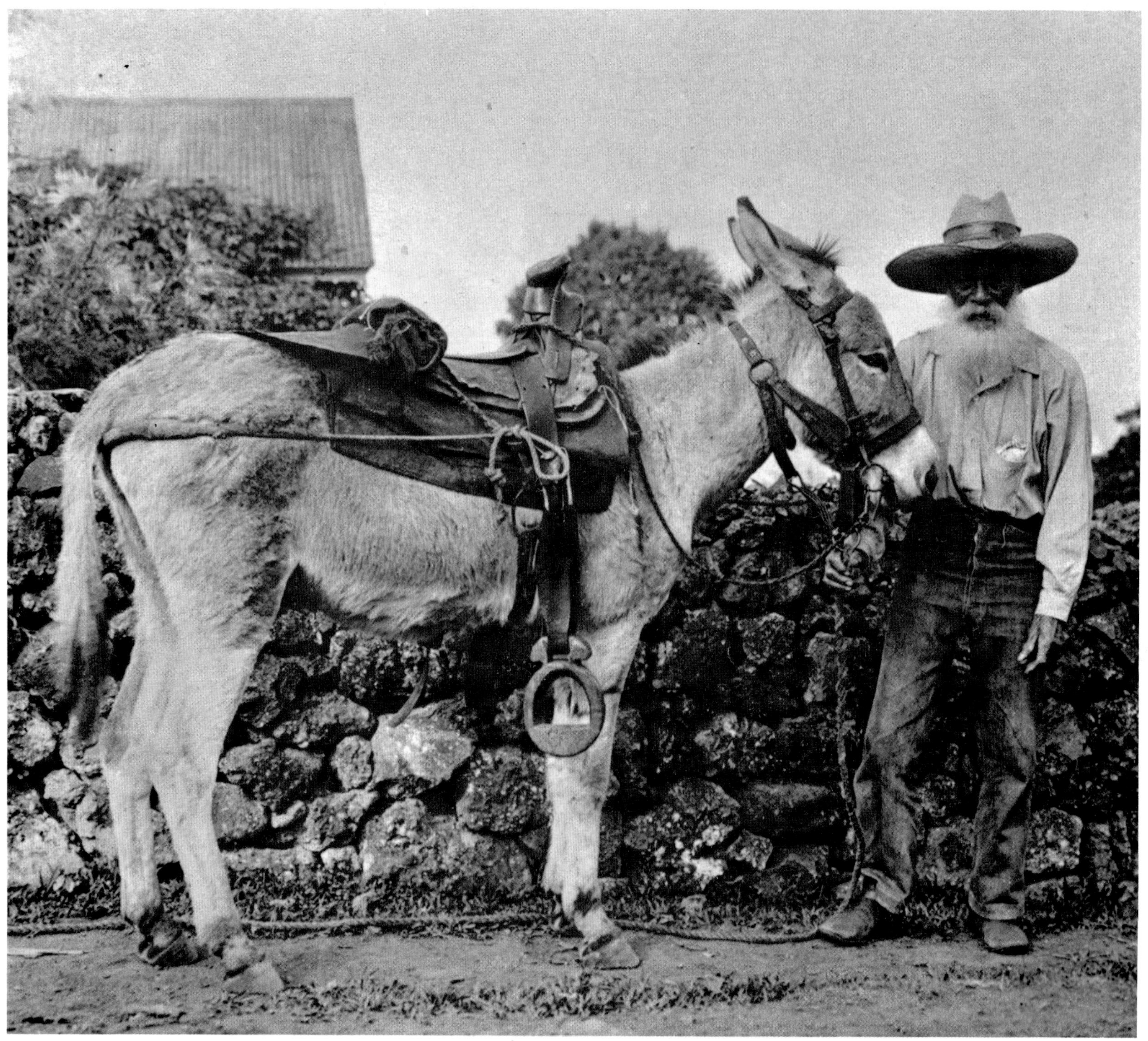

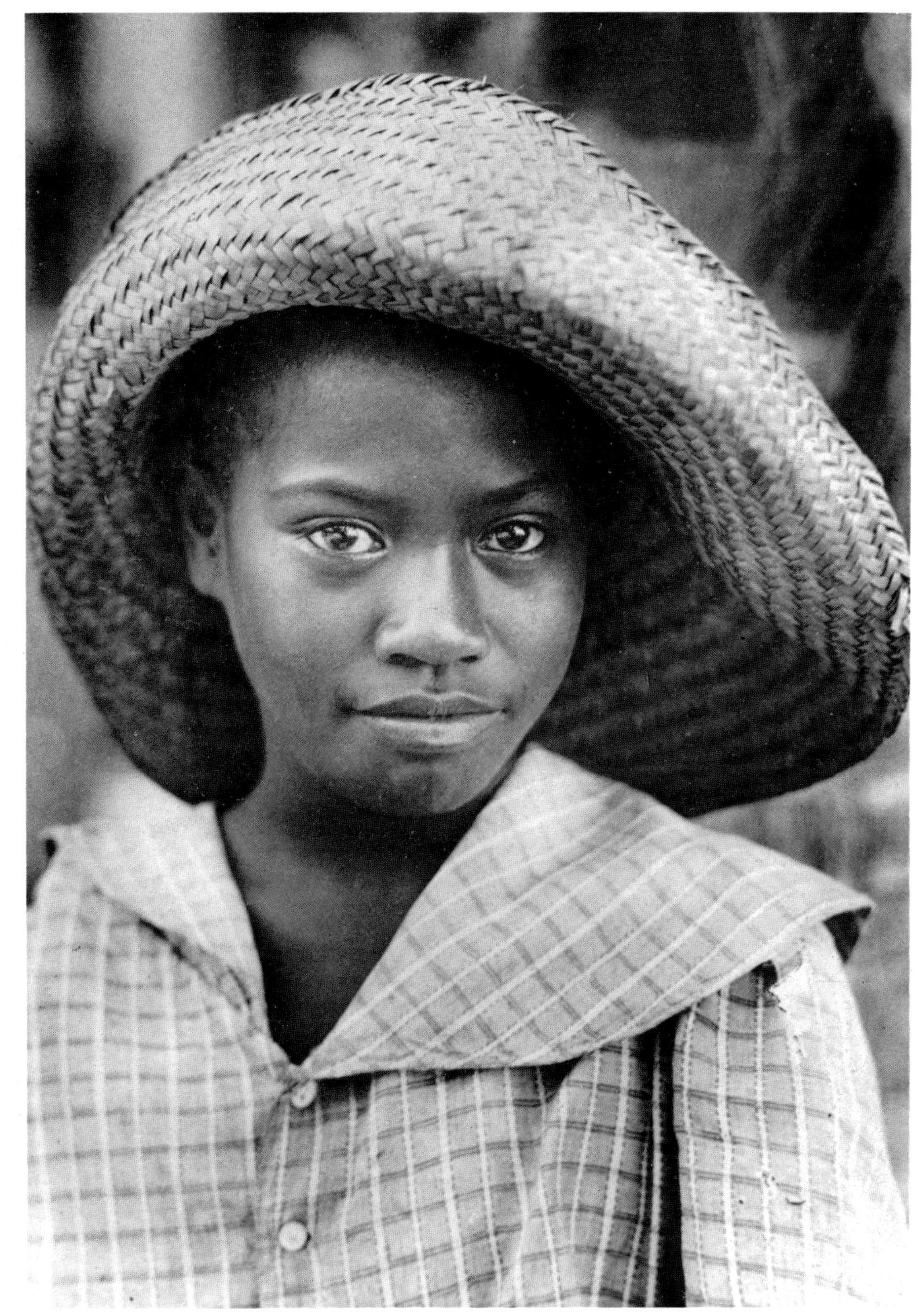

Left: Kona farmer in 1908. R. J. Baker. Hawaii State Archives.

Right: A Puerto Rican child at Lahaina, about 1912. R. J. Baker. Hawaii State Archives.

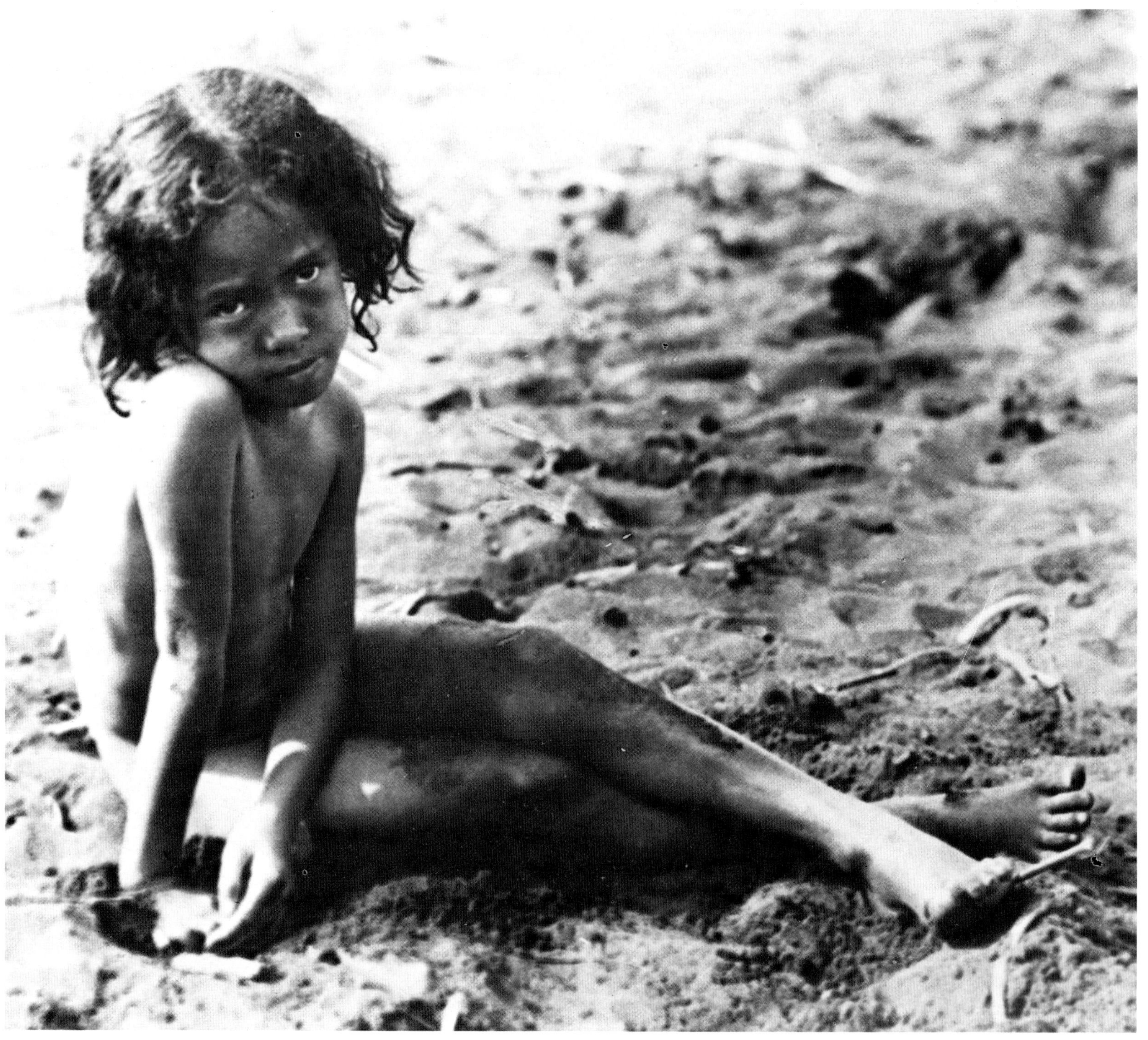

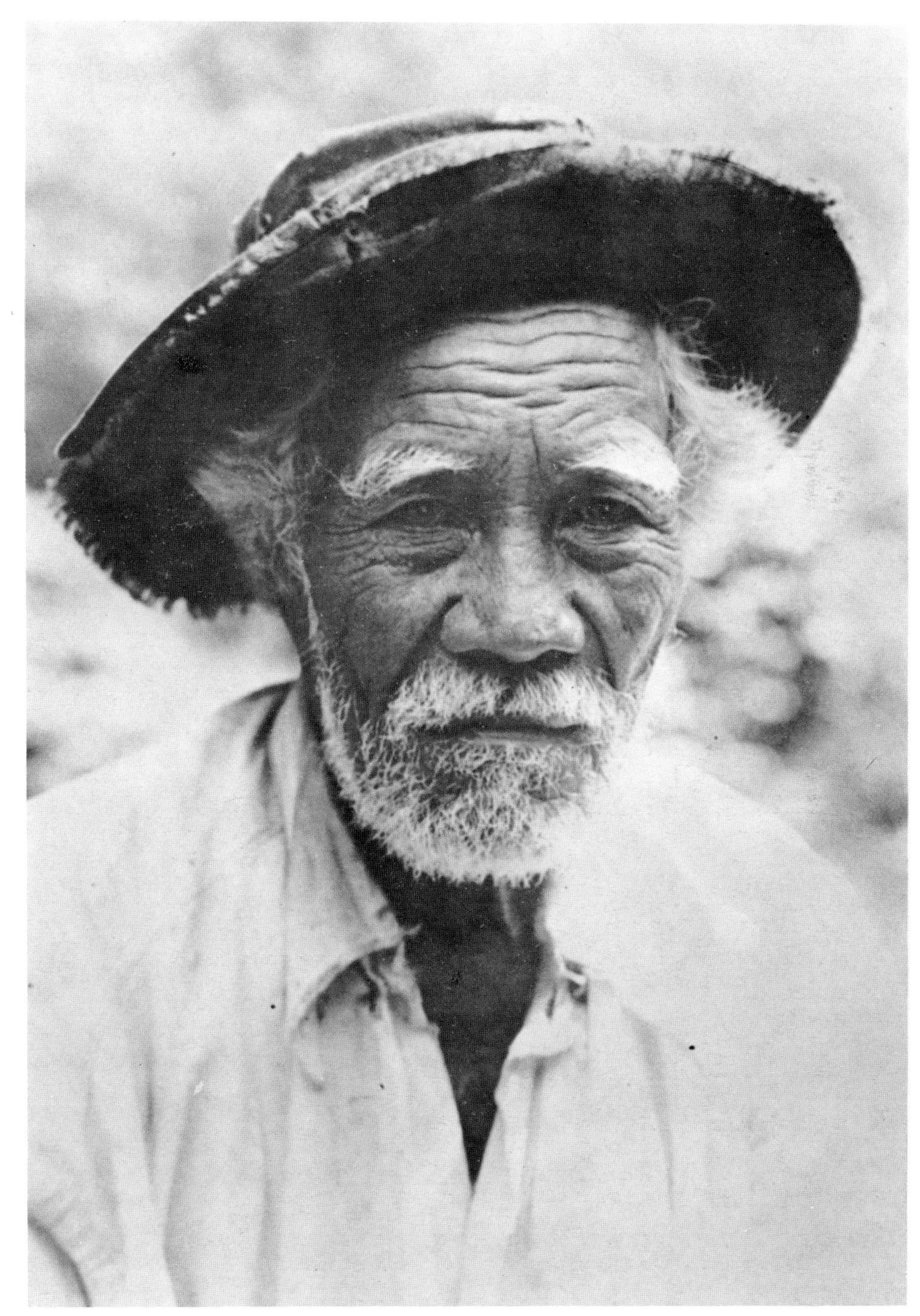

Left: On the beach at Waimea, Kauai, 1912. R. J. Baker. Hawaii State Archives.

Right: A Hawaiian man at Lahaina, Maui, 1911. R. J. Baker. Hawaii State Archives.

Right: A woman weaving lauhala mat, Molokai, 1913. R. J. Baker. Hawaii State Archives.

Below: Chinese child at Puunene, Maui, where his father served as a cook at the Puunene clubhouse, 1912. R. J. Baker. Hawaii State Archives.

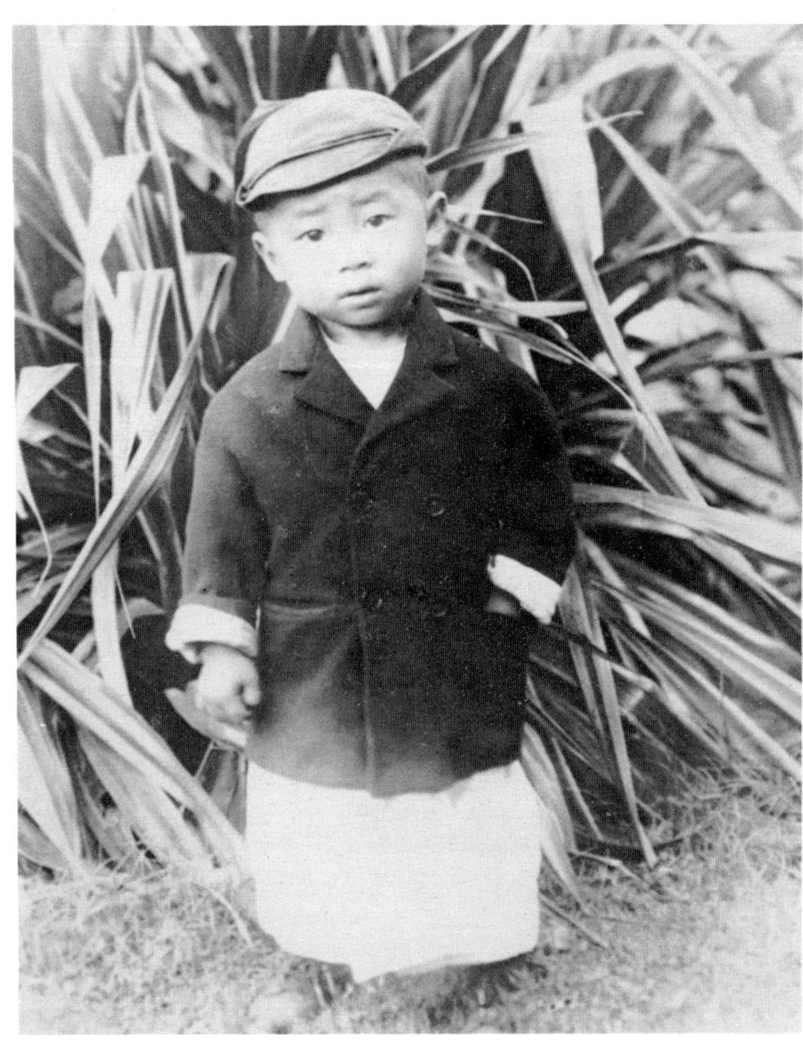

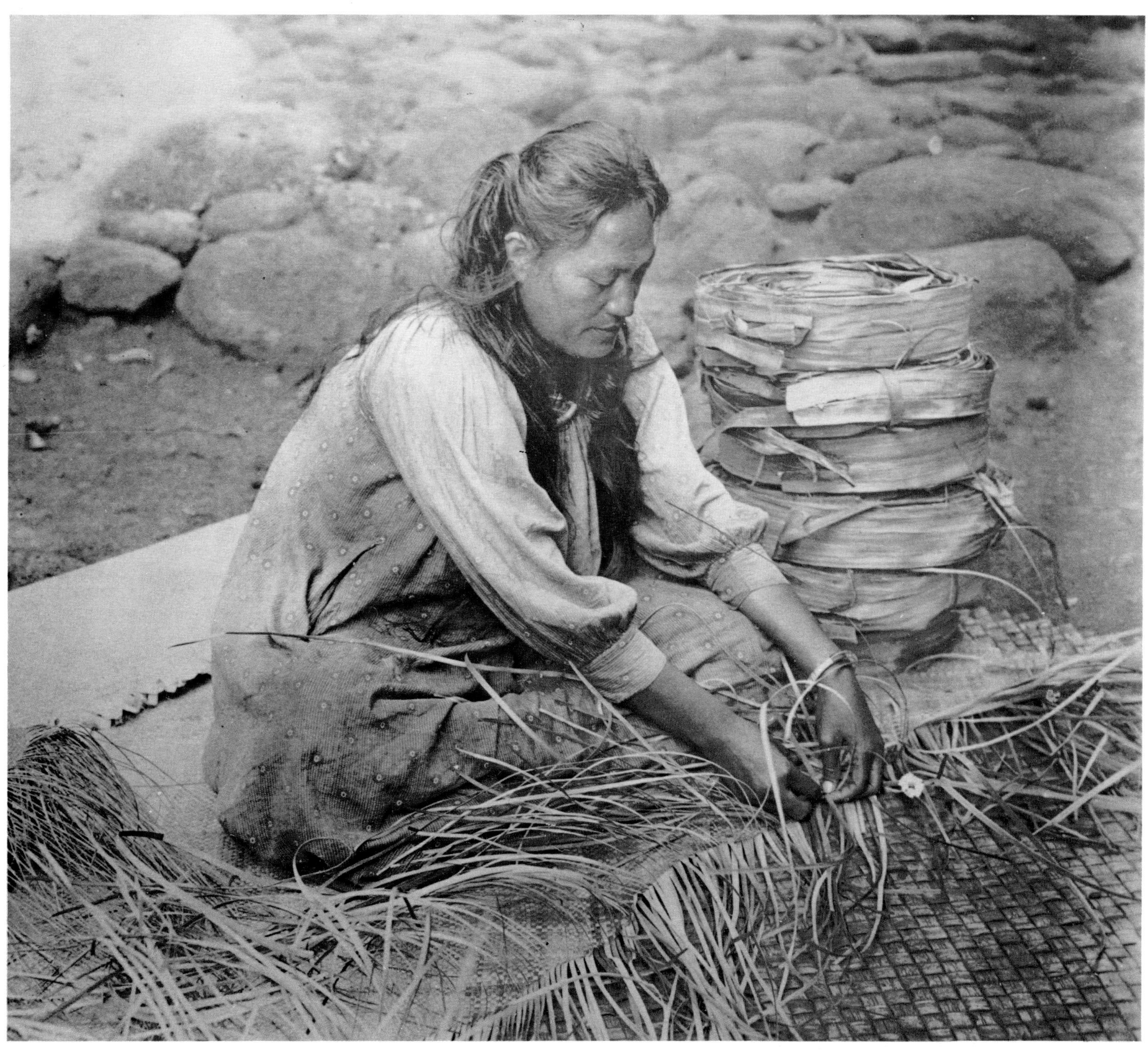

Acknowledgements

The assistance and encouragement of the following people made this book possible: Bruce Erickson, Honolulu photographer, formerly with Bishop Museum was largely responsible for the launching of this project. The initial idea of the book was developed together with Erickson and the initial work of collecting photographs was begun together. Erickson also trained me in the art of photocopying. University of Hawaii student Nelson Ho helped with photocopy work and printed the On Char material. University of Hawaii student Charles Brockman helped with some of the photo research. Rick Regan did most of the final prints for the book. The Stangenwald daguerreotypes were copied with the permission of the Mission Children's Society and the assistance of Elizabeth Larsen, librarian of the Hawaiian Mission Children's Society Museum. Orlando Lyman, director of the Lyman House Memorial Museum, along with Maralyn Herkes, museum librarian and Mary Helfrich, museum photographer, made possible the selection and printing of the Hitchcock material. Neal Walker, Hitchcock's grandson, formerly of Hilo, and Hildreth Walker, Hitchcock's daughter, of Kihei, Maui, provided information about Hitchcock and assistance in gaining Hitchcock photographs. Mr. and Mrs. L.C. Child of Kailua, Kona, permitted Mr. Erickson and me to disrupt their home in order to copy material from the Child photo albums. Mrs. Roger Williams of Kailua, Kona, Caroline Gurrey's daughter, provided information and photographs. Lyman Bond of Kohala provided the opportunity to explore the Bond home and copy photographs and daguerreotypes stored there. Joseph Feher of the Honolulu Academy of Arts provided space and assistance in the copying of Caroline Gurrey material. Donald Peterson and the staff of the Hawaii Volcano Observatory permitted the copying of Jaggar material from Kilauea Record Books. Mr. and Mrs. Howard Powers of Kula, Maui provided information on Jaggar's career. Mrs. Tai Sing Loo of Honolulu and her son and daughter provided photographs and information about Tai Sing Loo. June Gutmanis supplied information about Theodore Kelsey. Barbara Dunn, librarian of the Hawaiian Historical Society made the Kelsey photographic materials available. Lynn Davis of Bishop Museum provided assistance in selecting the On Char material. On Char spent hours talking about his life and provided photographs from his personal collection. Agnes Conrad and her helpful and efficient staff and the Hawaii State Archives provided space, patience and assistance for the collection of and copying of large numbers of photographs by most of the photographers represented in this volume as well as large numbers of photographs by photographers who have not been represented. To all of these people I owe warm thanks and an enormous debt of gratitude.